Marcus Tullius Cicero, Robert Yelverton Tyrrell

Cicero in His Letters

Edited with Notes by Robert Yelverton Tyrrell

Marcus Tullius Cicero, Robert Yelverton Tyrrell

Cicero in His Letters
Edited with Notes by Robert Yelverton Tyrrell

ISBN/EAN: 9783744687454

Printed in Europe, USA, Canada, Australia, Japan

Cover: Foto ©Thomas Meinert / pixelio.de

More available books at **www.hansebooks.com**

CICERO IN HIS LETTERS

CICERO IN HIS LETTERS

EDITED WITH NOTES

BY

ROBERT YELVERTON TYRRELL,
M.A., LITT.D.

D.LITT. QU. UNIV., LL.D. EDIN.,
FELLOW OF TRINITY COLLEGE AND REGIUS PROFESSOR OF GREEK, DUBLIN ;
EXAMINER IN LATIN TO THE LONDON UNIVERSITY

London
MACMILLAN AND CO.
AND NEW YORK
1891

PREFACE

A GREAT many editions have been published, both in Germany and in England, of letters selected from the correspondence of Cicero. Yet I think there is room for this new collection, because it has been made on a principle different from that which has been the basis of all the " Selections " hitherto offered to the world. The latter have invariably chosen those letters which throw light on Cicero as a politician, as a public man ; and the same letters have been again and again presented by successive editors, though in some cases they are epistolary only in form, like the long and celebrated document addressed to Lentulus, in the year 54, and preserved as Fam. i. 9, which is really rather a political *manifesto* or *pro vita sua apologia* than a communication to a private friend. Such compositions are highly important and interesting, but they have already received sufficient attention. At all events they are quite unavailable for my purpose, which is to present to my readers what will show Cicero in the character of a private gentleman, and throw light on his everyday life, his home

amusements, and his domestic worries.   Hence I
have given such letters as refer to his family and
personal friends, their misunderstandings and recon-
ciliations, his studies and his literary preferences, the
pleasures and drawbacks of country and suburban
life, his ailments and those of his friends, his tastes
in art, his views about public shows and combats
between men and beasts, his criticism on Lucretius,
his journey to his province.   We shall see him complaining to Atticus of the ingratitude of his freedman
the Greek Dionysius, and Tigellius the Sardinian
musician, and excusing himself for having thoroughly
enjoyed a dinner at the house of Volumnius, though
Cytheris reclined opposite to him.   We may perhaps
smile when he discusses the suitability of a certain
lady to be the successor of the divorced Terentia,
adding, 'She is as ugly a woman as I ever saw';
when he complains to Atticus (xv. 15) of the insolence of a courtier of Cleopatra's, after it was
evident that that lady had failed in her attempt to
fascinate Cicero; and when he tells Trebatius how
on going home from dining with him, though *bene
potus*, he looked up a law point which they had been
discussing, and found that he was in the right.   We
shall escape all those letters which discuss, in wearying
detail, the fears and hopes of men who were candi-
dates for the consulship nearly two thousand years
ago, the recurrence of which topic is as tiresome as
the gout in the letters of Walpole.   I have also made

room for *characteristic* letters of every kind, a couple of his incoherent wails from exile; the *bella epistula* in which he tries to persuade Lucceius to drop the thread of his history and devote a special book to '*natam me consule Romam*'; the notes written in covert and enigmatic Greek about the fraudulent attempts of Philotimus, where Milo appears as 'the Crotoniate tyrannicide,' Milo's freedman Timotheus as 'the namesake of Conon's father,' and Rome as 'the seven-hilled city.' Again, I have introduced several examples of the sportive vein found in his letters to Trebatius, Paetus, and Volumnius, and a couple of specimens of the jerky vigour of Caelius.

The fact that I have adopted a new principle of choice has naturally brought about the result that my Selection hardly ever coincides with that of my predecessors. Indeed, I have aimed at including in preference new letters, if in other respects suitable ; so that the student who may find time to read my little book, after studying the valuable work of Mr. Watson, will find that he not only meets Cicero in a new aspect, but that he has before him new and *characteristic* specimens of the correspondence of Cicero. My edition does not coincide with that of Mr. Watson, except in Epp. iv., l., lx., lxi., lxvi., lxxiii., lxxviii., and of these seven letters four must be introduced into every collection—the letter of Sulpicius and the answer to it, the dinner with Caesar in Cicero's villa near Puteoli, and the fine letter of

Matius about Caesar. Thus, the great majority of the letters now presented have not appeared before in any Selection, and very few of the letters from xl. to lxxx. have ever been commented on in English or German before; the letters from i. to xl. have already been treated in the *Correspondence of Cicero*, by Mr. Purser and myself.

In the Introduction, in dealing with Cicero as a public man, I have confined myself to those epochs in his career in which, as it seems to me, his character and motives have been misapprehended or deliberately misrepresented. The Introduction is for the most part abridged from the *Correspondence of Cicero*, where the subjects here treated are dealt with in greater detail than seems necessary for those for whom the present volume is intended, namely, boys in the higher forms at the schools of Great Britain and America.

I have had the invaluable aid of my colleague and *collaborateur*, Mr. L. C. Purser, in my comments on the letters not yet included in our joint edition of the *Correspondence*. To him my best thanks are due. But he himself would wish me to acknowledge even a greater debt of obligation to one who, though not a colleague, and influenced only by his love of letters, and the kindliness of his disposition, has conferred on me a favour which I could not overrate. I refer to Dr. Reid, of Gonville and Caius, Cambridge, who has been good enough to read over all

my notes, and who has allowed me to append many
of his own comments, thus enriching my little
edition with the fruits of a Ciceronian erudition
unrivalled in this kingdom at least. His notes will
be found enclosed between square brackets at the
end of my own comment in each case. Many very
important annotations of his I was obliged to omit,
as being above the heads of the students to whom
my edition is offered. It is not, of course, to be
inferred that Dr. Reid has sanctioned by his approval
every comment on which he has made no remark ;
again, I have not thought it necessary to record his
assent to my views except when he has added something of his own. It will be observed that I have
sometimes recorded his direct dissent. I think where
two views may be held consistently with grammar
and sense, there is no reason why both should not be
put before both teachers and learners. Many of the
letters in this Selection have never been explained
before except in the very sparse comments of Schütz
and Billerbeck, so that there may be a positive
advantage in putting forward divergent views, if
both are consistent with grammar and context.

I have been in the habit of setting free translations
from the letters as exercises for composition in Latin,
and I think I can recommend the practice to teachers.
As an illustration of the usefulness of the letters as
a model for Latin prose composition, I have appended
to the Introduction half a dozen exercises in the style

of the Epistles of Cicero written by myself and some of my friends.

I must add my tribute of testimony to the rare merits of Messrs. R. and R. Clark's reader. I am myself a wretched corrector of the Press. Messrs. R. and R. Clark's reader is evidently himself a good Latin scholar, and is admirably careful and attentive.

CONTENTS

CONTENTS

INTRODUCTION

I

CICERO AS A PUBLIC MAN

I HAVE prefixed to the text of this Selection a few
sentences which trace the chief events in Cicero's life up
to the year in which his extant correspondence begins.
The main incidents of his subsequent life will be familiar
to such students as will use this Selection, and if any one
desires a rapid survey of them, he will find the article even
in the abridged edition of Smith's *Dictionary of Biography*
adequate for his needs.   It is in the *interpretation* of the
acts of Cicero that historians have ever differed, and
will probably for ever differ.   Gaston Boissier has been
the most eloquent of his recent advocates, and all that
can be said against him has been concentrated into a few
scathing epigrams by the great history-maker Theodor
Mommsen.   I have already protested against the outrage
which Mommsen has committed on the fair fame of
Cicero.   Like Marina in *Pericles Prince of Tyre*, I have
spoken holy words to the Lord Lysimachus—I have
endeavoured to vindicate by arguments the character of

one whom I regard as a great and good man. For my present purpose it will be sufficient to put forward a few plain statements of facts.

There is no ground for saying that Cicero, in his early life, coquetted with democracy. He was doubtless a representative of the Equestrian class, and thus on the whole opposed to the Optimates ; but we do not find that his political principles, whatever they were, led him to the picking and choosing of his briefs at the beginning of his career. His object was to attain to an eminent position in the political life of Rome. With his amazing intellectual gifts, the obvious avenue to this was the Bar, and Cicero seized every opportunity of showing his powers as an advocate, without much considering the political aspects of the various cases which he undertook. It has been alleged that he defended Catiline, charged with extortion in Africa, with a view to improving the chances of his candidature for the consulship of 63. It is well-nigh certain that Cicero did not defend Catiline (see note on Ep. iv.) ; but, if he had done so, he would have done nothing immoral or unprofessional. Catiline was not at the time the declared champion of the democracy. He was a dissolute young noble who, like other Roman governors, had misused the power which the State had entrusted to him. If it be urged that, even apart from politics, it was unworthy of Cicero to think of defending the oppressor of his province, one may answer that moral standards differ in different periods of history. England, happily for her subjects, does not look on proconsular malversation with the lenient eyes of ancient Rome. If he had lived in the last century of the Roman Republic, Burke might have defended Sir Elijah Impey after his impeachment of Warren Hastings, without incurring any serious reprobation. But it is highly probable that a Roman of that epoch would have completely failed to see the applicability of the attribute honesty to certain quite legitimate transactions on the Turf and the Stock Exchange of our own day.

Cicero and the Equites were driven to the side of the nobility by the conspiracy of Catiline, in which Caesar undoubtedly took a part. Cicero was now a great power. He could give a voice to the party which he espoused. And no one discerned this so clearly as Caesar, who strained every nerve to secure the advocacy of the great consular. But Cicero had by this time begun to indulge the dream of a restored Republic of the Scipios; his watchwords are *senatus auctoritas* and *ordinum concordia*, and he claims Catulus as his political predecessor. In Pompeius he saw the natural instrument of this policy, to which he clung, even though painfully conscious of all the shortcomings of Pompeius, and fascinated by the nobility of Caesar's character and demeanour, as well as the majesty of his genius. His letters are never so gloomy as when for a moment he lets his gaze wander from this enchanting *mirage*. The celebrated letter to Lentulus (Fam. i. 9), written shortly after his restoration from exile, is rather an apology for, than a defence of, his political attitude; and he never fails to reproach himself bitterly for defections, even in thought, from the *causa optima*. This *causa optima*, or complete harmony between the Senate and the Optimates, was realised for the brief period of Cicero's consulate and the succeeding three years. And even then it did not absolutely attain to Cicero's ideal, for it cannot be said to have had Pompeius at its head. We cannot fail to observe how Cicero sneers at Pompeius as long as the latter kept up friendly relations with the popular leaders. Sampsi-ceramus, Arabarches, Hierosolymarius are all jibes at the possible despot. It is only when Pompeius has broken with the revolutionary party that Cicero uses towards him the language of sympathy and respect. But he never had for Pompeius that affectionate admiration against which he struggled in the case of Caesar. We have in a letter to Atticus a strong expression of his belief that in Pompeius lay the only hope of the Republic: 'His is the only influence which touches my feelings; nothing else; not the talk of the patriots, now really an extinct class; not the cause itself, which has hitherto inspired no resolute action, and is destined per-haps to issue in crime. It is to Pompeius I must accord the unique position, though he does not ask for it, nor is the cause his own, as he says, but the State's.'[1] His comment on the death of Pompeius does not speak the language of real grief: 'I cannot but feel grief for his sad death; I found him an upright, good, and worthy man.'[2]

[1] *Me quidem alius nemo movet; non sermo bonorum qui nulli sunt, non causa quae acta timide est, agetur improbe; uni, uni hoc damus, ne id quidem roganti, nec suam causam, ut ait, agenti sed publicam.*—Att. ix. 1, 4.

[2] *Non possum eius casum non dolere; hominem enim integrum et castum et gravem cognovi.*—Att. xi. 6, 5.

The conspiracy of Catiline cannot be regarded as having been really a move in the struggle for democracy, or a serious attempt to revolutionise the State. Catiline was not the political successor of the Gracchi, Saturninus, Drusus, Sulpicius, and Cinna. He drifted into the ranks of the insurgents, who were at best political desperadoes like Caesar, and was easily crushed by Cicero, who deliberately exaggerated the dimensions of the conspiracy to enhance his own glory in putting it down.

There can be little doubt that, had Cicero chosen, the Triumvirate might have been a Quattuorvirate ;[1] but he is faithful to his *causa optima*, the defection of Pompeius from which he regrets in expressive phrase (Att. ii. 21, 3, 4). His only comfort is that he has now no rival in Pompeius for the plaudits of posterity (Att. ii. 17, 2). Clodius having gained his tribunate by concealing his designs against Cicero (a strong proof that Cicero was not the object of popular resentment), at once proceeds to his revenge. After several enactments, having a tendency to conciliate the various classes of Roman society,

---

[1] This is stated in so many words by Cicero in the *or. de provinciis consularibus*, § 41, *me in tribus sibi coniunctissimis consularibus esse voluit.* And this pronouncement is abundantly confirmed by Cicero's private letters of this period. See Att. ii. 1, 6, and 7, to the words *non minus esset probanda medicina quae sanaret vitiosas partes reipublicae quam quae exsecaret ;* again Att. ii. 3, 3, from the words *Nam fuit apud me Cornelius,* where he distinctly says that he might have been a member of the coalition, but that he preferred to adhere to the policy and party which from his boyhood he looked on as the party of patriotism and constitutionalism. In fine, he resolves that his motto shall be : εἷς οἰωνὸς ἄριστος ἀμύνεσθαι περὶ πάτρης.

he proposes a law enacting that any one who had put
Roman citizens to death without trial should be inter-
dicted from fire and water.   Caesar having in vain tried
to gain Cicero as an adherent—having in vain sought
even to afford him an opportunity for retiring from a
perilous position with honour—now abandons him to his
fate.   Indeed Cicero's presence in Rome as a declared
opponent of the Triumvirate might have proved an
obstacle to his own departure for Gaul.   Pompeius
betrayed him to whom he had so often pledged his word.
The treason of Pompeius and the jealousy of Hortensius
wellnigh cost the world some of the noblest of the
speeches and essays of Cicero, for often during his exile
the victim of Clodius was on the point of self-destruction.
He often regrets that he had not opposed force to force,
even though he should have perished in the employment
of it : and still more he deplores the fatal step which he
took in leaving Rome before he was directly impeached.
But he invariably attributes his fall—first, to the
treason of Pompeius against the Optimates, and consequently against himself : secondly, to the jealousy felt
towards him by the rival aspirants to the leadership of
the Optimate party.

The recall of Cicero cannot be ascribed to a sudden
rapprochement on the part of Pompeius to the nobility.
Nor is it true to the authorities to say that the terms on
which the nobility accepted the overtures of Pompeius
were the re-establishment of the senatorial government
and the recall of Cicero.   The exile of Cicero was due to
the jealousy of the nobility as much as to the treason of

Pompeius. But jealousy is a sentiment which, though it grows terribly while its object is still in a position to excite it, yet is capable of being allayed by the humiliation of the once envied rival. Cicero recalled from exile, even with all the honours which attended his recall, was no longer the triumphant *parvenu*, the irresistible *moqueur*, unstained by a humiliation, and unabashed by a repulse. And to this must be added the effect of that essentially personal factor in history which is so generally treated with disdain by the historians of to-day. A quarrel about the safe keeping of an Armenian princeling brought about an incurable rupture between Pompeius and Clodius, and obtained for Cicero the good offices of Pompeius in procuring his restoration. Moreover, the people, whose instincts led them to acquiesce in the punishment of a man who had undoubtedly strained the constitution, yet felt that he had amply atoned his *coup d'état*, and welcomed back the saviour of his country. No doubt the rabble hissed, but the people (especially the Italians) were enthusiastic in the cause of his restoration, and Pompeius, through hatred for Clodius, enrolled himself on the same side. The Senate strained every nerve, and there seems to have been an organised 'whip' of Italian voters. Nor were the bravoes of Milo an unimportant factor in the result achieved.[1] Thus the restoration of Cicero was brought about mainly by the unconstitutional means by which it might more easily have been averted.

Cicero's exile was a period of deep depression. The

---

[1] Dio Cass. xxxix. 8.

pigritia, or 'listlessness,' which now sapped all the sources
of his energy has left its mark on his style.   The letters
from exile show little of his powers of expression.   Like
Hamlet, he has not skill to reckon his groans.   His pre-
cision of expression is gone ; he has not the heart to
achieve it.   He says himself in a letter to Atticus that
he would write more but that grief has paralysed all his
faculties, and especially his powers of letter-writing.[1]   It
is the period immediately succeeding his restoration which
has been seized on by his detractors as an opportunity
for depicting him as a political apostate or a time-serving
trimmer.   His situation was indeed difficult.   'How do
you suppose I feel?' he writes to Atticus (iv. 6, 2).   'If
I say what duty bids I am looked on as a madman ; as a
time-server if I follow the dictates of expediency ; and if
I hold my peace I am said to be browbeaten and in
thraldom.'[2]   His detractors represent him as halting
between two parties, the Optimates and the Triumvirate.
The fact is, there was now no longer an Optimate party.
'I am not sure that they are not an extinct species,' says
Cicero, *nescio an nulli sint.*   Nor yet was there a Triumvirate ; at least there was not a Triumvirate which
possessed anything like that clear-cut solidity which it
now presents to readers of the history of the time.   To

---

[1] *Ego et saepius ad te et plura scriberem, nisi mihi dolor meus
cum omnes partes mentis* tum maxime huius generis facultatem
adcmisset.—Att. iii. 7, 3.

[2] *Ego vero qui si loquor de republica quod oportet insanus, si
quod opus est servus existimor, si taceo oppressus et captus, qua
dolore esse debeo ?*—Att. iv. 6, 2.

Cicero the Triumvirate practically meant Pompeius. He
does not use the expression at all.   The Triumvirs figure
in his letters sometimes as *dynastae*, or *populares*, or *illi
qui tenent*, or *qui tenent omnia* ; sometimes they are the
master (Pompeius) and his supporters (*qua dominus qua
advocati*).[1]   Moreover, his old friends the aristocracy, for
whom he had suffered so much, were offended at the
enthusiasm of his restoration.   ' Those who had clipped
his wings did not care to see them sprouting again.'
When he was bold enough to announce on April 5, in
the year 56, his intention of calling on the Senate to
review on May 15 the legislation of Caesar's consulate in
59, especially the allotment of the Campanian lands
under the agrarian law of that year, he made a bid for
his old position as champion of the aristocracy, he gave a
direct challenge to Caesar, and he raised for the Optimates a banner round which to rally.   He received no
support.   The Optimates would not rally round the flag,
but they would gladly have seen him wave it, because
they thought the disagreeably clever *parvenu* would thus
irritate Caesar' and alienate Pompeius.   This treachery
was too much for Cicero.   He lent a ready ear to the
suggestion of Pompeius that he should withdraw his
motion.   Quintus made himself surety for the good conduct of his brother when he met Pompeius in Sardinia ;
and shortly afterwards the Triumvirate was placed on a
firmer basis by the conference at Luca.   Cicero's *palinode*,
as he calls his speech *de provinciis consularibus*, was

[1] This seems certainly to be the meaning of Att. ii. 19. 3.   See
note in *Correspondence of Cicero*.

written expressly to make this step irrevocable (Att. iv.
5, 1). He confesses (Att. iv. 5, 1) that he was 'a downright ass' (*asinum germanum*) for not having made
common cause with the Triumvirs before, and for having
so long believed in the feeble and treacherous aristocrats.
But at this time Cicero despairs of society. Writing to
Curio he says: 'I am afraid when you come you will
find nothing here to interest you; public life is in such a
state of syncope, indeed almost complete collapse';[1] and
he writes to his brother Quintus: 'Nothing can be more
desperate than the state to which society has come.'[2]
We must remember that Cicero was now drawn to
Pompeius by old political associations, and to Caesar by
the consistent courtesy, kindness, and respect which
Caesar showed him; and that the Optimates, having
deliberately effaced themselves, had treacherously tried
to efface Cicero too. In these circumstances Cicero
might have followed the *Equites* in their shift over to
Caesar and the democrats. But no. The refuge to which
he sought to betake himself was cultured leisure; what
we would now call *otium cum dignitate*. 'If through his
desire for *otium* he somewhat sacrificed his *dignitas*, let
us remember that he was really not so much a politician
as a man of letters thrust into political life by his unex-
ampled literary endowments. And above all things let
us remember that it was only when the cause of Pompeius

---

[1] *Vereor mehercule ne cum veneris non habeas iam quod cures : ita
sunt omnia debilitata ac iam prope exstincta.* —Fam. ii. 5. 2.
[2] *Nihil est perditius his hominibus, his temporibus.* —Q. Fr. iii.
9, 1.

became really desperate that Cicero's heart went out to him. 'I never wanted to share his prosperity,' he writes to Atticus; 'would rather that I had shared his downfall.'[1] The ruin of Pompeius drew Cicero closer to him than his most splendid triumphs. Cato was not the only Roman in whose eyes the vanquished found more favour than the victorious cause.

The attitude of Cicero towards Caesar on the one hand, and Pompeius on the other, before the outbreak of the civil war, has been largely misrepresented. It has been urged that Cicero did not really believe in Pompeius as the champion of the Republic; that he knew that Pompeius was only using the Constitution as a peg on which to hang his personal pretensions; in short, that what both rivals were aiming at was one and the same thing—a *tyrannis*. It is true that there are many expressions in his letters which would seem to support this theory, but we must remember that we have in these letters (and this is what gives them their profound interest) the private and unstudied record of every passing phase in the mind of one whose literary genius enables him to stereotype each flitting smile or sigh in some matchlessly expressive and subtile phrase. Thus the correspondence of Cicero supplies us with apt texts in support of almost every conceivable theory of his character and principles. As once was said about the Holy Scriptures—

[1] *Numquam illius victoriae socius esse volui, calamitatis mallem fuisse.*— Att. ix. 12, 4.

Hic liber est in quo quaerit sua dogmata quisque,
    Invenit et pariter dogmata quisque sua.

This being so, it is unfair to set against the prevailing tone of his letters the hasty expression of a momentary fear, the feverish outburst of distracted petulance. Cicero does speak of Pompeius as being, like Caesar, actuated only by personal motives, but it is in the tone in which many a good Tory often said of Beaconsfield, 'I declare he is as bad as Gladstone.' A full and fair examination of the letters shows that he did regard Pompeius as the champion of the Republic, and Caesar as its declared foe. I propose, therefore, by means of quotations from the letters, to summarise as briefly as possible the evidence afforded by the letters for the settlement of this question.

I. Cicero did not look on neutrality as at all a possible course for a man of honour.

Quid ergo, inquis, acturus es ? idem quod pecudes, quae dispulsae sui generis sequuntur greges : ut bos armenta, sic ego bonos viros, aut eos quicunque dicentur boni, sequar, etiam si ruent. (Att. vii. 7, 7.)

Si erit bellum, cum Pompeio esse constitui. (Att. vii. 26, 3.)

(Depugnabo) cum bona quidem spe vel vincendi vel in libertate moriendi. (Att. vii. 9, 4.)

Si enim castris res geretur, video cum altero vinci satius esse quam cum altero vincere. (Att. vii. 1, 4.)

Sin bellum geretur non deero officio nec dignitati meae. (Att. vii. 17, 4.)

Sive enim ad concordiam res adduci potest sive ad bonorum victoriam, utriusvis rei me aut adiutorem velim esse, *aut certe non expertem*. (Att. vii. 1, 2.)

II. Cicero is resolved to follow Pompeius.

(1) Through gratitude and affection :—

Quia de me erat optime meritus. (Att. vii. 1, 2.)

Unus Pompeius me movet beneficio non auctoritate. (Att. viii. 1, 4.)

Cum merita Pompeii summa erga salutem meam, familiaritasque quae mihi cum eo est, tum ipsa reipublicae causa me adducit, ut mihi vel consilium meum cum illius consilio, vel fortuna cum fortuna coniungenda esse videatur. (Att. viii. 3, 2.)

Εἰ τοῖς εὐεργέταις καὶ φίλοις συγκινδυνευτέον ἐν τοῖς πολιτικοῖς κἂν μὴ δοκῶσιν εὖ βεβουλεῦσθαι περὶ τῶν ὅλων. (Att. ix. 4, 2.)

Quid si non ἑταίρῳ solum sed etiam εὐεργέτῃ ? (Att. ix. 5, 3.)

Beneficium sequor, mihi crede, non causam . . . causa igitur non bona est ? immo optima : sed agetur (memento) foedissime. (Att. ix. 7, 3.)

Nec mehercule hoc facio reipublicae causa quam funditus deletam puto ; sed ne quis me putet ingratum in eum qui me levavit iis incommodis quibus idem adfecerat. (Att. ix. 19, 2.)

Ego pro Pompeio lubenter emori possum. Facio pluris omnium hominum neminem. Sed non ita : 'uno in eo iudico spem de salute reipublicae.' (Att. viii. 2, 4.)

(2) As leader of the Optimates :—

Si maneo et illum comitatum optimorum et clarissimorum civium desero. (Att. viii. 3, 1.)

Dabimus hoc Pompeio quod debemus. Nam me quidem alius nemo movet ; non sermo bonorum qui nulli sunt ; non causa quae acta timide est, agetur improbe. Uni, uni hoc damus, ne id quidem roganti, nec suam causam (ut ait) agenti, sed publicam. (Att. ix. 1, 4.)

Εἰ καὶ μὴ δοκιμάζοντα τὴν διὰ πολέμου κατάλυσιν τῆς τυραννίδος, συναπογραπτέον ὅμως τοῖς ἀρίστοις. (Att. ix. 4, 2.)

(3) As about to restore the Republic :—

Quando Pompeius rempublicam recuperarit.   (Att. viii. 3, 2.)

Sed me movet unus vir ; cuius fugientis comes, rempublicam recuperantis, videor esse debere.   (Att. viii. 14, 2.)

Tali viro talem causam agenti.   (Att. ix. 5, 3.)

III. Cicero,. however, sees faults many and serious in the Optimate side and Pompeius.

(1) He despises their dilatoriness, irresolution, weakness, and abandonment of principle.

Bellum nostri nullum administrant.   (Att. vii. 20, 1.)

Nulla causa, nullae vires, nulla sedes quo concurrant qui rempublicam defensam velint.   (Att. viii. 3, 4.)

Quem fugiam habeo, quem sequar non habeo.   (Att. viii. 7, 2.)   See also to end of this letter.

At ille tibi, πολλὰ χαίρειν τῷ καλῷ dicens, pergit Brundisium. (Att. viii. 8, 2.)

Quid hoc miserius, quam alterum plausum in foedissima causa quaerere, alterum offensiones in optima ? alterum existimari conservatorem inimicorum, alterum desertorem amicorum ? (Att. viii. 9, 3.)

Nihil fieri potest miserius, nihil perditius, nihil foedius. (Att. viii. 11, 4.)

(2) He fears that if victorious they will inflict a terrible vengeance on their enemies.

Iovi ipsi iniquum.   (Att. viii. 15, 2.)

Homini magis ad vastandam Italiam quam ad vincendum parato.   (Att. viii. 16, 2.)

Bellum crudele et exitiosum suscipi a Pompeio intellegebam. (Att. ix. 6, 7.)

Mirandum in modum Gnaeus noster Sullani regni similitudinem concupivit . . . (causa) agetur . . . foedissime. (Att. ix. 7, 3.)

Huius belli genus fugi, et eo magis quod crudeliora etiam cogitari et parari videbam. (Att. ix. 10, 3.)

Bellum . . . comparat non iniustum ille quidem sed cum pium tum etiam necessarium, suis tamen civibus exitiabile nisi vicerit, calamitosum etiam si vicerit. (Att. x. 4, 3.)

(3) He fears that Pompeius and the Optimates strive for tyranny as well as Caesar.

De sua potentia dimicant homines hoc tempore, periculo civitatis. (Att. vii. 3, 4.)

Ex victoria cum multa mala tum certe tyrannus exsistet. (Att. vii. 5. 4.)

Si viceris tamen servias. (Att. vii. 7, 7.)

Uterque regnare vult. (Att. viii. 11, 2.)

Quorum utrique semper patriae salus et dignitas posterior sua dominatione . . . fuit. (Att. x. 4, 4.)

IV. Caesar's side he will not, cannot, join.

(1) He looks on Caesar as a leader of revolutionists, and regards his as *the wrong side*.

Omnes damnatos, omnes ignominia adfectos, omnes damnatione ignominiaque dignos illac facere. (Att. vii. 3, 5.)

Nec in caede principum clementiorem hunc fore quam Cinna fuerit, nec moderatiorem quam Sulla in pecuniis locupletum. (Att. vii. 7, 7.)

Numquam improbi cives habuerunt paratiorem ducem. (Fam. xvi. 11, 3.)

Χρεῶν ἀποκοπὰς, φυγάδων καθόδους, sescenta alia scelera moliri. (Att. vii. 11, 1.)

Mirus invaserat furor non solum improbis sed etiam his qui boni habentur ut pugnare cuperent. (Fam. xvi. 12, 2.)

Foedissima causa. (Att. vii. 9, 3.)

Qui hic potest se gerere non perdite? Vetant vita, mores,
ante facta, ratio suscepti negotii, socii, vires bonorum aut etiam
constantia? (Att. ix. 2a, 2.)

Ardet furore et scelere . . . nec iam recusat sed quodam-
modo postulat ut, quemadmodum est, sic etiam appelletur
tyrannus. (Att. x. 4, 2.)

(2) Caesar is called *perditus civis* (Att. vii. 13);
perditissimus (Att. viii. 2); *tyrannus* (Att. vii. 20, and
passim). His conduct is *furor* (Att. vii. 14), and *scelus*
(*passim*).

(3) Cicero could not face the odium of such a course.

αἰδέομαι Τρῶας, nec solum civis sed etiam amici officio revocor.
(Att. vii. 12, 3.)

Audio . . . hanc cunctationem nostram non probari, multaque in me et severe in conviviis tempestivis quidem disputari;
cedamus igitur. (Att. ix. 1, 3.)

Nec enim ferre potero sermones istorum quicunque sunt—
non sunt enim certe ut appellantur boni. (Att. ix. 2a, 3.)

(4) To join Caesar would be *dishonourable.*

Fac posse tuto; multi enim hortantur. Num etiam honeste?
Nullo modo. (Att. vii. 22, *fin.*)

Cautior certe est mansio; honestior existimatur traiectio.
Malo interdum multi me non caute, quam pauci non honeste,
fecisse existiment. (Att. viii. 15, 2.)

Quid rectum sit apparet; quid expediat obscurum est.
(Fam. v. 19, 2.)

Ab illis est periculum, si peccaro; ab hoc, si recte fecero.
(Att. x. 8, 5.)

V. As Cicero is not blind to the weaknesses of
Pompeius and his side, so he clearly discerns the strong

points in Caesar's conduct and character, as, for instance, his tolerance and wise moderation.

Si mehercule neminem occiderit, nec cuiquam quidquam ademerit, ab his qui eum maxime timuerant maxime diligetur. (Att. viii. 13, 1.)

So that it was not through a mere recoil from Caesar that Cicero threw himself into the cause of Pompeius.

Max Budinger, in an able article on *Cicero und der Patriciat,* has shown what cordial feelings existed both before and after the outbreak of the civil war between Cicero and Caesar, not as politicians, but as men of the world.   A few references will be sufficient here.   For a favourable view of Caesar see Orat. de prov. cons. (delivered 56), § 40 ff. ; in Vatin. §§ 16, 22 (delivered same year) ; pro Sest. §§ 16, 132 (delivered same year) ; Fam. iv. 4, 3-4 (written 47) ; Fam. iv. 6, 3 (written 45) ; Fam. vi. 6, §§ 8, 9, 10, 13 (written 46).   See also the fine eulogy in Phil. ii. 116.   Caesar dedicated the De Analogia to Cicero (Brut. § 253).

In Att. vii. 20, 2, Cicero writes that the considerations which urge him to fly from Rome to the camp of Pompeius are 'his friendship with Gnaeus, the Optimate cause, the shamefulness of making common cause with a tyrant, about whom one could not be sure whether he was destined to prove a Phalaris or a Pisistratus.' A reference to a letter of Cicero to Sulpicius (Fam. iv. 4, 3-4) will show how conspicuously Caesar proved himself to be not a Phalaris, but a Pisistratus, and something far more than a Pisistratus.

Accordingly, the whole state of Cicero's mind before

the outbreak of the civil war may thus be summed up :—
What Cicero hoped for was an arrangement (*compositio,
concordia*).　Anything should be surrendered rather than
have war.[1]　War will bring the *tyrannis*.　Therefore Cicero
hesitates, and does not openly join Pompeius, whose
flight from Italy he condemns, while he despises the in-
capacity, dilatoriness, cowardice (almost) of his supporters.
Moreover, peace is what Cicero most desires : now peace
Pompeius will not have :[2] he even fears it.[3]　Yet Cicero
hopes he will be able to influence Pompeius.[4]　On the
other hand, Caesar is very powerful, very active, and
very conciliatory.　But Cicero says 'he is running a-
muck' (*ruit*) ; he is *perditus ;* he is a *tyrannus ;* his acts
are *furor, scelus*.　If war is unavoidable, Cicero *must*
join Pompeius ; not to do so would be inglorious, dishonourable, ungrateful.　Yet, again, to think of the
recklessness of the Optimates and the violence which
would follow their victory.　No matter : Pompeius alone
moves Cicero ; the acts of him and his side have been a
tissue of blunders : but his side is the right one.　'Mihi
σκάφος,' he writes, Att. vii. 3, 5, 'unum erit quod a
Pompeio gubernabitur.'

---

[1] *Ego is sum qui illi concedi putem utilius esse quod postulat,
quam signa conferri.*—Att. vii. 5, 5.

[2] *Quod quaeris ecquae spes pacificationis sit quantum ex Pompeii multo et accurato sermone perspexi,* ne voluntas quidem est.—
Att. vii. 8, 4.

[3] *Non modo non expetere pacem istam* sed etiam timere *visus
est.*—Att. vii. 8, 5.

[4] *Ipsum Pompeium separatim ad concordiam hortabor.*—Att.
vii. 3, 5.

The later life of Cicero does not present the same difficulties as have been found in his relations with the democracy in his early career, his subsequent attitude towards the Triumvirs, and his choice of a side in the civil war. His government of his province was astonishingly pure for his age, though we find that it realised for him a considerable fortune; that he was not firm enough to persevere in his refusal to favour Brutus in his rapacious claims on the citizens of Salamis in Cyprus; and that he made no attempt to develop the material resources of the country.

The restoration of the Commonwealth of the Scipios was but a dream; still it was a beautiful dream, and Cicero gave his life for it. We may thus sum up the motives of principles which guided him.

Cicero, like every politician, was actuated by mixed motives in the line which he took. He desired to achieve the commanding position to which he felt that his powers entitled him; but he did not wish to reach by crooked paths an eminence, however great. He was ambitious to rise, but he was ambitious to rise by inspiring his fellow-countrymen with a strong and abiding sense of those pre-eminent abilities of which he was conscious, and to use his power, when attained, in the honest service of the best interests of the State, as he conceived them. That vanity and self-laudation, which is so repugnant to our sense of fitness, was a vice not only of the man, but also of the age, though no doubt he was vain to a degree conspicuous even then. How different from ours was the spirit of the time when even Caesar, on whose ' marvel-

lous serenity' Mommsen dwells so lovingly, could send
such a letter to the senate as *veni, vidi, vici*. With
what ridicule would such a despatch now be received by
Parliament and the Press. Cicero lived in an epoch
when pro-consuls sought and found their 'laurels in a
must cake,' and on their return to Rome enjoyed the
empty pageantry of a triumph or a *supplicatio*, which
was often but a mockery of their demonstrated incom-
petence. But, in spite of characteristic weaknesses,
Cicero was a great power in his age. In the opinion
of his contemporaries he saved Rome in the time of
Catiline, and did his best to save it in the time of
Antonius. When once fairly embarked in politics, Cicero
was eminently serviceable to the party of his adoption.
For these services he has been condemned by Mommsen,
but has won the enthusiastic praise of Pliny, who rightly
sees the splendid triumphs of a born orator, not the en-
forced drudgery of a slighted hireling, in the speeches
which persuaded the people to abandon the Agrarian
Law, 'that is, their food,'[1] and to spare Roscius ; and
which induced the descendants of the Sullan proscripts
to relinquish their claim to office. It was the same
magic power which extorted from the *iudices* the condemnation of Verres, and which sent Catiline half
stunned from the Senate. It would be very easy to
add to Pliny a long array of enthusiastic admirers of
Cicero among ancient writers. The eloquent eulogy of
Velleius Paterculus (ii. 66) has often been quoted, and
Quintilian (Inst. Or. xii. 1, 15) has given a noble testi-

[1] Plin. Nat. Hist. vii. 31.

mony to the patriotism of Cicero : Cremutius Cordus, quoted by Seneca (Suas. vii.), writes that he was 'conspicuous not only for the greatness but the number of his virtues'; and Livy (Sen. *ibid.*) says that 'to praise him as he deserves we ought to have another Cicero.' But these witnesses are superfluous to him who reads the letters as they have been read by all historians from Niebuhr to Merivale ; while Mommsen and Drumann would no doubt dismiss their evidence with a sneer, and again betake themselves to their *acte d'accusation.*[1]

[1] I quote here the concluding words of an admirably just and learned account of the life of Cicero in the 'Quarterly Review,' by Mr. Strachan-Davidson, of Balliol College, Oxford :—

'His is one of those characters whose faults lie on the surface ; and the preservation of his most secret letters has withdrawn the veil which hides the weakness and the pettiness of most men from the eyes of posterity. His memory has thus been subjected to a test of unprecedented sharpness. Nevertheless, the faithful friends who resolved to present to the world his confidential utterances, unspoiled by editorial garbling, have not only earned our gratitude by the gift of a unique historical monument, but have judged most nobly and most truly what was due to the reputation of Cicero. As it was in his lifetime, so it has been with his memory : those who have known him most intimately have commonly loved him best. He is no demi-god to be set on a pedestal for the worship of the nations, but a man with human virtues and human weaknesses, and withal possessed of a charm of grace and goodness which makes us think of him as of some familiar and beloved friend. The calm retrospective judgment of Caesar Augustus, recorded for us by Plutarch (Life of Cicero, ch. 49), sums up not unfairly the story of Cicero's life.

' " It happened many years after, that Caesar once found one of his grandsons with a work of Cicero in his hands. The boy was frightened and hid the book under his gown ; but Caesar took it

II

CICERO IN HIS PRIVATE LIFE

Cicero is presented to us even at the very commence-
ment of his correspondence as being in easy circumstances.
He already possesses his estates at Formiae and Tusculum. We find him in the year 67 looking out for
objets d'art for his *gymnasium* at Tusculum, and he is in
a position to pay some £170 for certain statues made of
the κογχίτης λίθος, for which Megara was famous. He
had inherited from his father an estate in Arpinum, in
the neighbourhood of the two country houses of his
brother Quintus, Arcanum and Laterium; and a house
in Rome on the Carinae, which he seems to have made
over to his brother Quintus,[1] when he himself, after his
consulate, bought for nearly £30,000 the magnificent
house of M. Crassus on the Palatine, which brought on
him so much envy and misconstruction. The marriage
portion which he received on marrying Terentia, at the
age of 29, amounted to about £3400. But even before
this time he was in a position, in the years 79, 78, to
make a tour through Greece and Asia. What, then,
were the sources of Cicero's income, for there is no

from him, and standing there motionless he read through a great
part of the book; then he gave it back to the boy and said,
*This was a great orator, my child, a great orator and a man who
loved his country well."* '

[1] Plut. Cic. viii.

evidence that his father left him any great fortune?
The chief source, no doubt, was his practice at the Bar,
especially as the advocate of foreign States and Kings.
For though the Cincian Law[1] forbade the feeing of
advocates, yet there is abundant evidence that the thank-
fulness of successfully-defended clients generally took a
substantial form. We may perhaps infer from Att. i.
20, 7, that the gratitude of L. Papirius Pætus showed
itself in the appropriate present of his library, and the
tone of this passage leads us to surmise that the Lex
Cincia de Muneribus, now nearly 150 years old, had to
a great extent become obsolete.[2] Cicero, then, who devoted himself to the Bar at the early age of 25, must
have made a considerable income by his profession. For
there seems to have been but one other source of income
to him—legacies left by grateful clients or admiring
friends. Plutarch tells us that early in life he was bequeathed a sum of about £3000, but his receipts under
this head are probably much exaggerated.[3] For instance,
we are asked to believe that in 59 the Stoic Diodotus,

[1] This law was really an aristocratic measure. It shut the
career of an advocate to all who did not possess some fortune.
It denied the necessities of life to the advocate, while it gave him
the luxuries, which came in the form of handsome presents from
wealthy clients. The Bar then, as a political career, until very
recent times, was the privilege of the well-to-do.

[2] It is possible, indeed, that the remark here may be merely
playful, as there is no evidence that Cicero ever acted as advocate
for Papirius Pætus. But, besides this passage, there is abundant
proof that this law was practically a dead letter.

[3] Cicero boasts (Phil. ii. 40) that he had received in bequests
above £170,000, but this is probably a rhetorical hyperbole.

who had been for some time an inmate of Cicero's house, left him heir to a sum equal to about £85,000 ! Of a truth—

Sapiens uno minor est Iove, dives,
Liber, honoratus, pulcher, rex denique regum,

if he can make such bequests to his friends or hosts. But the grandeur of the legacy is as nothing compared with the coolness of the legatee, *Diodotus mortuus est ; reliquit nobis II. S. fortasse centies* (Att. ii. 20, 6), and then he passes to other trifling topics. Malaspina is no doubt right in reading *sestertia centum*, about £850. At the age of 61, in the year 45, Cicero did receive a very large legacy from Cluvius, which he tells us brought in nearly £700 a-year, and afterwards over £800 : *vehementer me Cluviana delectant*,[1] he says to his friend Atticus when he discovers how valuable his legacy is about to prove. Cicero appears [2] to have been able to serve the interests of this rich Puteolan by using in his favour his influence with Q. Thermus, who governed Asia as pro-praetor in 51. There seems to have existed in Ancient Rome a testamentary mania, in consequence of which distinguished public characters often became the heirs of men personally quite unknown to them. The obscure *millionaire* loved at his death to divide his riches between two or three of the most eminent public characters of the day. It was not a tribute to the character or the politics of the legatee. Such bequests were thought to reflect distinction on the testator. Caesar and Cicero were co-heirs of Cluvius; and Cicero was

---

[1] Att. xiv. 9, 1.   [2] Fam. xiii. 56.

coupled with the detested Clodius in the will of the architect Cyrus. This vagary of human folly ought not to cause much surprise. Are there not now those who during life devote their resources to the entertaining of distinguished persons, whose society they dislike; or the purchase of works of art, the merits of which they cannot appreciate; or who, at their death, apply to ostentatious charity wealth equitably due to dependents or benefactors?

Such, then, were the main sources of Cicero's income, for he refused to avail himself of the ordinary avenues to wealth in Rome. These were, first and chiefly, the plunder of the provinces. Cicero turned his back on this means of enriching himself by waiving his claim to a province after his praetorship and his consulate. When, in the year 51, he did accept the government of Cilicia, he set his face against the illegal practices by which Appius had 'depleted' the province. We may form an estimate of the wealth to be amassed by an unscrupulous governor, when we learn from Cicero himself that, in spite of the rigorous purism of his administration, he laid by in his provincial life nearly £19,000. This sum, which was in *cistophori*, the Asiatic currency, he deposited in the hands of certain *publicani* in Ephesus.[1] Another

---

[1] Cicero distinctly tells Rufus (Fam. v. 20, 9) that Pompeius appropriated this money. Yet we read in the early letters of the eleventh book to Atticus of this sum of money apparently still intact. It seems impossible to escape from the inference of Boot that the statement made by Cicero to Rufus was untrue, and that it was made with the design of comforting Rufus, who had recently sustained a pecuniary loss. Rufus was his quaestor.

road to a fortune neglected by Cicero was the practice of usury.[1] It is a singular feature in the social life of this period, that men of the highest distinction lent money on interest to individuals and corporations.   Brutus, though according to Shakspere he condemned Cassius for his itching palm, had large transactions of this kind, and it was thus that Atticus amassed the wealth which he knew so well how to keep.   Nor was this trade confined to men.   There is much reason to believe that Terentia seriously embarrassed her husband by speculations, in which she allowed herself to be defrauded by her steward and freedman Philotimus.   Caerellia,[2] too, seems to have had extensive business transactions.   From these Cicero

---

[1] This mode of acquiring wealth was by no means deemed disreputable in Rome.   But Cicero does not seem to have sought thus to add to his resources.   He uses, in one of his letters to Quintus (Q. Fr. i. 3, 6), an expression which seems designedly employed to show that his means were more honourably acquired. Writing from exile, he speaks of himself as one who once was *liberis, coniuge, copiis*, genere ipso pecuniae, *beatissimus.*   Cicero did not look down on trade.   In Parad. 6 he writes, *qui honeste rem quaerunt mercaturis faciendis ;* but he aspires, for himself, to the function which Scipio, in the Republic (i. 35), claims, *cum mihi sit unum opus hoc a parentibus maioribusque meis relictum, procuratio atque administratio reipublicae.*

[2] This interesting woman (the loss of whose correspondence with Cicero is much to be regretted) for many years afforded to him that intelligent sympathy in his literary labours which he sought in vain from Terentia.   She was the Stella of Cicero.   That the intimacy partook in no degree of the nature of an intrigue is plain from the friendly relations which subsisted between Caerellia and Terentia.   Yet the rancour of Dio Cassius has not recoiled even from this aspersion.   Like Swift, Comte, and Goethe, Cicero felt

always held aloof, though we find him ever ready to lend to a friend, and very frequently obliged to borrow.[1] His exile and its consequences involved him in difficulties, from which he never wholly emerged. Yet he cannot have ever been deeply in debt, for we find him throughout his life in possession of half a dozen country residences in the most delightful parts of Italy, together with 'lodges,' or *deversoria*, at Tarracina, Sinuessa, Cales, and Anagnia, which the want of hotels rendered necessary for persons of distinction who would travel in a manner befitting their rank. In the matter of money lent to him, Cicero shows a fastidious sense of honour quite in advance of his age. He feels it incumbent on him to apply to the repayment of his debt to Caesar the money which he had received for the expenses of his triumph, 'because it looks ugly to be in debt to a political opponent.'[2] Again, on leaving Rome after the death of

the charm of a woman's sympathy ; but Caerellia never had reason to regret that she had extended it to him. In his respect for the sanctity of domestic life Cicero presents a strong contrast to the manners of his age. Other traits in his character, too, show an approximation to modern modes of feeling and thought—notably his refined repugnance to the cruel sports of the amphitheatre.— Fam. vii. 1, 3.

[1] Cicero walks under his load of difficulties with a light step, which reminds us of Sheridan, with whom, indeed, the *scurra consularis* has other affiuities. He says of his country houses at Tusculum and Pompeii, *me, illum ipsum vindicem aeris alieni, aere non Corinthio sed hoc circumforaneo obruerunt* (Att. ii. 1, 11); and again (Fam. v. 6, 2), *itaque nunc me scito tantum habere aeris alieni, ut cupiam coniurare, si quis me recipiat.*

[2] *Est enim ἄμορφον ἀντιπολιτευομένου χρεωφειλέτην esse.*—Att. vii. 8, 5.

Caesar,[1] he writes to Atticus : — 'I am owed money enough to satisfy all claims on me ; yet it often happens that debtors fail to pay in due time.   If anything of this sort should happen, pray consult only my reputation. Borrow afresh to meet the demands of my creditors, or even raise money by selling my property.'

His married life with Terentia was decorous, but destitute of real sympathy.   His early letters from exile are full of tender expressions, but he seems to have become gradually estranged.   He suspects her of frittering away his money under the evil influence of Philotimus.   His last letter[2] to her reminds us of the celebrated 'chops and tomato sauce,' which the counsel for Mrs. Bardell found so difficult to construe into the language of affection.   Cicero has been blamed for his divorce of Terentia, and his remarriage with the youthful Publilia at the age of 63.   But it must be remembered that 63 was not then thought so advanced an age as it is now.   Men began life much later than in modern times.   Cicero cannot be said to have begun his political life till he was nearly 40 years of age, and Caesar began his career as a great general at an age at which Alexander was dead and Napoleon had been conquered.

Nor was the career of his son Marcus a source of happiness to Cicero.   Finding him intractable under the

---

[1] Att. xvi. 2, 2.

[2] *In Tusculanum nos venturos putamus aut Nonis aut postridie. Ibi ut sint omnia parata.   Plures enim fortasse nobiscum erunt et, ut arbitror, diutius ibi commorabimur.   Labrum si in balineo non est, ut sit ; item cetera, quae sunt ad victum et valetudinem necessaria.*—Fam. xiv. 20.

hands of his tutor Dionysius, his father sent him to Athens (as to an University) to complete his education. His allowance seems very ample, amounting, as it did, to about £850 a-year. Yet the youth squanders this on carousing and entertainments, while his tutor Gorgias abets his extravagances and dissipations, reminding us of Doctor Pangloss in the *Heir-at-Law*. Young Marcus seems never to have thoroughly cast off the vices of his youth. In the letter to Tiro (Fam. xvi. 21), in which he announces his complete reformation, we cannot help feeling that the young man 'protests too much,' and we hear that, even after Augustus raised him to the consulate, he distinguished himself by his drunken excesses.[1] It is a sad reflection to think what the consulate was when the great orator had to strain every nerve to gain it, and what it was when, as a late return for the services of the father, the Emperor conferred it, as a piece of patronage, on a brainless profligate.

[1] Brutus, however, commended his services at Pharsalia, and the delighted father dedicated to young Marcus the De Officiis. It is very interesting to observe how, under the profligacy and superficial cultivation of the declining Republic, still we may occasionally catch a glimpse of the old Roman qualities, by which *fortis Etruria crevit*. We can still see the iron hand in war. Quintus lays down his bloody axe and well-worn scourge ; young Marcus casts the reveller's chaplet from his brow ; to wield the sword with all the energy of Camillus or Scipio. Plutarch remarks that by a singular coincidence Divine justice reserved the completion of the punishment of Antonius for the house of Cicero : after the capture of the fleet of Antonius, which was immediately followed by his death, it was to the new consul, M. Cicero, that the official despatch announcing the victory was sent.

It is in his daughter Tullia that Cicero finds his solace and pride. Like Francis Atterbury, he found in the society of a daughter his one refuge from the changes and chances of a troublous life. He is never wearied of recounting her virtues. Indeed, he so eulogises her intellectual powers and her acquired knowledge, that he has almost earned for her the unenviable reputation of an *esprit fort*, or even a blue-stocking. Her infatuation for Dolabella, her third husband, is quite consistent with her father's account of her. We often find women of really exceptional intellect yielding to the fascinations of a handsome, shallow, somewhat clever Bohemian. Such was the blind admiration which the Brontë sisters felt for their worthless brother ; such was the love of George Eliot's Romola for Tito ; and such was the strange infatuation which made Tullia cling to Dolabella, in spite of his wicked extravagance, which squandered her dower, and his insulting infidelities with Caecilia Metella, which he hardly took the trouble to conceal. Tullia had lost her first husband, the noble Piso, by death ; she was then married to Crassipes. It was when her father was absent in Cilicia that her hand was sought for the third time. Among her suitors was Tiberius Nero, the father of the Emperor. Tullia died in childbirth,[1] at the age of 31, at her father's house in Tusculum, where she had taken refuge from the outrages of Dolabella. Cicero never recovered her loss. He never forgave Publilia, who betrayed joy at her death, and never again received her into his house, in spite of the girl's earnest

[1] She had had no children by her previous marriages.

entreaties for the forgiveness of her aged husband. One cannot but smile to find Cicero at once preparing to deify his dead daughter, as Hadrian afterwards deified his beloved slave. We owe to the death of Tullia the letter of Sulpicius, written to console the bereaved father (Ep. lx.) This is by far the best of the extant letters *to* Cicero, which, as a rule, show an amazing inferiority to the letters of the orator himself. There is a good letter from Matius (Ep. lxxiii.), and many amusing letters from others, but this is the only great letter, not by Cicero himself, in the whole correspondence. It is sad to see how little real consolation Sulpicius could offer to his friend. He urges him to moderate his grief for his daughter; to see her father so wretched would wound her loving heart were she alive; perhaps it wounds her even now, *si qui etiam inferis sensus est.*

In his romantic love for his daughter and his indifference to his wife, the character of Cicero presents a trait familiar in modern French life. Again, we have a view very characteristic of the modern Frenchman in the lightness with which he assigns to Terentia religion as her department, while his own business is with men.[1] Another

---

[1] *Neque Di quos tu castissime coluisti, neque homines quibus ego semper servivi.*—Fam. xiv. 5, 1; cf. also Fam. xiv. 7, 1. We find often in Cicero casual hints at his agnosticism, for instance, in Att. iv. 10, 1, *fors viderit, aut si qui est qui curet Deus;* and in the Pro Cluent. 171, we have this remarkable passage:—*nam nunc quidem quid tandem illi mali mors attulit? Nisi forte ineptiis et fabulis ducimur, ut existimemus illum apud inferos impiorum supplicia perferre . . . quae si falsa sunt, id quod omnes intellegunt, quid ei tandem aliud mors eripuit praeter*

thoroughly French feature in his disposition is his hatred for provincial life. 'I cannot express to you,' he writes (Att. v. 11, 1), 'how I am consumed with longing for the town, how intolerably insipid is this provincial life.' A letter to Caelius (Fam. ii. 12, 2), in the passage beginning *Urbem, urbem, mi Rufe, cole, et in ista luce vive,* breathes the very spirit of the *salon* and *boulevard.*

It is singular that the correspondence of another great letter-writer should be marked by the same overflowing love for a daughter. Madame de Sévigné's love for 'the prettiest girl in France' certainly was not so well placed as the love of Cicero for Tullia. Madame de Grignan seems to have been selfish, extravagant, and cold-hearted —not, indeed, nearly so lovable as her brother Charles de Sévigné. Indeed we can hardly acquit the clever Frenchwoman of assuming a *rôle,* and posing in the picturesque attitude of the adoring mother.

Cicero speaks in the highest terms of his father and

---

sensum doloris? In the speech for Rabirius (29) Cicero anticipates an eternal existence for the souls of the good, basing it on the instinctive belief of mankind : again, in the De Har. Resp. (19), he affirms his belief in the existence of gods, grounding it on the evidences of design in Nature. Again, in De Nat. Deor. (i. 37), and in De Rep. (vi. 16), he speaks of an overruling Providence. But it is strange how lightly his beliefs sit upon him, and how little they influence his conduct : in Tusc. i. 74 he says that the God who holds authority in our breast forbids us to leave our post without his leave ; yet we know that during his exile he clearly and deliberately contemplates the commission of this act, and we hear nothing at all about any prohibition of conscience, or even a hint that self-destruction is unworthy of a good man. See note on Ep. lx. 6.

mother. Of the former he writes (De Or. ii. 1) as *optimi ac prudentissimi viri*, and there is good reason to think that the beginning of his poem on his consulship was devoted to an elaborate eulogy of his father.[1] Cicero has often been accused of want of filial feeling, because he has been supposed to have curtly announced the death of his father to Atticus in the words *pater nobis decessit a. d. iiii. Kal. Decembris* (Att. i. 6, 2 ; Ep. iii.) In my notes on that passage I have fully discussed the soundness of the text. It is enough here to observe that even if the text be sound, it is quite probable that Cicero had announced to Atticus in more fitting terms his father's death, and is here (in answer to a question from Atticus) merely reminding his friend of the date—'the date of my poor father's death (for this is the force of *nobis*) was Nov. 27.'[2]

While acquitting Cicero in this particular instance, one cannot help noticing, even in the most refined of the ancient Romans, an absence of sensibilities which polish, and even sweeten, the intercourse of modern life. In Att. i. 3 Cicero announces to Atticus the death of the grandmother of Atticus in jesting phrase, which good taste must condemn. It seems that the lady was not dear to Atticus, and that he was not at all likely to feel real grief for her ; yet there is certainly a coarseness of tone in the letter. A sentiment of reverence

[1] See note on Att. i. 19, 10, in *Correspondence of Cicero.*

[2] For strong expressions of real sorrow for the death of a slave, and again, of a mere acquaintance, we have to go no farther than Att. i. 12, 4, and iv. 6, 1.

should be inspired by the thought of death, and even if it be not felt, it should be assumed. In such a case, if ever, hypocrisy is a homage to good taste.

In connection with this vindication of Cicero from attributed want of affection, it will be pertinent to examine briefly a few other charges brought against Cicero on the authority of his own letters.

In Att. iii. 12, 2, Cicero says, ' I am shocked that my speech against Curio has become public. I wrote it under the influence of anger, and as a reply to his attack on me. But I thought I had prevented any chance of its getting into circulation. However, inasmuch as I happen never to have had any verbal altercation with him, and inasmuch as it is written with less than my usual care, I think a good case could be made to show it was not by me.' When Cicero wrote this he was in an agony of suspense about the success or failure of the attempts to bring about his restoration. A speech against Curio and Clodius, of the literary execution of which he was ashamed, and which was extremely likely to inflame still more against him the resentment of his enemies, had, in spite of Cicero's efforts to prevent it, somehow got into public circulation. Cicero accordingly wished that it could be represented not to be his. It seems to me that even at the present day, if a public man wrote something which, on reflection, appeared likely to injure him, and also was unworthy of him in style, he would feel a desire to disown the article, or at least would refrain from acknowledging it to be his, which would probably have very much the same effect. It is, however, extremely unlikely that the supposed modern statesman, even in a letter to an intimate friend, would own his real feelings. And this very fact must be placed to the credit of modern society. Christianity and chivalry have made certain acts and sentiments impossible for a gentleman to avow.

One is bound to take into account the different points of view from which an act presents itself to the moral sense at different epochs of society. Cicero did favour his friend Brutus in a dispute with the Salaminians; but Brutus could hardly understand why Cicero should take the Salaminians into account at all. Cicero was in advance of his age in every way, and behind the present age, not in obedience to the dictates of the moral sense, but only in the education and refinement of it. This consideration, I think, entitles Cicero to an acquittal in the two following cases.

We learn (Att. vi. 6, 4) that Cicero was desirous of securing the good will of Caelius for his friend Atticus; so he dictated to the copyist of Atticus, who happened to be with him, a letter in praise of Caelius, which he read to Caelius as having come from Atticus.[1] Cicero, in all *naïveté* exclaims, *at te apud eum, di boni! quanta in gratia posui, eique legi litteras non tui sed librarii tui.* It never occurred to Cicero that it was base to stoop to a fabrication even to serve a friend.

In the year 47 B.C. a packet of letters from Quintus, directed to various friends, fell accidentally into the hands of Marcus. Some of them he forwarded to their destination. But on learning from these persons that

[1] Att. xi. 9, 2.

the letters forwarded by him were full of atrocious reflections upon himself, he opened the remaining missives,
and sent them to Atticus, leaving it to him to decide
whether they should be retained or sent to their destination. 'The fact that they have been opened,' he suggests,
'makes no matter, for I fancy Pomponia has his seal-
ring.' This, of course, strongly conflicts with modern
notions about honour, but the writer is supremely uncon-
scious that the act is in any way questionable.[1] Yet of
those who would now look on such an act as worse than
a crime, how few would be capable of the high-mindedness
with which Cicero acted on his discovery of his brother's
treachery ! He wrote to Caesar a letter (of which we still
preserve the copy which he sent to Atticus ; Att. xi. 12,
2) completely absolving his brother from the suspicion
of having instigated his own hostility against Caesar, or
having urged him to fly to Greece, and begging the good
offices of Caesar for a brother under the recent sense of
whose baseness to him he must have been still smarting.
It seems to me that this is an act of large nobleness and
truly chivalrous feeling, quite startling when we remember the times in which Cicero lived.

The character of Quintus is very remarkable. One is
familiar with the domestic bully, who in the world is an
obsequious sycophant. But in Quintus we have the
exactly opposite type. With his friends he is

> Jealous in honour, sudden and quick in quarrel :

---

[1] The same observations apply to a practice which Cicero
acknowledges that he adopts in giving introductory letters to
friends : see Fam. xiii. 6a.

the violence of his expressions [1] makes us feel that in his
tragedies he must have 'torn the passion to tatters': in
his province he is a wild beast in ferocity, though he
seems to have sought to be just, and he certainly was
not rapacious; he returned from Asia as poor as he left
Rome; but woe to the luckless provincial who was
caught tripping; the scourge was not cruel enough for
Quintus, nor the axe sufficiently expeditious.   Not
Shakspere's Richard was more ready to cry 'Off with his
head!' [2] But in private life he was the humblest of men.
Haec ego patior cotidie is his plaintive ejaculation
when Pomponia insults him in presence of his brother
Marcus, and refuses to sit at table because Quintus
had sent his slave Statius on before to see if dinner
were ready (Ep. xxvi.) No doubt the undue influence
accorded to Statius in domestic matters was resented
by the mistress of the household; but the paramount
position of that slave seems to show that (in his private
life), had Quintus been emancipated from the tyranny of
Pomponia, he would have experienced but a change of
rulers.   The letters of Marcus are full of affection
towards his brother Quintus.   Nor does he fail in solici-
tude for him and his son even after he has discovered

---

[1] Cicero, writing to Atticus (xv. 29, 2), says of Quintus, *ego
tamen suspicior hunc,* UT SOLET, *alucinari:* for examples of the
violence of Quintus, see Q. Fr. i. 2, 6.

[2] I write 'Shakspere's Richard' advisedly. Shakspere's
Richard more than once cries 'Off with his head!' The oft-quoted
line—'Off with his head! So much for Buckingham' is not from
Shakspere, but from Colley Cibber.

their base treachery in seeking to prejudice him with Caesar.

T. Pomponius Atticus, who stood to Cicero in the relation which Sir Horace Mann occupied to the Cicero of English letter-writing, Horace Walpole, is not a pleasing person. His persistent neutrality in politics[1] was a course which, though nowise reprehensible in our own times, must have been very much condemned in the days of Cicero. Yet he seems to have escaped to a great extent from adverse criticism; and, though connected with the unfortunate Sulpicius, he succeeded in living uninjured by Cinnan or Sullan, and in affording pecuniary assistance to Marius in his flight. He was intimate with the best Romans, from Sulla to Augustus; he was on good terms with both Caesar and Pompeius; he had the warm friendship of Brutus, Hortensius, and Cicero, and excited the enthusiastic admiration of Cornelius Nepos, the friend of Catullus. This he accomplished partly by availing himself of the shelter of his philosophic opinions. The Epicurean was speculatively bound to prefer the life of thought to the life of action. But he could not have preserved his complete tranquillity had he not early migrated to Athens, and there remained for about twenty years. In Athens we find him leading the life of a cultured gentleman, a recognised patron of literature and the fine arts, and recommending himself to his adopted fellow-citizens by gifts of corn grown, no

---

[1] As regards actions at least. He had, it appears, the strongest political feelings. We are told that Atticus exclaimed *periisse causam si* (Caesar) *funere elatus esset.*

doubt, on his Epirote estate—a Roman practice which Cicero seems disposed to condemn.[1] As a thorough man of business,[2] a ready lender of money, and a literary critic of the first order, Atticus was, of course, very useful to Cicero, but no doubt the keen *negotiator* found not a little that was negotiable in his relations with the great *littérateur*. Atticus kept large numbers of *librarii*, or slaves who acted as copyists. These, no doubt, executed many copies of the masterpieces of Cicero, and thus contributed not a little to fill the coffers of their master. Atticus seems to have neglected none of the avenues to wealth, and even to have discovered some new ones for himself. Not only do we find him practising money-lending on a large scale, but we even read of his buying and training bands of gladiators, to be hired out to the Aediles for their public shows.[3] And the wealth thus accumulated was preserved by a consistent parsimony in his household *ménage*, on which Cicero often rallies him. In Att. vi. 1, 13, he takes him to task for serving up cheap vegetables on expensive plate, and asks what would be his fare if his service were of earthenware ; and in Att. xvi. 3, 1, he sends Atticus his treatise De Gloria, which he asks him to have copied on large paper, and, in suggesting that he should read it for his guests at a dinner which he

---

[1] Att. vi. 6, 2, *Heus tu πυροὺς εἰς δῆμον Athenis ! Placet hoc tibi ?*

[2] Nepos tells us (ch. 6) *nullius rei neque praes neque manceps factus est.*

[3] Att. iv. 4*b*, 2 (Ep. xiii.) ; iv. 8*a*, 2.

was about to give, Cicero adds: 'but give them a decent entertainment, an you love me; else they will vent on my treatise their indignation against you. Nepos (Vit. Att. 13) says that he knows as a fact that the amount allowed by Atticus for household expenses was 3000 *asses*, or about six guineas of our money, a-month.

Nothing seemed more important to Atticus than to conceal as much as possible his business relations, and to appear before the world as a literary gentleman living on his estates in Epirus and elsewhere. When we find that his uncle, the odious Caecilius, from whom Cicero tells us even his own relations could not get a farthing under twelve per cent, adopted Atticus, and left him heir to a large fortune, one is a little tempted to think that the usurer Caecilius was in reality a secret partner of Atticus, taking much of the profits and all the obloquy, and not unwilling on those terms to play Jorkins to the Spenlos of his influential nephew.

One cannot much admire the character of the man who was on terms of intimate friendship with Clodius during his persecution of Cicero, and who, after the murder of Cicero, was the friend and entertainer of Fulvia, the wife of Antonius. His knowledge of business was, no doubt, of much service to Cicero; but we find that Cicero even here was able to repay him in kind. The very last letter of Cicero to Atticus[1] shows the keen interest which Cicero took in the material interests of his friend.

[1] Att. xvi. 16.

Atticus married Pilia in February 56 at the age of 53. Of this marriage the only issue was a daughter, born in 51, who was married to M. Agrippa, and whose daughter, Vipsania Agrippina, was the wife of the Emperor Tiberius. We are told that, believing that he was suffering from an incurable disease, he destroyed himself by abstaining from food for five days (Vit. Att. 22).

The other correspondents of Cicero who figure in this Selection may here be briefly described.

Q. Caecilius Metellus Nepos (Ep. xi.) served as lieutenant of Pompeius in Asia 67-64. He became tribune in December 63 and violently opposed Cicero. He it was who prevented Cicero from addressing the people on laying down his office and only allowed him to take the usual oath, whereon Cicero swore that he had saved the State. He was praetor in 60, and consul with Lentulus Spinther in 57. He did not oppose Cicero's recall from exile, and died in 55.

M. Fadius Gallus (Epp. xii. xvi. lxiii. lxiv.), a man of learning and taste, a close friend of Cicero and Atticus. He was a lieutenant of Caesar's, and was a follower of Epicurus. He wrote an eulogy on Cato of Utica.

L. Lucceius (Ep. xiv.) seems to have had some quarrel with Atticus which Cicero endeavoured to compose. He was a candidate for the consulship in 60 with Julius Caesar, but was defeated. He then withdrew from public life and devoted himself to literature. He projected a contemporaneous history of Rome, beginning from the Social or Marsic War. In 55 Cicero wrote to him the letter (Ep. xiv. of this Selection) in which he begged

Lucceius to deal separately with the history of his own
life from his consulship to his recall from exile.   Lucceius
promised to comply, but seems never to have carried out
his design.   In 49 he embraced the cause of Pompeius,
and was subsequently pardoned by Caesar and allowed
to live in Rome, where he enjoyed the society of Cicero.

For M. Marius (Ep. xvii.) Cicero expresses the
highest admiration and esteem (Q. Fr. ii. 8, 2).   He
was very delicate, and of the most refined tastes and
habits.

C. Trebatius Testa (Epp. xxii.-xxv. lxxix.), a Roman
jurist of great eminence, was an intimate friend of Cicero,
who recommended him to Caesar when on his Gallic
campaigns.   He followed Caesar's party when the civil
war broke out.   Cicero dedicated to him his Topica,
and Horace addressed to him the first Satire of the
second book.   He is often cited as an authority in the
Digest, but not even fragments of his books De iure civili
and De religionibus survive.   He was an Epicurean, and
was tribune in 47.

M. Caelius Rufus (Epp. xxvii. xxxi.), a young noble of
great promise, preserved the friendship of Cicero in spite
of the profligacy of his life.   He was distinguished for
his eloquence, and his letters show great vivacity of
intellect.   He was the lover of Clodia, the enemy of
Cicero, the *belle dame sans merci* who has been identified
with the Lesbia of Catullus.   He was quaestor in 57,
and was prosecuted in 56 on the charge of having
borrowed money from Clodia to procure the death of
Dion, the head of the embassy sent by Ptolemy Auletes

to Rome, and of having attempted to poison Clodia herself. He was defended by Cicero in the masterly oration
still extant. In 52 Caelius was one of the ten tribunes
who passed the *rogatio* that Caesar should be allowed to
become a candidate for the consulship without coming to
Rome. In 50 he was curule aedile, and in January 49
he fled to the camp of Caesar, with whom he went to
Spain in the April of that year. He became praetor in
48, but offended the other Caesarian magistrates by
furiously radical proposals, including the abolition of
debts. Being deprived of his office, he fled to the south
of Italy, and summoned Milo, his rival in profligacy and
extravagance, from Massilia to join him. Milo was killed
in an attack on Cosa, near Thurii ; and Caelius was put
to death in Thurii at the age of thirty-seven, by some of
Caesar's Gallic and Spanish cavalry, whom he attempted
to seduce from their allegiance.

P. Volumnius Eutrapelus (Ep. xxxiii.) was a Roman
knight, an intimate friend of Antonius as well as of
Cicero. Cicero describes a dinner at his house in Ep. liv.,
and justifies his own presence at it. Volumnius was
praefectus fabrum to Antonius. He used his influence
with him to save the life of Atticus.

L. Papirius Paetus (Epp. xxxiv. lii.-liv.) was the
receiver of some of Cicero's brightest and wittiest letters.
He gave to Cicero the library which Sev. Claudius had left
him, and seems to have been regarded by Cicero as a person
of great taste, not only in gastronomy, but in literature.

Tiro (Epp. xl. lxx. lxxx.) was a slave and afterwards a
freedman of Cicero's. He it was (most probably) who made

the collections of Cicero's letters which we now possess.
He appears in the correspondence of Cicero as habitually
ailing.   Cicero is constantly sending him prescriptions and
admonitions about preserving his health. He is said to have
lived to a hundred years of age. He set out for Cilicia with
Cicero when going to his province, but fell ill on the way,
and was left by Cicero with Lyso in Patrae in Achaia.

C. Cassius Longinus (Epp. lvi. lvii. lxxviii.) is the
friend of Brutus and murderer of Julius Caesar.   In 53
he was quaestor to Crassus in his campaign against the
Parthians, against whom he gained successes in 52 and
51.   In 49 he was tribune of the plebs, and fled with
Pompeius from Rome.   After the battle of Pharsalia he
surrendered to Caesar, who forgave him, and even promised him the province of Syria on his becoming praetor
in 44.   But Cassius never could forgive Caesar, and was
the chief mover in the conspiracy which ended in his
murder.   He slew himself on the field of battle at
Philippi in 42.   He was married to the half-sister of
Brutus, and was a man of considerable cultivation, and a
follower of the philosophy of Epicurus.

Servius Sulpicius (Epp. lx. lxi.) was an orator and
jurist; quaestor, 74 ; curule aedile, 69 ; praetor, 65 ;
consul with M. Claudius Marcellus, 51.   He embraced
Caesar's cause in the civil war, and was made by Caesar
pro-consul of Achaia in 46.   He died in 43 in the camp
of M. Antonius, who was besieging Dec. Brutus in
Mutina.   No selection from the correspondence of Cicero
can omit his eloquent letter to Cicero (Ep. lx.) consoling
him on the occasion of his daughter's death.

M. Curius (Epp. lxv. lxvii.) was an intimate private friend of Cicero and Atticus, to whom he bequeathed the whole of his property, which he had amassed by successful practice of the trade of a *negotiator* for many years at the Achaean town of Patrae, which was largely used as a place of debarcation from Italy.

C. Matius Calvena (Ep. lxxiii.), a common friend of Cicero and Trebatius, was a warm admirer of Caesar, and a steady adherent to his cause. Cicero nicknames him *Madarus* and *Calvena* on account of his baldness. His manly letter to Cicero (Ep. lxxiii.) on the proper attitude towards the dead Caesar has always been much admired. It and the letter of Sulpicius on the death of Tullia are the only letters in the correspondence which at all bear comparison with those of Cicero himself. Matius and Postumius undertook the management of the public games given by Octavius, and did not satisfy Cicero by their action in this matter. Prof. Palmer in his Introduction to Horace, Sat. ii. 4, vigorously defends the theory that this Matius is the person satirised there under the disguise of Catius. We are told by Columella that Matius wrote a treatise of cookery, and books on fish and pickles, and aimed at making Gastronomy one of the fine arts.

C. Asinius Pollio (Ep. lxxvii.), the celebrated poet, orator, and historian of the Augustan Court, born B.C. 76, died A.D. 4, in the eightieth year of his age. He was the friend of Catullus, of Cicero, of Julius Caesar, and afterwards of Augustus, and the patron of Virgil and Horace, and the critic of Sallust and Livy.

III

§ 1. ON THE FORM OF THE LETTERS

In the time of Cicero the letter was written either (1) on thin tablets of wood or ivory covered with wax, in which the letters were cut in uncial characters by the *stilus,* the characters being protected from defacement by the projecting rim of the tablets ; or (2) they were written on paper or parchment with a reed pen and ink.   It seems probable that the longer letters of Cicero were written in the second fashion.   We have frequent allusions to *charta* in the letters ; for instance, in Fam. vii. 18 Cicero asks Trebatius whether he wrote on a palimpsest, and if so, what could have been the writing so worthless as to make way for the letter.   So in Q. Fr. ii. 14 (15*b*), 1, it is plain that *charta, calamus,* and *atramentum* were used.   The same inference is to be drawn from Att. v. 4, 4, and perhaps from the passage already adverted to above (Att. vi. 6, 4), where Cicero avails himself of the services of the copying slave of Atticus to pass off on Caelius the letter written by himself, but purporting to come from Atticus ; for Cicero's handwriting on *charta* with a pen would have been much more easily recognised than his uncials carved with a *stilus* on wax.   Moreover, the use of pen and paper would be so obviously more suitable for long letters that we can hardly doubt that it was the vehicle used by Cicero for his correspondence.   Nor is there any real evidence to set against the passages adduced above, for expressions like *tabella, exaravi,* etc., are applied to the use of pen and paper as well as to the use of *cera* and *stilus.*[1] When the letter was finished the *tabellae* were bound together by a thread, which was sealed at the knot. This seal was generally looked on as the formal guaranty of genuineness, for the handwriting was generally that of a slave, if the writer possessed sufficient means to keep a *servus a manu* or *ab epistulis.*

There being no postal arrangements whatever in the time of Cicero, it was necessary either to employ private messengers, or to avail oneself of the services of the *tabellarii* of the *publicani,* who were constantly travelling between Rome and the provinces.

For further information about modes of addressing letters in Cicero's time, see note on Ep. xxxiii. § 1.

The earliest letter of the correspondence is written in the year 68 B.C., the latest in the year 43 B.C. I have already expressed my opinion of the great historical value of these letters, especially the private letters. Indeed, if we except Caesar and the epitome of the lost Books of Livy, they are the only basis for the history of the

---

[1] That in old times *cera* and *stilus* were employed in letter-writing there can be no doubt. We have all the materials enumerated together, the *stilus,* the wax, the thread, the tablets, and the signet-ring, in Plaut. Bacch. iv. 3, 78 *seq.* ; such phrases as *exarare* and *tabellae* would be survivals from the ancient usage ; nor is it at all improbable that *chartae* would be enclosed between tablets of wood or ivory and bound by a thread, so that the *tabellae,* even though actually thus employed, would not necessarily imply the use of the *cera.*

period of which they treat. If Sallust be looked on as a political pamphleteer, we have no better authorities than Velleius Paterculus and Suetonius, who cannot be trusted unless they give their authority; and Appian, Plutarch, and Dio Cassius, who lived two centuries after Cicero, and wrote without any critical spirit.

Cicero himself never edited or collected his letters. But even in his lifetime there was some such project formed. The well-known *locus classicus* on the subject is Att. xvi. 5, 5, *mearum epistularum nulla est συν-αγωγή, sed habet Tiro instar septuaginta. Et quidem sunt a te quaedam sumendae. Eas ego oportet per-spiciam, corrigam ; tum denique edentur.* Two years before this he had written to Tiro a letter (Fam. xvi. 17), in which he jestingly condemns his use of the adverb *fideliter* in the phrase *valetudini fideliter inserviendo,* and says that he ought to be more careful if he wishes his letters to be included in the volume.[1] But it is universally agreed that no collection of the letters was published during the life of Cicero. The *Epistulae ad Familiares* [2] and *ad Atticum* were probably published at

---

[1] The words are *tuas quoque epistulas vis referri in volumina.* It is to be observed that these words do not imply that any collection of Cicero's letters existed at that time, but only that Cicero desired that such a collection should be made. The words might merely mean, 'are you, too (like myself), set on a collection of your letters ?' or 'do you want to make a collection of your letters as well as mine ?'

[2] This title has no classical authority, and the name is not free from objections, for some of Cicero's correspondents were in no sense his *familiares.* However, the correspondence may con-

the same time, and edited by the same editor ; this has
been inferred from the fact that there is evidence of the
strict observance of the rule to exclude from one collection letters published in the other. This rule is only
twice violated. We find enclosed to Atticus (Att. x. 9a)
a letter from Caelius to Cicero which appears as Fam.
viii. 16 ; and in the same way a letter from Cicero to
Dolabella (Fam. ix. 14) is published again among the
letters to Atticus (Att. xiv. 17a). That the letters to
Atticus did not appear before the death of Atticus
(32 B.C.) is probable from the testimony of Corn. Nepos.
The letters to Quintus and Brutus were published with
the letters to Atticus.

The Books of the *ad Fam.* are entitled according to
the person to whom the earlier letters in each Book are
addressed. Thus the first is *ad Lentulum*, the second *ad
Curionem*, the third *ad Appium Claudium Pulchrum*.
The eighth consists solely of letters from Caelius to
Cicero. It is probable that the editor first published
twelve books, and subsequently added four others, the
thirteenth and fifteenth being *addenda* to the first
edition, the fourteenth consisting solely of letters to his
family, and the sixteenth of letters to Tiro, who, as we
shall see, was probably the editor of the collection.
Subsequent to the extant collections we have evidence of
the existence of much larger volumes, of which only
scanty fragments remain. These were probably made in

veniently be so named, as *most* of his correspondents were
familiares. *Ad Diversos* is bad Latin. Suetonius calls such a
series *amicorum epp.* See note on Att. ii. 13, 1.

the Augustan period, and perhaps from them were gleaned materials for the books of *addenda* (Fam. xiii. xv.) But the original xii. books were not remodelled on the basis of the later collection, for from the four books *ad Pompeium* and the three *ad Caesarem*, which the now lost edition is said on good authority to have contained, we should doubtless have had copious extracts. Now the *Epp. ad Fam.* contain only one letter to Pompeius (Fam. v. 7) and three to Caesar (Fam. vii. 5 ; xiii. 15, 16).

The *Epp. ad Fam.* (and therefore the whole correspondence) were probably edited by Tiro because—(1) we know that he had formed such a design; (2) *ad Fam.* xvi. contains many letters addressed to him (some even not by Cicero) which would hardly have found their way into the volume had it not been edited by Tiro ; (3) there are no letters from Tiro, just as in the other volume there are no letters from Atticus, though Tiro's letters were carefully preserved by Cicero, as we are told in Att. ix. 10, 4, *evolvi volumen epistularum tuarum quod ego sub signo habeo servoque diligentissime ;* (4) to these arguments for the editorship of Tiro may be added one drawn from a passage in Att. ii. 1, 3 :—' Fuit enim mihi commodum, quod in eis orationibus, quae Philippicae nominantur, enituerat civis ille tuus Demosthenes, et quod se ab hoc refractariolo iudiciali dicendi genere abiunxerat, ut σεμνότερός τις καὶ πολιτικώτερος videretur, curare ut meae quoque essent orationes, quae consulares nominarentur. Quarum una est in senatu Kal. Ian., altera ad populum de lege agraria, tertia de

Othone, quarta pro Rabirio, quinta de proscriptorum filiis, sexta, quum provinciam in contione deposui, septima, qua Catilinam emisi, octava, quam habui ad populum postridie quam Catilina profugit, nona in contione, quo die Allobroges invulgarunt, decima in senatu, Nonis Decembr. Sunt praeterea duae breves, quasi ἀποσπασμάτια legis agrariae. Hoc totum σῶμα curabo ut habeas. Et quoniam te cum scripta tum res meae delectant, iisdem ex libris perspicies et quae gesserim et quae dixerim, aut ne poposcisses : ego enim tibi me non offerebam.' If, as seems probable, this passage is spurious, there is much reason for accepting the theory of Orelli, that it was inserted by Tiro to vouch for the authenticity of the three last speeches against Catiline, which (according to Orelli) were not written by Cicero, but probably by Tiro. It would certainly have been an attractive subject for one who wished to foist his own work on posterity as a speech written by the great orator, and his position as editor of the letters would have given him an opportunity to almost ensure the success of his forgery.

Nake believes that Atticus was the editor, because we know from the letters that he bought and sold whole libraries,[1] that he kept a large establishment of copyists,[2] that he in various ways assisted Cicero's literary pursuits, suggesting to him subjects on which to employ his pen, replying carefully to questions of Cicero on literary points, and correcting and criticising his work. Thus Cicero in one place says that in his work De Gloria Atticus had

---

[1] Att. i. 4, 3 ; ii. 4, 1.   [2] Att. xii. 40, 1.

selected for praise the very best bits, which were now enhanced in his own estimation by the approval of his friend; 'for,' he writes, 'I was in great dread of those bits of red wax of yours'[1] which pointed out defects. The most important testimony in support of Nake's view is a passage in Att. ii. 1, 2, *tu si tibi placuerit liber curabis ut et Athenis sit et in ceteris oppidis Graeciae,* which shows clearly that Atticus was in the habit of actually publishing works of Cicero, the book here referred to being a memoir of his consulship, written in Greek. However, all these arguments do not in my opinion counterbalance the evidence for the editorship of Tiro, given above, and to it may be added a passage in Fam. xvi. 23, 2, where Cicero, writing to Tiro, says, *Atticus noster, quia quondam me commoveri* πανικοῖς *intellexit, idem semper putat, nec videt quibus praesidiis philosophiae saeptus sim, et hercle quod timidus ipse est,* θορυβοποιεῖ. Surely this contemptuous judgment on himself would not have been permitted by Atticus to survive in his edition. Moreover, the only objection against the theory that Tiro was the editor is the defective arrangement of the books above referred to; but this is completely explained by the theory of a plurality

---

[1] Att. xvi. 11, 1, *cerulas enim tuas miniatulas extimescebam.* It was the habit of the ancients to stick pieces of coloured wax on the margin of books to mark exceptionable passages. *Cerula* could not mean 'a kind of crayon,' as Lewis and Short explain it. The Greeks called these *cerulae* παραπλάσματα. For other testimonies to the editorship of Atticus, see Att. i. 19, 10; 20, 6; xiii. 37, 3; xiii. 43, 3; xvi. 6, 4; vi. 2, 3, Phliasios dici sciebam, et *ita fac ut habeas.* Cp. also Fronto, Ep. vii. 20 (Naber).

of editions, which, as we have seen, is more than probable. Nor can we accept the view of Nake that the
collection which we now have was posterior to the much
fuller collection, of which there is undoubted evidence.
The paucity of letters to such remarkable personages as
Caesar and Pompeius is fatal to such a supposition ; for
we know that the large collection contained books of such
letters : how, then, can we account for the fact that the
smaller collection which we possess presents us with very
few letters to those eminent persons? The argument on
which Nake most relies for his theory that the letters,
as we now have them, were first published in the beginning of the second century A.D., is the fact that Fronto [1]
made a collection of elegant extracts from Cicero's letters
—a fact which seems to me in no way to support his
hypothesis, but rather to tend to subvert it.[2]

[1] *Memini me excerpsisse ex Ciceronis epistulis ea duntaxat
quibus inesset aliqua de eloquentia vel de philosophia vel de Rep.
disputatio; praeterea si quid elegantius aut verbo notabili dictum
videretur, excerpsisse . . . Omnes autem Ciceronis epistulas legen-
das censeo mea sententia, vel magis quam eius omnes orationes.
Epistulis Ciceronis nihil est perfectius.*—Front. ad Antoniu. ii. 5
(ed. Mai, 1823).

[2] L. Gurlitt, in an able essay (Göttingen, 1879), maintains that
there never was any larger collection than those which we have.
He explains the allusions of Nonius and other grammarians as referring to the collections which we possess, or as being corrupt, or
as instances of negligence or stupidity on the part of the grammarian. With regard to Nonius, he quotes with approbation the
words of Bücheler (Rhein. Mus. 596), *quocum qui comparari
posset levitate et stupiditate neque antiquitas neque nostra aetas
ullum grammaticum tulit.*

Gurlitt strongly holds the theory that Tiro was the editor.

The three books *ad Quintum Fratrem* embrace a period of six years, from 694-700 (B.C. 60-54). They are highly interesting, though not written with that complete *abandon* which characterises the letters to Atticus. Indeed one is greatly struck and somewhat puzzled by the stately and respectful courtesy of the great consular to his younger and comparatively undistinguished brother in the first letter of this correspondence. It is, however, rather a formal essay on provincial government than a letter, and was intended as a return for the letter of Quintus on the duties of a candidate, commonly called *De petitione consulatus*.

§ 2. ON THE STYLE OF THE LETTERS

We have in the letters of Cicero an almost unique literary monument. The history of one of the most interesting epochs in the annals of the world is unfolded to us in a series of cabinet pictures by a master hand. We contemplate, passed in review before us, a procession of those Roman nobles who in the last few decades of the Republic wielded a greater power than is now given to kings, and lived with far greater splendour. The Senate has been called a mob of kings. Most of its members had held, or would at some time hold, governments more irresponsible and not less important than the Governor General of India now administers. And all these we see in the letters in the aspect which they presented to their friends and associates, not in the aspect which they presented to the world and to the historian. We see Pompeius, with his embroidered toga and with his chalked bandages on his legs, sulking because no one would thrust on him that greatness which he might have grasped if he had but put forth his hand. We hear how Lucullus thought more about teaching his bearded mullets to eat out of his hand than about the interests of the *causa optima* so dear to Cicero. In Caelius and Dolabella we have a type of the *jeunesse dorée* of Rome ; in Trebatius, of the genial professional man. To each of these Cicero writes in a tone suitable to his correspondent's years and views. Whether he exchanges *rumusculi* with Caelius, jokes with Paetus, or politics with Lentulus—whether he complains or apologises, congratulates or condoles— whether he lectures his brother Quintus on his violence of temper, or addresses himself to the kindly task of bantering Trebatius out of his discontent with the camp of Caesar in Gaul, we never miss the sustained brilliancy and fertility of thought and language. It is most interesting to observe the superiority of his letters to those of his correspondents. We have, it is true, many charming letters from Caelius and others of Cicero's correspondents, notably the exquisite letter of Sulpicius before referred to. These, however, are quite exceptional, and the net result of the comparison of the letters of Cicero with those of his contemporaries is a greatly strengthened belief in the amazing literary endowments of Cicero.[1] But the quality in Cicero's letters [2] which makes them

---

[1] For points of difference between the letters of Cicero and his correspondents, see pp. xc-xciv.

[2] Of course I here refer to the private letters. The public

most valuable is that they were not (like the letters of
Pliny, and Seneca, and Madame de Sévigné) written to
be published. The letters are absolutely trustworthy;
they set forth the failures and foibles of their writer as
well as his virtues and his triumphs. The portraits with
which they abound were never to be shown to his in-
voluntary sitters, so there was no reason why they should
not be faithful. In his speeches this is not so : according
to the requirements of his brief, his subjects are glorified
or caricatured beyond recognition.

As a motto for the whole correspondence may be taken
his own words[1] in which he exalts the letter of Atticus
over the oral description of Curio. He should be a good
talker who could surpass the vivacity of Cicero's letters.
But it is a serious error to ascribe carelessness to them.
His style is colloquial, but thoroughly accurate. Cicero
is the most precise of writers. Every sentence corresponds to a definite thought, and each word gives its aid
to the adequate expression of the whole. Those who
think that the speeches are a mere effusion of rhetoric, a
piling up of superlatives for most of which another superlative might easily be substituted without any injury to
the meaning or effect of the passage, have (it seems to
me) not read Cicero aright. Every adjective is set down
with as careful a pen as ever was plied by a master-

---

letters have not this quality. For an instance of the degree to
which Cicero disguises his real feelings in his public letters see
Att. xiv. 13*b*, where he sends to Atticus a copy of a letter to
Antonius.

[1] *Ubi sunt qui aiunt ζώσης φωνῆς* ? Att. ii. 12, 2.

hand; each is almost as essential to the sentence as the principal verb. We have an amusing testimony to the carefulness—one might say purism—of his letters in Att. vii. 3, 10, where he so earnestly defends his use of *in* before *Piraeum* (while he avows with shame that he should have written *Piraeum* not *Piraeea*), on the ground that Piraeus cannot be regarded as a *town;* citing in defence of his usage Dionysius and Nicias Cous, and quoting a passage in point from Caecilius, whom he candidly allows to be but a poor authority, as well as one from Terence, whose *elegantia* he considers to be beyond dispute. All this, too, at a time when one might have supposed that he would have been more concerned in deciding on the political position to be assumed by him on his return to Rome, which he was fast approaching, and from which were constantly reaching him *miri terrores Caesariani,* and reports which he describes as *falsa, spero, sed certe horribilia.* We should, therefore, in my opinion, never admit the theory of carelessness in the writer to influence our opinion about the soundness or unsoundness of a phrase or construction.

In treating of the Latinity of these letters one must, of course, in an Introduction dwell mainly on the general aspects of the style, for details referring the student to the notes and to special treatises on the style of the letters, such as Stinner's and Paul Meyer's, afterwards to be mentioned; as well as elaborate histories of Latin style, such as Nägelsbach's *Stilistik,* and Dräger's *Historische Syntax.* Having pointed out, therefore, what seem to me to be the distinctive characteristics of the correspondence as a whole, I shall give a general sketch of the broad peculiarities of this branch of literature as regards the *use* of words, and offer a few observations on the distinctions which may be observed between the letters of Cicero and of his correspondents.

A

There is a very remarkable characteristic of the style of these letters, not hitherto dwelt on,[1] so far as I am aware—a very close parallelism between their diction and the diction of the comic drama.[2] It is, indeed, to be expected *a priori* that the language of familiar letter-writing would closely resemble the language of familiar dialogue. In both cases the language may be expected to be largely tinged with the idiom of the *sermo vulgaris*, or *colloquialism*.[3] Cicero, in an important

---

[1] Stinner (*de eo quo Cicero in Epistulis usus est sermone*, Oppeln, E. Franck, 1879) notices this feature in the letters, but does not pursue the subject.

[2] Cicero has in a passage already quoted expressed his high opinion of the *elegantia* of Terence: in Off. i. 104 he lays down that there are two kinds of humour—*unum illiberale, petulans, flagitiosum, obscaenum; alterum elegans, urbanum, ingeniosum, facetum;* and of the latter he makes Plautus a type, in this judgment differing from the verdict of Horace (Ep. in Pis. 270 ; Epp. ii. 1, 170) and of Quintilian (x. 1, 99), but afterwards corroborated by Gellius (vii. 17, 4), who pronounces Plautus *homo linguae atque elegantiae in verbis Latinae princeps*.

[3] It must be borne in mind that *archaism* is a large ingredient in *colloquialism*, as has been pointed out (p. 127) in the very able treatise of Paul Meyer, *Untersuchung über die Frage der Echtheit des Briefwechsels* Cicero ad Brutum. Stuttgart, 1881.

passage,[1] recognises the *colloquial* character of his letters, referring, no doubt, especially to those which we have spoken of as his more private letters, namely, those to Atticus, Trebatius, Caelius, and his brother Quintus. It would be impossible for me here to enter into an elaborate comparison between the language of Cicero's letters and that of the comic stage. But in order to show that the subject well deserves a full treatment, I will here point out some of the coincidences which have struck me. I will first take one play, the *Miles Gloriosus*, and note the coincidences ; then add such general resemblances as have not been touched.

(1) In the following examples it is not contended that in every case the usage adduced is *confined* to Cic. Epp. and the comic drama ; but that it is far more prevalent there than elsewhere, and that this circumstance is not fortuitous, but arises from the fact that the usage referred to partakes of that *colloquial* character which the Germans call *Vulgarismus*.

Mil. i. 1, 11, *tam bellatorem :* for *tam* with predic. subst. cf. *tam Lynceus*, Fam. ix. 2, 2 ; *tam corruptrice provincia*, Q. Fr. i. 1, 19 ; *tam matula*, Pl. Pers. iv. 3, 64 ; *parum leno*, Ter. Phorm. 507.

Mil. i. 1, 44, *sic memini tamen :* for *sic* = ' as things now stand ' cf. *sed sic me privas*, Fam. v. 20, 4 ; *sic vero fallaces sunt*, Q. Fr. i. 1, 16. See under *sic* v. 3 in Lewis and Short.

---

[1] *Quid enim simile habet epistola aut iudicio aut contioni ? Quin ipsa iudicia non solemus omnia tractare uno modo ; privatas causas et eas tenues agimus subtilius, capitis aut famae ornatius. Epistolas vero cotidianis verbis texere solemus.*—Fam. ix. 21, 1.

Mil. i. 1, 67, *dare operam*, 'to attend to': see L. S., *opera*, ii. A 1.

Mil. ii. 2, 62, *tibi ego dico:* cf. *narro tibi* in Cic. Epp. See n. on Ep. vii. 1.

Mil. ii. 2, 95, *quid agimus:* for this emphatic use of pres. indic. instead of delib. subjunc. cf. *nunc quid respondemus*, Att. xvi. 7, 4.

Mil. ii. 3, 1, *certo . . . scio:* *certo* is found only in comic poets and in Cic., nearly always in his letters.

Mil. ii. 6, 103, *irae:* for abstract substantives in plural cf. in Pl. *opulentiae*, Trin. ii. 4, 89 ; *parsimoniae*, ib. iv. 3, 21 ; *perfidiae*, Capt. iii. 3, 7 ; *industriae*, Most. ii. 1, 1 ; *paces*, Pers. v. 5, 1 ; *superbiae*, Stich. ii. 2, 27. In Cic. Epp. we find *iracundiae*, Q. Fr. i. 1, 39 ; *admurmurationes*, Q. Fr. ii. 1, 3 ; *aestimationes*, Fam. ix. 18, 4 ; *apparitiones*, Q. Fr. i. 1, 12 ; *compellationes*, Fam. xii. 25, 2 ; *compotationes* and *concenationes*, Fam. ix. 24, 3 ; *dementiae*, Att. ix. 9, 8 ; *desperationes*, Fam. ii. 16, 6 ; *iocationes*, Fam. viii. 16, 7 ; *avaritiae*, Q. Fr. i. 1, 40 ; *iucunditates*, Att. x. 8, 9 ; *tranquillitates*, Att. vi. 8, 4 ; *urbanitates*, Fam. xvi. 21, 7.

Mil. iii. 1, 41, *nota noscere:* cf. *actum agere*, Ter. Phorm. 419 ; *inventum inveni*, Pl. Capt. ii. 3, 81 ; *perditum perdamus*, Fam. xiv. 1, 5 ; *impeditum impedire*, Att. xv. 15, 3.

Mil. iii. 1, 148, *odiorum Ilias:* cf. *malorum impendet* Ἰλιάς, Att. viii. 11, 3.

Mil. iii. 2, 38, *loculi:* Pl. affects strange diminutives, like this from *locus*; e.g. *recula*, from *res ;* *specula*, from *spes ;* *ralla*, for *rarula ;* *celocula ;* *nepotulus ;* *uxorcula.*

Vid. infra, pp. lxxxvi, lxxxvii, for a list of dimin. in Cic. Epp.

Mil. iv. 2, 102, *tago ;* old form of *tango :* cf. *tagax*, Att. vi. 3, 1.

Mil. iv. 3, 17, *nihil huius :* cf. *quod huius*, *quod eius*, etc., in Cic. Epp. *passim*. This expression is also common in legal formulae.

Mil. iv. 5, 43, *hariolatur :* used in Att. viii. 11, 3 ; very frequent in comic poets ; elsewhere only in Cic. de Div. i. 134. The dialogues of Cic. naturally present points of contact with the letters ; for instance, the *tmesis* of *per* with adjectives and verbs is common to the letters and dialogues of Cic. and the comic drama, but does not occur elsewhere in classical Latin.

(2) Thus the examination of one play of Plautus yields a dozen coincidences between the drama and the letters. I now add such general stylistic resemblances as have not been necessarily suggested by the *Miles*.

(*a*) The prevalence of such interjections as *st, hui, sodes, amabo te ; ast* for *at ; absque* for *sine ; mi* for *mihi*.

(*b*) Such phrases as *nullus venit*, 'not a bit of him came'; *ab armis nullus discedere*, 'not to move an inch from one's post'; *Corumbus nullus adhuc*, 'not a sign of Corumbus yet'; *nullus tu quidem domum*, 'don't stir a foot to visit him.' [1]

(*c*) *Teneo, habeo* in sense of *scio*, especially in imper.

---

[1] Att. xi. 24, 4 ; xv. 22, 1 ; xiv. 3, 1 ; xv. 29, 1. For similar usage in the comic poets, Ter. Eun. ii. 1, 10 ; Hec. i. 2, 4 ; Andr. ii. 2, 33 ; Plaut. Trin. iii. 1, 5.

sic habeto, tantum habeto with accus. and infin.; and *habeo = possum* with infin.

(*d*) Copious use of ejaculatory phrases: *at te Romae non fore!* Att. v. 20, 7; *O tempora! fore cum dubitet,* Att. xii. 49, 1; *facinus indignum! epistolam . . . neminem reddidisse,* Att. ii. 13, 1; *esse locum tam prope Romam ubi,* Att. ii. 6, 2; *hui! totiensne me dedisse,* Att. v. 11, 1; *me miserum! te incidisse,* Fam. xiv. 1, 1; *hem! mea lux,* Fam. xiv. 2, 2.

(*e*) Isolated agreements in the employment of a peculiar word (or phrase), as *susque deque est,* which is found only in Plautus and Cic. Epp. among classical writers. Paul Meyer (*Untersuchung,* p. 127) defends *expedire = narrare* in Epp. ad Brut. i. 15, 1, on the ground that it is an archaism. On similar grounds I would introduce *accuderim* in Att. i. 1, 2, as a Plautine word, and PIPULO *ac convicio* for *populi convicio* in Q. Fr. ii. 10 (12), 1. On a like principle Meyer (p. 134) vindicates *tardare* intrans. in Att. vi. 7, 2 by *durare* intrans. in Plautus. Such cases as these will be noticed in the notes where they occur.

(*f*) A very striking coincidence with the diction of the comic stage is illustrated by the phrase *quid mi auctor es,* Att. xiii. 40, 2; *quid sim tibi auctor,* Fam. vi. 8, 2, where *auctor es* is treated as a verb and takes an object in the accusative. This construction is very common in Plautus, e.g. *ubi quadruplator quempiam iniexit manum,* Pers. i. 2, 18; *sitis gnarures hanc rem,* Most. i. 2, 17; *quod gravida est,* Amph. iii. 1, 18, where see Ussing's note.

(*g*) In Plautus words like *videlicet, scilicet, ilicet,* are, as it were, resolved into their component elements and govern a case, as if (e.g.) *videlicet* were *videre licet.* A very good example of this is found in Pl. Stich. iv. 1, 49, 51:—

> *videlicet,* parcum fuisse illum senem . . .
> *videlicet,* fuisse illum nequam adolescentem.

Hence, I believe it is unsound criticism to change *tum videlicet datas,* the ms. reading in Att. v. 11, 7, to *datae,* which, indeed, would not stand without *sunt,* as Boot observes.

(*h*) Another use of the accus., which the letters and the *comici* have in common, is illustrated by *scelus hominis,* 'a villain,' Att. xi. 9, 2. This usage is pushed very far by Pl., who not only has *scelus viri,* Mil. v. 41, but even *hallex viri,* Poen. v. 5, 31; *hominum mendicabula* = *mendicos,* Aul. iv. 8, 3.

(*i*) An accusative of cognate or homogeneous objects is very common both in the letters and in comedy. Under this head come such accusatives as *si quidquam* (*i.e.* ullum amorem) *me amas,* Att. v. 17, 5 : cf. *id gaudeo,* Ter. And. ii. 2, 25; *quid gaudeam,* Pl. Capt. iv. 2, 62. Cf. also *quidquid valebo . . . valebo tibi,* Fam. vi. 6, 13, where T badly gives *conciliabo tibi.*

(*j*) The use of the *ethical dative* is far more common in the letters and in comedy than elsewhere in classical literature. In fact the ethical dative without *en* or *ecce* is very rare in the other writings of Cicero. For this reason I would defend TIBI of the mss. in Att. iv. 2, 4, *vix tandem* TIBI *de mea voluntate concessum est,* 'after

all, at last, *lo and behold you with my consent*, the point
was conceded.'   The vigorous exclamation is justified by
the *unexpected* announcement that Cicero himself was
for conceding the request of Serranus, which was so
adverse to his interests.   It seems to me most unscientific to read *illi*, or *id ei*, or *homini* for *tibi*.   Surely no
copyist, however stupid, finding any of these readings,
all of which yield an obvious sense, would have written
tibi, which at first sight seems to give no sense at all.

(*k*) A passage in the letters *ad Fam.* affords an
example, in my opinion, of a characteristic idiom borrowed from the comic stage.   The passage, Fam. vii.
1, 1, runs thus :—

Neque tamen dubito quin tu *ex* illo cubiculo tuo, ex quo tibi
Stabianum perforasti et patefecisti Misenum, per eos dies matutina tempora *lectiunculis* consumpseris.

All editors have either changed *ex* to *in* or changed
lectiunculis to *spectiunculis*.   But the ms. reading as
given above is right.   What Cicero means is this : he
had said above that the leisure of Marius (gained by
absenting himself from the games) would not be rightly
employed unless he did something useful.   Now to take
' little dips into books' might fairly be called useful as
compared with dozing over hackneyed farces.   *Spectiunculis*, 'taking little peeps' at the beauties of the bay of
Naples would hardly satisfy this condition ; again, *spectiunculis* is against the mss. ; finally, the word *spectarent*
would not have been used after *spectiunculis*.   Accordingly, nearly all the edd., retaining *lectiunculis*, change
ex to *in* before *illo cubiculo*.   But if Cicero wrote the

easy *in illo cubiculo*, why do *all* the mss. give us the difficult *ex illo cubiculo* ? The fact is, that in *ex illo cubiculo
tuo ex quo* we have an example of that *inverse attraction*
which is common in Plautus : cf.—

indidem unde oritur facito ut facias stultitiam sepelibilem.
Pl. Cist. i. 1, 63.

ego te hodie reddam madidum si vivo probe
tibi quoi decretumst bibere aquam.
Aul. iii. 6, 38

quid illum facere vis qui *tibi quoi* divitiae domi maximae sunt
. . . amicis numum nullum habes.
Epid. iii. 1, 8.

A familiar example in Greek of this *inverse attraction*
is βῆναι κεῖθεν ὅθενπερ ἥκει.—Soph. O. C. 1226.

I think I have now shown sufficient reason for regarding the usage of the comic stage as having an important
bearing on the criticism of the letters. I have adopted
this view as a principle in my recension of the text.
In the criticism of Tacitus a parallelism from Virgil is
almost as decisive in favour of a disputed reading as a
parallel passage from the works of Tacitus himself ; for
it is certain that the very keynote of the prose of Tacitus
is the imitation of the verse of Virgil. In the criticism
of Cicero's letters we may go farther, and say that to
quote an analogous usage in Plautus or Terence is far
more relevant than to quote an analogous usage from
the oratory or philosophy of Cicero himself.[1]

---

[1] We have seen that the dialogues, as might be expected, have
far greater affinities with the letters, as regards the diction, than
have speeches and rhetorical essays of Cicero.

B

This coincidence between the letters and the stage might, as I have said, have been expected *a priori*, and we might also expect to find an extremely *delicate use of language*. When a writer has to treat of very delicate subjects at a time when there exists no secure postal transmission, he must express himself with caution, and this Cicero does with consummate skill. The difficulty of the letters is often thus greatly increased. The merest hint of the writer's thought must be confided to paper. Cicero often couches his meaning in riddles, which he fears that even Atticus may be unable to decipher. It is amazing that the cases are so few in which the ingenuity of scholars has not arrived at a solution at least plausible.

(1) Perhaps in no part of Latin literature is there such a delicate usage of the subjunctive as may be found in these letters. I have not neglected in my notes to call the attention of readers to such cases. Here I shall only quote one passage in which the joke depends altogether on the use of the subjunctive, and would vanish were the indicative substituted. He is telling (Att. vi. 1, 25 : Ep. xxxv.) how among the goods of Vedius (which were accidentally included among the assets of Pompeius Vindullus deceased) were found images or portrait models of certain Roman ladies. This compromised the characters of these ladies, for Vedius was a notorious profligate. Among these models was one of Junia, sister of

Brutus, and wife of Lepidus. Neither Brutus nor
Lepidus took any notice of the matter, and Brutus still
kept up his intimacy with Vedius. This is Cicero's way
of telling it—*in his* (*sc.* rebus Vedii) *inventae sunt
quinque imagunculae matronarum, in quibus una sororis
amici tui hominis Bruti qui hoc utatur, et uxoris illius
Lepidi qui haec tam neglegenter ferat*, 'among which was
a model of the sister of your friend Brutus (a brute part,[1]
indeed, to keep up the fellow's acquaintance), and wife
of Lepidus (funny, indeed, to take the matter so coolly).'
Here, but for the subjunctive, there would be no play on
the words *Brutus* and *Lepidus*.

(2) The phrase *ita . . . ut* is very delicately employed in the letters, and it is often hard to find an exact
equivalent in English for this Latin idiom. For instance,
Att. i. 1, 1, *ita negant vulgo ut mihi se debere dicant*,
'their refusal generally takes the form of a statement
that they are pledged to me'; Att. i. 19, 8, *ita tamen
his novis amicitiis implicati sumus ut vafer ille Siculus
insusurret cantilenam illam suam*, 'involved as I am in
many new acquaintanceships, yet I do not let them prevent me from having constantly in my ears the refrain of
the astute Sicilian'; Q. Fr. i. 1, 10, *quem scio ita laborare de existimatione sua ut . . . etiam de nostra laboret*,
'in whom I know a keen regard for his own reputation
is yet compatible with as keen a regard for ours'; Att.
ii. 4, 7, *magni aestimo . . . fructum palaestrae Pala-*

---

[1] Cf. Hamlet, iii. 2 : *Polonius.* I did enact Julius Caesar. I
was killed in the Capitol. Brutus killed me. *Ham.* It was a
brute part of him to kill so capital a calf there.

*tinae, sed ita tamen ut nihil minus velim quam Pom-
poniam versari in timore ruinae,* 'I greatly value the
enjoyment of my *palaestra* on the Palatine, not, however, so much as to prevent my feeling that anything is
better than to keep Pomponia in constant fear of the
falling of the wall.' There are other good instances in
Att. ii. 21, 1 ; ii. 24, 2 ; iii. 15, 2 ; and in the letter of
Quintus, *De petitione consulatus,* § 13.

(3) Caution often compels Cicero to use covert language
when dealing with dangerous topics. Hence the enigmatic Greek in which he refers to the dishonesty of
Philotimus in some letters of the 6th book to Atticus.
This caution has left its impression on the *diction* of the
letters in the use of the *plural* when only one person is
meant, e.g. *veteres hostes novos amicos* in referring to
Caesar, Fam. v. 7, 1 ; and in Att. i. 17, 3, *meos* means
Quintus, *tuos* Pomponia ; *invidorum* refers to Hortensius
in Att. iii. 7, 2. So Pompeius is often referred to by a
plural attribute. Somewhat like this is the *pluralis
modestiae* (as Draeger calls it, Hist. Synt. i. 25), whereby
a man speaking of himself in a somewhat boastful tone
softens the arrogance by the use of the plural : see
Fam. v. 4, 2 : again, in that same letter *tuorum*
refers to Clodius alone, but is made plural *invidiae
minuendae causa.*

(4) The use of epistolary tenses is familiar to readers
of the letters, and is commented on in the notes. For
the emphatic *ego* pointing to the fact that the sentence
in which it occurs is an answer to a question, see Ep.
viii. § 1.

C

(1) A very interesting feature in these letters is Cicero's use of *Greek words and phrases*. They were the *argot* of literary Rome. I have so treated them in translating passages in which they occur. I have done so even when I was forced to introduce a metaphor not even hinted at in the Greek word. For instance, in Att. i. 1, 2, where Cicero says *ut mihi videatur non esse ἀδύνατον Curium obducere*, I render 'that it seems to me *on the cards* to carry Curius against them.' If Cicero uses a Greek word where he could quite as easily have used a Latin, we must take this circumstance into account in translating. Greek words are also frequently used as part of the terminology of rhetoric and politics; but the most interesting point connected with this feature in the style of the letters is the fact that very often Greek words are called in to supply a deficiency in the Latin language, and that in these very cases in a number of instances our own language fails, and we are obliged to borrow from the French; so that a French word is not only the best, but the only, word to express the meaning of the Greek term in the letter. This fact is always taken notice of in the notes; but the following list may be given here of Greek words *naturalised* by Cicero to supply a want in Latin, and translatable by us only in naturalised French words: ἀκηδία, *ennui*; ἀδιαφορία, *nonchalance*; δυσωπία, *mauvaise honte*; ὁδοῦ πάρεργον, *en passant*; μετέωρος, *distrait*; μείλιγμα,

f

douceur ; νεωτερισμός, *bouleversement ;* ῥιξόθεμις (?),
fracas ; σκυλμός, *émeute ;* μάλ' ἀριστοκρατικῶς, *en grand
seigneur ;* καχέκτης, *mauvais sujet ;* ἀπρακτότατος, *mala-
droit, fainéant ;* ἀφελής, *ingénu, naïf ;* ἀποσόλοικον, *a
bêtise ;* σφάλμα, a *faux pas ;* ἀπροσδιόννυσον, ἄκυρον,
mal à propos ; ὑπόμνημα, *mémoire ;* περίστασις, *en-
tourage ;* πρόσνευσις, *penchant ;* δύσχρηστα, *désagré-
mens ;* σύγχυσιν τῆς πολιτείας, *coup d'état ;* λέσχη,
causerie ; ἀνεμοφόρητα, *canards ;* ἀποφθέγματα, *bons
mots ;* ἀμφιλαφία, *embarras de richesse ;* while ἀπό-
τευγμα corresponds very nearly to the Italian *fiasco.* In
all or very nearly all of these the Latin actually wants a
word, and has borrowed it from the Greek, while we, to
supply a like *lacuna* in our own tongue, have recourse to
the French.

(2) Sometimes, as I have observed above, the Greek
word answers rather to our slang or cant phrases : of
this we have examples in ἀτίσια, 'impecuniosity' ;
ἄμορφον, 'bad form'; πολίτευμα, 'platform'; τριο-
αρειοπαγίτης, 'a bigwig'; ἐξοχή, 'a lead'; ἄνω κάτω,
'topsy-turvy'; ἐκτένεια, 'gush'; ἐξακανθίζειν, 'to pick
holes'; ἐπίτηκτα, 'veneering'; ὀξύπεινος, 'sharpset' ;
θορυβοποιεῖ, 'he is an alarmist.'[1]   And often we find
that, by a curious coincidence, Cicero borrows an expres
sion from the Greek where we have recourse not to
French or to any vernacular *argot*, but to Latin. Where
we should say *de mortuis nil nisi bonum*, or more briefly

---

[1] Modern physicians still write their prescriptions in Latin, and
affect the use of Latin terms in hygienic or sanitary matters. The
letters affect Greek terms in these cases. (See note on Ep. iv. § 1.)

de mortuis, Cicero invariably has οὐχ ὁσίη φθιμένοισιν,[1] and the proverb *ne sutor supra crepidam* (often wrongly quoted *ultra*)[2] appears in Cicero in its Greek dress as ἔρδοι τις.[3] Again, μηδὲ δίκην[4] is *audi alteram partem ;* a *lapsus memoriae* is a μνημονικὸν ἁμάρτημα; *viva voce* is ζῶσα φωνή; *seriatim* is κατὰ μίτον or κατὰ λεπτόν; *corpus* (in the sense in which we use the word in the phrase *Corpus Poetarum*) is σῶμα ; and *muta persona* is κωφὸν πρόσωπον.

D

The following are the most characteristic uses of words :—

(1) Strange words coined to suit a momentary need, such as *Pseudo-Cato* ('Cato's ape ') ; *Pseudo-damasippus ;* the curious verbal *facteon* formed on the analogy of φιλοσοφητέον which immediately precedes it ; *Fulviaster*

---

[1] The verse is οὐχ ὁσίη κταμένοισιν ἐπ' ἀνδράσιν εὐχετάασθαι, Hom. Od. xxii. 412. But Cic. writes φθιμένοισιν : see Att. iv. 7, 2. He makes a similar μνημονικὸν ἁμάρτημα in writing *Agamemno* for *Ulixes* in de Div. ii. 63.

[2] The proverb is derived from the story of Apelles, who accepted the cobbler's criticism when it referred to the loop (*ansa*) of a sandal (*crepida*) ; but when, elated by his success, the cobbler began to criticise the leg of the statue (*cavillante circa crus*) Apelles warned him *ne super crepidam iudicaret,* ' you must not criticise *higher up than* the sandal,' Plin. H. N. xxxv. 36, 12. *Supra* is the word used by Valerius Maximus also in telling the same story ; *ultra* has no authority, and, indeed, no meaning.

[3] ἔρδοι τις ἣν ἕκαστος εἰδείη τέχνην.—Ar. Vesp. 1431.

[4] μηδὲ δίκην δικάσῃς πρὶν ἂν ἀμφοῖν μῦθον ἀκούσῃς.—Phocylides.

or *Fulviniaster* (which is often regarded as corrupt, but is defended by *Antoniaster*, Fragm. Or. Var. 8); desideratives like *petiturit*, 'he is keen about standing'; *Sullaturit*, 'he is bent on a *coup d'état*'; *proscripturit*, 'he is eager for a proscription': we have also *salaco*, 'a swaggerer'; *tocullio*, 'a bit of a usurer'; and strangest of all, the singular substantives *Appietas* and *Lentulitas*, meaning 'your mere possession of the name Appius or Lentulus,' in a very manly and dignified letter, Fam. iii. 7, 5.   Cf. Tennyson's 'Aylmerism.'

Like these are strange words arising directly from the context, such as *consponsor*, *inhibitio* (remigum), *traductor* (ad plebem), *breviloquens*, *levidensis*, *tagax*; and from the fact that things are spoken of in the letters which are not likely to be mentioned elsewhere, such as *glutnator* (applied to a certain class of bookbinders), *apparitio* (the office of an *apparitor*); to which may be added strangely-formed words, such as *inconsiderantia*, *obvamitio*.

(2) A great prevalence of diminutives, such as the following, of which those printed in italics are not found amongst classical writers save in Cicero : *actuariolum*, *aedificatiuncula*, *ambulatiuncula*, animula, assentatiuncula, *atriolum*, auricula, *captiuncula*, *cerula*, *chartula* *classicula*, *commotiuncula*, *contiuncula*, *deliciolae*, *deversoriolum*, *dextella*, diecula, febricula, filiolus, furcilla *gloriola*, *imagunculae*, *laureola*, *lectiunculae*, *lintriculus*, litterulae, *membranula*, *memoriola*, *nauseola*, *negotiolum*, *nervuli*, ocelli, olusculum, oppidulum, *pagella*, *paginula*, *plangunculae* (probably a corruption of *imagunculae*),

lebecula, *porticula, possessiuncula, raudusculum, ripula,*
rumusculi, *rutula, sedecula, servula, simiolus, sportella,*
ectoriolum, tocullio, villula, *vindemiola, vocula, vulticulus;*
to which add the proper names *Atticula, Tulliola,* and
(if I am right in my view of Att. ii. 1, 8) *Romula.*[1]

To these must be added the following adjectival
diminutives : *argutulus, hilarulus,* integellus, *lentulus,*
ligneolus, limatulus, longulus, maiusculus, minusculus,
miniatulus, misellus, *pulchellus, putidiusculus, rabiosulus,*
refractariolus, subturpiculus, tenuiculus, and the adverbial
diminutive *meliuscule.*

(3) There are many ἅπαξ εἰρημένα in the letters
which we may hold to be due to chance ; that is, we feel
that, had we larger remains from antiquity, we should
probably have other instances of their employment. It
would be uninstructive to supply any list of such words
(not elsewhere found in *classical* Latin) as *peregrinator,*
adiunctor,[2] *corruptrix, aberratio, remigatio, consolabilis,*
petasatus, candidatorius, sanguinarius ; but the following adverbs, though to many of them what I have just
said is applicable, may be set down : *assentatorie, de-*
speranter, furenter, immortaliter (gaudeo), *impendio,*
inhumaniter, pervesperi, turbulenter, vulgariter, and
utique, which occurs about twenty times in the letters,
and only thrice in all the other works of Cicero.

[1] This list and the following are chiefly taken from A. Stinner,
De eo quo Cicero in Epistulis usus est sermone. Oppeln, Franck,
1879. The classification is my own.

[2] Cicero in his letters affects words in *-tor.* We have besides
those already quoted the following rare examples : *approbator, con-*
vector, ioculator(?), *expilator, propugator* ; to which add *corruptrix.*

(4) Moreover, nearly every adjective and adverb in the language is intensified by the prefix *per-*[1] and mitigated by the prefix *sub-*. This is to be expected, owing to the need arising in letters for conveying delicate shades of meaning. This need demands also that minute graduation of the force of a word which the use of the comparative and superlative can so well supply in Latin. Hence the extraordinary richness of the letters in comparative and superlative forms both in adjectives and adverbs, for which see Stinner, pp. 12-15. These prefixes are rarer in the case of verbs, but we have the following: *pergaudere, perplacere, pertaedet, pervincere, subdiffidere, subdocere, subdubitare, subinvidere, subinvitare, subnegare, suboffendere, subringi* (= διαμυλλαίνειν), *subvereri, suppaenitet, suppudet.* Of other verbs the most strange are *cenitare, flaccere, fruticari, itare, muginari, pigrari, suppetiari, tricari, edolare, repungere, restillare, oblanguescere.* Cicero in his letters also affects rare compositions with *e, ex,* as *eblandiri, effligere, elugere, emonere, exhilarare.*

(5) The following very rare words cannot be brought under any of the above classes. They are simply due to the caprice of the moment: *combibo,* 'a boon companion' (though we have *compotor* in Phil. ii. 42); *obiratio, involatus* (of a bird); *itus* (for *abitus*); *reflatus* ('a contrary wind'); *sponsus* (gen. *-us;* for *sponsum*); *noctuabundus, involgare* (?). In all these cases there were other terms quite as suitable to express the exact shade

---

[1] *Tmesis* of *per* with adjectives and verbs is found only in the comic poets and the letters and dialogues of Cicero.

of meaning; it was merely a whim to use these very rare
words.

(6) There is nothing more characteristic of the style
of the letters than the extremely bold use of *ellipse*.
Some commentators strain this figure in the most violent
manner, and understand words which it would require
not an Atticus or Caelius, but an Oedipus or Teiresias to
supply. The following, however, are undoubtedly instances of *ellipse*, and are in some cases very bold
indeed :—

De illo domestico scrupulum quem non ignoras (*sc.*
tolle), Att. v. 13, 3. *Illa fefellerunt, facilem quod
putaramus* (*sc.* fore), Att. ix. 18, 1. *At ille adiurans
nusquam se unquam libentius* (*sc.* fuisse), Fam. ix. 19, 1.
*De Caesaris adventu, scripsit ad me Balbus non ante
Kalendas Sextiles* (*sc.* futurum), Att. xiii. 21, 6. *Quintus
enim altero die se aiebat* (*sc.* perventurum Romam esse),
Att. xvi. 4, 1. *Quod Tullia te non putabat hoc tempore
ex Italia* (*sc.* abiturum esse), Att. x. 8, 10. *Atticam
doleo tamdiu* (*sc.* aegrotare), Att. xii. 6, 4. *De tertio
pollicetur se deinceps* (*sc.* scripturum), Att. xvi. 11, 4.
Natio me hominis impulit, ut ei recte putarem (*sc.* me
commendare), Fam. xv. 20, 1. *Miror te nihildum cum
Tigellio* (*sc.* locutum esse), Att. xiii. 50, 3. *Illud accuso,
non te, sed illam, ne salutem quidem* (*sc.* adscripsisse),
Att. xiii. 22, 5. *Quintus filius mihi pollicetur se
Catonem* (*sc.* futurum), Att. xvi. 1, 6. *Nec mirabamur
nihil a te litterarum* (*sc.* ad nos missum esse), Fam. xvi.
7, 1. *Video te bona perdidisse; spero idem istuc familiares tuos* (*sc.* passos esse), Fam. ix. 18, 4.

(7) *Esse* with adverbs is justly pointed to as a character-
acteristic feature in the style of the letters by Paul
Meyer, p. 161. The following are examples : *sic esse ut
sumus,* Fam. xvi. 12, 4 ; *tamquam si tu esses ita fuerint,*
Q. Fr. iii. 2, 2 ; *Lucretii poemata ita sunt,* Q. Fr. ii.
9 (11), 4.

So we find *esse* with *recte,* Att. vii. 17, 1 ; *commodis-
sime,* Fam. xiv. 7, 2 ; *tuto,* Att. xiv. 20, 3 ; *honeste,* Fam.
xiv. 14, 1 ; *flagitiose et turpiter,* Att. vi. 3, 9 ; *hilare et
libenter,* Fam. xvi. 10, 2 ; *libenter et sat diu,* Att. xv.
3, 2.

A stranger use of *esse* with adverbs is where the adverb
is predicative, and takes the place, as it were, of an adj.:
e.g. *haec tam esse quam audio non puto,* Q. Fr. i. 2, 5 ;
utinam tam (sc. integra), *in periculo fuisset,* Att. iii. 13,
2. See also Q. Fr. ii. 13 (15a), 4 (Ep. xx.), *quem ad
modum me censes oportere esse . . . ita et esse et fore,
oricula infima scito molliorem.*

E

In treating of the style of the letters of Cicero, I have
in nearly every case taken my examples from the letters
of Cicero himself, but the same views are broadly applicable to the ninety letters of his correspondents. I have
already pointed out how inferior they are, as a rule, in
style to the great master with whom it was their privilege to correspond. But even in syntax and in the use
of words—in dealing with the raw material of literature
—they show themselves not to be by any means so care-

ul or exact as Cicero himself. Subjoined are examples
? words and phrases not to be found in Cicero, but
occurring in the letters of his correspondents : [1]—

(1) In the undoubtedly genuine letter of Brutus,
'am. xi. 2, we find, in § 2, *aliud libertate*, 'different
rom (other than) liberty.' This abl. of comparison is
found only in Varro, R. R. iii. 16, 23, *aliud melle ;* Hor.
Sat. ii. 3, 208, *alias veris ;* id. Ep. i. 16, 20, *alium
sapiente ;* and in Phaedrus and Apuleius.

Ibid. *facultatem decipiendi nos ;* cf. *spatium confirm-
andi sese*, Asinius Pollio, Fam. x. 33, 5.

(2) Balbus, Att. viii. 15a, 1, writes *dignissimam tuae
virtutis ;* for *dignus* with gen. (which is un-Ciceronian)
cf. Pl. Trin. v. 2, 29.

(3) Bithynicus, Fam. vi. 16, uses *intermoriturum ;*
no part of *intermori*, but *intermortuus* is found in Cicero.

(4) Galba, Fam. ix. 30, 3, 4, has *dexterius* and
sinisterius.

(5) Plancus, Fam. x. 8, 4, has *diffiteri ;* Fam. x. 15,
4, *praecognoscere ;* Fam. x. 18, 3, *sollicitiorem ;* and in
Fam. x. 11, 1, *ut . . . me civem dignum . . . praestem ;*
whereas Cicero uses *se praestare* with a predicative
accusative only in the case of a pronoun or adjective.

(6) Quintus Cicero, Fam. xvi. 27, 2, has *dissuaviabor*.

(7) Servius Sulpicius, Fam. iv. 5, 2, has *existimare*
with genitive of price ; Fam. iv. 5, 5, *perfunctum esse*.

---

[1] I do not take into account the letter of Quintus, *de petitione
consulatus*, as being really rather a rhetorical treatise than a letter ;
nor the Brutine correspondence, as involving a still unsettled
question.

(8) The language of Caelius is marked throughout by peculiarities, in most cases taking the form of archaism and approximation to the language of the stage. The following may be quoted here :—

(*a*) Colloquial and redolent of the comic stage : *quod illorum capiti sit*, Fam. viii. 1, 5, cf. Ter. Phorm. iii. 2, 6 ; *nunquam = non*, 14, 1, cf. Donatus on Ter. Andr. ii. 4, 7 ; *frigore frigescimus*, 6, 4, cf. *curriculo transcurre*, Plaut. Mil. ii. 6, 43, *ornatu ornatus*, iv. 3, 41 ; *nisi si*, 15, 1 ; *hui*, 15, 2 ; *quam* with the *positive* of the adj., as *quam clementer*, 8, 2.

(*b*) Rare words and usages : *susurratores*, 1, 4 ; *sub-rostrani*, 1, 5 ; *incile*, 5, 3 ; *conglaciare*, 6, 3 ; *cohorti-cula*, 6, 4 ; *aquarius*, 'a water-commissioner,' 6, 4 ; *velificari*, 'to give a lift to,' 10, 2 ; *vapulare*, 'to be thrashed,' 1, 4 ; *ferventer = magnopere*, 8, 2, cf. 6, 3 ; *moretur* (passive), 5, 2 ; the remarkable Graecism *nosti Marcellum quam tardus et parum efficax sit*, 10, 3.

(*c*) Archaic forms : *quoius* for *cuius*, 1, 1 ; 14, 1 ; 16, 2 ; 17, 1 ; *quoi* for *cui*, 2, 1 ; 8, 2 ; 12, 2 ; *illi* for *illic*, 15, 2 ; *istoc* for *istuc*, 4, 1 ; *rusus* for *rursus*, 8, 3. *Pelia* for *Pelias*, Quintil. i. 5, 61.

The examples which I have adduced may seem hardly to warrant the assertion that the letters of Cicero's correspondents display a laxity as compared with those of Cicero. Yet when we remember what a large body of literature Cicero's extant works afford,[1] it is strange that Brutus, for instance, in one of the two extant letters

---

[1] I suppose three-fourths of our Latin Dictionaries are extracts from Cicero.

which are certainly genuine, should twice hit on an un-
Ciceronian usage, and that in one of these violations
there should be associated with him another of Cicero's
correspondents, Asinius Pollio.   Again, Cicero, we may
suppose, must have had some reason for not using *dignus*
with the genitive, or *existimare* with the genitive of
price; this reason must have been unknown to Balbus
and Sulpicius, or else deliberately rejected by them.
Finally, we may be surprised not to find in the seven
hundred and fifty letters of Cicero more words ἅπαξ
εἰρημένα in classical Latin, when in the two letters of
Quintus Cicero we find one, and in the twelve letters of
Plancus three.

The conclusion seems to be that the correspondents of
Cicero are even less careful than he is to avoid the vul-
garisms and laxities which beset the speech of daily life.
A confirmation of this is to be found in their respective
usage (pointed out by Lieberkühn) with regard to a
phrase which occurs repeatedly in the letters.   Cicero
always (except in two places, Att. v. 10, 1 ; viii. 14, 1)
writes *mihi crede*.   On the other hand, *crede mihi* is the
phrase of Brutus, Fam. xi. 26 ; Cassius, Fam. xii. 12, 4 ;
Caelius, Fam. viii. 17, 1.   According to Böckel (Epistulae selectae, 8th ed., p. 323) *crede mihi* is a vulgarism,
or, at least, belongs especially to familiar speech.   Such
distinctions, however, are perhaps too fine-drawn to find
favour out of Germany.   Among such may be classed the
acute observation of Wölfflin (Philol. xxxiv. p. 134) that,
while in his earliest speeches and letters Cicero greatly
prefers *abs te*, he gradually seems to show a growing

preference for the form *a te*, which is the only form found
after the year 700 (B.C. 54).

IV

CRITICAL

For the letters *ad Familiares*, our ms. authorities
are the following :—

(1) M, the *Medicean*.   This ms. is of the eleventh
century.   It has always been held until quite lately that
we owe all our knowledge of the letters of Cicero to
Petrarch.   It is certain that about the year 1345 he
found (at Verona probably) the letters to Atticus, Q.
Cicero, and Brutus.   It has been generally supposed that
a few years later he found at Vercelli the letters *ad
Familiares*.   The Vercelli ms. still exists, together with
a copy ascribed to Petrarch.   The Verona ms. is lost,
and a copy of it (also ascribed to Petrarch) is our chief
authority for the letters to Atticus, Quintus, and
Brutus.

This opinion, which has been held since the revival of
learning, has recently been vigorously and successfully
(as it seems to me) assailed by Dr. Anton Viertel.[1]   He
leaves untouched the belief that Petrarch was the dis-
coverer of the ms. containing the letters to Atticus,
Quintus, and Brutus.   This is plain from the famous

---

[1] Die Wiederauffindung von Cicero's Briefen durch Petrarcha
(Königsberg, Hartung, 1879).

letter of Petrarch to Cicero in the other world, dated
'*apud superos* Verona, June 16th, 1345'; that the place
of finding the ms. was Verona has been inferred (not on
sufficient grounds) from the fact that Petrarch's letter is
dated *Verona*.   The extant copy of this ms., according
to Dr. Viertel, is not by Petrarch.

But Dr. Viertel maintains that not only did Petrarch
not discover the ms. containing the letters *ad Fam.*, but
that he did not even know of the existence of these
letters.   The grounds on which he rests his argument
are these :—

(*a*) Petrarch never refers to the *Epp. ad Fam.*,
though he constantly quotes from *Epp. ad Att., Quint.,
Brut.*

(*b*) He never mentions a second discovery in his extant
letters.

(*c*) In the preface to his own letters, 1359, he contrasts the number of his own correspondents with the
fewness of the correspondents of ancient letter-writers,
referring to Brutus, Atticus, Quintus, and Cicero's son as
the correspondents of Cicero.

(*d*) In 1372 he speaks of the letters of Cicero as com-
prising *tria volumina*, plainly those to Atticus, Quintus,
and Brutus.

(2) The *codices Harleiani* in the British Museum.
They have recently been carefully examined by Franz
Rühl, who has given the results of his inquiry in the
Rhein. Mus. 1875, vol. xxx., pp. 26 ff.   The best and
oldest of these (Harleianus A), which I will call H^a,
is numbered 2682, is of folio size, on parchment, belongs

to the eleventh century, and consists of twenty-five quaternions. It contains the Epp. ad Fam. ix.-xvi., together with the letter to Augustus Octavianus, the *De petitione cons.*, the Laelius, Cato Maior, De Officiis, the Philippics, the Verrines, the speeches in Sallustium, pro Milone, de Imperio Pompeii, pro Marcello, pro Ligario, and pro Deiotaro ; together with some other authors, as Fulgentius *de abstrusis sermonibus.* Each book of the *Epp. ad Fam.* has a separate index. The letters and part of the speeches are corrected by two hands throughout.

H^a is independent of M ; as is sufficiently shown—- (*a*) by the fact that H^a omits altogether Fam. xi. 13 *a*, which is not referred to in the index to Fam. xi. in H^b. (*b*) The letters Fam. xii. 22-30 are lumped together as one letter in M, but are given separately in H^a.

But H^a and M are undoubtedly from the same archetype.

The second of the *codices Harleiani*, H^b, is numbered 2773. Rühl says it came originally from the Hospital of St. Nicolaus, at Kues. It is on parchment, folio, and in two columns. It belongs to the twelfth century. It contains from the beginning of Fam. i. 1 to the words *puto etiam si ullam spem*, Fam. viii. 9, 3. It is certainly independent of M. It wants from Fam. i. 9, 20, *non solum praesenti*, to Fam. ii. 1, *dignitate es consecutus.* There is no distinction made between the first and second books. Accordingly book iii. is in H^b called book ii., book iv. is book iii., and so on. There are no separate *indices* to each book of the letters, as in H^a.

H^b and T (the *codex Turonensis* afterwards to be

described) present a remarkable agreement throughout. But they are independent : see Fam. i. 2, 4, where II[b] and M agree in *agatur*, while T gives *agantur*. More- over, T's curious transposition in Fam. i. 9, 17, is not in H[b].

(3) The *Codex Turonensis*, commonly called T, is in the Library of Tours, No. 688. It was included in Haenel's *Catalogi librorum manuscriptorum qui in bibliothecis Galliae Helvetiae Belgiae Britanniae magnae Hispaniae Lusitaniae asservantur :* Lipsiae, 1829. It is a parchment quarto, in two columns. M. Charles Thurot, in a valuable pamphlet, entitled *Notice sur un manuscrit du xiie siècle* (published by the *Bibliothèque de l'école des hautes études :* Paris, 1874), has given a full account of this ms. It has from Fam. i. to Fam. vii. 32, 1, *me conferri ;* omitting from Fam. ii. 16, 4, *hac orbis terrarum*, to Fam. iv. 3, 4, *appareat cum me co.* It wants the last three and a half letters of the second book, the whole of the third, and the first three and a half of the fourth. Orelli believes it not to be earlier than the end of the fourteenth century, on the not very strong ground that it contains, together with the letters, some of the philosophical works of Cicero, which combination, he says, his experience teaches him to be the mark of a late *codex.* M. Thurot holds it to be of the end of the twelfth century—(*a*) on the authority of M. L. Delisle, *qui est si profondément versé dans la connaissance des manuscrits des bibliothèques de Paris et des départements.* (*b*) The writing *a bien les caractères de l'écriture de la fin du xiie siècle.* (*c*) T presents in

its text a great improvement on M, and there was not enough scholarship at the end of the twelfth century to make these improvements by the exercise of conjecture. M. Thurot holds that T comes from the same archetype (A) as M, but is independent of M.

(4) Hofmann claims an independent place for P, a *Codex Parisinus*, including from Fam. i. to *impediendi moram*, Fam. viii. 8, 6; and the same claim is made by some editors for one page of a Turin palimpsest, which includes Fam. vi. 9 and part of 10. Orelli, while classing the Wolfenbüttel ms. with the other *codices* ultimately traceable to M, has remarked how desirable would be a thorough collation of the *codex Guelferbytanus*. R. Heine (*Jahn's Jahrb.*, 1878, Seite 784) has examined the ms., and pronounces it to belong to the fifteenth century, and to have no value independent of M.

(5) Very important in the criticism of the letters are the *Editio Neapolitana* (1474), and the editions of Victorius, published—one in Venice 1536, another in Florence 1558—as well as an edition preserved in the library of Zurich, of which the time and place of publication are unknown, the last leaf of the copy being lost. This is called A by Orelli, i.e. *Editio Antiquissima*, but must not be confounded with A, the supposed archetype of M, H, and T; nor with A, the *Codex Antonianus*, containing the letters to Atticus, Quintus, and Brutus, of which I shall have presently to treat. In this edition A will mean the *Codex Antonianus*. The other two are very seldom mentioned, and when they are mentioned each will be given its full title.

For the letters to Atticus, Quintus, and Brutus, we have the following authorities :—

(6) M, the Medicean. This ms. was discovered by Petrarch, perhaps at Verona, about 1345. The copy which we possess of it was probably procured by Pasquino of Milan for Coluccio Salutato of Florence. In two letters, from the word *reperire*, Att. i. 18, 1, to *isus est et talis*, nearly the last words of Att. i. 19, we lose the guidance of M, some leaves of the ms. having perished. But for Att. i. 19 we have the assistance of a *Codex Poggianus* in the Medicean Library, collated by Th. Mommsen, the celebrated historian, who has conferred such a benefit on students of the letters by arranging those to Quintus in their true order.

(7) C. This is a name given to a ms. of which we have no knowledge except from the marginal notes in Cratander's edition of 1528, which, however, show it to have been independent of M.

(8) W. Some leaves of a ms. of these letters are preserved at Munich and others at Wurzburg (whence the leaves at both places are designated W): these contain portions of books xi. and xii. They coincide closely with the marginal readings in Cratander's edition, and are by some supposed to have formed a part of C.

(9) Z. The *Codex Tornaesianus*, now lost, our knowledge of which is derived from the notes of Lambinus and a few quotations by Turnebus.

In addition to these real sources of knowledge, the fabricated *codices* of Bosius were till quite lately believed

in, and carefully regarded in the arrangement of the
text. Just as Henri Estienne (the famous Stephanus)
vitiated the criticism of Euripides by recommending his
own usually excellent conjectures by the authority of
imaginary mss., so this other and almost equally able
Frenchman, Simeon Du Bos, a native of Limoges, born
1535, imposed on the most learned men of three
centuries with his imaginary *Decurtatus* and *Crusellinus*,
and his pretended or falsified citations from the real'y
existing Z. Even Orelli was deceived by the imposture.
Indeed the great critic of Zurich would probably have
left little to be added by his successors had he been
aware of the fictitious character of the *codices* of Bosius.
And yet Bosius' own account of the manner in which he
gained possession of his *vetustissimi codices* might have
excited suspicion. His *Decurtatus* (commonly quoted as
Y) he obtained from a private soldier who had rescued it
in the sack of a monastery, in which it had been deposited. Of his *Crusellinus* (X) he does not tell his
readers the source in his edition published at Limoges,
1580, but he gives the following rather vague details :—
*adiutus sum praeterea codice quodam excusso Lugduni
qui olim fuerat Petri Cruselli, medici apud nostrates
celeberrimi; ad cuius libri oras doctus ille vir varias
lectiones appinxerat, a se, ut ipse dicebat, diligentissime
et summa fide e vetustissimo et castigatissimo libro
Novioduni descriptas.* The imposture, however, escaped
detection for nearly three hundred years, and it was not
until the year 1855 that Maurice Haupt discovered that
no such mss. as the *Decurtatus* (Y) and *Crusellinus* (X)

of Bosius ever existed. The discovery of Haupt acquired
the certainty of a demonstration when Mommsen found
that a ms. deposited in Paris contained the rough draft of
Bosius' notes for the last seven books of the Epp. ad
Att. On comparing these with the published commentary of Bosius, Mommsen found that Bosius had frequently ascribed one reading to the mss. in his first draft,
and another in the published commentary. In each case
he recommended his own conjecture by the authority of
the fabricated ms.; and in some cases he changed his
view of a passage in the time intervening between the
first draft and the ultimate publication, and accordingly changed his account of the reading of his ms.
For instance, in Ep. ad Att. x. 6, 2, Bosius in his published edition reads *De Quincto filio fit a me sedulo ;* on
which he states that his *Codex Decurtatus* has *de Q. F.*,
and his *Crusellinus, de Q. filio.* In his unpublished
première ébauche, found by Mommsen, he had given *de
Q. frat.* as the reading of the *Decurtatus,* adding
'Victorius legit *de Q. filio,* quam scripturam in meis
non reperio.' Baiter hardly transcends that emphasis of
expression which is warranted by the case, when after
narrating the circumstances just referred to he adds,
'Bosium cito *scelus suum* morte luisse a latronibus
trucidatum.'

To the above sources of information may be added
(10) A (*Codex Antonianus*) and (11) F (*Codex Faër-
ninus*), in so far as their readings are reported by Malaspina; but these mss. must be viewed with some
suspicion. We cannot be sure that we have not in

Malaspina something of the Bosius, whom he rivals in the brilliancy of his conjectures. The title of the work of Malaspina (which is extremely rare) is, *Malaspinae emendationes et suspiciones in epistulas ad Atticum, Brutum, et Quintum fr.*; it was published in Venice in 1563-64.

(12) The most ancient editions are the *editio Romana* (R), published at Rome in 1470, and the *ed. Iensoniana* (I), published in Venice in the same year. These are founded on M, R giving generally the reading *a prima manu*, while I, as a rule, presents the marginal or superscribed corrections.

The following is a conspectus of the chief corrections of the mss. adopted in this edition, or recorded with approval in the notes :—

Ep.	MS. Reading.	Generally received Reading.	Conjecture accepted in Text, or recorded with approbation in Notes.	Author of Conjecture.
v. 8	Asiani	...	Asiani	Malaspina
ix. 1	non solum vitae sed etiam dignitatis	...	*non dignitatis sed vitae*	Ed.
xi. 2	omnium reservandorum	omnium servandorum	*nominum Reip. reservandorum*	"
xiii. 2	emisisti locum	emisti ludum	emisti λόχον	Bosius
xvii. 1	Stabianum perforasti	...	*tablinum perforasti*	Boot
xix. 1	populi convicio	...	pipulo convicio	Ed.
xxii. 1	in extremo sero sapiunt	in extremo: ' sero sapiunt'	'in extremo sero sapiunt'	"
xxiv. 1	Seius	Zeius	Seius	Klotz
xxv. 1	arbitrarere	...	arbitrare	Ed.
xxvi. 1	meo (M), in eo (Rav.)	...	mei in eo	"
xxvi. 2	DCCC. aperuisti	...	de DCCC. aperuisti	"
xxvii. 1	quo ius M, quid ius II	cuius	quoius	Becher
xxix. 1	ΑΚΡΑΤΗΡΕωΝ iura	ἀκρωτηρίων οὖρα	ἄκρα Γυρέων οὖρα	L. Dindorf

Ep.	MS. Reading.	Generally received Reading.	Conjecture accepted in Text, or recorded with approbation in Notes.	Author of Conjecture.
xxix. 2	ad te statim	::	a te statim	Ed.
xxx. 3	plura scribebam	::	epistolam sciebam	Gronovius
xxxii. 1	superioris quod idem	superiores. Quod idem	superioris quadriennii ; quod idem	Ed.
xxxv. 17	CENS. . . . Cos.	::	Cos. . . . CENS.	,,
xxxvii. 2	κληρονομήσας	::	κληρονομῆσαι	
xli. 1	praesidiis	::	praediis	Klotz
xli. 4	sin autem etiam	sin pax aut etiam	sin aut otium aut etiam	Purser
xlii. 1	quorum ego	::	quorum ergo	Bosius
ibid.	inanes	::	ad Nonas inanes	Boot
ibid.	itinarum	Attianarum	Appianarum	Lipsius
xliii. 3	Gnaeum ire Br. desertum	† desertum	Gnaeum B. ire, Dom. iri desertum	Ed.
xliv. 1	certior	::	cerritior	Bosius
ibid.	tum eum isse	::	timuisse	Ed.
ibid.	sed meam mans.	::	sed en meam mans.	,,
xlv. 2	exspect. Corfiniensi	ἀσμένυστον	exspect. de re Corfiniensi	Purser
xlv. 3	ACMENICTON	::	ἀσμενιστὸν	Ed.
ibid.	vita mores		vetant mores	Boot
xlvi. 1	scripta	aperta	stricta	Ed.
xlvi. 3	id si cras	id si ἀκραὲs	inde si ἀκραὲs	Reid

Ep.	MS. Reading.	Generally received Reading.	Conjecture accepted in Text, or recorded with approbation in Notes.	Author of Conjecture.
xlvii. 1	fuere infantia	...	*fuerunt fatua*	Reid
xlix. 2	nam etsi	...	tametsi	Cratander
xlix. 7	popilium . . . denarium	...	popilium . . . thunna-rium	Rutilius
ibid.	non eo sis	...	non est quod eo sis	Wesenberg
xlix. 10	sannonum *or* sanniorum	sannionum	saniorum	Ed.
li. 2	φλδδημον	...	φλειδήμονα	Popma
liii. 2	ex artis	exquisitae artis	ἐξοχῆς	Ed.
lvii. 2	quod velis	quod cum velis	quod quae velis	?
lix. 1	loqueretur	...	videretur	Klotz
ibid.	me etiam gravius esse	me etiam gravius esse affectum	mi etiam gravius esse	Orelli
ibid.	illae	...	illi	Ed.
ibid.	ut ego nollem	...	ut ego avolem. Nollem	Madvig
lx. 3	an . . . credo doles ?	at . . . credo doles	an . . . credo doles ?	Ed.
lx. 5	imitare	...	imitari	Cratander
lxi. 3	maior . . . vatio	maior levatio	maius . . . ratio	H. and T.
lxiv. 1	nisi istum	...	ne si istum	Baiter
lxvi. 1	tam gravem ἀμετ.	...	gravem, tamen ἀμετ.	Boot
ibid.	mutavit	...	*mutivit*	
lxviii. 2	itaque abutor coronis	...	itaque ut ab utro coronas	Ed.?

Ep.	MS. Reading.	Generally received Reading.	Conjecture accepted in Text, *or recorded with approbation in Notes.*	Author of Conjecture.
lxix. 1	Caninium	...	C. Asinium	Boot
ibid.	recta	...	recte	Reid
lxix. 2	meam	...	en meam	Ed.
ibid.	magni sedebant	magni esse debebant	ἄγιοι esse debebant	Boot
lxx. 1	de legem quid egerit	de lege quid egerit	de lege en quid egerit	Lehmann
lxxvi. 1	delectari	...	delectare	Boot

APPENDIX TO INTRODUCTION

DINERS OUT

ALL great cities abound with little men, whose object it is to be stars of the dinner-table, and grand purveyors of all the stray jokes of the town. So long as these confine themselves to fetch and carry for their masters they succeed tolerably well, but the moment they set up for originality, and turn manufacturers instead of retailers, they are ruined. Like the hind wheel of the carriage which is in constant pursuit of the fore without ever overtaking it; so these become the doubles of a Selwyn or a Sheridan, but without ever coming up to them. They are constantly near wit without being witty, as his valet is always near a great man without being great.

A MOTLEY CREW

BUT with every care the camp still presented an irregular and uncouth appearance. A spy who was sent from England about the middle of October reports as follows :—They consist of an odd medley of grey beards and no beards—old men fit to drop into the grave, and young boys whose swords are near equal to their weight, and I really believe more than their length. Four or five thousand may be very good determined men, but the rest are mean, dirty, villainous-looking rascals, who seem more anxious for plunder than their prince, and would be better pleased with four shillings than a crown.

CONVIVIORUM CIRCULATORES

Non desunt per urbes magnas homunculi quidam qui lecti imi derisores agunt, et facetiarum institores si quid ridiculi sub basilicis emanet. Quibus quamdiu satis videtur patronorum logos baiulare et quasi τὴν καπηλικὴν facere, satis belle vivitur ; at siquando salinas, ut ita dicam, suas exercere affectant, conturbant ilico. Scis enim Persianum illud

frustra sectabere canthum
Si rota posterior curras et in axe secundo.

Ita fit ut Laeliastri sive Luciliastri evadant sanniones nostri, Laelii aut Lucilii nequaquam ; et, quemadmodum regis pedisequus ad magnum creber accedat, ad magnitudinem nunquam, sic inter lepores semper versati vivant ipsi illepidi.

ΣΤΡΦΕΤΟΣ

Sed ne summa quidem diligentia prohiberi potuit quin aliquid inconditi et imparati castra prae se ferrent. Speculator missus e Britannia circiter Idus Octobres renunciavit, exercitum e senibus barbatis et pueris imberbibus mire commixtis esse conflatum ; homines capulares et adulescentulos gladiorum pondere leviores, longitudine mediusfidius breviores, una tendere ; ad quattuor vel quinque milia strenuos sane fortesque viros ; ceteros vero meras quisquilias, sordidos et truculentos latrones, praedarum quam principis cupidiores, centussim Caesari praelaturos.

GREAT EXPECTATIONS

There will be mistakes at first as there are in all changes. All young ladies will imagine that as soon as this bill is carried they will be instantly married. Schoolboys believe that gerunds and supines will be abolished, and that currant tarts must ultimately come down in price. The corporal and sergeant are sure of double pay; bad poets expect a demand for their epics. Fools will be disappointed, as they always are; reasonable men who know what to expect will find that a very serious good has been obtained.

TO ALL WHOM IT MAY CONCERN

We understand that discharged soldiers who re-enlist are now allowed to count their previous service, together with other advantages; and that if they present themselves at the offices of the recruiting districts, or at the headquarters of a regiment, they will be entitled to ten shillings levy-money, which will cover their expenses.

PINTO

'Well, now I shall begin my dinner,' he said to Pinto when he was at length served. 'What surprises me most in you is your English. There is not a man who speaks such good English as you do.'—'English is an expressive language,' said Mr. Pinto, 'but not difficult to master. Its range is limited. It consists, so far as I can observe, of four words, *nice, jolly, charming,* and *bore,* and some grammarians add *fond.*'

ΟΥ ΤΑΥΤΟΝ ΕΙΔΟΣ

PRIMO quidem, ut in rebus novis ferme fit, erunt qui fallantur. 'Hac rogatione perlata unaquaeque puella nil morae futurum quin nuptum detur existimabit. Pueri qui Minervam colunt sibi persuasum habebunt fore ut leges grammaticae antiquentur et crustulorum annona tandem aliquando laxior fiat. Tesserarii et centuriones duplex stipendium sibi promittent ; Bavius et Maevius libros suos nunc demum Sosiis aera merituros credent. Stulti, ut semper, frustra erunt ; homines vero perspicaces, quibus quid liceat sperare notum, nil parvum profici intellegent.

PRAEMIA MILITIAE

ACCEPIMUS fore ut militibus exauctoratis aera procedant, et alia accedant commoda si denuo nomina edant ; et si apud con-quisitores vel ad stativa cuiusque legionis profiteantur, viritim deberi conscriptionis mercedem et viaticum IIS sexagenos.

SERMO CONVIVIALIS

CIBO tandem apposito 'iam cenare libet,' Pisoni dixit et 'ideo potissimum mihi admirationem moves quod tam perite Anglice loqueris ut nemo possit melius.'—'Lingua Anglica,' respondit Piso, 'quamvis arguta sit tamen ea est quam quis facile calleat. Fines eius parum ampli : quippe quattuor tantum, quod sciam, nomina habeat. Ei enim res quaevis est aut *lepida* aut *festiva* aut *dulcis* aut *insulsa;* praeterea apud nonnullos auctores est et *in deliciis.*'

PITT

His powerful intellect was ill supplied with knowledge. Of this he had no more than a man can acquire while he is a student at college. The stock of general information which he brought with him from Cambridge, extraordinary for a boy, was far inferior to what Fox possessed, and beggarly when compared with the massy, the splendid, the various treasures laid up in the large mind of Burke. He had no leisure to learn more than what was necessary for the purposes of the day which was passing over him.

XOPHΓΙA ΠΟΛΙΤΙΚΗ

INGENIO validus, doctrina impar; nec plura tenuit quam quivis adolescens tirocinium apud philosophos emeritus. Sane ea rerum peritia quam Rhodo reportavit, quamvis in puero memorabilis, vel a Lucullo longe superata est; eadem mera inopia esse videbitur, si cum ampla et multiplici et lautissima ubertate conferatur, quam immensae Varronis facultates continuere. Nempe non erat otium ad plura discenda quam quae in diem opus essent.

CICERO IN HIS LETTERS

CICERO'S extant correspondence commenced B. C. 68. Cicero was then 38 years of age. Ten years before he had returned from his travels in Greece and Asia, and shortly after his return (aged about 29) had married Terentia. At the age of 17 he had served under Cn. Pompeius Strabo in the Marsic War. He had distinguished himself by his speech for P. Quinctius (B.C. 81), and by his daring defence of Sex. Roscius Amerinus, and an Arretine woman (B.C. 80), against the power of Sulla. He had afterwards, in his defence of Q. Roscius Comoedus (B.C. 76), more clearly shown his great qualifications for the Bar, and had filled the quaestorship at the age of 31 (B.C. 75). But it was not until he was 36 years old (two years before the date of these letters) that his public life may be said to have begun with the prosecution of Verres (B.C. 70). The year after this famous prosecution he became curule aedile, and while holding that office defended A. Caecina, and made the speech for M. Fonteius, charged with misgovernment in Gaul. Except the treatise *De Inventione Rhetorica* (B.C. 86), Cicero had, at the time when his extant correspondence opens, contributed to literature only translations from the Greek, most of which he afterwards retouched, as, for instance, the *Prognostica* of Aratus. Of these translations we preserve only fragmentary remains.

B

I. TO ATTICUS, at Athens (Att. i. 5)

ROME, A.U.C. 686; B.C. 68; AET. CIC. 38

De L. Ciceronis fratris patruelis morte, de Q. fratris animo in uxorem suam, Attici sororem, et placando et regendo, de intermissione litterarum, de negotio Acutiliano, de Lucceii offensione lenienda, de re Tadiana, de Epirotica emptione Attici, de ornando Tusculano, de Terentiae valetudine et humanitate.

1. Quantum dolorem acceperim et quanto fructu sim privatus et forensi et domestico Lucii fratris nostri morte in primis pro nostra consuetudine tu existimare potes. Nam mihi omnia, quae iucunda ex humanitate alterius et moribus homini accidere possunt, ex illo accidebant. Qua re non dubito quin tibi quoque id molestum sit, cum et meo dolore moveare et ipse omni virtute officioque ornatissimum tuique et sua sponte et meo sermone amantem, adfinem, amicumque amiseris. 2. Quod ad me scribis de sorore tua, testis erit tibi ipsa quantae mihi curae fuerit, ut Quinti fratris animus in eam esset is, qui esse deberet. Quem cum esse offensiorem arbitrarer, eas litteras ad eum misi, quibus et placarem ut fratrem et monerem ut minorem et obiurgarem ut errantem. Itaque ex iis, quae postea saepe ab eo ad me scripta sunt, confido ita esse omnia, ut et oporteat et velimus. 3. De litterarum missione sine causa abs te accusor. Numquam enim a Pomponia nostra certior sum factus esse cui dare litteras possem, porro autem neque mihi accidit ut haberem qui in Epirum proficisceretur nequedum te Athenis esse audiebamus. 4. De Acutiliano autem negotio quod mihi

mandaras, ut primum a tuo digressu Romam veni, confeceram, sed accidit ut et contentione nihil opus esset, et
ut ego, qui in te satis consilii statuerim esse, mallem
Peducaeum tibi consilium per litteras quam me dare.
Etenim cum multos dies aures meas Acutilio dedissem,
cuius sermonis genus tibi notum esse arbitror, non mihi
grave duxi scribere ad te de illius querimoniis, cum eas
audire, quod erat subodiosum, leve putassem. Sed abs te
ipso, qui me accusas, unas mihi scito litteras redditas esse,
cum et otii ad scribendum plus et facultatem dandi maiorem
habueris. 5. Quod scribis, etiam si cuius animus in te
esset offensior, a me recolligi oportere, teneo quid dicas,
neque id neglexi, sed est miro quodam modo adfectus.
Ego autem, quae dicenda fuerunt de te, non praeterii:
quid autem contendendum esset ex tua putabam voluntate statuere me oportere: quam si ad me perscripseris,
intelleges me neque diligentiorem esse voluisse, quam tu
esses, neque neglegentiorem fore, quam tu velis. 6. De
Tadiana re, mecum Tadius locutus est te ita scripsisse,
nihil esse iam quod laboraretur, quoniam hereditas usu
capta esset. Id mirabamur te ignorare, de tutela legitima,
in qua dicitur esse puella, nihil usu capi posse. 7. Epiroticam emptionem gaudeo tibi placere. Quae tibi mandavi
et quae tu intelleges convenire nostro Tusculano, velim,
ut scribis, cures, quod sine molestia tua facere poteris.
Nam nos ex omnibus molestiis et laboribus uno illo in
loco conquiescimus. 8. Q. fratrem cotidie exspectamus.
Terentia magnos articulorum dolores habet. Et te et
sororem tuam et matrem maxime diligit; salutemque
tibi plurimam ascribit, et Tulliola, deliciae nostrae. Cura

ut valeas et nos ames et tibi persuadeas te a me fraterne
amari.

II. TO ATTICUS, at Athens (Att. i. 7)

ROME, A.U.C. 686 ; B.C. 68 ; AET. CIC. 38

De matre Attici Caecilia, de pecunia L. Cincio constituta, de
signis mittendis, de bibliotheca ab Attico conficienda.

Apud matrem recte est, eaque nobis curae est.   L.
Cincio HS xxcd constitui me curaturum Idibus Februariis.
Tu velim ea, quae nobis emisse te et parasse scribis, des
operam ut quam primum habeamus, et velim cogites, id
quod mihi pollicitus es, quem ad modum bibliothecam
nobis conficere possis.   Omnem spem delectationis nostrae,
quam, cum in otium venerimus, habere volumus, in tua
humanitate positam habemus.

III. TO ATTICUS, at Athens (Att. i. 6)

ROME, A.U.C. 687 ; B.C. 67 ; AET. CIC. 39

De mutuo litterarum commercio, de domo Rabiriana Neapoli
a M'. Fonteio empta, de animo Q. fratris in Pomponiam, de
patris morte, de Tusculano ornando.

1. Non committam posthac ut me accusare de epistolarum neglegentia possis.   Tu modo videto in tanto otio ut
par mihi sis.   Domum Rabirianam Neapoli, quam tu iam

dimensam et exaedificatam animo habebas, M'.Fonteius
emit HS ccciɔɔɔxxx.   Id te scire volui, si quid forte ea
res ad cogitationes tuas pertineret. 2. Q. frater, ut
mihi videtur, quo volumus animo est in Pomponiam, et
cum ea nunc in Arpinatibus praediis erat et secum
habebat hominem χρηστομαθῆ, D. Turranium.   Pater
nobis decessit A.D. IIII. Kal. Decembris.   Haec habebam
fere quae te scire vellem.   Tu velim, si qua ornamenta
γυμνασιώδη reperire poteris, quae loci sint eius, quem tu
non ignoras, ne praetermittas.   Nos Tusculano ita
delectamur, ut nobismet ipsis tum denique, cum illo
venimus, placeamus.   Quid agas omnibus de rebus et
quid acturus sis fac nos quam diligentissime certiores.

IV. TO ATTICUS, at Athens (Att. i. 2)

ROME, A.U.C. 689 ; B.C. 65 ; AET. CIC. 41

Exponit M. Cicero de filio sibi nato, de Catilina defendendo,
de Attici adventu ad hominum nobilium voluntatem sibi conciliandam a se exspectato.

1. L. Iulio Caesare C. Marcio Figulo consulibus
filiolo me auctum scito salva Terentia.   Abs te tam diu
nihil litterarum ?   Ego de meis ad te rationibus scripsi
antea diligenter.   Hoc tempore Catilinam, competitorem
nostrum, defendere cogitamus.   Iudices habemus, quos
voluimus, summa accusatoris voluntate.   Spero, si
absolutus erit, coniunctiorem illum nobis fore in ratione
petitionis : sin aliter acciderit, humaniter feremus.   2.

Tuo adventu nobis opus est maturo: nam prorsis summa hominum est opinio tuos familiares, nobil:s homines, adversarios honori nostro fore. Ad eorun voluntatem mihi conciliandam maximo te mihi usui fo:e video. Qua re Ianuario mense, ut constituisti, cura ut Romae sis.

V. TO ATTICUS, in Epirus (Att. i. 17)

ROME, A.U.C. 693; B.C. 61; AET. CIC. 45

M. Cicero de Q. fratris offensione et voluntate mutata erg ı Atticum exponit, causamque eius rei ipsam praesenti colloqui) reservans, adseverat de summo suo erga Atticum amore. Tun ı significat statum rei publicae et solutam paene coniunctionen: senatus et ordinis equestris; de consiliis suis capessendae re: publicae, de Lucceii aliorumque petitione consulatus.

1. Magna mihi varietas voluntatis et dissimilitudc opinionis ac iudicii Quinti fratris mei demonstrata est ex litteris tuis, in quibus ad me epistolarum illius exempla misisti. Qua ex re et molestia sum tanta adfectus, quantam mihi meus amor summus erga utrumque vestrum adferre debuit, et admiratione quidnam accidisset quod adferret Quinto fratri meo aut offensionem tam gravem aut commutationem tantam voluntatis. Atque illud a me iam ante intellegebatur, quod te quoque ipsum discedentem a nobis suspicari videbam, subesse nescio quid opinionis incommodae sauciumque eius esse animum et insedisse quasdam odiosas suspiciones; quibus ego mederi cum cuperem antea saepe et vehementius etiam post sorti-

tionem provinciae, nec tantum intellegebam ei esse offen-
sionis, quantum litterae tuae declarabant, nec tantum
proficiebam, quantum volebam. 2. Sed tamen hoc me
ipse consolabar, quod non dubitabam quin te ille aut
Dyrrhachii aut in istis locis uspiam visurus esset. Quod
cum accidisset, confidebam ac mihi persuaseram fore ut
omnia placarentur inter vos non modo sermone ac dis-
putatione, sed conspectu ipso congressuque vestro. Nam
quanta sit in Quinto fratre meo comitas, quanta iucun-
ditas, quam mollis animus ad accipiendam et ad depon-
endam offensionem, nihil attinet me ad te, qui ea nosti,
scribere. Sed accidit perincommode, quod cum nusquam
vidisti. Valuit enim plus, quod erat illi non nullorum
artificiis inculcatum, quam aut officium aut necessitudo
aut amor vester ille pristinus, qui plurimum valere debuit.
3. Atque huius incommodi culpa ubi resideat facilius
possum existimare quam scribere. Vereor enim ne, dum
defendam meos, non parcam tuis. Nam sic intellego, ut
nihil a domesticis vulneris factum sit, illud quidem, quod
erat, eos certe sanare potuisse. Sed huiusce rei totius
vitium, quod aliquanto etiam latius patet quam videtur,
praesenti tibi commodius exponam. 4. De iis litteris,
quas ad te Thessalonica misit, et de sermonibus, quos ab
illo et Romae apud amicos tuos et in itinere habitos putas,
ecquid tantum causae sit ignoro, sed omnis in tua posita
est humanitate mihi spes huius levandae molestiae. Nam,
si ita statueris, et irritabiles animos esse optimorum saepe
hominum et eosdem placabiles, et esse hanc agilitatem,
ut ita dicam, mollitiamque naturae plerumque boni-
tatis, et, id quod caput est, nobis inter nos nostra sive

incommoda sive vitia sive iniurias esse tolerandas, facile hacc, quem ad modum spero, mitigabuntur. Quod ego ut facias te oro. Nam ad me, qui te unice diligo, maxime pertinet neminem esse meorum, qui aut te non amet aut abs te non ametur. 5. Illa pars epistolae tuae minime fuit necessaria, in qua exponis quas facultates aut provincialium aut urbanorum commodorum et aliis temporibus et me ipso consule praetermiseris. Mihi enim perspecta est ingenuitas et magnitudo animi tui, neque ego inter me atque te quidquam interesse umquam dux practer voluntatem institutae vitae, quod me ambitio quaedam ad honorum studium, te autem alia minime reprehendenda ratio ad honestum otium duxit. Vera quidem laude probitatis, diligentiae, religionis neque me tibi neque quemquam antepono, amoris vero erga me, cum a fraterno [amore] domesticoque discessi, tibi primas defero. 6. Vidi enim, vidi penitusque perspexi in meis variis temporibus et solicitudines et laetitias tuas. Fuit mihi saepe et laudis nostrae gratulatio tua iucunda et timoris consolatio grata. Quin mihi nunc te absente non solum consilium, quo tu excellis, sed etiam sermonis communicatio, quae mihi suavissima tecum solet esse, maxime deest—quid dicam? in publica re, quo in genere mihi neglegenti esse non licet, an in forensi labore, quem antea propter ambitionem sustinebam, nunc, ut dignitatem tueri gratia possim, an in ipsis domesticis negotiis? in quibus ego cum antea tum vero post discessum fratris te sermonesque nostros desidero. Postremo non labor meus, non requies, non negotium, non otium, non forenses res, non domesticae, non publicae, non privatae carere diutius tuo

suavissimo atque amantissimo consilio ac sermone possunt.
7. Atque harum rerum commemorationem verecundia
saepe impedivit utriusque nostrum.   Nunc autem ea fuit
necessaria propter eam partem epistolae .tuae, per quam
te ac mores tuos mihi purgatos ac probatos esse voluisti.
Atque in ista incommoditate alienati illius animi et offensi
illud inest tamen commodi, quod et mihi et ceteris amicis
tuis nota fuit et abs te aliquando testificata tua voluntas
omittendae provinciae, ut, quod una non estis, non dissensione ac discidio vestro, sed voluntate ac iudicio tuo
factum esse videatur.   Qua re et illa, quae violata, expia-
buntur et haec nostra, quae sunt sanctissime conservata,
suam religionem obtinebunt.   8. Nos hic in re publica
infirma, misera commutabilique versamur.   Credo enim
te audisse nostros equites paene a senatu esse disiunctos:
qui primum illud valde graviter tulerunt, promulgatum
ex senatus consulto fuisse, ut de eis, qui ob iudicandum
accepissent, quaereretur.   Qua in re decernenda cum ego
casu non adfuissem sensissemque id equestrem ordinem
ferre moleste neque aperte dicere, obiurgavi senatum, ut
mihi visus sum, summa cum auctoritate et in causa non
verecunda admodum gravis et copiosus fui.   9. Ecce
aliae deliciae equitum vix ferendae! quas ego non solum
tuli, sed etiam ornavi. Asiam qui de censoribus con-
duxerunt, questi sunt in senatu se cupiditate pro-
lapsos nimium magno conduxisse: ut induceretur locatio,
postulaverunt.   Ego princeps in adiutoribus atque
adeo secundus: nam, ut illi auderent hoc postulare,
Crassus eos impulit. Invidiosa res, turpis postulatio
et confessio temeritatis. Summum erat periculum ne,

si nihil impetrassent, plane alienarentur a senatu. Huic quoque rei subventum est maxime a nobis, perfectumque ut frequentissimo senatu et libentissimo uterentur, multaque a me de ordinum dignitate et concordia dicta sunt Kal. Decembr. et postridie. Neque adhuc res confecta est, sed voluntas senatus perspecta. Unus enim contra dixerat Metellus consul designatus, cum erat dicturus—ad quem propter diei brevitatem perventui non est—heros ille noster Cato. 10. Sic ego conservans rationem institutionemque nostram tueor, ut possum, illam a me conglutinatam concordiam, sed tamen, quoniam ista sunt tam infirma, munitur quaedam nobis ad retinendas opes nostras tuta, ut spero, via, quam tibi litteris satis explicare non possum, significatione parva ostendam tamen. Utor Pompeio familiarissime. Video quid dicas. Cavebo quae sunt cavenda ac scribam alias ad te de meis consiliis capessendae rei publicae plura. 11. Lucceium scito consulatum habere in animo statim petere: duo enim soli dicuntur petituri. Caesar cum eo coire per Arrium cogitat, et Bibulus cum hoc se putat per C. Pisonem posse coniungi. Rides? Non sunt haec ridicula, mihi crede. Quid aliud scribam ad te? quid? Multa sunt, sed in aliud tempus. Si exspectare velis, cures ut sciam. Iam illud modeste rogo, quod maxime cupio, ut quam primum venias. Nonis Decembribus.

VI. TO ATTICUS, ON HIS WAY TO ROME (ATT. II. 2)

TUSCULANUM, A.U.C. 694; B.C. 60; AET. CIC. 46

M. Cicero Attico Ciceronem suum commendat, Dicaearchum

summis adficit laudibus, Herodem vituperat : deinde de adventu Antonii quaerit et Atticum, ut pridie Kal. secum sit, rogat.

1. Cura, amabo te, Ciceronem nostrum. Ei nos συννοσεῖν videmur. 2. Πελληναίων in manibus tenebam et hercule magnum acervum Dicaearchi mihi ante pedes exstruxeram. O magnum hominem ! et unde multo plura didiceris quam de Procilio. Κορινθίων et ᾿Αθηναίων puto me Romae habere. Mihi crede, si leges haec, dices 'mirabilis vir est.' ῾Ηρώδης, si homo esset, eum potius legeret quam unam litteram scriberet : qui me epistula petivit, ad te, ut video, comminus accessit. Coniurasse mallem quam restitisse coniurationi, si illum mihi audiendum putassem. 3. De Lollio, sanus non es : de vino, laudo. Sed heus tu, ecquid vides Kal. venire, Antonium non venire ? iudices cogi ? Nam ita ad me mittunt, Nigidium minari in contione se iudicem, qui non adfuerit, compellaturum. Velim tamen, si quid est de Antonii adventu quod audieris, scribas ad me et, quoniam huc non venis, cenes apud nos utique pridie Kal. Cave aliter facias. Cura ut valeas.

VII. TO ATTICUS, in Rome (Att. ii. 11)

FORMIAE, A.U.C. 695 ; B.C. 59 ; AET. CIC. 47

M. Cicero Attico scribit se in Formiano nihil fere quid Romae fiat accipere, rogat ut puero, quem miserit, ponderosam epistolam det, ipsum a se in Formiano usque ad prid. Nonas Mai. exspectari, Arpinum non posse invitari.

1. Narro tibi : plane relegatus mihi videor, postea

quam in Formiano sum.   Dies enim nullus erat, Antii cum essem, quo die non melius scirem Romae quid agaretur quam ii qui erant Romae.   Etenim litterae tuae non solum quid Romae, sed etiam quid in re publica, neque solum quid fieret, verum etiam quid futurum esset indicabant.   Nunc, nisi si quid ex praetereunte viatore exceptum est, scire nihil possumus.   Qua re quamquam iam te ipsum exspecto, tamen isti puero, quem ad me statim iussi recurrere, da ponderosam aliquam epistolam, plenam omnium non modo actorum, sed etiam opinionum tuarum, ac diem, quo Roma sis exiturus, cura ut sciam 2. Nos in Formiano esse volumus usque ad prid. Nonas Mai.   Eo si ante eam diem non veneris, Romae te fort- asse videbo.   Nam Arpinum quid ego te invitem ?

τρηχεῖ᾽, ἀλλ᾽ ἀγαθὴ κουροτρόφος.   οὔτ᾽ ἄρ᾽ ἔγωγε
ἧς γαίης δύναμαι γλυκερώτερον ἄλλο ἰδέσθαι.

Haec igitur, et cura ut valeas.

VIII. TO HIS FAMILY, in Rome (Fam. xiv. 4)

BRUNDISIUM, A.U.C. 696 ; B.C. 58 ; AET. CIC. 48

M. Tullius uxori Terentiae scribit se Brundisio per Mace- doniam Cyzicum proficisci et sollicitum esse de ipsa et liberis : de servis manu mittendis, de doloris sui solacio, de libertorum fide.

TULLIUS S. D. TERENTIAE ET TULLIOLAE ET CICERONI SUIS

1. Ego minus saepe do ad vos litteras quam possum.

propterea quod cum omnia mihi tempora sunt misera
tum vero, cum aut scribo ad vos aut vestras lego,
conficior lacrimis sic, ut ferre non possim.   Quod utinam
minus vitae cupidi fuissemus ! certe nihil aut non multum
in vita mali vidissemus.   Quod si nos ad aliquam ali-
cuius commodi aliquando reciperandi spem fortuna
reservavit, minus est erratum a nobis : si haec mala
fixa sunt, ego vero te quam primum, mea vita, cupio
videre et in tuo complexu emori, quando neque di, quos
tu castissime coluisti, neque homines, quibus ego semper
servivi, nobis gratiam rettulerunt.   2. Nos Brundisii
apud M. Laenium Flaccum dies XIII fuimus, virum
optimum, qui periculum fortunarum et capitis sui prae
mea salute neglexit neque legis improbissimae poena
deductus est quo minus hospitii et amicitiae ius officium-
que praestaret.   Huic utinam aliquando gratiam referre
possimus ! habebimus quidem semper.   3. Brundisio profecti sumus a. d. II. Kalendas Maias : per
Macedoniam Cyzicum petebamus.   O me perditum ! o
adflictum !   Quid enim ?   Rogem te ut venias ?   Mulierem
aegram et corpore et animo confectam ?   Non rogem ?
Sine te igitur sim ?   Opinor, sic agam : si est spes nostri
reditus, eam confirmes et rem adiuves : sin, ut ego
metuo, transactum est, quoquo modo potes, ad me fac
venias.   Unum hoc scito : si te habebo, non mihi videbor
plane perisse.   Sed quid Tulliola mea fiet ?   Iam id vos
videte :. mihi deest consilium.   Sed certe, quoquo modo
se res habebit, illius misellae et matrimonio et famae
serviendum est.   Quid, Cicero meus quid aget ?   Iste
vero sit in sinu semper et complexu meo.   Non queo

plura iam scribere : impedit maeror. Tu quid egeris
nescio : utrum aliquid teneas an, quod metuo, plane
sis spoliata. 4. Pisonem, ut scribis, spero fore semper
nostrum. De familia liberata nihil est quod te moveat.
Primum tuis ita promissum est, te facturam esse, ut
quisque esset meritus. Est autem in officio adhuc
Orpheus : praeterea magno opere nemo. Ceterorum.
servorum ea causa est, ut, si res a nobis abisset, libert.
nostri essent, si obtinere potuissent : sin ad nos pertineret, servirent, praeterquam oppido pauci. Sed haec
minora sunt. 5. Tu quod me hortaris, ut animo sim
magno et spem habeam reciperandae salutis, id velim sit
eius modi, ut recte sperare possimus. Nunc, miser
quando tuas iam litteras accipiam ? quis ad me perferet ?
quas ego exspectassem Brundisii, si esset licitum per
nautas, qui tempestatem praetermittere noluerunt. Quod
reliquum est, sustenta te, mea Terentia, ut potes,
honestissime. Viximus : floruimus : non vitium nostrum,
sed virtus nostra nos adflixit. Peccatum est nullum,
nisi quod non una animam cum ornamentis amisimus.
Sed si hoc fuit liberis nostris gratius, nos vivere, cetera,
quamquam ferenda non sunt, feramus. Atqui ego, qui
te confirmo, ipse me non possum. 6. Clodium Philhe-
taerum, quod valetudine oculorum impediebatur, hominem
fidelem, remisi. Sallustius officio vincit omnes. Pescennius est perbenevolus nobis : quem semper spero tui
fore observantem. Sica dixerat se mecum fore, sed
Brundisio discessit. Cura, quod potes, ut valeas, et sic
existimes, me vehementius tua miseria quam mea commoveri. Mea Terentia, fidissima atque optima uxor, et

mea carissima filiola et spes reliqua nostra, Cicero, valete. Pridie Kalendas Maias Brundisio.

IX. TO QUINTUS, in Rome (Q. Fr. i. 3)

THESSALONICA, A.U.C. 696; B.C. 58; AET. CIC. 48

M. Cicero Q. fratri de pueris sine epistola missis se excusat, de exsilii calamitate queritur, pro oblatis facultatibus gratias agit, monet de quorumdam fide suosque commendat.

MARCUS Q. FRATRI S.

1. Mi frater, mi frater, mi frater, tune id veritus es, ne ego iracundia aliqua adductus pueros ad te sine litteris miserim? aut etiam ne te videre noluerim? Ego tibi irascerer? tibi ego possem irasci? Scilicet, tu enim me adflixisti: tui me inimici, tua me invidia ac non ego te misere perdidi. Meus ille laudatus consulatus mihi te, liberos, patriam, fortunas, tibi velim ne quid eripuerit praeter unum me. Sed certe a te mihi omnia semper honesta et iucunda ceciderunt, a me tibi luctus meae calamitatis, metus tuae, desiderium, maeror, solitudo. Ego te videre noluerim? Immo vero me a te videri nolui. Non enim vidisses fratrem tuum, non eum, quem reliqueras, non eum, quem noras, non eum, quem flens flentem, prosequentem proficiscens dimiseras: ne vestigium quidem eius nec simulacrum, sed quamdam effigiem spirantis mortui. Atque utinam me mortuum prius vidisses aut audisses! utinam te non solum vitae, sed etiam dignitatis meae superstitem reliquissem! 2. Sed

testor omnes deos me hac una voce a morte esse revoca-
tum, quod omnes in mea vita partem aliquam tuae vitae
repositam esse dicebant. Qua in re peccavi scelerateque
feci. Nam si occidissem, mors ipsa meam pietatei
amoremque in te facile defenderet. Nunc commisi ut
me vivo careres, vivo me aliis indigeres: mea vox in
domesticis periculis potissimum occideret, quae saepe
alienissimis praesidio fuisset. Nam quod ad te pueri
sine litteris venerunt, quoniam vides non fuisse iracund·
iam causam, certe pigritia fuit et quaedam infinita vi
lacrimarum et dolorum. 3. Haec ipsa me quo fleti
putas scripsisse? Eodem quo te legere certo scio. At
ego possum aut non cogitare aliquando de te aut umquam
sine lacrimis cogitare? Cum enim te desidero, fratrem
solum desidero? Ego vero suavitate [fratrem prope]
aequalem, obsequio filium, consilio parentem. Quid
mihi sine te umquam aut tibi sine me iucundum fuit?
Quid, quod eodem tempore desidero filiam? qua pietate,
qua modestia, quo ingenio! effigiem oris, sermonis, animi
mei! Quod filium venustissimum mihique dulcissimum?
quem ego ferus ac ferreus e complexu dimisi meo, sapien-
tiorem puerum quam vellem. Sentiebat enim miser iam
quid ageretur. Quod vero tuum filium, quod imaginem
tuam, quem meus Cicero et amabat ut fratrem et iam ut
maiorem fratrem verebatur? Quid, quod mulierem miserri-
mam, fidelissimam coniugem, me prosequi non sum passus,
ut esset quae reliquias communis calamitatis, communes
liberos tueretur? 4. Sed tamen, quoquo modo potui,
scripsi et dedi litteras ad te Philogono, liberto tuo, quas
credo tibi postea redditas esse: in quibus idem te hortor et

rogo, quod pueri tibi verbis meis nuntiarunt, ut Romam
protinus pergas et properes.   Primum enim te praesidio
esse volui, si qui essent inimici quorum crudelitas nondum
esset nostra calamitate satiata.   Deinde congressus nostri
lamentationem pertimui, digressum vero non tulissem,
atque etiam id ipsum quod tu scribis, metuebam, ne a
me distrahi non posses.   His de causis hoc maximum
malum, quod te non vidi quo nihil amantissimis et coniunctissimis fratribus acerbius miseriusve videtur accidere
potuisse, minus acerbum, minus miserum fuit, quam
fuisset cum congressio tum vero digressio nostra.   5.
Nunc, si potes, id quod ego, qui tibi semper fortis videbar, non possum, erige te et confirma, si qua subeunda
dimicatio erit.   Spero, si quid mea spes habet auctoritatis, tibi et integritatem tuam et amorem in te civitatis
et aliquid etiam misericordiam nostri praesidii laturam.
Sin eris ab isto periculo vacuus, ages scilicet, si quid agi
posse de nobis putabis.   De quo scribunt ad me quidem
multi multa et se sperare demonstrant, sed ego quid
sperem non dispicio, cum inimici plurimum valeant, amici
partim deseruerint me, partim etiam prodiderint, qui in
meo reditu fortasse reprehensionem sui sceleris pertimes-
cant.   Sed ista qualia sint tu velim perspicias mihique
declares.   Ego tamen, quam diu tibi opus erit, si quid
periculi subeundum videbis, vivam : diutius in hac vita
esse non possum.   Neque enim tantum virium habet ulla
aut prudentia aut doctrina, ut tantum dolorem possit
sustinere.   6. Scio fuisse et honestius moriendi tempus
et utilius, sed non hoc solum, multa alia praetermisi,
quae si queri velim praeterita, nihil agam nisi ut augeam

dolorem tuum, indicem stultitiam meam.   Illud quidem
nec faciendum est nec fieri potest, me diutius, quam aut
tuum tempus aut firma spes postulabit, in tam misera
tamque turpi vita commorari, ut, qui modo fratre fuerim,
liberis, coniuge, copiis, genere ipso pecuniae beatissimus,
dignitate, auctoritate, existimatione, gratia non inferior
quam qui umquam fuerunt amplissimi, is nunc in hac
tam adflicta perditaque fortuna neque me neque meos
lugere diutius possim.   7. Qua re quid ad me scripsisti
de permutatione? quasi vero nunc me non tuae facultates
sustineant, qua in re ipsa video miser et sentio quid
sceleris admiserim, cum tu de visceribus tuis et filii tui
satis facturus sis quibus debes, ego acceptam ex aerario
pecuniam tuo nomine frustra dissiparim.   Sed tamen et
M. Antonio, quantum tu scripseras, et Caepioni tantum-
dem solutum est: mihi ad id, quod cogito, hoc, quod
habeo, satis est.   Sive enim restituimur sive desperamur,
nihil amplius opus est.   Tu, si forte quid erit molestiae,
te ad Crassum et ad Calidium conferas, censeo.   8.
Quantum Hortensio credendum sit nescio.   Me summa
simulatione amoris summaque adsiduitate cotidiana
sceleratissime insidiosissimeque tractavit, adiuncto Q.
Arrio: quorum ego consiliis, promissis, praeceptis desti-
tutus in hanc calamitatem incidi.   Sed haec occultabis,
ne quid obsint.   Illud caveto—et eo puto per Pomponium
fovendum tibi esse ipsum Hortensium—ne ille versus,
qui in te erat collatus, cum aedilitatem petebas, de lege
Aurelia, falso testimonio confirmetur.   Nihil enim tam
timeo quam ne, cum intellegant homines quantum miseri-
cordiae nobis tuae preces et tua salus adlatura sit, op-

pugnent te vehementius.   9. Messallam tui studiosum esse arbitror : Pompeium etiam simulatorem puto.   Sed haec utinam ne experiare ! quod precarer deos, nisi meas preces audire desissent.   Verum tamen precor, ut his infinitis nostris malis contenti sint : in quibus tamen nullius inest peccati infamia, sed omnis dolor est, quod optime factis poena maxima est constituta.   10. Filiam meam et tuam Ciceronemque nostrum quid ego, mi frater, tibi commendem? quin illud maereo, quod tibi non minorem dolorem illorum orbitas adferet quam mihi. Sed te incolumi orbi non erunt.   Reliqua, ita mihi salus aliqua detur potestasque in patria moriendi, ut me lacrimae non sinunt scribere !   Etiam Terentiam velim tueare mihique de omnibus rebus rescribas.   Sis fortis, quoad rei natura patiatur.   Idibus Iuniis, Thessalonicae.

X. TO ATTICUS, in Rome (Att. iii. 20)

THESSALONICA, A.U.C. 696 ; B.C. 58 ; AET. CIC. 48

M. Cicero gratulatur Attico de eius adoptione per Q. Caecilium avunculum iam mortuum facta, de condicione et spe sua, de domo sua et ceteris rebus suis, quas universas Attico commendat, de humanitate Attici, de rogatione Sestii.

CICERO S. D. Q. CAECILIO Q. F. POMPONIANO ATTICO

1. Quod quidem ita esse et avunculum tuum functum esse officio vehementissime probo, gaudere me tum dicam, si mihi hoc verbo licebit uti.   Me miserum ! quam omnia essent ex sententia, si nobis animus, si consilium, si fides eorum, quibus credidimus, non defuisset ! quae colligere

nolo, ne augeam maerorem. Sed tibi venire in mentem
certo scio quae vita esset nostra, quae suavitas, quae
dignitas. Ad quae recuperanda, per fortunas! incumbe,
ut facis, diemque natalem reditus mei cura ut in tuis
aedibus amoenissimis agam tecum et cum meis. Ego
huic spei et exspectationi, quae nobis proponitur maxim i,
tamen volui praestolari apud te in Epiro, sed ita ad me
scribitur, ut putem esse commodius non eisdem in loc s
esse. 2. De domo et Curionis oratione, ut scribis, ita es i.
In universa salute, si ea modo nobis restituetur, inerunt
omnia, ex quibus nihil malo quam domum. Sed til i
nihil mando nominatim, totum me tuo amori fideiqu ;
commendo. Quod te in tanta hereditate ab omni oc-
cupatione expedisti, valde mihi gratum est. Quod
facultates tuas ad meam salutem polliceris, ut omnibus
rebus a te praeter ceteros iuver, id quantum sit praesidiun.
video intellegoque te multas partes meae salutis et sus-
cipere et posse sustinere neque, ut ita facias, rogandum
esse. 3. Quod me vetas quidquam suspicari accidisse ad
animum tuum quod secus a me erga te commissum aut
praetermissum videretur, geram tibi morem et liberabor
ista cura, tibi tamen eo plus debebo, quo tua in me
humanitas fuerit excelsior quam in te mea. Velim quid
videas, quid intellegas, quid agatur ad me scribas, tuosque
omnes ad nostram salutem adhortere. Rogatio Sestii
neque dignitatis satis habet nec cautionis. Nam et
nominatim ferri oportet et de bonis diligentius scribi,
et id animadvertas velim. Data IIII. Non. Octobr.
Thessalonicae.

XI. TO THE CONSUL, METELLUS NEPOS,
in Rome (Fam. v. 4)

DYRRHACHIUM, A.U.C. 697; B.C. 57; AET. CIC. 49

M. Cicero Q. Metelli consulis opem implorat.

M. CICERO S. D. Q. METELLO COS.

1. Litterae Quinti fratris et T. Pomponii, necessarii mei, tantum spei dederant, ut in te non minus auxilii quam in tuo collega mihi constitutum fuerit.   Itaque ad te litteras statim misi, per quas, ut fortuna postulabat, et gratias tibi egi et de reliquo tempore auxilium petii.   Postea mihi non tam meorum litterae quam sermones eorum, qui hac iter faciebant, animum tuum immutátum significabant: quae res fecit ut tibi litteris obstrepere non auderem.   2. Nunc mihi Quintus frater meus mitissimam tuam orationem, quam in senatu habuisses, perscripsit, qua inductus ad te scribere sum conatus et abs te, quántum tua fert voluntas, peto quaesoque, ut tuos mecum serves potius quam propter adrogantem crudelitatem <u>tuorum</u> me oppugnes.   Tu tuas inimicitias ut rei publicae donares, te vicisti: alienas ut contra rem publicam confirmes, adduceris?   Quod si mihi tua clementia opem tuleris, omnibus in rebus me fore in tua potestate tibi confirmo: sin mihi neque magistratus neque senatum neque populum auxiliari propter eam vim, quae me cum re publica vicit, licuerit, vide ne, cum velis revocare tempus ‸omnium <u>reservandorum</u>, cum qui servetur non erit, non possis.

XII. TO M. FADIUS GALLUS (Fam. vii. 26)

TUSCULANUM, A.U.C. 697; B.C. 57; AET. CIC. 49

M. Cicero narrat Gallo herbas in augurali cena suaviter conditis et a se avidius comesas sibi morbum attulisse.

CICERO S. D. GALLO

1. Cum decimum iam diem graviter ex intestinis laborarem neque iis, qui mea opera uti volebant, me probarem non valere, quia febrim non haberem, fugi in Tusculanum, cum quidem biduum ita ieiunus fuissem, ut ne aquam quidem gustarem. Itaque confectus languore et fame magis tuum officium desideravi, quam a te requir putavi meum. Ego autem cum omnes morbos reformido, tum, in quo Epicurum tuum Stoici male accipiunt, quia dicat στραγγουρικὰ καὶ δυσεντερικὰ πάθη sibi molesta esse, quorum alterum morbum edacitatis esse putant, alterum etiam turpioris intemperantiae. Sane δυσεντερίαν pertimueram. Sed visa est mihi vel loci mutatio vel animi etiam relaxatio vel ipsa fortasse iam senescentis morbi remissio profuisse. 2. Ac tamen, ne mirere unde hoc acciderit quo modove commiserim, lex sumptuaria, quae videtur λιτότητα attulisse, ea mihi fraudi fuit. Nam dum volunt isti lauti terra nata, quae lege excepta sunt, in honorem adducere, fungos, helvellas, herbas omnes ita condiunt, ut nihil possit esse suavius. In eas cum incidissem in cena augurali apud Lentulum, tanta me διάρροια adripuit, ut hodie primum videatur coepisse consistere. Ita ego, qui me ostreis et muraenis facile abstinebam, a beta et

a malva deceptus sum. Posthac igitur erimus cautiores. Tu
tamen cum audisses ab Anicio—vidit enim me nauseantem
—non modo mittendi causam iustam habuisti, sed etiam
visendi. Ego hic cogito commorari, quoad me reficiam :
nam et vires et corpus amisi. Sed, si morbum depulero,
facile, ut spero, illa revocabo.

XIII. TO ATTICUS, in Italy, on his Journey to Rome (Att. iv. 4*b*)

ANTIUM, A.U.C. 698 ; B.C. 56 ; AET. CIC. 50

De bibliotheca sua a Tyrannione, ope librariorum Attici, iam
restituenda et de exspectato Attici adventu.

1. Perbelle feceris, si ad nos veneris. Offendes desig-
nationem Tyrannionis mirificam librorum meorum [biblio-
theca], quorum reliquiae multo meliores sunt quam
putaram. Etiam velim mihi mittas de tuis librariolis
duos aliquos, quibus Tyrannio utatur glutinatoribus, ad
cetera administris, iisque imperes, ut sumant membranu-
lam ex qua indices fiant, quos vos Graeci, ut opinor,
σιλλύβους appellatis. 2. Sed haec, si tibi erit commodum. Ipse vero utique fac venias, si potes in his
locis adhaerescere et Piliam adducere. Ita enim et
aequum est et cupit Tullia. Medius fidius ne tu emisti
λόχον praeclarum : gladiatores audio pugnare mirifice.
Si locare voluisses, duobus his muneribus liber esses. Sed
haec posterius. Tu fac venias, et de librariis, si me
amas, diligenter.

XIV. TO LUCCEIUS (Fam. v. 12)

ARPINUM, A.U.C. 698 ; B.C. 56 ; AET. CIC. 50

M. Cicero L. Lucceium scriptorem historicum non ignobilem hac epistola summa arte composita rogat, ut de rebus a se in consulatu suo gestis et de discessu redituque commentarios componat.

M. CICERO S. D. L. LUCCEIO Q. F.

1. Coram me tecum eadem haec agere saepe conantem deterruit pudor quidam paene subrusticus, quae nunc expromam absens audacius : epistola enim non erubescit. Ardeo cupiditate incredibili neque, ut ego arbitror, reprehendenda, nomen ut nostrum scriptis illustretur et celebretur tuis. Quod etsi mihi saepe ostendisti te esse facturum, tamen ignoscas velim huic festinationi meae. Genus enim scriptorum tuorum etsi erat semper a me vehementer exspectatum, tamen vicit opinionem meam meque ita vel cepit vel incendit, ut cuperem quam celerrime res nostras monimentis commendari tuis. Neque enim me solum commemoratio posteritatis ad spem quamdam immortalitatis rapit, sed etiam illa cupiditas, ut vel auctoritate testimonii tui vel iudicio benevolentiae vel suavitate ingenii vivi perfruamur. 2. Neque tamen, haec cum scribebam, eram nescius quantis oneribus premere susceptarum rerum et iam institutarum, sed quia videbam Italici belli et civilis historiam iam a te paene esse perfectam, dixeras autem mihi te reliquas res ordiri, deesse mihi nolui quin te admonerem, ut cogitares coniunctene malles cum reliquis rebus nostra contexere

an, ut multi Graeci fecerunt, Callisthenes Phocium
bellum, Timaeus Pyrrhi, Polybius Numantinum, qui
omnes a perpetuis suis historiis ea, quae dixi, bella
separaverunt, tu quoque item civilem coniurationem ab
hostilibus externisque bellis sciungeres. Equidem ad
nostram laudem non multum video interesse, sed ad
properationem meam quiddam interest non te exspectare,
dum ad locum venias, ac statim causam illam totam et
tempus adripere. Et simul, si uno in argumento unaque
in persona mens tua tota versabitur, cerno iam animo
quanto omnia uberiora atque ornatiora futura sint.
Neque tamen ignoro quam impudenter faciam, qui
primum tibi tantum oneris imponam—potest enim mihi
denegare occupatio tua,—deinde etiam, ut ornes me,
postulem. Quid, si illa tibi non tanto opere videntur
ornanda? 3. Sed tamen, qui semel verecundiae fines
transierit, eum bene et naviter oportet esse impudentem.
Itaque te plane etiam atque etiam rogo, ut et ornes ea
vehementius etiam quam fortasse sentis, et in eo leges
historiae neglegas, gratiamque illam, de qua suavissime,
plenissime quodam in prooemio scripsisti, a qua te deflecti
non magis potuisse demonstras quam Herculem Xeno-
phontium illum a Voluptate, eam, si me tibi vehementius
commendabit, ne aspernere, amorique nostro plusculum
etiam quam concedet veritas largiare. Quod si te ad-
ducemus ut hoc suscipias, erit, ut mihi persuadeo,
materies digna facultate et copia tua. 4. A principio
enim coniurationis usque ad reditum nostrum videtur
mihi modicum quoddam corpus confici posse, in quo et
illa poteris uti civilium commutationum scientia vel in

explicandis causis rerum novarum vel in remediis incom-
modorum, cum et reprehendes ea, quae vituperanda
duces, et quae placebunt exponendis rationibus compro-
babis et, si liberius, ut consuesti, agendum putabis, multorum in nos perfidiam, insidias, proditionem notabis.
Multam etiam casus nostri varietatem tibi in scribendo
suppeditabunt plenam cuiusdam voluptatis, quae vehementer animos hominum in legendo, te scriptore, retinere
possit.   Nihil est enim aptius ad delectationem lectoris
quam temporum varietates fortunaeque vicissitudines :
quae etsi nobis optabiles in experiendo non fuerunt, in
legendo tamen erunt iucundae : habet enim praeteriti
doloris secura recordatio delectationem.   5. Ceteris vero
nulla perfunctis propria molestia, casus autem alienos
sine ullo dolore intuentibus, etiam ipsa misericordia est
iucunda.   Quem enim nostrum ille moriens apud Man-
tineam Epaminondas non cum quadam miseratione
delectat? qui tum denique sibi evelli iubet spiculum,
postea quam ei percontanti dictum est clipeum esse salvum,
ut etiam in vulneris dolore aequo animo cum laude more-
retur.   Cuius studium in legendo non erectum Themistocli fuga redituque retinetur?   Etenim ordo ipse
annalium mediocriter nos retinet quasi enumeratione
fastorum : at viri saepe excellentis ancipites variique
casus habent admirationem, exspectationem, laetitiam,
molestiam, spem, timorem : si vero exitu notabili con-
cluduntur, expletur animus iucundissima lectionis voluptate.   6. Quo mihi acciderit optatius, si in hac sententia
fueris, ut a continentibus tuis scriptis, in quibus perpetuam
rerum gestarum historiam complecteris, secernas hanc

quasi fabulam rerum eventorumque nostrorum: habet enim
varios actus mutationesque et consiliorum et temporum.
Ac non vereor ne adsentatiuncula quadam aucupari tuam
gratiam videar, cum hoc demonstrem, me a te potissimum
ornari celebrarique velle. Neque enim tu is es, qui quid
sis nescias et qui non eos magis, qui te non admirentur,
invidos quam eos, qui laudent, adsentatores arbitrere.
Neque autem ego sum ita demens, ut me sempiternae
gloriae per eum commendari velim, qui non ipse quoque
in me commendando propriam ingenii gloriam consequatur.
7. Neque enim Alexander ille gratiae causa ab Apelle
potissimum pingi et a Lysippo fingi volebat, sed quod
illorum artem cum ipsis tum etiam sibi gloriae fore
putabat. Atque illi artifices corporis simulacra ignotis
nota faciebant: quae vel si nulla sint, nihilo sint tamen
obscuriores clari viri. Nec minus est Spartiates Agesilaus
ille perhibendus, qui neque pictam neque fictam imaginem
suam passus est esse, quam qui in eo genere laborarunt;
unus enim Xenophontis libellus in eo rege laudando facile
omnes imagines omnium statuasque superavit. Atque
hoc praestantius mihi fuerit et ad laetitiam animi et ad
memoriae dignitatem, si in tua scripta pervenero, quam
si in ceterorum, quod non ingenium mihi solum suppedita-
tum fuerit tuum, sicut Timoleonti a Timaeo aut ab
Herodoto Themistocli, sed etiam auctoritas clarissimi et
spectatissimi viri et in rei publicae maximis gravissi-
misque causis cogniti atque in primis probati: ut mihi
non solum praeconium, quod, cum in Sigeum venisset,
Alexander ab Homero Achilli tributum esse dixit, sed
etiam grave testimonium impertitum clari hominis

magnique videatur.   Placet enim Hector ille mihi
Naevianus, qui non tantum 'laudari' se laetatur, sed
addit etiam 'a laudato viro.'   8. Quod si a te non
impetraro, hoc est, si quae te res impedierit—neque enim
fas esse arbitror quidquam me rogantem abs te non
impetrare,—cogar fortasse facere, quod non nulli saepe
reprehendunt : scribam ipse de me, multorum tamen
exemplo et clarorum virorum.   Sed, quod te non fugit,
haec sunt in hoc genere vitia : et verecundius ipsi de sese
scribant necesse est, si quid est laudandum, et praetereant,
si quid reprehendendum est.   Accedit etiam, ut minor sit
fides, minor auctoritas, multi denique reprehendant et
dicant verecundiores esse praecones ludorum gymnicorum,
qui cum ceteris coronas imposuerint victoribus eorumque
nomina magna voce pronuntiarint, cum ipsi ante ludorum
missionem corona donentur, alium praeconem adhibeant,
ne sua voce se ipsi victores esse praedicent.   9. Haec nos
vitare cupimus et, si recipis causam nostram, vitabimus,
idque ut facias rogamus.   Ac ne forte mirere cur, cum
mihi saepe ostenderis te accuratissime nostrorum temporum consilia atque eventus litteris mandaturum, a te id
nunc tanto opere et tam multis verbis petamus, illa nos
cupiditas incendit, de qua initio scripsi, festinationis,
quod alacres animo sumus, ut et ceteri viventibus
nobis ex libris tuis nos cognoscant et nosmet ipsi
vivi gloriola nostra perfruamur.   10. His de rebus
quid acturus sis, si tibi non est molestum, rescribas
mihi velim.   Si enim suscipis causam, conficiam commentarios rerum omnium : sin autem differs me in
tempus aliud, coram tecum loquar.   Tu interea non

cessabis et ea, quae habes instituta, perpolies nosque
diliges.

XV. TO ATTICUS, in Rome (Att. iv. 9)

CUMANUM, A.U.C. 699; B.C. 55; AET. CIC. 51

M. Cicero ab Attico de censura a tribunis impedita certior fieri
cupit, de Pompeio, quocum una fuerit, de Lucceio, de Q. fratre, de
itinere suo de Cumano in Pompeianum.

1. Sane velim scire num censum impediant tribuni
diebus vitiandis—est enim hic rumor—totaque de
censura quid agant, quid cogitent. Nos hic cum
Pompeio fuimus. Multa mecum de re publica, sane sibi
displicens, ut loquebatur—sic est enim in hoc homine
dicendum,—Syriam spernens, Hispaniam iactans : hic
quoque, ut loquebatur, et, opinor, usquequaque, de hoc
cum dicemus, sit hoc quasi καὶ τόδε Φωκυλίδου. Tibi
etiam gratias agebat, quod signa componenda suscepisses,
in nos vero suavissime hercule est effusus. Venit etiam
ad me in Cumanum. Etsi nihil minus velle mihi visus
est quam Messallam consulatum petere : de quo ipso si
quid scis, velim scire. 2. Quod Lucceio scribis te nostram
gloriam commendaturum et aedificium nostrum quod
crebro invisis, gratum. Quintus frater ad me scripsit se,
quoniam Ciceronem suavissimum tecum haberes, ad te
Nonis Maiis venturum. Ego me de Cumano movi ante
diem v. Kal. Maias. Eo die Neapoli apud Pactum.
Ante diem iv. Kal. Maias iens in Pompeianum bene mane
haec scripsi.

XVI. TO FADIUS GALLUS (Fam. vii. 23)

ROME, A.U.C. 699; B.C. 55; AET. CIC. 51

M. Cicero scribit de signis et statuis a M. Fadio Gallo sibi emp-
tis, quae sibi emi noluisse dicit, sed tamen rata se velle habere:
tum de domo a Gallo prope se conducta.

M. CICERO S. D. M. FADIO GALLO

1. Tantum quod ex Arpinati veneram, cum mihi a te
litterae redditae sunt: ab eodemque accepi Avianii litteras, in quibus hoc inerat liberalissimum, nomina se
facturum, cum venisset, qua ego vellem die. Fac, quaeso,
qui ego sum, esse te: estne aut tui pudoris aut nostri,
primum rogare de die, deinde plus annua postulare? Sed
essent, mi Galle, omnia facilia, si et ea mercatus esses,
quae ego desiderabam, et ad eam summam, quam volu-
eram. Ac tamen ista ipsa, quae te emisse scribis, non
solum rata mihi erunt, sed etiam grata: plane enim intellego te non modo studio, sed etiam amore usum quae
te delectarint,—hominem, ut ego semper iudicavi, in omni
iudicio elegantissimum,—quia me digna putaris, coëmisse.
2. Sed velim maneat Damasippus in sententia: prorsus
enim ex istis emptionibus nullam desidero. Tu autem
ignarus instituti mei, quanti ego genus omnino signorum
omnium non aestimo, tanti ista quattuor aut quinque
sumpsisti. Bacchas istas cum Musis Metelli comparas.
Quid simile? primum ipsas ego Musas numquam tanti
putassem atque id fecissem Musis omnibus appro-
bantibus: sed tamen erat aptum bibliothecae studiisque
nostris congruens. Bacchis vero ubi est apud me locus?

—At pulchellae sunt.—Novi optime et saepe vidi.
Nominatim tibi signa mihi nota mandassem, si probas-
sem. Ea enim signa ego emere soleo, quae ad similitudinem gymnasiorum exornent mihi in palaestra locum.
Martis vero signum quo mihi pacis auctori? Gaudeo
nullum Saturni signum fuisse : haec enim duo signa
putarem mihi aes alienum attulisse. Mercurii mallem
aliquod fuisset : felicius, puto, cum Avianio transigere
possemus. 3. Quod tibi destinaras trapezophorum, si te
delectat, habebis : sin autem sententiam mutasti, ego
habebo scilicet.—Ista quidem summa ne ego multo
libentius emerim deversorium Tarracinae, ne semper
hospiti molestus sim. Omnino liberti mei video esse
culpam, cui plane res certas mandaram, itemque Iunii,
quem puto tibi notum esse, Avianii familiarem. Exhedria quaedam mihi nova sunt instituta in porticula
Tusculani. Ea volebam tabellis ornare : etenim, si quid
generis istius modi me delectat, pictura delectat. Sed
tamen, si ista mihi sunt habenda, certiorem velim me
facias ubi sint, quando arcessantur, quo genere vecturae.
Si enim Damasippus in sententia non manebit, aliquem
Pseudodamasippum vel cum iactura reperiemus. 4. Quod
ad me de domo scribis iterum, iam id ego proficiscens
mandaram meae Tulliae : ea enim ipsa hora acceperam
tuas litteras. Egeram etiam cum tuo Nicia, quod is
utitur, ut scis, familiariter Crasso. Ut redii autem prius
quam tuas legi has proximas litteras, quaesivi, de mea
Tullia quid egisset. Per Liciniam se egisse dicebat (sed
opinor Crassum uti non ita multum sorore), eam porro
negare se audere cum vir abesset—est enim profectus in

Hispaniam † Dexius †—illo et absente et insciente migrare.
Est mihi gratissimum tanti a te aestimatam consuetu-
dinem vitae victusque nostri, primum, ut eam domum
sumeres, ut non modo prope me, sed plane mecum habi-
tare posses, deinde ut migrare tanto opere festines. Sed
ne vivam, si tibi concedo, ut eius rei tu cupidior sis quan.
ego sum. Itaque omnia experiar. Video enim quid mea
intersit, quid utriusque nostrum. Si quid egero, faciam.
ut scias. Tu et ad omnia rescribes et quando te exspectem facies me, si tibi videtur, certiorem.

XVII. TO M. MARIUS, in his Villa on the Bay of Naples (Fam. vii. 1)

ROME, A.U.C. 699; B.C. 55; AET. CIC. 51

M. Cicero probat, quod M. Marius ludos a Pompeio II cos.
editos spectatum non venerit. Se quoque interea Caninii causam
egisse narrat et optare se ait, ut, omissis rebus forensibus, libere
possit in villis et cum Mario vivere.

M. CICERO S. D. M. MARIO

1. Si te dolor aliqui corporis aut infirmitas valetudinis
tuae tenuit quo minus ad ludos venires, fortunae magis
tribuo quam sapientiae tuae: sin haec, quae ceteri
mirantur, contemnenda duxisti et, cum per valetudinem
posses, venire tamen noluisti, utrumque laetor, et sine
dolore corporis te fuisse et animo valuisse, cum ea, quae
sine causa mirantur alii, neglexeris; modo ut tibi constiterit fructus otii tui, quo quidem tibi perfrui mirifice
licuit, cum esses in ista amoenitate paene solus relictus.

Neque tamen dubito quin tu ex illo cubiculo tuo, ex quo
tibi † Stabianum † perforasti et patefecisti Misenum, per
eos dies matutina tempora lectiunculis consumpseris, cum
illi interea, qui te istic reliquerunt, spectarent comminus
mimos semisomni. Reliquas vero partes diei tu con-
sumebas iis delectationibus, quas tibi ipse ad arbitrium
tuum compararas, nobis autem erant ea perpetienda,
quae Sp. Maccius probavisset. 2. Omnino, si quaeris,
ludi apparatissimi, sed non tui stomachi: coniecturam
enim facio de meo. Nam primum honoris causa in
scaenam redierant ii, quos ego honoris causa de scaena
decesse arbitrabar. Deliciae vero tuae, noster Aesopus,
eius modi fuit, ut ei desinere per omnes homines liceret.
Is iurare cum coepisset, vox eum defecit in illo loco: *Si
sciens fallo.* Quid tibi ego alia narrem? nosti enim
reliquos ludos: qui ne id quidem leporis habuerunt, quod
solent mediocres ludi: apparatus enim spectatio tollebat
omnem hilaritatem, quo quidem apparatu non dubito quin
animo aequissimo carueris. Quid enim delectationis habent
sescenti muli in Clytaemnestra aut in Equo Troiano
creterrarum tria milia aut armatura varia peditatus et
equitatus in aliqua pugna? quae popularem admirationem
habuerunt, delectationem tibi nullam attulissent. 3.
Quod si tu per eos dies operam dedisti Protogeni tuo,
dum modo is tibi quidvis potius quam orationes meas
legerit, ne tu haud paullo plus quam quisquam nostrum
delectationis habuisti. Non enim te puto Graecos aut
Oscos ludos desiderasse, praesertim cum Oscos ludos vel
in senatu vestro spectare possis, Graecos ita non ames,
ut ne ad villam quidem tuam via Graeca ire soleas.

Nam quid ego te athletas putem desiderare, qui gladiatores contempseris? in quibus ipse Pompeius confitetu·
se et operam et oleum perdidisse. Reliquae sunt venationes binae per dies quinque, magnificae—nemo negat.
—sed quae potest homini esse polito delectatio, cum
aut homo imbecillus a valentissima bestia laniatur aut
praeclara bestia venabulo transverberatur? Quae tamen,
si videnda sunt, saepe vidisti, neque nos, qui haec spectavi-
mus, quidquam novi vidimus. Extremus elephantorum
dies fuit, in quo admiratio magna vulgi atque turbae,
delectatio nulla exstitit. Quin etiam misericordia quaedam consecuta est atque opinio eius modi, esse quamdam
illi beluae cum genere humano societatem. 4. His ego
tamen diebus, ludis scaenicis, ne forte videar tibi non
modo beatus, sed liber omnino fuisse, dirupi me paene in
iudicio Galli Caninii, familiaris tui. Quod si tam
facilem populum haberem, quam Aesopus habuit, libenter
mehercule artem desinerem tecumque et cum similibus
nostri viverem. Nam me cum antea taedebat, cum et
aetas et ambitio me hortabatur et licebat denique quem
nolebam non defendere, tum vero hoc tempore vita nulla
est. Neque enim fructum ullum laboris exspecto et
cogor non numquam homines non optime de me meritos
rogatu eorum, qui bene meriti sunt, defendere. 5. Itaque
quaero causas omnes aliquando vivendi arbitratu meo,
teque et istam rationem otii tui et laudo vehementer et
probo, quodque nos minus intervisis, hoc fero animo
aequiore, quod, si Romae esses, tamen neque nos lepore
tuo neque te—si qui est in me—meo frui liceret propter
molestissimas occupationes meas: quibus si me relaxaro

—nam ut plane exsolvam non postulo—te ipsum, qui multos annos nihil aliud commentaris, docebo profecto quid sit humaniter vivere. Tu modo istam imbecillitatem valetudinis tuae sustenta et tuere, ut facis, ut nostras villas obire et mecum simul lecticula concursare possis. 6. Haec ad te pluribus verbis scripsi quam soleo non otii abundantia, sed amoris erga te, quod me quadam epistola subinvitaras, si memoria tenes, ut ad te aliquid eius modi scriberem, quo minus te praetermisisse ludos paeniteret. Quod si adsecutus sum, gaudeo : sin minus, hoc me tamen consolor, quod posthac ad ludos venies nosque vises neque in epistolis relinques meis spem aliquam delectationis tuae.

XVIII. TO QUINTUS, IN SOME SUBURBAN DWELLING
(Q. FR. II. 9 [11])

ROME, A.U.C. 700 ; B.C. 54 ; AET. CIC. 52

M. Cicero Q. fratri scribit, cum nihil quod scribat habeat, de libertate Tenediis negata, de laudibus Q. fratris et de Lucretii ac Salustii poëmatis.

1. Epistolam hanc convitio efflagitarunt codicilli tui. Nam res quidem ipsa et is dies, quo tu es profectus, nihil mihi ad scribendum argumenti sane dabat. Sed quem ad modum, coram cum sumus, sermo nobis deesse non solet, sic epistolae nostrae debent interdum alucinari. 2. Tenediorum igitur libertas securi Tenedia praecisa est, cum eos praeter me et Bibulum et Calidium et Favonium nemo defenderet. 3. De te a Magnetibus ab Sipylo mentio est

honorifica facta, cum te unum dicerent postulationi L.
Sestii Pansae restitisse.   Reliquis diebus si quid erit quod
te scire opus sit, aut etiam si nihil erit, tamen scribam
cotidie aliquid.   Pridie Id. neque tibi neque Pomponio
deero.   4. Lucretii poëmata ut scribis ita sunt, multis
luminibus ingenii, multae tamen artis.   Sed cum
veneris. Virum te putabo, si Sallustii Empedoclea legeris,
hominem non putabo.

XIX. TO QUINTUS, in the Country
(Q. Fr. ii. 10 [12])

ROME, A.U.C. 700 ; B.C. 54 ; AET. CIC. 52

M. Cicero Q. fratri de Commageni regis causa a se acta et de
litteris a Caesare ad se missis refert.

1. Gaudeo tibi iucundas esse meas litteras, nec tamen
habuissem scribendi nunc quidem ullum argumentum,
nisi tuas accepissem.   Nam pridie Id. cum Appius
senatum infrequentem coëgisset, tantum fuit frigus, ut
pipulo, convicio coactus sit nos dimittere.   2. De Commageno, quod rem totam discusseram, mirifice mihi et
per se et per Pomponium blanditur Appius.   Videt
enim, hoc genere dicendi si utar in ceteris, Februarium
sterilem futurum.   Eumque lusi iocose satis, neque solum
illud extorsi oppidulum eius † quod erat positum in
Euphrati Zeugmate, † praeterea togam sum eius praetextam, quam erat adeptus Caesare consule, magno hominum risu cavillatus.   3. 'Quod vult,' inquam, 'renovari

honores eosdem, quo minus togam praetextam quotannis interpolet, decernendum nihil censeo. Vos autem homines nobiles, qui Bostrenum praetextatum non ferebatis, Commagenum feretis?' Genus vides et locum iocandi. Multa dixi in ignobilem regem, quibus totus est explosus. Quo genere commotus, ut dixi, Appius totum me amplexatur. Nihil est enim facilius quam reliqua discutere. Sed non faciam ut illum offendam, ne imploret fidem Iovis Hospitalis, Graios omnes convocet, per quos mecum in gratiam redit. 4. Theopompo satis faciemus. De Caesare fugerat me ad te scribere. Video enim quas tu litteras exspectaris. Sed ille scripsit ad Balbum, fasciculum illum epistolarum, in quo fuerat mea et Balbi, totum sibi aqua madidum redditum esse, ut ne illud quidem sciat, meam fuisse aliquam epistolam. Sed ex Balbi epistola pauca verba intellexerat, ad quae rescripsit his verbis: 'De Cicerone te video quiddam scripsisse, quod ego non intellexi: quantum autem coniectura consequebar, id erat eius modi, ut magis optandum quam sperandum putarem.' 5. Itaque postea misi ad Caesarem eodem illo exemplo litteras. Locum autem illius de sua egestate ne sis aspernatus. Ad quem ego rescripsi nihil esse quod posthac arcae nostrae fiducia conturbaret, lusique in eo genere et familiariter et cum dignitate. Amor autem eius erga nos perfertur omnium nuntiis singularis. Litterae quidem ad id, quod exspectas, fere cum tuo reditu iungentur, reliqua singulorum dierum scribemus ad te, si modo tabellarios tu praebebis. Quamquam eius modi frigus impendebat, ut summum periculum esset ne Appio suae aedes urerentur.

XX. TO QUINTUS, on his way to Caesar's Camp in Britain (Q. Fr. ii. 13 [15*a*])

ROME, A.U.C. 700 ; B.C. 54 ; AET. CIC. 52

M. Cicero Caesaris in se amorem et liberalitatem laudat atque eius se studiosissimum profitetur : de eiusdem favore in Trebatium et Curtium : de rei publicae statu.

1. A. d. iiii. Non. Iun., quo die Romam veni, accepi tuas litteras, datas Placentia : deinde alteras postridie, datas Blandenone cum Caesaris litteris, refertis omni officio, diligentia, suavitate. Sunt ista quidem magna vel potius maxima. Habent enim vim magnam ad gloriam et ad summam dignitatem. Sed mihi crede, quem nosti, quod in istis rebus ego plurimi aestimo, id iam habeo : te scilicet primum tam inservientem communi dignitati ; deinde Caesaris tantum in me amorem, quem omnibus iis honoribus, quos me a se exspectare vult, antepono. Litterae vero eius una datae cum tuis, quarum initium est, quam suavis ei tuus adventus fuerit et recordatio veteris amoris, deinde se effecturum ut ego in medio dolore ac desiderio tui te, cum a me abesses, potissimum secum esse laetarer, incredibiliter delectarunt. 2. Qua re facis tu quidem fraterne, quod me hortaris, sed mehercule currentem nunc quidem, ut omnia mea studia in istum unum conferam. Ego vero ardenti quidem studio, ac fortasse efficiam, quod saepe viatoribus, cum properant, evenit, ut, si serius quam voluerint forte surrexerint, properando etiam citius, quam si de nocte vigilassent, perveniant quo velint : sic ego, quoniam˙in isto

homine colendo tam indormivi diu, te mehercule saepe excitante, cursu corrigam tarditatem cum equis tum vero, quoniam tu scribis poëma ab eo nostrum probari, quadrigis poëticis. Modo mihi date Britanniam, quam pingam coloribus tuis, penicillo meo. Sed quid ago? quod mihi tempus, Romae praesertim, ut iste me rogat, manenti, vacuum ostenditur? Sed videro. Fortasse enim, ut fit, vincet tuus amor omnes difficultates. 3. Trebatium quod ad se miserim, persalse et humaniter etiam gratias mihi agit. Negat enim in tanta multitudine eorum, qui una essent, quemquam fuisse qui vadimonium concipere posset. M. Curtio tribunatum ab eo petivi—nam Domitius se derideri putasset, si esset a me rogatus: hoc enim est eius cotidianum, se ne tribunum militum quidem facere: etiam in senatu lusit Appium collegam, propterea isse ad Caesarem, ut aliquem tribunatum auferret—sed in alterum annum. Id et Curtius ita volebat. 4. Tu, quem ad modum me censes oportere esse et in re publica et in nostris inimicitiis, ita et esse et fore oricula infima scito molliorem. 5. Res Romanae se sic habebant: erat non nulla spes comitiorum, sed incerta: erat aliqua suspicio dictaturae, ne ea quidem certa: summum otium forense, sed senescentis magis civitatis quam acquiescentis. Sententia autem nostra in senatu eius modi, magis ut alii nobis adsentiantur quam nosmet ipsi.

Τοιαῦθ' ὁ τλήμων πόλεμος ἐξεργάζεται.

XXI. TO QUINTUS, in Britain (Q. Fr. iii. 7)

TUSCULANUM, A.U.C. 700 ; B.C. 54 ; AET. CIC. 52

M. Cicero Q. fratri Romae ingentem adluviem fuisse scribit.

1. Romae et maxime . . . et Appia ad Martis mira
alluvies ; Crassipedis ambulatio ablata, horti, tabernae
plurimae, magna vis aquae usque ad piscinam publicam
Viget illud Homeri :

Ἦμἀτ' ὀπωρινῷ, ὅτε λαβρότατον χέει ὕδωρ
Ζεύς, ὅτε δή ῥ' ἄνδρεσσι κοτεσσάμενος χαλεπήνῃ.

Cadit enim in absolutionem Gabinii :

Οἳ βίῃ εἰν ἀγορῇ σκολιὰς κρίνωσι θέμιστας,
Ἐκ δὲ δίκην ἐλάσωσι, θεῶν ὄπιν οὐκ ἀλέγοντες.

Sed haec non curare decrevi. 2. Romam cum venero,
quae perspexero, scribam ad te et maxime de dictatura,
et ad Labienum et ad Ligurium litteras dabo. Hanc
scripsi ante lucem ad lychnuchum ligneolum, qui mihi
erat periucundus, quod cum te aiebant, cum esses Sami,
curasse faciendum. Vale, mi suavissime et optime frater.

XXII. TO TREBATIUS, in the Camp of Caesar in Britain (Fam. vii. 16)

ROME, A.U.C. 700 ; B.C. 54 ; AET. CIC. 52

Facete M. Cicero laudat C. Trebatii sapientiam in vitando belli
discrimine, ut timiditatis eum arguat.

1. In Equo Troiano scis esse : *in extremo sero sapiunt.*

Tu tamen, mi vetule, non sero.   Primas illas

rabiosulas sat fatuas

dedisti : deinde . . . Quod in Britannia non nimis φιλοθέωρον te praebuisti, plane non reprehendo : nunc vero in
hibernis <u>intectus</u> mihi videris : itaque te commovere non
curas.

Usque quaque sapere oportet : id erit telum acerrimum.

2. Ego si foris cenitarem, Cn. Octavio familiari tuo non
defuissem : cui tamen dixi, cum me aliquoties invitaret :

Oro te, quis tu es ?

Sed mehercules, extra iocum, homo bellus est : vellem
cum tecum abduxisses.   3. Quid agatis et ecquid in
Italiam venturi sitis hac hieme fac plane sciam.   Balbus
mihi confirmavit te divitem futurum.   Id utrum
Romano more locutus est, bene nummatum te futurum ;
an, quo modo Stoici dicunt 'omnes esse divites, qui
caelo et terra frui possint,' postea videbo.   Qui istinc
veniunt superbiam tuam accusant, quod negent te percontantibus respondere.   Sed tamen est quod gaudeas.
Constat enim inter omnes neminem te uno Samarobrivae
iuris peritiorem esse.

XXIII. TO TREBATIUS, in Britain (Fam. vii. 11)

ROME, A.U.C. 701 ; B.C. 53 ; AET. CIC. 53

M. Cicero iocatur cum C. Trebatio de interregnis, suadet, ut, si e re sua sit, maneat in provincia : sin minus, se in urbem recipiat.

1. Nisi ante Roma profectus esses, nunc eam certe relinqueres. Quis enim tot interregnis iure consultum desiderat? Ego omnibus, unde petitur, hoc consilii dederim, ut a singulis interregibus binas advocationes postulent. Satisne tibi videor abs te ius civile didicisse? 2. Sed heus tu, quid agis? ecquid fit? Video enim te iam iocari per litteras. Haec signa meliora sunt quam in meo Tusculano. Sed quid sit scire cupio. Consuli quidem te a Caesare scribis, sed ego tibi ab illo consuli mallem. Quod si aut fit aut futurum putas, perfer istam militiam et permane : ego enim desiderium tui spe tuorum commodorum consolabor : sin autem ista sunt in- aniora, recipe te ad nos. Nam aut erit hic aliquid aliquando aut, si minus, una mehercule collocutio nostra pluris erit quam omnes Samarobrivae. Denique, si cito te rettuleris, sermo nullus erit : si diutius frustra afueris, non modo Laberium, sed etiam sodalem nostrum Valerium pertimesco. Mira enim persona induci potest Britannici iure consulti. 3. Haec ego non rideo, quamvis tu rideas, sed de re severissima tecum, ut soleo, iocor. Remoto ioco tibi hoc amicissimo animo praecipio, ut, si istic mea commendatione tuam dignitatem obtinebis, perferas nostri desiderium, honestatem et facultates tuas augeas : sin autem ista frigebunt, recipias te ad nos. Omnia

tamen quae vis et tua virtute profecto et nostro summo erga te studio consequere.

XXIV. TO TREBATIUS, in Gaul (Fam. vii. 12)

ROME, A.U.C. 701 ; B.C. 53 ; AET. CIC. 53

Per iocum exagitat M. Cicero Epicureos ipsumque adeo Trebatium, quem Epicureum esse factum narraverat Pansa.

1. Mirabar quid esset quod tu mihi litteras mittere intermisisses. Indicavit mihi Pansa meus Epicureum te esse factum. O castra praeclara! Quid tu fecisses, si te Tarentum et non Samarobrivam misissem? Iam tum mihi non placebas, cum idem tu tuebare quod Selius familiaris meus. 2. Sed quonam modo ius civile defendes, cum omnia tua causa facias, non civium? Ubi porro illa erit formula fiduciae, UT INTER BONOS BENE AGIER OPORTET? Quis enim bonus est, qui facit nihil nisi sua causa? Quod ius statues COMMUNI DIVIDUNDO, cum commune nihil possit esse apud eos, qui omnia voluptate sua metiuntur? Quo modo autem tibi placebit IOVEM LAPIDEM iurare, cum scias Iovem iratum esse nemini posse? Quid fiet porro populo Ulubrano, si tu statueris πολιτεύεσθαι non oportere? Qua re si plane a nobis deficis moleste fero : sin Pansae adsentari commodum est, ignosco. Modo scribe aliquando ad nos quid agas et a nobis quid fieri aut curari velis.

M. Cicero C. Trebatio causam exponit intermissionis epistolarum sibique gratum esse significat iocis interpositis, quod amicus iam libentius in provincia versetur.

1. Adeone me iniustum esse existimasti, ut tibi irascerer, quod parum mihi constans et nimium cupidus decedendi viderere, ob eamque causam me arbitrare litteras ad te iam diu non misisse? Mihi perturbatio animi tui, quam primis litteris perspiciebam, molestiam attulit. Neque alia ulla fuit causa intermissionis epistolarum, nisi quod ubi esses plane nesciebam. Hic tu me etiam insimulas nec satisfactionem meam accipis? Audi, Testa mi: utrum superbiorem te pecunia facit an quod te imperator consulit? Moriar, ni, quae tua gloria est, puto te malle a Caesare consuli quam inaurari. Si vero utrumque est, quis te feret praeter me, qui omnia ferre possum? 2. Sed, ut ad rem redeam, te istic invitum non esse vehementer gaudeo, et, ut illud erat molestum, sic hoc est iucundum. Tantum metuo, ne artificium tuum tibi parum prosit: nam, ut audio, istic

> non ex iure manum consertum, sed magi' ferro
> rem repetunt,

et tu soles ad vim faciundam adhiberi: neque est quod illam exceptionem in interdicto pertimescas; QUO TU PRIOR VI HOMINIBUS ARMATIS NON VENERIS: scio enim te non esse procacem in lacessendo. Sed, ut ego quoque

te aliquid admoneam de vestris cautionibus, Treviros vites
censeo : audio capitales esse : mallem auro, argento, aere
essent. Sed alias iocabimur. Tu ad me de istis rebus
omnibus scribas velim quam diligentissime. D. IV. Non.
Mart.

XXVI. TO ATTICUS, in Rome (Att. v. 1)

MINTURNAE, A.U.C. 703 ; B.C. 51 ; AET. CIC. 55

Cum M. Ciceroni a.u.c. 703 Cilicia provincia suscipienda esset,
iam Attico ex hoc ipso itinere hanc et, quae deinceps sequuntur.
epistolas mittit. Et in hac quidem prima agit de Annio Saturnino,
de satisdationibus praediorum, de negotio cum Oppio transigendo,
de uxore Q. fratris, sorore Attici eiusque inhumanitate in Q.
fratrem, de mandatis suis, de A. Torquato, quem Minturnis
amantissime dimiserit.

1. Ego vero et tuum in discessu vidi animum et mei
in eo sum ipse testis. Quo magis erit tibi videndum ne
quid novi decernatur, ut hoc nostrum desiderium ne plus
sit annuum. 2. De Annio Saturnino curasti probe. De
satis dando vero te rogo, quoad eris Romae, tu ut satis
des. Et sunt aliquot satisdationes secundum mancipium,
veluti Menuianorum praediorum vel Atilianorum. De
Oppio factum est ut volui, et maxime, quod⟨de⟩DCCC.
aperuisti : quae quidem ego utique vel versura facta *berre*
solvi volo, ne extrema exactio nostrorum nominum *money*
exspectetur. 3. Nunc venio ad transversum illum *a debt*
extremae epistolae tuae versiculum, in quo me admones
de sorore. Quae res se sic habet. Ut veni in Arpinas,
cum ad me frater venisset, in primis nobis sermo isque

multus de te fuit : ex quo ego veni ad ea, quae fueramus
ego et tu inter nos de sorore in Tusculano locuti.   Nihil
tam vidi mite, nihil tam placatum, quam tum meus
frater erat in sororem tuam, ut etiam, si qua fuerat ex
ratione sumptus offensio, non appareret.   Illo sic die.
Postridie ex Arpinati profecti sumus.   Ut in Arcano
Quintus maneret dies fecit, ego Aquini, sed prandimus
in Arcano.   Nosti hunc fundum.   Quo ut venimus,
humanissime Quintus : 'Pomponia,' inquit, 'tu invita
mulieres, ego viros ascivero.'   Nihil potuit, mihi quidem
ut visum est, dulcius, idque cum verbis tum etiam animo
ac voltu.   At illa audientibus nobis : 'Ego sum,' inquit,
'hic hospita.'   Id autem ex eo, ut opinor, quod ante-
cesserat Statius, ut prandium nobis videret.   Tum
Quintus : 'En,' inquit mihi, 'haec ego patior cotidie.'
4. Dices : 'Quid, quaeso, istuc erat?' Magnum : itaque me
ipsum commoverat : sic absurde et aspere verbis vultuque
responderat.   Dissimulavi dolens.   Discubuimus omnes
praeter illam, cui tamen Quintus de mensa misit ; illa
reiecit.   Quid multa ? nihil meo fratre lenius, nihil asperius
tua sorore mihi visum est, et multa praetereo, quae tum
mihi maiori stomacho quam ipsi Quinto fuerunt.   Ego
inde Aquinum, Quintus in Arcano remansit et Aquinum ad
me postridie mane venit mihique narravit cum discessura
esset, fuisse eius modi, qualem ego vidissem.   Quid quaeris ?
Vel ipsi hoc dicas licet, humanitatem ei meo iudicio illo
die defuisse.   Haec ad te scripsi fortasse pluribus, quam
necesse fuit, ut videres tuas quoque esse partes instituendi
et monendi.   5. Reliquum est, ut ante quam proficiscare
mandata nostra exhaurias, scribas ad me omnia, Pompti-

num extrudas, cum profectus eris, cures ut sciam, sic
habeas, nihil mehercule te mihi nec carius esse nec suavius.
A. Torquatum amantissime dimisi Minturnis, optimum
virum : cui me ad te scripsisse aliquid in sermone
significes velim.

XXVII. FROM CAELIUS TO CICERO, on his Journey to his Province (Fam. viii. 1)

ROME, A.U.C. 703 ; B.C. 51 ; AET. CIC. 55

M. Caelius mittit ad M. Ciceronem Ciliciae procos. commentarium
rerum urbanarum et se excusat, quod eum non ipse confecerit.
Addit de comitiis Transpadanorum, de successione Galliarum, de
Cn. Pompeio, de C. Caesare et Domitio, de M. Cicerone et Q.
Pompeio, de Planco, de Ciceronis libris politicis.

1. Quod tibi decedenti pollicitus sum, me omnes res
urbanas diligentissime tibi perscripturum, data opera
paravi qui sic omnia persequeretur, ut verear ne tibi
nimium arguta haec sedulitas videatur. Tametsi tu scio
quam sis curiosus et quam omnibus peregrinantibus
gratum sit minimarum quoque rerum, quae domi gerantur,
fieri certiores, tamen in hoc te deprecor, ne meum hoc
officium adrogantiae condemnes, quod hunc laborem alteri
delegavi, non quin mihi suavissimum sit et occupato et
ad litteras scribendas, ut tu nosti, pigerrimo tuae memoriae
dare operam, sed ipsum volumen, quod tibi misi, facile,
ut ego arbitror, me excusat. Nescio quoius otii esset non
modo perscribere haec, sed omnino animadvertere : omnia
enim sunt ibi senatus consulta, edicta, fabulae, rumores :

quod exemplum si forte minus te delectarit, ne molestia:n
tibi cum impensa mea exhibeam, fac me certiorem. .2.
Si quid in re publica maius actum erit, quod isti operarii
minus commode persequi possint, et quem ad modum
actum sit et quae existimatio secuta quaeque de eo spes
sit diligenter tibi perscribemus. Ut nunc est, nulla
magno opere exspectatio est. Nam et illi rumores de
comitiis Transpadanorum Cumarum tenus caluerunt :
Romam cum venissem, ne tenuissimam quidem aud -
tionem de ea re accepi. Praeterea Marcellus, quod adhu:
nihil rettulit de successione provinciarum Galliarum et i ı
Kalendas Iunias, ut mihi ipse dixit, eam distulit rela-
tionem, sanc-quam eos sermones <u>expressit</u>, qui de eo tum
fuerunt, cum Romae nos essemus. 3. Tu si Pompeium,
ut volebas, offendisti, qui tibi visus sit et quam orationem habuerit tecum quamque ostenderit voluntatem—
solet enim aliud sentire et loqui neque tantum valer⸗
ingenio ut non appareat quid cupiat—fac mihi perscribas.
4. Quod ad Caesarem, crebri et non <u>belli</u> de eo rumores,
sed susurratores dumtaxat veniunt : alius equitem per -
didisse, quod, opinor, certe fictum est : alius septiman
legionem vapulasse, ipsum apud Bellovacos circumseder
interclusum ab reliquo exercitu : neque adhuc certi quid
quam est neque haec incerta tamen vulgo iactantur, sec
inter paucos, quos tu nosti, palam secreto narrantur : al
Domitius, <u>cum manus ad os apposuit</u>. 5. Te a. d. ix.
Kal. Iunias subrostrani—quod illorum capiti sit !—dissi-
parant perisse : urbe ac foro toto maximus rumor fuit tc
a Q. Pompeio in itinere occisum. Ego, qui scirem Q.
Pompeium Baulis iam πεινητικὴν facere, et usque eo, ut

ego miserer eius, esurire, non sum commotus, et hoc
mendacio, si qua pericula tibi impenderent, ut defun-
geremur optavi. Plancus quidem tuus Ravennae est et
magno congiario donatus a Caesare nec beatus nec bene
instructus est. Tui πολιτικοὶ libri omnibus vigent.

XXVIII. TO ATTICUS, in Rome (Att. v. 9)

ON THE JOURNEY TO HIS PROVINCE, NEAR ATHENS, A.U.C. 703; B.C. 51; AET. CIC. 55

M. Cicero Attico gratias agit de muneribus sibi Actium missis
et exponit de ratione itineris sui, de provincia abstinenter admini-
stranda, Attici litteras de negotiis suis Romanis exspectat et cum
rogat, ut omnia faciat ne sibi provincia plus quam annua sit, addit
de Cicerone suo, de Dionysio.

1. Actium venimus a. d. XVII. Kal. Quinct., cum quidem et Corcyrae et Sybotis muneribus tuis, quae et Areus
et meus amicus Eutychides opipare et φιλοπροσηνέστατα
nobis congesserant, epulati essemus Saliarem in modum.
Actio maluimus iter facere pedibus, qui incommodissime
navigassemus, et Leucatem flectere molestum videbatur.
Actuariis autem minutis Patras accedere sine his impedi-
mentis non satis visum est decorum. Ego, ut saepe tu
me currentem hortatus es, cotidie meditor, praecipio
meis, faciam denique, ut summa modestia et summa
abstinentia munus hoc extraordinarium traducamus.
Parthus velim quiescat et fortuna nos iuvet: nostra
praestabimus. 2. Tu, quaeso, quid agas, ubi quoque
tempore futurus sis, quales res nostras Romae reliqueris,

E

maxime de xx. et DCCC., cura ut sciamus. Id unis
diligenter litteris datis, quae ad me utique perferantur,
consequere. Illud tamen—quoniam nunc abes, cum il
non agitur, aderis autem ad tempus, ut mihi rescripsti—
memento curare per te et per omnes nostros, in primis
per Hortensium, ut annus noster maneat suo statu, ne
quid novi decernatur. Hoc tibi ita mando, ut dubiterı
an etiam te rogem, ut pugnes ne intercaletur. Sed non
audeo tibi omnia onera imponere. Annum quidem
utique teneto. 3. Cicero meus, modestissimus et suavis-
simus puer, tibi salutem dicit. Dionysium sempe·
equidem, ut scis, dilexi : sed cotidie pluris facio, e ;
mehercule in primis, quod te amat nec tui mentionen
intermitti sinit.

XXIX. TO ATTICUS, in Rome (Att. v. 12)

OFF DELOS, A.U.C. 703 ; B.C. 51 ; AET. CIC. 55

M. Cicero Attico exponit de molestiis cursus maritimi Atheniε
Delum confecti, de Messalla de ambitu reo, de exspectatis Attic:
litteris, de rebus urbanis, de negotiis suis Romanis.

1. Negotium magnum est navigare atque id mense
Quinctili. Sexto die Delum Athenis venimus. Pridie
Nonas Quinctil. a Piraeeo ad Zostera, vento molesto, qui
nos ibidem Nonis tenuit. A. d. VIII. Idus ad Ceo
iucunde. Inde Gyarum saevo vento, non adverso : hinc
Syrum, inde Delum, utroque citius quam vellemus cursum
confecimus. Iam nosti aphracta Rhodiorum : nihil quod
minus fluctum ferre possit. Itaque erat in animo nihil

festinare nec me Delo movere, nisi omnia ἄκρα Γυρέων ⸱⸱. Β
pura vidissem. 2. De Messalla a te statim ut audivi de
Gyaro dedi litteras, et—id ipsum consilium nostrum—
etiam ad Hortensium, cui quidem valde συνηγωνίων.
Sed tuas de eius iudicii sermonibus et mehercule omni
de rei publicae statu litteras exspecto, πολιτικώτερον
quidem scriptas, quoniam meos cum Thallumeto nostro
pervolutas libros, eius modi, inquam, litteras ex quibus
ego non quid fiat—nam id vel Helonius, vir gravissimus,
potest efficere, cliens tuus—sed quid futurum sit sciam.
Cum haec leges, habemus consules. Omnia perspicere
poteris de Caesare, de Pompeio, de ipsis iudiciis. 3.
Nostra autem negotia, quoniam Romae commoraris,
amabo te, explica. Cui rei fugerat me rescribere, de
strue laterum, plane rogo, de aqua, si quid poterit fieri,
eo sis animo, quo soles esse : quam ego cum mea sponte
tum tuis sermonibus aestimo plurimi. Ergo tu id conficies. Praeterea, si quid Philippus rogabit, quod in tua
re faceres, id velim facias. Plura scribam ad te, cum
constitero : nunc eram plane in medio mari.

XXX. TO ATTICUS, in Rome (Att. v. 15)

LAODICEA, A.U.C. 703; B.C. 51; AET. CIC. 55

M. Cicero Attico scribit se Laodiceam pervenisse, abstinenter
vivere, iter suscepisse Laodicea in Lycaoniam, sed sibi negotium
provinciae molestum esse, itaque instat amico ut operam det ne
sibi provincia prorogetur, ab eoque petit ut sibi de rebus urbanis
scribat.

1. Laodiceam veni pridie Kal. Sext. Ex hoc die

clavum anni movebis. Nihil exoptatius adventu meo, nihil carius. Sed est incredibile quam me negctii taedeat. Non habeat satis magnum campum ille t bi non ignotus cursus animi, et industriae meae praeclara opera cesset? Quippe. Ius Laodiccae me dicere, cum Romae A. Plotius dicat? et cum exercitum noster amicus habeat tantum, me nomen habere duarum legionum exilium? Denique haec non desidero: lucem, forum, urbem, domum, vos desidero. Sed feram, it potero, sit modo annuum. Si prorogatur, actum est. Verum perfacile resisti potest, tu modo Romae sis. 2. Quaeris quid hic agam? Ita vivam ut maximos sumptus facio. Mirifice delector hoc instituto. Admirabilis abstinentia ex praeceptis tuis, ut verear ne illud, qued tecum permutavi, versura mihi solvendum sit. Ap[ii vulnera non refrico, sed apparent nec occuli possunt. 3. Iter Laodicea faciebam a. d. III. Non. Sext., cum has litteras dabam, in castra in Lycaoniam: inde ad Taurum cogitabam, ut cum Moeragene signis collatis, si possem, de servo tuo decernerem.

Clitellae bovi impositae sunt, plane non est nostrum onus: sed feremus, modo, si me amas, sim annuus. Adsis tu ad tempus, ut senatum totum excites. Mirifice sollicitus sum, quod iam diu ignota sunt mihi ista omnia. Qua re, ut ad te ante scripsi, cum cetera tum res publica cura ut mihi nota sit. Epistolam sciebam tarde tibi redditur i iri, sed dabam familiari homini ac domestico, C. Andronico Puteolano. Tu autem saepe dare tabellarii s publicanorum poteris per magistros scripturae et portu i nostrarum dioecesium.

XXXI. CAELIUS TO CICERO, in his Province (Fam. viii. 5)

ROME, A.U.C. 703; B.C. 51; AET. CIC. 55

M. Caelius metuere se M. Ciceroni significat ex Parthici belli fama ob paucitatem copiarum eius. Addit de successione provinciarum eiusque tarditate.

1. Qua tu cura sis, quod ad pacem provinciae tuae finitimarumque regionum attinet, nescio: ego quidem vehementer animi pendeo. Nam si hoc more moderari possemus, ut pro viribus copiarum tuarum belli quoque exsisteret magnitudo, et, quantum gloriae triumphoque opus esset, adsequeremur, periculosam et gravem illam dimicationem evitaremus, nihil tam esset optandum. Nunc si Parthus movet aliquid, scio non mediocrem fore contentionem. Tuus porro exercitus vix unum saltum tueri potest. Hanc autem nemo ducit rationem, sed omnia desiderantur ab eo—tamquam nihil denegatum sit ei, quo minus quam paratissimus esset,—qui publico negotio praepositus est. 2. Accedit huc, quod successionem futuram propter Galliarum controversiam non video. Tametsi hac de re puto te constitutum quid facturus esses habere, tamen, quo maturius constitueres, cum hunc eventum providebam, visum est ut te facerem certiorem. Nosti enim haec tralaticia: de Galliis constituetur; erit qui intercedat; deinde alius exsistet qui, nisi libere liceat de omnibus provinciis decernere senatui, reliquas impediat. Sic multum ac diu ludetur atque ita diu, ut plus biennium in his tricis moretur. 3. Si quid

novi de re publica quod tibi scriberem haberem, usus
essem mea consuetudine, ut diligenter et quid actum esset
et quid ex eo futurum sperarem perscriberem. Sane
tamquam in quodam _incili_ iam omnia adhaeseru it.
Marcellus idem illud de provinciis urget, neque adhuc
frequentem senatum efficere potuit. Hoc si praeterito
anno Curio tribunus et eadem actio de provinciis intio-
ibit, quam facile tunc sit omnia impedire et quam hoc
Caesar iique, qui _in_ sua causa rem publicam non curci t,
sperent non te fallit.

XXXII. TO ATTICUS, on the way to Epirus (Att. v. 20)

CILICIA, A.U.C. 703 ; B.C. 51 ; AET. CIC. 55

M. Cicero Attico res a se in Cilicia gestas et maxime Pinden-
issi oppidi Eleutherocilicum munitissimi expugnationem exponit.
Addit de abstinentia sua, de Ariobarzane sua opera regnum
obtinente, de Bruto a se excitato, de litteris Romam publice de h s
rebus gestis mittendis, de metu ne sibi provincia prorogetur, de
rebus urbanis, de quibus omnibus per Philogenem libertum Atti i
certiorem se factum scribit, dein de rebus familiaribus ac domesticis. Scripta epistola est in castris ad Pindenissum tertio die
Saturnaliorum.

1. Saturnalibus mane se mihi Pindenissitae dediderunt,
septimo et quinquagesimo die, postquam oppugnare eos
coepimus. Qui, malum ! isti Pindenissitae ? qui sunt '
inquies : nomen audivi numquam. Quid ergo faciam '
num potui Ciliciam Aetoliam aut Macedoniam reddere'
Hoc iam sic habeto, nec hoc exercitu nec hic tanta
negotia geri potuisse. Quae cognosce ἐν ἐπιτομῇ. Sic

enim concedis mihi proximis litteris. Ephesum ut
venerim nosti, qui etiam mihi gratulatus es illius diei
celebritatem, qua nihil me unquam delectavit magis.
Inde in oppidis iis, † que erant † mirabiliter accepti Laodiceam pridie Kal. Sext. venimus. Ibi morati biduum
perillustres fuimus honorificisque verbis omnes iniurias
revellimus superioris quadriennii; quod idem dein Apameae
quinque dies morati et Synnadis triduum, Philomelii quinque dies, Iconii decem fecimus. Nihil ea iuris dictione
aequabilius, nihil lenius, nihil gravius. 2. Inde in castra
veni a. d. VII. Kal. Septembr. A. d. III. exercitum
lustravi apud Iconium. Ex his castris, cum graves
de Parthis nuntii venirent, perrexi in Ciliciam per
Cappadociae partem eam, quae Ciliciam attingit, eo
consilio, ut Armenius Artavasdes et ipsi Parthi Cappadocia
se excludi putarent. Cum dies quinque ad Cybistra
castra habuissem, certior sum factus Parthos ab illo aditu
Cappadociae longe abesse, Ciliciae magis imminere. Itaque
confestim iter in Ciliciam feci per Tauri pylas. 3.
Tarsum veni a. d. III. Non. Octobr. Inde ad Amanum
contendi, qui Syriam a Cilicia in aquarum divortio dividit,
qui mons erat hostium plenus sempiternorum. Hic a. d.
III. Idus Octobr. magnum numerum hostium occidimus.
Castella munitissima nocturno Pomptini adventu, nostro
matutino cepimus, incendimus : imperatores appellati
sumus. Castra paucos dies habuimus ea ipsa, quae contra
Dareum habuerat apud Issum Alexander, imperator haud
paullo melior quam aut tu aut ego. Ibi dies quinque
morati, direpto et vastato Amano, inde discessimus. Scis
enim dici quaedam πανικά, dici item τὰ κενὰ τοῦ πολέμου.

Rumore adventus nostri et Cassio, qui Antiochia teneba-
tur, animus accessit et Parthis timor iniectus est.   Itaque
eos cedentes ab oppido Cassius insecutus rem bene gessit.
Qua in fuga, magna auctoritate Osaces, dux Parthorum,
vulnus accepit eoque interiit paucis post diebus.   Erat
in Syria nostrum nomen in gratia.   4. Venit interim
Bibulus.   Credo, voluit appellatione hac inani nobis esse
par.   In eodem Amano coepit lorcolam in mustacco
quaerere.   At ille cohortem primam totam perdidit cen-
turionemque primi pili, nobilem sui generis, Asinium
Dentonem, et reliquos cohortis eiusdem et Sex. Lucilium,
T. Gavii Caepionis, locupletis et splendidi hominis, filium,
tribunum militum.   Sane plagam odiosam acceperat cum
re tum tempore.   5. Nos ad Pindenissum, quod oppidum
munitissimum Eleutherocilicum omnium memoria in armis
fuit.   Feri homines et acres et omnibus rebus ad
defendendum parati.   Cinximus vallo et fossa, aggere maximo, vineis, turre altissima, magna tormentorum copia,
multis sagittariis : magno labore, apparatu, multis sauciis
nostris, incolumi exercitu, negotium confecimus.   Hilara
sane Saturnalia, militibus quoque, quibus mancipiis
exceptis reliquam praedam concessimus : mancipia veni-
bant Saturnalibus tertiis, cum haec scribebam : in
tribunali res erat ad HS cxx.   Hinc exercitum in hi-
berna agri male pacati deducendum Quinto fratri dabam.
Ipse me Laodiceam recipiebam.   6. Haec adhuc.   Sed
ad praeterita revertamur.   Quod me maxime hortaris
et quod pluris est quam omnia, in quo laboras, ut
etiam Ligurino μώμῳ satis faciamus, moriar, si quidquam
fieri potest elegantius.   Nec iam ego hanc continentiam

appello, quae virtus voluptati resistere videtur. Ego in
vita mea nulla umquam voluptate tanta sum adfectus,
quanta adficior hac integritate. Nec me tam fama, quae
summa est, quam res ipsa delectat. Quid quaeris? Fuit
tanti : me ipse non noram nec satis sciebam quid in hoc
genere facere possem : recte πεφυσίωμαι. Nihil est prae-
clarius. Interim haec λαμπρά. Ariobarzanes opera mea
vivit, regnat. 'Εν παρόδῳ, consilio et auctoritate et quod
insidiatoribus eius ἀπρόσιτον me non modo ἀδωροδό-
κητον praebui, regem regnumque servavi. Interea e
Cappadocia ne pilum quidem.—Brutum abiectum quantum potui excitavi, quem non minus amo quam tu, paene
dixi, quam te.—Atque etiam spero toto anno imperii
nostri teruncium sumptus in provincia nullum fore. 7.
Habes omnia. Nunc publice litteras Romam mittere
parabam. Uberiores erunt, quam si ex Amano misissem.
At te Romae non fore! Sed est totum, quod Kal. Mart.
futurum est. Vereor enim ne, cum de provincia agetur,
si Caesar resistet, nos retineamur. His tu si adesses,
nihil timerem. 8. Redeo ad urbana : quae ego diu
ignorans ex tuis iucundissimis litteris a. d. xv. Kal. Ian.
denique cognovi. Eas diligentissime Philogenes, libertus
tuus, curavit perlonga et non satis tuta via perferendas.
Nam quas Laenii pueris scribis datas, non acceperam.
Iucunda de Caesare et quae senatus decrevit et quae tu
speras : quibus ille si cedit, salvi sumus. Incendio Plac-
toriano quod Seius ambustus est, minus moleste fero.
Lucceius de Q. Cassio cur tam vehemens fuerit et quid
actum sit aveo scire. 9. Ego, cum Laodiceam venero,
Quinto, sororis tuae filio, togam puram iubeor dare, cui

moderabor diligentius.   Deiotarus, cuius auxiliis magi is
usus sum, ad me, ut scripsit, cum Ciceronibus Laodiceam
venturus erat.   Tuas etiam Epiroticas exspecto litters s,
ut habeam rationem non modo negotii, verum etiam ot ii
tui.   Nicanor in officio est et a me liberaliter tractatu :
quem, ut puto, Romam cum litteris publicis mittam, ut
et diligentius perferantur et idem ad me certa de te et a
te referat.   Alexis quod mihi totiens salutem ascribit,
est gratum.   Sed cur non suis litteris idem facit, quod
meus ad te Alexis facit?   Phemio quaeritur κέρας.   Sed
haec hactenus.   Cura ut valeas et ut sciam quando cogites
Romam.   Etiam atque etiam vale.   10. Tua tuosque
Thermo et praesens Ephesi diligentissime commendarar i
et nunc per litteras, ipsumque intellexi esse perstudiosur i
tui.   Tu velim, quod antea ad te scripsi, de domo Pam-
meni des operam, ut, quod tuo meoque beneficio puc :
habet, cures ne qua ratione convellatur.   Id cum honestum
utrique nostrum existimo, tum mihi erit pergratum.

XXXIII. TO P. VOLUMNIUS EUTRAPELUS,
in Rome (Fam. vii. 32)

CILICIA, A.U.C. 703 ; B.C. 51 ; AET. CIC. 55

M. Cicero P. Volumnio scribit de dictis, de iudiciis, de re
publica, de Dolabella nondum genero.

1. Quod sine praenomine familiariter, ut debebas, ad
me epistolam misisti, primum addubitavi num a Volumnio
senatore esset, quocum mihi est magnus usus, deinde

εὐτραπελία litterarum fecit, ut intellegerem tuas esse. Quibus in litteris omnia mihi periucunda fuerunt praeter illud, quod parum diligenter possessio salinarum mearum a te procuratore defenditur. Ais enim, ut ego discesserim, omnia omnium dicta, in his etiam Sestiana, in me conferri. Quid? tu id pateris? nonne defendis? nonne resistis? Equidem sperabam ita notata me reliquisse genera dictorum meorum, ut cognosci sua sponte possent. 2. Sed quoniam tanta faex est in urbe, ut nihil tam sit ἀκύθηρον quod non alicui venustum esse videatur, pugna, si me amas, nisi acuta ἀμφιβολία, nisi elegans ὑπερβολή, nisi παράγραμμα bellum, nisi ridiculum παρὰ προσδοκίαν, nisi cetera, quae sunt a me in secundo libro DE ORATORE per Antonii personam disputata de ridiculis, ἔντεχνα et arguta apparebunt, ut sacramento contendas mea non esse. Nam de iudiciis quod quereris, multo laboro minus. Trahantur per me pedibus omnes rei, sit vel Selius tam eloquens, ut possit probare se liberum : non laboro. Urbanitatis possessionem, amabo, quibusvis interdictis defendamus : in qua te unum metuo, contemno ceteros. Derideri te putas? Nunc demum intellego te sapere. 3. Sed mehercules extra iocum : valde mihi tuae litterae facetae elegantesque visae sunt. Illa, quamvis ridicula essent, sicut erant, mihi tamen risum non moverunt. Cupio enim nostrum illum amicum in tribunatu quam plurimum habere gravitatis, id cum ipsius causa — est mihi, ut scis, in amoribus — tum mehercule etiam rei publicae : quam quidem, quamvis in me ingrata sit, amare non desinam. Tu, mi Volumni, quoniam et instituisti et mihi vides esse gratum, scribe

ad me quam saepissime de rebus urbanis, de re publica.
Iucundus est mihi sermo litterarum tuarum.   Praeterea
Dolabellam, quem ego perspicio et iudico cupidissimum
esse atque amantissimum mei, cohortare et confirma et
redde plane meum ; non mehercule, quo quidquam desi·,
sed quia valde ei cupio, non videor nimium laborare.

XXXIV. TO LUCIUS PAPIRIUS PAETUS,
in Rome (Fam. ix. 25)

LAODICEA, A.U.C. 704 ; B.C. 50 ; AET. CIC. 56

Cum M. Cicero procos. Ciliciam obtineret, misit ad eum L.
Paetus litteras de re militari, quibus facete exagitatis amico M.
Fadium commendat Cicero.

1. Summum me ducem litterae tuae reddiderunt :
plane nesciebam te tam peritum esse rei militaris.
Pyrrhi te libros et Cineae video lectitasse.   Itaque
obtemperare cogito praeceptis tuis : hoc amplius, navi-
cularum habere aliquid in ora maritima : contra equitem
Parthum negant ullam armaturam meliorem inveniri
posse.   Sed quid ludimus? nescis quo cum imperatore
tibi negotium sit.   Παιδείαν Κύρου, quam contriveram
legendo, totam in hoc imperio explicavi.   2. Sed iocabimur alias coram, ut spero, brevi tempore.   Nunc ades
ad imperandum vel ad parendum potius : sic enim
antiqui loquebantur.   Cum M. Fadio, quod scire te
arbitror, mihi summus usus est, valdeque eum diligo cum
propter summam probitatem eius ac singularem modes-
tiam tum quod in iis controversiis, quas habeo cum tuis

combibonibus Epicuriis, optima opera eius uti soleo. 3.
Is cum ad me Laodiceam venisset mecumque ego cum
esse vellem, repente percussus est atrocissimis litteris, in
quibus scriptum erat fundum Herculanensem a Q.
Fadio fratre proscriptum esse, qui fundus cum eo
communis esset. Id M. Fadius pergraviter tulit existi-
mavitque fratrem suum, hominem non sapientem,
impulsu inimicorum suorum eo progressum esse. Nunc,
si me amas, mi Paete, negotium totum suscipe : molestia
Fadium libera. Auctoritate tua nobis opus est et consilio et etiam gratia. Noli pati litigare fratres et
iudiciis turpibus conflictari. Matonem et Pollionem
inimicos habet Fadius. Quid multa? non mehercule tam
perscribere possum quam mihi gratum feceris, si otiosum
Fadium reddideris. Id ille in te positum esse putat
mihique persuadet.

XXXV. CICERO TO ATTICUS, on his way
to Rome (Att. vi. 1, §§ 17–26)

LAODICEA, A.U.C. 704 ; B.C. 50 ; AET. CIC. 56

De errore a Metello in subscriptione statuae Africani facto non
excusando, similibus erroribus a Graecis auctoribus commissis, de
Philotimo, de admonitione Attici, de M. Octavii postulatis, de
Lepta, de filiola Attici et Pilia. Iam breviter respondet ad epistolam quamdam minorem de multis variisque rebus et hominibus.
Litteras Attici ait se exspectare, de Caesare, de Pompeio, de P.
Vedio eiusque deversatione apud Pompeium Vindullum Laodiceae,
de monumento Appii Eleusine, de monumento quod sui ipse velit
esse Athenis.

17. De statua Africani — ὦ πραγμάτων ἀσυγκλώστων!

sed me id ipsum delectavit in tuis litteris—ain tι ?
Scipio hic Metellus proavum suum nescit censorem ncn
fuisse ? Atqui nihil habuit aliud inscriptum nisi COS.
ea statua, quae ad Opis per te posita in excelso est, in
illa autem, quae est ad Πολυκλέους Herculem, inscriptum est CENS. quam esse eiusdem status, amictus, anulus, imago ipsa declarat.   At mehercule ego cum in turma
inauratarum equestrium, quas hic Metellus in Capitolio
posuit, animadvertissem in Serapionis subscriptione Afr-
cani imaginem, erratum fabrile putavi, nunc video Metell .
O ἀνιστορησίαν turpem !   18. Nam illud de Flavio et
fastis, si secus est, commune erratum est, et tu bell?
ἠπόρησας et nos publicam prope opinionem secuti sumus,
ut multa apud Graecos.   Quis enim non dixit Εἴπολι,
τὸν τῆς ἀρχαίας, ab Alcibiade navigante in Siciliam
deiectum esse in mare ?   Redarguit Eratosthenes : adfer?
enim quas ille post id tempus fabulas docuerit.   Num
idcirco Duris Samius, homo in historia diligens, quod
cum multis erravit, irridetur ?   Quis Zaleucum lege.?
Locris scripsisse non dixit ?   Num igitur iacet Theophrastus, si id a Timaeo, tuo familiari, reprehensum est ?
Sed nescire proavum suum censorem non fuisse turpe est
praesertim cum post eum consulem nemo Cornelius illc
vivo censor fuerit.   19. Quod de Philotimo et de solu-
tione HS xxDC. scribis, Philotimum circiter Kal. Ianu-
arias in Chersonesum audio venisse : at mihi ab eo nihil
adhuc.   Reliqua mea Camillus scribit se accepisse : ea
quae sint nescio et aveo scire.   Verum haec posterius et
coram fortasse commodius.   20. Illud me, mi Attice, in
extrema fere parte epistolae commovit : scribis enim sic,

τί λοιπόν; deinde me obsecras amantissime, ne obliviscar vigilare et ut animadvertam quae fiant. Num quid de quo inaudisti? Etsi nihil eius modi est. Πολλοῦ γε καὶ δεῖ. Nec enim me fefellisset nec fallet. Sed ista admonitio tua tam accurata nescio quid mihi significare visa est. 21. De M. Octavio iterum iam tibi rescribo te illi probe respondisse, paullo vellem fidentius. Nam Caelius libertum ad me misit et litteras accurate scriptas et de pantheris et a civitatibus. Rescripsi alterum me moleste ferre, si ego in tenebris laterem nec audiretur Romae nullum in mea provincia nummum nisi in aes alienum erogari, docuique nec mihi conciliare pecuniam licere nec illi capere, monuique eum, quem plane diligo, ut, cum alios accusasset, cautius viveret, illud autem alterum alienum esse existimatione mea, Cibyratas imperio meo publice venari. 22. Lepta tua epistola gaudio exsultat. Etenim scripta belle est meque apud eum magna in gratia posuit. Filiola tua gratum mihi fecit, quod tibi diligenter mandavit ut mihi salutem ascriberes : gratum etiam Pilia, sed illa officiosius, quod mihi, quem [iam pridem] numquam vidit. Igitur tu quoque salutem utrique ascribito. Litterarum datarum dies pr. Kal. Ianuar. suavem habuit recordationem clarissimi iuris iurandi, quod ego non eram oblitus. Magnus enim praetextatus illo die fui. Habes ad omnia, non, ut postulasti, χρύσεα χαλκείων, sed paria paribus [respondimus]. 23. Ecce alia autem pusilla epistola, quam non relinquam ἀναντιφώνητον. † Bene mehercule potuit Lucceius Tusculanum, nisi forte — solet enim — cum suo tibicine,† et velim scire qui sit status eius. Lentulum

quidem nostrum omnia praeter Tusculanum proscripsisse
audio.   Cupio hos expeditos videre, cupio etiam Sestium,
adde, sis, Caelium, in quibus omnibus est,

αἰδεσθεν μὲν ἀνήνασθαι, δεῖσαν δ' ὑποδέχθαι.

De Memmio restituendo ut Curio cogitet te audiisse
puto.   De Egnatii Sidicini nomine nec nulla nec magna
spe sumus.   Pinarium, quem mihi commendas, diligentissime Deiotarus curat graviter aegrum.   Respondi etiam
minori.   24. Tu velim, dum ero Laodiceae, id est, ad
Idus Maias, quam saepissime mecum per litteras
colloquare, et cum Athenas veneris—iam enim sciemus
de rebus urbanis, de provinciis, quae omnia in mensem
Martium sunt collata—utique ad me tabellarios mittas.
25. Et heus tu, iamne vos a Caesare per Herodem
talenta Attica L. extorsistis? in quo, ut audio, magnum
odium Pompeii suscepistis.   Putat enim suos nummos
vos comedisse, Caesarem in Nemore aedificando diligen tiorem fore.   Haec ego ex P. Vedio, magno nebulone, sed
Pompeii tamen familiari, audivi.   Hic Vedius venit mihi
ob viam cum duobus essedis et reda equis iuncta et
lectica et familia magna pro qua, si Curio legem
pertulerit, HS centenos pendat necesse est.   Erit
praeterea cynocephalus in essedo nec deerant onagri.
Numquam vidi hominem nequiorem.   Sed extremum
audi.   Deversatus est Laodiceae apud Pompeium
Vindullum : ibi sua deposuit, cum ad me profectus est.
Moritur interim Vindullus, quae res ad Magnum
[Pompeium] pertinere putabatur.   C. Vennonius domum
Vindulli venit : cum omnia obsignaret in Vedianas res

incidit. In his inventae sunt quinque imagunculae matronarum, in quibus una sororis amici tui, hominis 'bruti,' qui hoc utatur, et uxoris illius 'lepidi,' qui haec tam neglegenter ferat. Haec te volui παριστορῆσαι. Sumus enim ambo belle curiosi. 26. Unum etiam velim cogites. Audio Appium πρόπυλον Eleusine facere. Num inepti nos fuerimus, si nos quoque Academiae fecerimus? Puto, inquies. Ergo id ipsum scribes ad me. Equidem valde ipsas Athenas amo. Volo esse aliquod monumentum meum. Odi falsas inscriptiones statuarum alienarum. Sed ut tibi placebit, faciesque me in quem diem Romana incidant mysteria certiorem et quo modo hiemaris. Cura ut valeas. Post Leuctricam pugnam die septingentesimo sexagesimo quinto.

XXXVI. TO ATTICUS, on his way to Rome (ATT. vi. 4)

TARSUS, A.U.C. 704; B.C. 50; AET. CIC. 56

M. Cicero Attico scribit se Tarsum venisse et cum de aliis rebus tum de eo sollicitum esse, quem provinciae praeficiat in decessu suo, ei omnia sua, quando Romam venerit, commendat, de re sua familiari, quam sequenti epistola uberius explicat, μυστικώτερον Graecis verbis scribit.

1. Tarsum venimus Nonis Iuniis. Ibi me multa moverunt: magnum in Syria bellum, magna in Cilicia latrocinia, mihi difficilis ratio administrandi, quod paucos dies habebam reliquos annui muneris, illud autem difficillimum: relinquendus erat ex senatus consulto qui praeesset. Nihil minus probari poterat quam quaestor

F

Mescinius. Nam de Caelio nihil audiebamus. Rec:is-
simum videbatur Q. fratrem cum imperio relinquere : in
quo multa molesta, discessus noster, belli periculum,
militum improbitas, sescenta praeterea. O rem tot·m
odiosam ! Sed haec fortuna viderit, quoniam consilio ron
multum uti licet. 2. Tu, quando Romam salvus, ut
spero, venisti, videbis, ut soles, omnia, quae intelleges
nostra interesse, in primis de Tullia mea, cuius de con·i-
cione quid mihi placeret scripsi ad Terentiam, cum tu in
Graecia esses : deinde de honore nostro : quod enim tu
afuisti, vereor ut satis diligenter actum in senatu sit de
litteris meis. 3. Illud praeterea μυστικώτερον ad te
scribam, tu sagacius odorabere : τῆς δάμαρτός μου ὁ
ἀπελεύθερος—οἶσθα ὃν λέγω—ἔδοξέ μοι πρώην, ἐξ ὃν
ἀλογευόμενος παρεφθέγγετο, πεφυρακέναι τὰς ψήφους ἐκ
τῆς ὠνῆς τῶν ὑπαρχόντων τοῦ Κροτωνιάτου τυρανιο-
κτόνου· δέδοικα δή, μή τι οὐ νοήσῃς· εἰς δήπου τοῦτο δὴ
περισκεψάμενος τὰ λοιπὰ ἐξασφάλισαι. Non queo tantum, quantum vereor, scribere. Tu autem fac ut mihi
tuae litterae volent obviae. Haec festinans scripsi in
itinere atque agmine. Piliae et puellae Caeciliae bell:s-
simae salutem dices.

XXXVII. TO ATTICUS, in Rome (Att. vi. 5)

TARSUS, A.U.C. 704; B.C. 50; AET. CIC. 56

De exspectato Attici adventu in urbem, ab eo cupit sibi litter. s
obvias mitti, in primis de rationibus turbatis in re sua familiari p·r
libertum uxoris suae, quam rem Graece ἐν αἰνιγμοῖς exponit ·t

maximae curae Attico esse vult : se in ipso decessu suo sollicitudine provinciae maxime urgeri, de Bibulo sibi non molesto, de brevitate huius ipsius epistolae.

1. Nunc quidem profecto Romae es : quo te, si ita est, salvum venisse gaudeo : unde quidem quam diu afuisti, magis a me abesse videbare, quam si domi esses : minus enim mihi meae notae res erant, minus etiam publicae. Qua re velim, etsi, ut spero, te haec legente aliquantum iam viae processero, tamen obvias mihi litteras quam argutissimas de omnibus rebus crebro mittas, in primis de quo scripsi ad te antea : τῆς ξυναόρου τῆς ἐμῆς οὐξελεύ-θερος ἔδοξέ μοι θαμὰ βατταρίζων καὶ ἁλίων ἐν τοῖς ξυλλό-γοις καὶ ταῖς λέσχαις ὑπό τι πεφιρακέναι τὰς ψήφους ἐν τοῖς ὑπάρχουσι τοῖς τοῦ Κροτωνιάτου. 2. Hoc tu indaga, ut soles ; ast hoc magis : ἐξ ἄστεως ἑπταλόφου στείχων παρέδωκεν μνῶν κδ'. μή. ὀφείλημα τῷ Καμίλλῳ· ἑαυτόν τε ὀφείλοντα μνᾶς κδ'. ἐκ τῶν Κροτωνιατικῶν καὶ ἐκ τῶν Χερρονησιτικῶν μή. καὶ μνᾶς κληρονομῆσαι χμ'. χμ'. τούτων δὲ μηδὲ ὀβολὸν διευλυτῶσθαι, πάντων ὀφειλη-θέντων τοῦ δευτέρου μηνὸς τῇ νουμηνίᾳ· τὸν δὲ ἀπελεύθερον αὐτοῦ, ὄντα ὁμώνυμον τῷ Κόνωνος πατρί, μηδὲν ὁλοσ-χερῶς πεφροντικέναι. ταῦτα οὖν, πρῶτον μὲν ἵνα πάντα σώζηται, δεύτερον δὲ ἵνα μηδὲ τῶν τόκων ὀλιγωρήσῃς τῶν ἀπὸ τῆς προεκκειμένης. ἡμέρας ὅσας αὐτὸν ἠνέγκαμεν σφόδρα δέδοικα. καὶ γὰρ παρῆν πρὸς ἡμᾶς κατασκε-ψόμενος καί τι σχεδὸν ἐλπίσας· ἀπογνοὺς δ' ἀλόγως ἀπέστη, ἐπειπών, εἴκω· αἰσχρόν τοι δηρόν τε μένειν· meque obiurgavit vetere proverbio τὰ μὲν διδόμενα. 3. Reliqua vide et quantum fieri potest prospice. Nos etsi annuum tempus prope iam emeritum habebamus—dies

enim xxxiii. erant reliqui—sollicitudine provinciae tamen vel maxime urgebamur. Cum enim arderet Syria bello et Bibulus in tanto maerore suo maximam curam belli sustineret ad meque legati eius et quaestor et amici eius litteras mitterent ut subsidio venirem, etsi exercitum infirmum habebam, auxilia sane bona, sed ea Galataruia, Pisidarum, Lyciorum—haec enim sunt nostra robora—tamen esse officium meum putavi exercitum habere quam proxime hostem, quoad mihi praeesse provinciae per senatus consultum liceret. Sed, quo ego maxime delectabar, Bibulus molestus mihi non erat : de omnibus rebus scribebat ad me potius, et mihi decessionis dies λελήθότος obrepebat : qui cum advenerit, ἄλλο πρόβλημα, quem praeficiam, nisi Caldus quaestor venerit, de quo adhuc nihil certi habebamus. 4. Cupiebam mehercule longiorem epistolam facere, sed nec erat res de qua scriberem nec iocari prae cura poteram. Valebis igitur et puellae salutem Atticulae dices nostraeque Piliae.

XXXVIII. TO ATTICUS, in Rome (Att. vi. 8)

EPHESUS, A.U.C. 704 ; B.C. 50 ; AET. CIC. 56

Litteras Attici Ephesi sibi redditas a Batonio gratas fuisse significat, sed Batonium meros terrores Caesarianos ad se attulisse : de tarditate navigationis suae, de rebus urbanis vult edoceri et quid Atticus de triumpho suo cogitet.

1. Cum instituissem ad te scribere calamumque sumpsissem Batonius e navi recta ad me venit domum Ephesi et epistolam tuam reddidit pridie Kal. Octobres. Laeta-

tus sum felicitate navigationis tuae, opportunitate Piliae, etiam hercule sermone ciusdem de coniugio Tulliae meae. 2. Batonius autem meros terrores ad me attulit Caesarianos, cum Lepta etiam plura locutus est, spero falsa, sed certe horribilia, exercitum nullo modo dimissurum, cum illo praetores designatos, Cassium tribunum pl., Lentulum consulem facere, Pompeio in animo esse urbem relinquere. 3. Sed heus tu, num quid moleste fers de illo, qui se *gaudivi* solet anteferre patruo sororis tuae filii? At a quibus victus? Sed ad rem. 4. Nos etesiae vehementissime tardarunt. Detraxit xx. ipsos dies etiam aphractus Rhodiorum. Kal. Octobr. Epheso conscendentes hanc epistolam dedimus L. Tarquitio, simul e portu egredienti, sed expeditius naviganti. Nos Rhodiorum aphractis ceterisque longis navibus tranquillitates aucupaturi eramus: ita tamen properabamus, ut non posset magis. 5. De raudusculo Puteolano gratum. Nunc velim dispicias res Romanas, videas quid nobis de triumpho cogitandum putes, ad quem amici me vocant. Ego, nisi Bibulus, qui, dum unus hostis in Syria fuit, pedem porta non plus extulit quam domi domo sua, adniteretur de triumpho, aequo animo essem. Nunc vero αἰσχρὸν σιωπᾶν. Sed explora rem totam, ut, quo die congressi erimus, consilium capere possimus. Sat multa, qui et properarem et ei litteras darem, qui aut mecum aut paullo ante venturus esset. Cicero tibi plurimam salutem dicit. Tu dices utriusque nostrum verbis et Piliae tuae et filiae.

XXXIX. TO ATTICUS, in Rome (Att. vi. 9)

ATHENS, A.U.C. 704 ; B.C. 50 ; AET. CIC. 56

M. Cicero Attico scribit se eius litteras ab Acasto servo suo
accepisse, e quibus cognosset eum febriculam habere, se sperare
iam melius ei esse factum : de re sua familiari, de Q. fratre provinciae non praefecto, de litterarum commercio.

1. In Piraeca cum exissem pridie Idus Octobr. accepi
ab Acasto, servo meo, statim tuas litteras, quas quidem
cum exspectassem iam diu, admiratus sum, ut vi li
obsignatam epistolam, brevitatem eius, ut aperui, rursus
σύγχυσιν litterularum, quia solent tuae compositissime
et clarissimae esse, ac, ne multa, cognovi ex eo, quod iia
scripseras, te Romam venisse a. d. xii. Kal. Octobr. cum
febri. Percussus vehementer nec magis quam debui
statim quaero ex Acasto.   Ille et tibi et sibi visum et
ita se domi ex tuis audisse, ut nihil esset incommode.
Id videbatur approbare, quod erat in extremo, febriculam
tum te habentem scripsisse.   Sed te amavi tamen admira-
tusque sum, quod nihilo minus ad me tua manu scripsisses.   Qua re de hoc satis.   Spero enim, quae tui
prudentia et temperantia est, et hercule, ut me iubet
Acastus, confido te iam ut volumus valere.   2. A Tu-
ranio te accepisse meas litteras gaudeo.   Παραφύλαξοι,
si me amas, τὴν τοῦ φυρατοῦ φιλοτιμίαν αὐτότατα.
Hanc quae mehercule mihi magno dolori est—dilexi
enim hominem—procura, quantulacumque est, Precianam
hereditatem prorsus ille ne attingat.   Dices nummo;
mihi opus esse ad apparatum triumphi, in quo, ut

praecipis, nec me κενὸν in expctendo cognosces nec
ἄτυφον in abiiciendo. 3. Intellexi ex tuis litteris te
ex Turranio audisse a me provinciam fratri traditam.
Adeon ego non perspexeram prudentiam litterarum
tuarum? Ἐπέχειν te scribebas. Quid erat dubitatione
dignum, si esset quidquam cur placeret fratrem et talem
fratrem relinqui? Ἀθέτησις ista mihi tua, non ἐποχὴ
videbatur. Monebas de Q. Cicerone puero, ut eum
quidem neutiquam relinquerem. Τοὐμὸν ὄνειρον ἐμοί.
Eadem omnia, quasi collocuti essemus, vidimus. Non
fuit faciendum aliter, meque ἐπιχρονία ἐποχὴ tua dubitatione liberavit. Sed puto te accepisse de hac re epistolam scriptam accuratius. 4. Ego tabellarios postero die
ad vos eram missurus, quos puto ante venturos quam
nostrum Saufeium. Sed eum sine meis litteris ad te
venire vix rectum erat. 5. Tu mihi, ut polliceris, de
Tulliola mea, id est, de Dolabella, perscribes, de re
publica, quam praevideo in summis periculis, de censoribus, maximeque de signis, tabulis quid fiat, referaturne.
Idibus Octobr. has dedi litteras, quo die, ut scribis,
Caesar Placentiam legiones quattuor. Quaeso, quid
nobis futurum est? In arce Athenis statio mea nunc
placet.

XL. CICERO AND HIS SON TO TIRO, ON HIS WAY TO ROME (FAM. XVI. 9)

BRUNDISIUM, A.U.C. 704; B.C. 50; AET. CIC. 56

M. Cicero describit navigationis suae cursum et ad curandam
valetudinem Tironem cohortatur.

1. Nos a te, ut scis, discessimus a. d. IV. Non. Nov-

cmbr. Leucadem venimus a. d. VIII. Idus Novembr., a.
d. VII. Actium : ibi propter tempestatem a. d. VI. Idus
morati sumus. Inde a. d. V. Idus Corcyram bellissime
navigavimus. Corcyrae fuimus usque ad a. d. XVI.
Kalend. Decembr. tempestatibus retenti. A. d. XV.
Kalend. in portum Corcyraeorum ad Cassiopen stadia
CXX. processimus. Ibi retenti ventis sumus usque ad
a. d. VIIII. Kalendas. Interea, qui cupide profecti sur t,
multi naufragia fecerunt. 2. Nos eo die cenati solvimus.
Inde austro lenissimo, caelo sereno, nocte illa et die postero
in Italiam ad Hydruntem ludibundi pervenimus eodemque
vento postridie—id erat a. d. VII. Kalend. Decembr.--
hora quarta Brundisium venimus, eodemque tempo e
simul nobiscum in oppidum introiit Terentia, quae e
facit plurimi. A. d. V. Kalend. Decembr. servus C.1.
Plancii Brundisii tandem aliquando mihi a te exspect i-
tissimas litteras reddidit, datas Idibus Novembr., quæ e
me molestia valde levarunt : utinam omnino liberassent !
Sed tamen Asclapo medicus plane confirmat propediem
te valentem fore. 3. Nunc quid ego te horter, ut omnem
diligentiam adhibeas ad convalescendum ? Tuam prudentiam, temperantiam, amorem erga me novi : scio te omnia
facturum, ut nobiscum quam primum sis : sed tamen ita
velim, ut ne quid properes. Symphoniam Lysonis velle i
vitasses, ne in quartam hebdomada incideres. Sed quor-
iam pudori tuo maluisti obsequi quam valetudini, reliqu i
cura. Curio misi, ut medico honos haberetur et til i
daret quod opus esset : me cui iussisset curaturum. Ecum
et mulum Brundisii tibi reliqui. Romae vereor ne e::
Kalend. Ian. magni tumultus sint. Nos agemus omnia

modice. 4. Reliquum est ut te hoc rogem et a te petam,
ne temere naviges—solent nautae festinare quaestus sui
causa—cautus sis, mi Tiro—mare magnum et difficile tibi
restat—si poteris cum Mescinio—caute is solet navigare
—si minus, cum honesto aliquo homine, cuius auctoritate
navicularius moveatur. In hoc omnem diligentiam si
adhibueris teque nobis incolumem stiteris, omnia a te
habebo. Etiam atque etiam, noster Tiro, vale. Medico,
Curio, Lysoni de te scripsi diligentissime. Vale et salve.

XLI. TO ATTICUS, in Rome (Att. vii. 17)

FORMIAE, A.U.C. 705 ; B.C. 49 ; AET. CIC. 57

M. Cicero Attico scribit de pueris in Graeciam transportandis,
si ipse Hispaniam peteret, de Attici commoratione in urbe cum
Sexto, de responsis ad Caesaris responsa scriptis a P. Sestio, quae
ipse a Caesare non acceptum iri existimat, de Trebatii litteris
rogatu Caesaris ad se missis et quid Trebatio ipse responderit, et
de consiliis suis, a se Capua reverso in Formiano mulieres suas
exspectari, ipsum velle Non. Febr. Capuae esse.

1. Tuae litterae mihi gratae iucundaeque sunt. De
pueris in Graeciam transportandis tum cogitabam, cum
fuga ex Italia quaeri videbatur. Nos enim Hispaniam
peteremus, illis hoc aeque commodum non erat. Tu ipse
cum Sexto etiam nunc mihi videris Romae recte esse
posse. Etenim minime amici Pompeio nostro esse
debetis. Nemo enim umquam tantum de urbanis
praediis detraxit. 2. Videsne me etiam iocari? Scire
iam te oportet L. Caesar quae responsa referat a
Pompeio, quas ab eodem ad Caesarem ferat litteras.

Scriptae enim et datae ita sunt, ut proponerentur in publico: in quo accusavi mecum ipse Pompeium, qui cum scriptor luculentus esset, tantas res atque eas, quae in omnium manus venturae essent, Sestio nostro scribendas dederit. Itaque nihil umquam legi scriptum σηστιωδέστερον. Perspici tamen ex litteris Pompeii potest nihil Caesari negari omniaque et cumulate quae postulet dari, quae ille amentissimus fuerit nisi acceperit, praesertim cum impudentissime postulaverit. Quis enim tu es, qui dicas: 'Si in Hispaniam profectus erit, si praesidia dimiserit.' Tamen conceditur: minus honeste nunc quidem, violata iam ab illo re publica illatoque bello, quam si olim de ratione habenda impetrasset, et tamen vereor ut his ipsis contentus sit. Nam cum ista mandata dedisset L. Caesari, debuit esse paullo quietior, dum responsa referrentur, dicitur autem nunc esse acerrimus. 3. Trebatius quidem scribit se ab illo IX. Kal. Febr. rogatum esse, ut scriberet ad me, ut essem ad urbem: nihil ei me gratius facere posse. Haec verbis plurimis. Intellexi ex dierum ratione, ut primum de discessu nostro Caesar audisset, laborare eum coepisse ne omnes abessemus. Itaque non dubito quin ad Pisonem, quin ad Servium scripserit. Illud admiror non ipsum ad me scripsisse, non per Dolabellam, non per Caelium egisse, quamquam non aspernor Trebatii litteras, a quo me unice diligi scio. 4. Rescripsi ad Trebatium—nam ad ipsum Caesarem, qui mihi nihil scripsisset, nolui—quam illud hoc tempore esset difficile, me tamen in praediis meis esse neque dilectum ullum neque negotium suscepisse. In quo quidem manebo, dum spes pacis erit:

sin bellum geretur, non deero officio nec dignitati meae, pueros ὑπεκθέμενος in Graeciam. Totam enim Italiam flagraturam bello intellego. Tantum mali est excitatum partim ex improbis, partim ex invidis civibus. Sed haec paucis diebus ex illius ad nostra responsa responsis intellegentur quorsum evasura sint. Tum ad te scribam plura, si erit bellum: sin aut otium aut etiam indutiae, te ipsum, ut spero, videbo. 5. Ego IIII. Non. Febr., quo die has litteras dedi, in Formiano, quo Capua redieram, mulieres exspectabam, quibus quidem scripseram tuis litteris admonitus, ut Romae manerent. Sed audio maiorem quemdam in urbe timorem esse. Capuae Non. Febr. esse volebam, quia consules iusserant. Quidquid huc erit a Pompeio adlatum, statim ad te scribam, tuasque de istis rebus litteras exspectabo.

XLII. TO ATTICUS, in Rome (Att. vii. 20)

CAPUA, A.U.C. 705 ; B.C. 49 ; AET. CIC. 57

Desperata pace queritur M. Cicero tamen bellum non parari a consulibus, a Caesare omnia acerrime agitari. Quaerit ab Attico quid sibi agendum putet.

1. Breviloquentem iam me tempus ipsum facit. Pacem enim desperavi, bellum nostri nullum administrant. Cave enim putes quidquam esse minoris his consulibus: quorum ergo spe audiendi aliquid et cognoscendi nostri apparatus maximo imbri Capuam veni pridie Nonas, ut eram iussus. Illi autem nondum venerant, sed erant venturi ad Nonas, inanes, imparati.

Gnaeus autem Luceriae dicebatur esse et adire cohor es
legionum Appianarum, non firmissimarum. At illum
ruere nuntiant et iam iamque adesse, non ut manum
conserat — quicum enim ? — sed ut fugam intercludat.
2. Ego autem in Italia κἂν ἀποθανεῖν — nec te id
consulo — sin extra, quid ago ? Ad manendum hiems,
lictores, improvidi et neglegentes duces, ad fugam
hortatur amicitia Gnaei, causa bonorum, turpitudo
coniungendi cum tyranno : qui quidem incertum est
Phalarimne an Pisistratum sit imitaturus. Haec velim
explices et me iuves consilio, etsi te ipsum istic iam
calere puto. Sed tamen quantum poteris. Ego si qu d
hic hodie novi cognoro, scies. Iam enim aderunt consul s
ad suas Nonas. Tuas cotidie litteras exspectabo. Ad
has autem, cum poteris, rescribes. Mulieres et Cicerones
in Formiano reliqui.

XLIII. TO ATTICUS, in Rome (Att. viii. 4)

FORMIAE, A.U.C. 705 ; B.C. 49 ; AET. CIC. 57

M. Cicero de ingrato Dionysii magistri Ciceronum animo quer -
tur et quae audierit de C. Atio Paeligno nuntiat, Attici litteras
exspectat.

1. Dionysius quidem tuus potius quam noster, cuius
ego cum satis cognossem mores, tuo tamen potius stabam
iudicio quam meo, ne tui quidem testimonii, quod ei saepe
apud me dederas, veritus superbum se praebuit in fortuna,
quam putavit nostram fore : cuius fortunae nos, quantun
humano consilio effici poterit, motum ratione quadam gu

bernabimus. Cui qui noster honos, quod obsequium, quae
etiam ad ceteros contempti cuiusdam hominis commendatio defuit ? ut meum iudicium reprehendi a Quinto fratre
vulgoque ab omnibus mallem quam illum non efferre laudibus, Ciceronesque nostros meo potius labore subdoceri
quam me alium iis magistrum quaerere. Ad quem ego quas
litteras, di immortales, miseram, quantum honoris significa-
cantes, quantum amoris!—Dicaearchum mehercule aut Aristoxenum diceres arcessi, non hominem omnium loquacis-
simum et minime aptum ad docendum. 2. 'Sed est
memoria bona.' Me dicet esse meliore.—Quibus litteris
ita respondit, ut ego nemini, cuius causam non reciperem.
Semper enim, 'si potero, si ante suscepta causa non
impediar,' numquam reo cuiquam tam humili, tam sor-
dido, tam nocenti, tam alieno tam praecise negavi quam
hic mihi plane sine ulla exceptione praecidit. Nihil
cognovi ingratius, in quo vitio nihil mali non inest. Sed
de hoc nimis multa. 3. Ego navem paravi : tuas litteras
tamen exspecto, ut sciam quid respondeant consultationi
meae. Sulmone C. Atium Paelignum aperuisse Antonio
portas, cum essent cohortes quinque, Q. Lucretium
inde effugisse scis, Gnaeum Brundisium ire, Domitium iri
desertum. Confecta res est.

XLIV. TO ATTICUS, in Rome (Att. viii. 5)

FORMIAE, A.U.C. 705 ; B.C. 49 ; AET. CIC. 57

M. Cicero Attico scribit Dionysium ipsum ad se venisse et se
sibi iam referri velle eam epistolam quam Attico misisset ad illum

perferendam.   Tum de exspectatione de re Corfiniensi, de Tirone M'. Curio commendando.

1. Cum ante lucem VIII. Kal. ad te [de Dionysio] litteras dedissem, vesperi ad nos eodem die venit ipse Dionysius, auctoritate tua permotus, ut suspicor.   Quid enim putem aliud?   Etsi solet eum, cum aliquid furiose fecit, paenitere.   Numquam autem cerritior fuit quam in hoc negotio.   Nam, quod ad te non scripseram, postea audivi a tertio miliario timuisse,

$$\pi o\lambda\lambda\grave{a}\ \mu\acute{a}\tau\eta\nu\ \kappa\epsilon\rho\acute{a}\epsilon\sigma\sigma\iota\nu\ \grave{\epsilon}\varsigma\ \mathring{\eta}\acute{\epsilon}\rho a\ \theta\upsilon\mu\acute{\eta}\nu a\nu\tau a,$$

multa, inquam, mala cum dixisset: suo capiti, ut aiunt. Sed en meam mansuetudinem!   Conieceram in fasciculum una cum tua vehementem ad illum epistolam: hanc id me referri volo, nec ullam ob aliam causam Pollicem servum a pedibus meis Romam misi.   Eo autem ad te scripsi, ut, si tibi forte reddita esset, mihi curares referendam, ne in illius manus perveniret.   2. Novi si quid esset, scripsissem.   Pendeo animi exspectatione de re Corfiniensi, in qua de salute rei publicae decernetur.   Tu fasciculum, qui est M'. CURIO inscriptus, velim cures ad eum perferendum, Tironemque Curio commendes et it det ei, si quid opus erit in sumptum, roges.

XLV. TO ATTICUS, in Rome (ATT. IX. 2)

FORMIAE, A.U.C. 705; B.C. 49; AET. CIC. 57

Quod Atticus epistola quadam scripserat se gaudere Cicerone n mansisse, iam quaerit Cicero utrum ipse eius sententiam parum

meminerit an ille sententiam mutaverit. Dubitare se scribit
de consilio ab Attico sibi dato, exponit de misera condicione
sua, si Caesaris partes sequatur, apud Pompeium se in offensa esse
non posse, quum ille se potius neglexerit, de adventu Postumi Curtii,
de nuntio Brundisio nondum adlato.

1. Etsi Nonis Martiis die tuo, ut opinor, exspectabam
epistolam a te longiorem, tamen ad eam ipsam brevem,
quam IIII. Nonas ὑπὸ τὴν λῆψιν dedisti, rescribendum
putavi. Gaudere ais te mansisse me, et scribis in
sententia te manere. Mihi autem superioribus litteris
videbare non dubitare quin cederem, ita, si et Gnaeus
bene comitatus conscendisset et consules transissent.
Utrum hoc tu parum commeministi an ego non satis
intellexi an mutasti sententiam? Sed aut ex epistola,
quam exspecto, perspiciam quid sentias aut alias abs te
litteras eliciam. Brundisio nihildum erat adlatum.

2. O rem difficilem planeque perditam! quam nihil
praetermittis in consilio dando! quam nihil tamen quod
tibi ipsi placeat explicas! Non esse me una cum
Pompeio gaudes, ac proponis quam sit turpe me adesse,
cum quid de illo detrahatur. Nefas esse approbare.
Certe. Contra igitur? Di, inquis, averruncent! Quid
ergo fiet, si in altero scelus est, in altero supplicium?
Impetrabis, inquis, a Caesare ut tibi abesse liceat et esse
otioso. Supplicandum igitur? Miserum. Quid, si non
impetraro? Et de triumpho erit, inquis, integrum.
Quid, si hoc ipso premar? Accipiam: quid foedius?
Negem: repudiari se totum, magis etiam quam olim in
xxviratu, putabit. Ac solet, cum se purgat, in me conferre omnem illorum temporum culpam: ita me sibi

fuisse inimicum, ut ne honorem quidem a se accipere vellem.   Quanto nunc hoc idem accipiet asperius?   Tanto
scilicet, quanto et honor hic illo est amplior et ipse
robustior.   3. Nam quod negas te dubitare quin magna
in offensa sim apud Pompeium hoc tempore, non video
causam cur ita sit, hoc quidem tempore.   Qui enim
amisso Corfinio denique certiorem me sui consilii fecit, is
queretur Brundisium me non venisse, quum inter me et
Brundisium Caesar esset?   Deinde etiam scit ἀπαρρησίαστον esse in ea causa querellam suam.   Me putat de
municipiorum imbecillitate, de dilectibus, de pace, de
urbe, de pecunia, de Piceno occupando plus vidisse quam
se.   Sin, cum potuero, non venero, iure erit inimicus;
quod ego non eo vereor ne mihi noceat—quid en m
faciet?

> Τίς δ' ἐστὶ δοῦλος, τοῦ θανεῖν ἄφροντις ὤν;—

sed quia ingrati animi crimen horreo.   Confido igitur
adventum nostrum illi, quoquo tempore fuerit, ut scribis,
ἀσμενιστὸν fore.   Nam quod ais, si hic temperatius
egerit, consideratius consilium te daturum, qui hic potest
se gerere non perdite?   Vetant mores, ante facta, ratio
suscepti negotii, socii, vires bonorum aut etiam constantia.
4. Vixdum epistolam tuam legeram, cum ad me currens
ad illum Postumus Curtius venit, nihil nisi classes
loquens et exercitus, eripiebat Hispanias, tenebat Asiam,
Siciliam, Africam, Sardiniam, confestim in Graeciam
persequebatur.   Eundum igitur est nec tam ut belli
quam ut fugae socii simus.   Nec enim ferre potero
sermones istorum, quicumque sunt: non sunt enim certe,

ut appellantur, boni. Sed tamen id ipsum scire cupio, quid loquantur, idque ut exquiras meque certiorem facias, te vehementer rogo. Nos adhuc quid Brundisii actum esset plane nesciebamus : cum sciemus, tum ex re et ex tempore consilium capiemus, sed utemur tuo.

XLVI. TO ATTICUS, in Rome (Att. x. 17)

POMPEII, A.U.C. 705 ; B.C. 49 ; AET. CIC. 57

De Hortensii ad se adventu, de Serapionis adventu cum epistola Attici, de lippitudine sua et valetudine Attici, de Ocella, denique, quod de diplomate Attici suspicatus erat, se excusat.

1. Pridie Idus Hortensius ad me venit scripta epistola. Vellem cetera eius. Quam in me incredibilem ἐκτένειαν ! qua quidem cogito uti. Deinde Serapion cum epistola tua, quam prius quam aperuissem, dixi ei te ad me de eo scripsisse antea, ut feceras. Deinde, epistola stricta, cumulatissime cetera : et hercule hominem bonum et doctum et probum existimo : quin etiam navi eius me et ipso convectore usurum puto. 2. Crebro refricat lippitudo, non illa quidem perodiosa, sed tamen quae impediat scriptionem meam. Valetudinem tuam iam confirmatam esse et a vetere morbo et a novis temptationibus gaudeo. 3. Ocellam vellem haberemus. Viderentur enim esse haec paullo faciliora. Nunc quidem aequinoctium nos moratur, quod valde perturbatum erat. Inde si ἀκραὲς erit, utinam idem maneat Hortensius ! si quidem, ut adhuc erat, liberalius esse nihil potest. 4. De diplomate, admiraris, quasi nescio cuius te flagitii insimularim. Negas enim

G

te reperire qui mihi id in mentem venerit. Ego autem,
quia scripseras, te proficisci cogitare—etenim audierum
nemini aliter licere,—eo te habere censebam, et q iia
pueris diploma sumpseras. Habes causam opinionis meae,
et tamen velim scire quid cogites, in primisque, si quid
etiam nunc novi est. XVII. Kal. Iun.

XLVII. TO ATTICUS, in Rome (Att. x. 18)

POMPEII, A.U.C. 705 ; B.C. 49 ; AET. CIC. 57

De partu Tulliae, de navigatione impedita adhuc, de custodis,
quibus adservetur, Attici epistolas exspectat, maxime si quid de
Hispaniis, de Balbo, de misera condicione sua.

1. Tullia mea peperit XIIII. Kal. Iun. puerum ἑπταμηνιαῖον. Quod εὐτόκησεν, est quod gaudeam. Quod
quidem est natum, perimbecillum est. Me mirifice
tranquillitates adhuc tenuerunt atque maiori impedimento
fuerunt quam custodiae, quibus adservor. Nam illa
Hortensiana omnia fuere infantia. Ita fiet : homo nequs-
simus a Salvio liberto depravatus est. Itaque posthic
non scribam ad te quid facturus sim, sed quid fecerim :
omnes enim Κωρυκαῖοι videntur subauscultare quae
loquor. 2. Tu tamen, si quid de Hispaniis sive quid
aliud, perge quaeso scribere, nec meas litteras exspectaris,
nisi cum quo opto pervenerimus aut si quid ex cursu, sed
hoc quoque timide scribo : ita omnia tarda adhuc et spissa.
Ut male posuimus initia, sic cetera sequuntur. Formius
nunc sequimur, eodem nos fortasse Furiae persequentur.
Ex Balbi autem sermone, quem tecum habuit, non pro

bamus de Melita. Dubitas igitur quin nos in hostium
numero habeat? Scripsi equidem Balbo te ad me de
benevolentia scripsisse et de suspicione. Egi gratias.
De altero ei me purgavi. 3. Ecquem tu hominem infeliciorem? Non loquor plura, ne te quoque excruciem.
Ipse conficior venisse tempus cum iam nec fortiter nec
prudenter quidquam facere possim.

XLVIII. TO ATTICUS (Att. xi. 1)

EPIRUS, A.U.C. 706 ; B.C. 48 ; AET. CIC. 58

M. Cicero Attico res suas domesticas suscipiendas et tuendas
commendat.

1. Accepi a te signatum libellum, quem Anteros attu-
lerat, ex quo nihil scire potui de nostris domesticis rebus :
de quibus acerbissime adflictor, quod qui eas dispensavit
neque adest istic neque ubi terrarum sit scio. Omnem
autem spem habeo existimationis privatarumque rerum
in tua erga me mihi perspectissima benevolentia, quam
si his temporibus miseris et extremis praestiteris, haec
pericula, quae mihi communia sunt cum ceteris, fortius
feram : idque ut facias, te obtestor atque obsecro. 2.
Ego in cistophoro in Asia habeo ad HS. bis et viciens.
Huius pecuniae permutatione fidem nostram facile tuebere,
quam quidem ego nisi expeditam relinquere me putassem,
credens ei, cui tu scis iam pridem minime me credere,
commoratus essem paullisper nec domesticas res impedi-
tas reliquissem ; ob eamque causam serius ad te scribo,

quod sero intellexi quid timendum esset. Te etiam atque etiam oro, ut me totum tuendum suscipias, ut, si ii salvi erunt, quibuscum sum, una cum iis possim incolumis esse salutemque meam benevolentiae tuae acceptam referre.

XLIX. TO PAETUS (Fam. ix. 16)

TUSCULANUM, A.U.C. 708 ; B.C. 46 ; AET. CIC. 60

M. Cicero L. Papirio Paeto scribit se nihil praetermisisse, ut Caesarianorum sibi benevolentiam conciliaret, nec boni civis aut sapientis hominis officium in se posse desiderari. Denique Paeti iocis iocosa reddit.

1. Delectarunt me tuae litterae, in quibus primum amavi amorem tuum, qui te ad scribendum incitavit verentem, ne Silius suo nuntio aliquid mihi sollicitudinis attulisset : de quo et tu mihi antea scripseras, bis quidem eodem exemplo, facile ut intellegerem te esse commotum, et ego tibi accurate rescripseram, ut quoquo modo in tali re atque tempore aut liberarem te ista cura aut certe levarem.　2. Sed quoniam proximis quoque litteris ostendis, quantae tibi curae sit ea res, sic, mi Paete, habeto : quidquid arte fieri potuerit—non enim iam satis est consilio pugnare : artificium quoddam excogitandum est,—sed tamen quidquid elaborari aut effici potuerit ad istorum benevolentiam conciliandam et colligendam, summo studio me consecutum esse, nec frustra, ut arbitror : sic enim color, sic observor ab omnibus iis, qui a Caesare diliguntur, ut ab iis me amari putem. Tametsi non facile diiudicatur amor verus et fictus, nisi aliquod

incidat eius modi tempus, ut quasi aurum igni, sic
benevolentia fidelis periculo aliquo perspici possit, cetera
sunt signa communia, sed ego uno utor argumento, quam
ob rem me ex animo vereque arbitrer diligi, quia et nostra
fortuna ea est et illorum, ut simulandi causa non sit. 3.
De illo autem, quem penes est omnis potestas, nihil video
quod timeam: nisi quod omnia sunt incerta, cum a iure
discessum est, nec praestari quidquam potest, quale
futurum sit, quod positum est in alterius voluntate, ne
dicam libidine. Sed tamen eius ipsius nulla re a me
offensus est animus. Est enim adhibita in ea re ipsa
summa a nobis moderatio. Ut enim olim arbitrabar esse
meum libere loqui, cuius opera esset in civitate libertas,
sic ea nunc amissa nihil loqui quod offendat aut illius
aut eorum, qui ab illo diliguntur, voluntatem. Effugere
autem si velim non nullorum acute aut facete dictorum
famam, fama ingenii mihi est abiicienda: quod, si id
possem, non recusarem. 4. Sed tamen ipse Caesar habet
peracre iudicium, et, ut Servius, frater tuus, quem littera-
tissimum fuisse iudico, facile diceret, 'hic versus Plauti
non est, hic est,' quod tritas aures haberet notandis
generibus poëtarum et consuetudine legendi, sic audio
Caesarem, cum volumina iam confecerit ἀποφθεγμάτων,
si quod adferatur ad eum pro meo, quod meum non sit,
reiicere solere: quod eo nunc magis facit, quia vivunt mecum
fere cotidie illius familiares. Incidunt autem in sermone
vario multa, quae fortasse illis cum dixi nec illitterata nec
insulsa esse videantur. Haec ad illum cum reliquis actis
perferuntur: ita enim ipse mandavit. Sic fit ut, si quid
praeterea de me audiat, non audiendum putet. Quam

ob rem Ocnomao tuo nihil utor: etsi posuisti loco versus
Accianos. 5. Sed quae est invidia aut quid mihi nunc
invideri potest? Verum fac posse omnia. Sic video
philosophis placuisse iis, qui mihi soli videntur vim virtutis tenere, nihil esse sapientis praestare nisi culpam:
qua mihi videor dupliciter carere, et quod ea senserim,
quae rectissima fuerunt, et quod, cum viderem praesidii
non satis esse ad ea obtinenda, viribus certandum cum
valentioribus non putarim Ergo in officio boni civis
certe non sum reprehendendus. Reliquum est, ne quid
stulte, ne quid temere dicam aut faciam contra potentes:
id quoque puto esse sapientis. Cetera vero, quid quisque
me dixisse dicat aut quo modo ille accipiat aut qua fide
mecum vivant ii, qui me adsidue colunt et observant,
praestare non possum. 6. Ita fit ut et consiliorum
superiorum conscientia et praesentis temporis moderatione
me consoler et illam Accii similitudinem non iam ad
invidiam, sed ad fortunam transferam, quam existimo
levem et imbecillam ab animo firmo et gravi tamquam
fluctum a saxo frangi oportere. Etenim cum plena sint
monumenta Graecorum, quem ad modum sapientissimi
viri regna tulerint vel Athenis vel Syracusis, cum servien-
tibus suis civitatibus fuerint ipsi quodam modo liberi, ego
me non putem tueri meum statum sic posse, ut neque
offendam animum cuiusquam nec frangam dignitatem
meam? 7 Nunc venio ad iocationes tuas, quoniam tu
secundum Ocnomaum Accii, non, ut olim solebat, Atel-
lanam, sed, ut nunc fit, mimum introduxisti. Quem tu
mihi pompilum, quem thunnarium narras? quam tyrotaric ii
patinam? Facilitate mea ista ferebantur antea: nunc

mutata res est.   Hirtium ego et Dolabellam dicendi discipulos habeo, cenandi magistros.   Puto enim te audisse,
si forte ad vos omnia perferuntur, illos apud me declami-
tare, me apud illos cenitare.   Tu autem quod mihi
bonam copiam eiures nihil est : tum enim, cum rem habebas, quaesticulis te faciebat attentiorem : nunc, cum tam
aequo animo bona perdas, non est quod eo sis consilio, ut,
cum me hospitio recipias, aestimationem te aliquam putes
accipere: etiam haec levior est plaga ab amico quam a debi-
tore. 8. Nec tamen eas cenas quaero, ut magnae reliquiae
fiant: quod erit, magnificum sit et lautum. Memini te mihi
Phameae cenam narrare : temperius fiat, cetera eodem
modo.   Quod si perseveras me ad matris tuae cenam
revocare, feram id quoque.   Volo enim videre animum,
qui mihi audeat ista, quae scribis, apponere aut etiam
polypum miniati Iovis similem.   Mihi crede, non aude-
bis.   Ante meum adventum fama ad te de mea nova
lautitia veniet : eam extimesces.   Neque est quod in
promulside spei ponas aliquid, quam totam sustuli.
Solebam enim antea debilitari oleis et lucanicis tuis.   9.
Sed quid haec loquimur ? liceat modo isto venire.   Tu
vero—volo enim abstergere animi tui metum,—ad tyro-
tarichum antiquum redi.   Ego tibi unum sumptum adferam, quod balneum calfacias oportebit : cetera more
nostro : superiora illa lusimus.   10. De villa Seliciana
et curasti diligenter et scripsisti facetissime.   Itaque puto
me praetermissurum.   Salis enim satis est, saniorum
parum.

L. TO PAETUS (Fam. ix. 18)

TUSCULANUM, A.U.C. 708; B.C. 46; AET. CIC. 60

M. Cicero causas exponit L. Papirio cur alios declamanlo
exercere coeperit. Tum iocatur de cenarum apparatu.

1. Cum essem otiosius in Tusculano, propterea quod
discipulos ob viam miseram, ut eadem me quam maxime
conciliarent familiari suo, accepi tuas litteras plenissimas
suavitatis, ex quibus intellexi probari tibi meum consilium,
quod, ut Dionysius tyrannus, cum Syracusis pulsus esset,
Corinthi dicitur ludum aperuisse, sic ego sublatis iudici s
amisso regno forensi ludum quasi habere coeperim. 2.
Quid quaeris? me quoque delectat consilium: multi
enim consequor: primum, id quod maxime nunc opus
est, munio me ad haec tempora. Id cuius modi sit
nescio: tantum video, nullius adhuc consilium me hui s
anteponere, nisi forte mori melius fuit: in lectulo, fateor,
sed non accidit: in acie non fui. Ceteri quidem,
Pompeius, Lentulus tuus, Scipio, Afranius foede perierunt
—At Cato praeclare.—Iam istuc quidem, cum volemus
licebit: demus modo operam ne tam necesse nobis sit
quam illi fuit: id quod agimus. 3. Ergo hoc primum.
Sequitur illud: ipse melior fio: primum valetudine,
quam intermissis exercitationibus amiseram: deinde
ipsa illa, si qua fuit in me, facultas orationis, nisi
me ad has exercitationes rettulissem, exaruisset. Extremum illud est, quod tu nescio an primum putes:
plures iam pavones confeci quam tu pullos columbinos.
Tu istic te Hateriano iure delectas, ego me hic Hirtiano

Veni igitur, si vir es, et disce a me προλεγομένας, quas quaeris : etsi sus Minervam. 4. Sed quo modo, videro. Si aestimationes tuas vendere non potes neque ollam- denariorum implere, Romam tibi remigrandum est. Satius est hic cruditate quam istic fame. Video te bona perdidisse : spero item istic familiares tuos. Actum igitur de te est, nisi provides. Potes mulo isto, quem tibi reliquum dicis esse, quoniam cantherium comedisti, Romam pervehi. Sella tibi erit in ludo tamquam hypo- didascalo proxima : eam pulvinus sequetur.

LI. TO ATTICUS (Att. xii. 6)

TUSCULANUM, A.U.C. 708 ; B.C. 46 ; AET. CIC. 60

De negotio Caeliano, de Tyrannionis quodam libro, de Oratore suo, de Caesare, de Atticae valetudine.

1. De Caelio, vide, quaeso, ne quae lacuna sit in auro. Ego ista non novi. Sed certe in collubo est detrimenti satis. Huc aurum si accedit . . . sed quid loquor? Tu videbis. Habes Hegesiae genus, quod Varro laudat. 2. Venio ad Tyrannionem. Ain tu? verum hoc fuit? sine me? At ego quotiens, cum essem otiosus, sine te tamen nolui? Quo modo hoc ergo lues? Uno scilicet, si mihi librum miseris : quod ut facias, etiam atque etiam rogo. Etsi me non magis liber ipse delectabit quam tua admiratio delectavit. Amo enim πάντα φιλειδήμονα, teque istam tam tenuem θεωρίαν tam valde admiratum esse gaudeo. Etsi tua quidem sunt eius modi omnia

Scire enim vis, quo uno animus alitur. Sed, quaeso, quid ex ista acuta et gravi refertur ad τέλος? * * * Sed longa oratio est et tu occupatus es in meo fortasse aliquo negotio. Et pro isto asso sole, quo tu abusus es in nostro pratulo, a te nitidum solem unctumque repetemus. Sed ad prima redeo. Librum, si me amas, mitte. Tuus est enim profecto, quoniam quidem est missus ad te.

3. *Chremes, tantumne ab re tua est oti tibi . . . ,*

ut etiam 'oratorem' legas? Macte virtute! Mihi quidem gratum est et erit gratius, si non modo in libris tuis, sed etiam in aliorum per librarios tuos 'Aristophanem' reposueris pro 'Eupoli.' 4. Caesar autem mihi irridere visus est 'quaeso' illud tuum, quod erat εὐπινές et urbanum. Ita porro te sine cura esse iussit, ut mihi quidem dubitationem omnem tolleret. Atticam doleo tam diu, sed quoniam iam sine horrore est, spero esse ut volumus.

LII. TO PAETUS (Fam. ix. 19)

ROME, A.U.C. 708; B.C. 46; AET. CIC. 60

Quod scripserat L. Paetus tenui apparatu Balbum fuisse contentum, M. Cicero ita iocatur, quasi ille accusationem incontinentiae suae intenderit.

1. Tamen a malitia non discedis? Tenuiculo apparatu significas Balbum fuisse contentum. Hoc videris dicere, cum reges tam sint continentes, multo magis consulares esse oportere. Nescis me ab illo omnia expiscatum; recta enim a porta domum meam venisse: neque hoc admiror,

quod non _suam_ potius, sed illud, quod non _ad suam_. Ego autem tribus primis verbis : ' Quid noster Paetus ?' At ille adiurans, nusquam se umquam libentius.   2. Hoc si verbis adsecutus es, aures ad te adferam non minus elegantes : sin autem opsonio, peto a te, ne pluris esse _balbos_ quam disertos putes.   Me cotidie aliud ex alio impedit.   Sed si me expediero, ut in ista loca venire possim, non committam ut te sero a me certiorem factum putes.

LIII. TO PAETUS (Fam. ix. 20)

ROME, A.U.C. 708 ; B.C. 46 ; AET. CIC. 60

Iocatur M. Cicero cum L. Paeto Epicureum se factum abiecta rei publicae cura lautiusque quam antea excipiendum esse.   Dein vitae suae et studiorum rationes perscribit.

1. Dupliciter delectatus sum tuis litteris, et quod ipse risi et quod te intellexi iam posse ridere.   Me autem a te, ut scurram velitem, malis oneratum esse non moleste tuli.   Illud doleo, in ista loca venire me, ut constitueram, non potuisse . habuisses enim non hospitem, sed contubernalem.   At_quem virum ! non eum, quem tu es solitus promulside conficere.   Integram famem ad ovum adfero : itaque usque ad assum vitulinum opera perducitur.   Illa mea, quae solebas antea laudare, ' O hominem facilem ! o hospitem non gravem !' abierunt. Nos omnem nostram de re publica curam, cogitationem de dicenda in senatu sententia, commentationem causarum abiecimus : in Epicuri nos adversarii nostri castra coniecimus, nec tamen ad hanc insolentiam, sed ad illam tuam

lautitiam, veterem dico, cum in sumptum habebas : etsi
numquam plura praedia habuisti.   2. Proinde te para :
cum homine et edaci tibi res est et qui iam aliquid i1-
tellegat : ὀψιμαθεῖς autem homines scis quam insolentes
sint.   Dediscendae tibi sunt sportellae et artolagani tui.
Nos iam ἐξοχῆς tantum habemus, ut Verrium tuum et
Camillum — qua munditia homines ! qua elegantia ! —
vocare saepius audeamus.   Sed vide audaciam : etiam
Hirtio cenam dedi, sine pavone tamen : in ea cena coquus
meus practer ius fervens nihil non potuit imitari.   3. Haec
igitur est nunc vita nostra : mane salutamus domi et
bonos viros multos, sed tristes, et hos laetos victores, qui
me quidem perofficiose et peramanter observant.   Uli
salutatio defluxit, litteris me involvo, aut scribo aut lego.
Veniunt etiam qui me audiunt quasi doctum hominem,
quia paullo sum quam ipsi doctior.   Inde corpori omne
tempus datur.   Patriam eluxi iam et gravius et diutius
quam ulla mater unicum filium.   Sed cura, si me amas
ut valeas, ne ego te iacente bona tua comedim.   Statu
enim tibi ne aegroto quidem parcere.

LIV. TO PAETUS (Fam. ix. 26)

ROME, A.U.C. 708; B.C. 46; AET. CIC. 60

M. Cicero describit et excusat cenam Volumnii liberiorem
habitam accumbente Cytheride.

1. Accubueram hora nona, cum ad te harum exemplum
in codicillis exaravi. Dices, ubi ? apud Volumnium
Eutrapelum et quidem supra me Atticus, infra

Verrius, familiares tui. Miraris tam exhilaratam esse servitutem nostram? Quid ergo faciam? te consulo, qui philosophum audis. Angar? excruciem me? quid adsequar? Deinde quem ad finem? Vivas, inquis, in litteris. An quidquam me aliud agere censes? aut possem vivere, nisi in litteris viverem? Sed est earum etiam non satietas, sed quidam modus. A quibus cum discessi, etsi minimum mihi est in cena—quod tu unum ζήτημα Dioni philosopho posuisti,—tamen quid potius faciam, prius quam me dormitum conferam, non reperio. 2. Audi reliqua. Infra Eutrapelum Cytheris accubuit. In eo igitur, inquis, convivio Cicero ille,

quem aspectabant, cuius ob os Graii ora obvertebant sua?

Non, mehercule, suspicatus sum illam adfore : sed tamen ne Aristippus quidem ille Socraticus erubuit, cum esset obiectum habere cum Laida : 'Habeo,' inquit, 'non habeor [a Laide].' Graece hoc melius : tu, si voles, interpretabere. Me vero nihil istorum ne iuvenem quidem movit umquam, ne nunc senem. Convivio delector : ibi loquor, quod in solum, ut dicitur, et gemitum in risus maximos transfero. 3. An tu id melius, qui etiam philosophum irriseris? qui cum ille, si quis quid quaereret, dixisset, cenam te quaerere a mane dixeris. Ille baro te putabat quaesiturum, unum caelum esset an innumerabilia. Quid id ad te? At hercule quis 'cena num quid ad te?' tibi praesertim? 4. Sic igitur vivitur : cotidie aliquid legitur aut scribitur : dein, ne amicis nihil tribuamus, epulamur una non modo non contra legem, si ulla nunc lex est, sed etiam intra legem et quidem aliquanto. Qua re nihil est

quod adventum nostrum extimescas.   Non multi cibi
hospitem accipies, sed multi ioci.

LV. TO ATTICUS (Att. xii. 11)

ANTIUM, A.U.C. 709; B.C. 45; AET. CIC. 61

De morte Seii, de Postumia Sulpicii, de Pompeii filia, de aliis
condicionibus.

Male de Seio.   Sed omnia humana tolerabilia ducenda.
Ipsi enim quid sumus aut quam diu haec curaturi sumus ?
Ea videamus, quae ad nos magis pertinent, nec tamen
multo : quid agamus de senatu.   Et, ut ne quid praeter-
mittam, Caesonius ad me litteras misit Postumiam
Sulpicii domum ad se venisse.   De Pompeii Magni fili
tibi rescripsi nihil me hoc tempore cogitare.   Alteram
vero illam, quam tu scribis, puto, nosti.   Nihil vidi
foedius.   Sed adsum.   Coram igitur.

Obsignata epistola accepi tuas.   Atticae hilaritatem
libenter audio : commotiunculis συμπάσχω.

LVI. TO CASSIUS (Fam. xv. 17)

ROME, A.U.C. 709; B.C. 45; AET. CIC. 61

M. Cicero queritur de tabellariis : narrat de P. Sullae morte
de bello Hispaniensi, de Pansae profectione in provinciam : Cassi
consilium probat Brundisinae mansionis : litteras mutuas poscit.

1. Praeposteros habes tabellarios, etsi me quidem non
offendunt.   Sed tamen, cum a me discedunt, flagitant

litteras : cum ad me veniunt, nullas adferunt.   Atque id
ipsum facerent commodius, si mihi aliquid spatii ad scribendum darent, sed petasati veniunt, comites ad portam
exspectare dicunt.   Ergo ignosces : alteras habebis has
breves, sed exspecta πάντα περὶ πάντων.   Etsi quid ego
me tibi purgo, cum tui ad me inanes veniant, ad te cum
epistolis revertantur ?   2. Nos hic—tamen ad te scribam
aliquid—Sullam patrem mortuum habebamus : alii a
latronibus, alii cruditate dicebant : populus non curabat :
combustum enim esse constabat.   Hoc tu pro tua sapientia
feres aequo animo: quamquam πρόσωπον πόλεως amisimus.   Caesarem putabant moleste laturum, verentem ne
hasta refrixisset.   Mindius Marcellus et Attius pigmen-
tarius valde gaudebant se adversarium perdidisse.   3. De
Hispania novi nihil, sed exspectatio valde magna: rumores
tristiores, sed ἀδέσποτοι.   Pansa noster paludatus a. d. III.
Kalend. [Ian.] profectus est, ut quivis intellegere posset
id, quod tu nuper dubitare coepisti, τὸ καλὸν δι' αὐτὸ
αἱρετὸν esse.   Nam quod multos miseriis levavit et quod
se in his malis hominem praebuit, mirabilis eum virorum
bonorum benevolentia prosecuta est.   4. Tu quod adhuc
Brundisii moratus es, valde probo et gaudeo, et mehercule
puto te sapienter facturum, si ἀκενόσπουδος fueris.   Nobis
quidem, qui te amamus, erit gratum.   Et, amabo te, cum
dabis posthac aliquid domum litterarum, mei memineris.
Ego numquam quemquam ad te, cum sciam, sine meis
litteris ire patiar.   Vale.

LVII. TO CASSIUS (Fam. xv. 16)

ROME, A.U.C. 709 ; B.C. 45 ; AET. CIC. 61

M. Cicero ridet opiniones Epicureorum et ipsum Cassium disci-
plinae Epicureae studiosum.

1. Puto te iam suppudere, cum haec tertia iam epistola
ante te oppresserit quam tu scïdam aut litteram. Sed
non urgeo : longiores enim exspectabo vel potius exiga n.
Ego si semper haberem cui darem, vel ternas in hora
darem. Fit enim nescio qui ut quasi coram adesse videa e,
cum scribo aliquid ad te, neque id κατ' εἰδώλων φαντασίι s,
ut dicunt tui amici novi, qui putant etiam διανοητικ ὶς
φαντασίας spectris Catianis excitari. Nam, ne te fugii t,
Catius Insuber, Epicureus, qui nuper est mortuus, quæ ἶ le
Gargettius et iam ante Democritus εἰδωλα, hic spect a
nominat. 2. His autem spectris etiam si oculi posse it
feriri, quod quae velis ipsa incurrunt, animus qui possit e:o
non video. Doceas tu me oportebit, cum salvus veneris,
in meane potestate sit spectrum tuum, ut, simul ac mi ii
collibitum sit de te cogitare, illud incurrat, neque solu n
de te, qui mihi haeres in medullis, sed, si insulam Brita i-
niam coepero cogitare, eius εἴδωλον mihi advolabit ¿d
pectus? 3. Sed haec posterius. Tempto enim te qio
animo accipias. Si enim stomachabere et moleste fere ,
plura dicemus postulabimusque, ex qua αἱρέσει VI HOMI-
NIBUS ARMATIS deiectus sis, in eam restituare. In h c
interdicto non solet addi IN HOC ANNO. Qua re si iaa
biennium aut triennium est, cum virtuti nuntium remisis i
delenitus illecebris voluptatis, in integro res nobis eri .

Quamquam quicum loquor? cum uno fortissimo viro, qui, postea quam forum attigisti, nihil fecisti nisi plenissimum amplissimae dignitatis. In ista ipsa αἱρέσει metuo ne plus nervorum sit quam ego putarim, si modo eam tu probas. Qui id tibi in mentem venit? inquies. Quia nihil habebam aliud quod scriberem. De re publica enim nihil scribere possum : nec enim quod sentio libet scribere.

LVIII. TO ATTICUS (ATT. XII. 12)

ASTURA, A.U.C. 709 ; B.C. 45 ; AET. CIC. 61

De dote, de Balbi condicione, de loco fani Tulliae aedificandi et aliis rebus privatis.

1. De dote, tanto magis perpurga. Balbi regia condicio est delegandi. Quoquo modo confice. Turpe est rem impeditam iacere. Insula Arpinas habere potest germanam ἀποθέωσιν, sed vereor ne minorem τιμὴν habere videatur ἐκτοπισμός. Est igitur animus in hortis : quos tamen inspiciam, cum venero. 2. De Epicuro, ut voles, etsi μεθαρμόσομαι in posterum genus hoc personarum. Incredibile est quam ea quidam requirant. Ad antiquos igitur : ἀνεμέσητον γάρ. Nihil habeo ad te quod perscribam, sed tamen institui cotidie mittere, ut eliciam tuas litteras, non quo aliquid ex his exspectem, sed nescio quo modo tamen exspecto. Qua re sive habes quid sive nil habes, scribe tamen aliquid teque cura.

LIX. TO ATTICUS (Att. xii. 32)

ASTURA, A.U.C. 709 ; B.C. 45 ; AET. CIC. 61

De Publilia, quae cum matre sua ad se venire velit, retinenda, d₃ sumptibus Ciceronis sui moderandis.

1. Publilia ad me scripsit, matrem suam, cum Publilio videretur, ad me cum illo venturam et se una, si ego paterer : orat multis et supplicibus verbis, ut liceat et u₃ sibi rescribam. Res quam molesta sit vides. Rescripsi mi etiam gravius esse quam tum, cum illi dixissen me solum esse velle, qua re nolle me hoc tempore ean ad me venire. Putabam, si nihil rescripsissem, illam cum matre venturam : nunc non puto. Apparebat enim illas litteras non illius esse. Illud autem, quod fore video, ipsum volo vitare, ne illi ad me veniant. Et una est vitatio ut ego avolem. Nollem, sed necesse est. Te hoc nunc rogo ut explores ad quam diem hic ita possim esse, ut ne opprimar. Ages, ut scribis, temperate. 2. Ciceroni velim hoc proponas, ita tamen, si tibi non iniquum videbitur, ut sumptus huius peregrinationis, quibus, si Romae esset domumque conduceret, quod facere cogitabat, facile contentus futurus erat, accommodet ad mercedes Argileti et Aventini, et cum ei proposueris, ipse velim reliqua moderere, quem ad modum ex iis mercedibus suppeditemus ei, quod opus sit. Praestabo nec Bibulum nec Acidinum nec Messallam, quos Athenis futuros audio, maiores sumptus facturos quam quod ex eis mercedibus recipietur. Itaque velim videas, primum, conductores qui sint et quanti, deinde, ut sint qui ad diem solvant, et,

quid viatici, quid instrumenti satis sit. Iumento certe
Athenis nihil opus est. Quibus autem in via utatur,
domi sunt plura quam opus erat, quod etiam tu animadvertes.

LX. SERVIUS SULPICIUS TO CICERO
(FAM. IV. 5)

ATHENS, A.U.C. 709 ; B.C. 45 ; AET. CIC. 61

Ser. Sulpicius Achaiae praefectus consolatur M. Ciceronem adflictum obitu filiae ex partu menso Febr. mortuae.

1. Postea quam mihi renuntiatum est de obitu Tulliae,
filiae tuae, sane quam pro eo ac debui graviter molesteque tuli communemque eam calamitatem existimavi,
qui, si istic adfuissem, neque tibi defuissem coramque
meum dolorem tibi declarassem. Etsi genus hoc consolationis miserum atque acerbum est, propterea quia, per
quos ea conferi debet propinquos ac familiares, ii ipsi
pari molestia adficiuntur neque sine lacrimis multis id
conari possunt, uti magis ipsi videantur aliorum conso-
latione indigere quam aliis posse suum officium praestare,
tamen quae in praesentia in mentem mihi venerunt,
decrevi brevi ad te perscribere, non quo ea te fugere
existimem, sed quod forsitan dolore impeditus minus ea
perspicias. 2. Quid est quod tanto opere te commoveat
tuus dolor intestinus? Cogita quem ad modum adhuc
fortuna nobiscum egerit: ea nobis erepta esse, quae
hominibus non minus quam liberi cara esse debent,
patriam, honestatem, dignitatem, honores omnes. Hoc

uno incommodo addito quid ad dolorem adiungi potuit?
aut qui non in illis rebus exercitatus animus callere iam
debet atque omnia minoris existimare? 3. An illius
vicem, cedo, doles? Quotiens in eam cogitationem
necesse est et tu veneris (et nos saepe incidimus), hisce
temporibus non pessime cum iis esse actum, quibus si ie
dolore licitum est mortem cum vita commutare? Quid
autem fuit quod illam hoc tempore ad vivendum magno
opere invitare posset? quae res? quae spes? quod animi
solacium? Ut cum aliquo adolescente primario con-
iuncta aetatem gereret? Licitum est tibi, credo, pro tua
dignitate ex hac iuventute generum deligere cuius fidei
liberos tuos te tuto committere putares! An ut ea liberos ex sese pareret, quos cum florentes videret, laetaretur?
qui rem a parente traditam per se tenere possent, honores
ordinatim petituri essent, in re publica, in amicorum
negotiis libertate sua usuri? Quid horum fuit quod non
prius, quam datum est, ademptum sit? At vero malum
est liberos amittere. Malum: nisi hoc peius est, haec
sufferre et perpeti. 4. Quae res mihi non mediocrem
consolationem attulit, volo tibi commemorare, si forte
eadem res tibi dolorem minuere possit. Ex Asia rediens
cum ab Aegina Megaram versus navigarem, coepi
regiones circumcirca prospicere. Post me erat Aegina,
ante me Megara, dextra Piraeeus, sinistra Corinthus:
quae oppida quodam tempore florentissima fuerunt, nunc
prostrata et diruta ante oculos iacent. Coepi egomet
mecum sic cogitare: 'Hem! nos homunculi indignamur,
si quis nostrum interiit aut occisus est, quorum vita
brevior esse debet, cum uno loco tot oppidûm cadavera

proiecta iacent? Visne tu te, Servi, cohibere et memi-
nisse hominem te esse natum?' Credo mihi, cogitatione
ea non mediocriter sum confirmatus. Hoc idem, si tibi
videtur, fac ante oculos tibi proponas. Modo uno
tempore tot viri clarissimi interierunt: de imperio
populi Romani tanta deminutio facta est: omnes provinciae conquassatae sunt: in unius mulierculae animula
si iactura facta est, tanto opere commoveris? quae si hoc
tempore non diem suum obisset, paucis post annis tamen
ei moriendum fuit, quoniam homo nata fuerat. 5.
Etiam tu ab hisce rebus animum ac cogitationem tuam
avoca atque ea potius reminiscere, quae digna tua persona sunt: illam, quam diu ei opus fuerit, vixisse: una
cum re publica fuisse: te, patrem suum, praetorem,
consulem, augurem vidisse: adolescentibus primariis
nuptam fuisse: omnibus bonis prope perfunctam esse:
cum res publica occideret, vita excessisse. Quid est
quod tu aut illa cum fortuna hoc nomine queri possitis?
Denique noli te oblivisci Ciceronem esse et eum, qui aliis
consueris praecipere et dare consilium, neque imitari
malos medicos, qui in alienis morbis profitentur tenere se
medicinae scientiam, ipsi se curare non possunt, sed
potius, quae aliis tute praecipere soles, ea tute tibi
subiice atque apud animum propone. 6. Nullus dolor
est quem non longinquitas temporis minuat ac molliat.
Hoc te exspectare tempus tibi turpe est ac non ei rei
sapientia tua te occurrere. Quod si qui etiam inferis
sensus est, qui illius in te amor fuit pietasque in omnes
suos, hoc certe illa te facere non vult. Da hoc illi
mortuae: da ceteris amicis ac familiaribus, qui tuo

dolore macrent : da patriae ut, si qua in re opus sit,
opera et consilio tuo uti possit. Denique, quoniam in
eam fortunam devenimus, ut etiam huic rei nobis serviendum sit, noli committere ut quisquam te putet non
tam filiam quam rei publicae tempora et aliorum victoriam lugere. Plura me ad te de hac re scribere pudet,
ne videar prudentiae tuae diffidere : qua re, si hoc unum
proposuero, finem faciam scribendi. Vidimus aliquotiens
secundam pulcherrime te ferre fortunam magnamque ex
ea re te laudem apisci : fac aliquando intellegamus ad-
versam quoque te aeque ferre posse neque id maius,
quam debeat, tibi onus videri, ne ex omnibus virtutibus
haec una tibi videatur deesse. Quod ad me attinet,
cum te tranquilliore animo esse cognoro, de iis rebus,
quae hic geruntur, quemadmodumque se provincia habet,
certiorem faciam. Vale.

LXI. CICERO TO SERVIUS SULPICIUS
(Fam. iv. 6)

ASTURA, A.U.C. 709 ; B.C. 45 ; AET. CIC. 61

Ser. Sulpicii superioribus litteris respondet, quas ait sibi magno
solacio fuisse : quam ob rem quamquam nemini quam sibi iustiores
dolendi causas fuisse dicit, maximam tamen sibi sperat leva-
tionem reditu et Servii consuetudine fore.

1. Ego vero, Servi, vellem, ut scribis, in meo gravis-
simo casu adfuisses. Quantum enim praesens me
adiuvare potueris et consolando et prope aeque dolendo
facile ex eo intellego, quod litteris lectis aliquantum

was co...d
acquievi. Nam et ea scripsisti, quae levare luctum
possent, et in me consolando non mediocrem ipse animi
dolorem adhibuisti. Servius tamen tuus omnibus officiis,
quae illi tempori tribui potuerunt, declaravit et quanti
ipse me faceret et quam suum talem erga me animum
tibi gratum putaret fore : cuius officia iucundiora scilicet
saepe mihi fuerunt, numquam tamen gratiora. Me autem
non oratio tua solum et societas paene aegritudinis, sed
etiam auctoritas consolatur. Turpe enim esse existimo
me non ita ferre casum meum, ut tu, tali sapientia prae-
ditus, ferendum putas. Sed opprimor interdum et vix
resisto dolori, quod ea me solacia deficiunt, quae ceteris,
quorum mihi exempla propono, simili in fortuna non
defuerunt. Nam et Q. Maximus, qui filium consularem,
clarum virum et magnis rebus gestis, amisit, et L.
Paullus, qui duo septem diebus, et vester Gallus et M.
Cato, qui summo ingenio, summa virtute filium perdidit,
iis temporibus fuerunt, ut eorum luctum ipsorum dignitas
consolaretur ea, quam ex re publica consequebantur.
2. Mihi autem, amissis ornamentis iis, quae ipse com-
memoras quaeque eram maximis laboribus adeptus,
unum manebat illud solacium, quod ereptum est. Non
amicorum negotiis, non rei publicae procuratione im-
pediebantur cogitationes meae : nihil in foro agere libe-
bat : aspicere curiam non poteram : existimabam, id quod
erat, omnes me et industriae meae fructus et fortunae
perdidisse. Sed cum cogitarem haec mihi tecum et cum
quibusdam esse communia, et cum frangerem iam ipse
me cogeremque illa ferre toleranter, habebam quo confugerem, ubi conquiescerem, cuius in sermone et suavitate

omnes curas doloresque deponerem. Nunc autem hoc tam gravi vulnere etiam illa, quae consanuisse videbantur, recrudescunt. Non enim, ut tum me a re publica maestum domus excipiebat quae levaret, sic nunc domo maerens ad rem publicam confugere possum, ut in eius bonis acquiescam. Itaque et domo absum et foro, quod nec eum dolorem, quem a re publica capio, domus iam consolari potest nec domesticum res publica. 3. Quo magis te exspecto teque videre quam primum cupio. Maius solacium afferre ratio nulla potest quam coniunctio consuetudinis sermonumque nostrorum : quamquam sperabam tuum adventum—sic enim audiebam—appropinquare. Ego autem cum multis de causis te exopto quam primum videre tum etiam, ut ante commentemur inter nos qua ratione nobis traducendum sit hoc tempus, quod est totum ad unius voluntatem accommodandum et prudentis et liberalis et, ut perspexisse videor, nec a me alieni et tibi amicissimi. Quod cum ita sit, magnae tamen est deliberationis quae ratio sit ineunda nobis, non agendi aliquid, sed illius concessu et beneficio quiescendi. Vale.

LXII. TO ATTICUS (ATT. XII. 45)

TUSCULANUM, A.U.C. 709; B.C. 45; AET. CIC. 61

De scriptis suis in Antiati confectis, de litterarum inter se commercio, de ἀκηδίᾳ Attici, de commoratione in Tusculano, de Caesare vicino, de Hirtii libro pervulgando.

1. Ego hic duo magna συντάγματα absolvi: nullo

enim alio modo a miseria quasi aberrare possum. Tu
mihi, etiam si nihil erit quod scribas, quod fore ita video,
tamen id ipsum scribas velim, te nihil habuisse quod
scriberes, dum modo ne his verbis. 2. De Attica,
optime. 'Ακηδία tua me movet, etsi scribis nihil esse.
In Tusculano eo commodius ero, quod et crebrius tuas
litteras accipiam et te ipsum non numquam videbo.
Nam ceteroqui ἀνεκτότερα erant Asturae : nunc haec,
quae refricant, hic me magis angunt. Etsi tamen, ubi-
cumque sum, illa sunt mecum. 3. De Caesare vicino
scripseram ad te, quia cognoram ex tuis litteris. Eum
σύνναον Quirini malo quam Salutis. Tu vero pervulga
Hirtium. Id enim ipsum putaram quod scribis, ut, cum
ingenium amici nostri probaretur, ὑπόθεσις vituperandi
Catonis irrideretur.

LXIII. TO FADIUS GALLUS (Fam. vii. 24)

TUSCULANUM, A.U.C. 709 ; B.C. 45 ; AET. CIC. 61

**Exponit M. Cicero M. Fadio Gallo, quam iniuste sibi Tigellius
iratus sit.**

1. Amoris quidem tui, quoquo me verti, vestigia : vel
proxime de Tigellio. Sensi enim ex litteris tuis valde te
laborasse. Amo igitur voluntatem. Sed pauca de re.
Cipius, opinor, olim : 'Non omnibus dormio': sic ego
non omnibus, mi Galle, servio. Etsi quae est haec servi-
tus? Olim, cum regnare existimabamur, non tam ab
ullis quam hoc tempore observor a familiarissimis Caesaris
omnibus praeter istum. Id ego in lucris pono, non ferre

hominem pestilentiorem patria sua, cumque addictum iam
tum puto esse Calvi Licinii Hipponacteo praeconio.   2.
At vide quid suscenseat.   Phameae causam receperam
ipsius quidem causa : erat enim mihi sane familiaris.   Is
ad me venit dixitque iudicem sibi operam dare constituisse
eo ipso die, quo de P. Sestio in consilium iri necesse erat.
Respondi nullo modo me facere posse : quem vellet alium
diem si sumpsisset, me ei non defuturum.   Ille autem,
qui sciret se nepotem bellum tibicinem habere et sit
bonum unctorem, discessit a me, ut mihi videbatu·,
iratior.   Habes Sardos venales, alium alio nequioren.
Cognosti meam causam et istius salaconis iniquitaten.
Catonem tuum mihi mitte : cupio enim legere.   Me adhuc
non legisse turpe utrique nostrum est.

LXIV. TO FADIUS GALLUS (Fam. vii. 25)

TUSCULANUM, A.U.C. 709 ; B.C. 45 ; AET. CIC. 61

M. Cicero M. Fadio epistolam conscissam non esse nuntiat : mo
nitus, ne incautius de Caesare loquatur, gratias agit, hortaturque,
ut stilum exercere pergat Fadius.

1. Quod epistolam conscissam doles, noli laborare :
salva est : domo petes, cum libebit.   Quod autem me
mones, valde gratum est, idque ut semper facias rogo.
Videris enim mihi vereri ne, si istum * habuerimus,
rideamus γέλωτα σαρδόνιον.   Sed heus tu, manum de
tabula : magister adest citius quam putaramus.   Vereor
ne in catonium Catoninos.   2. Mi Galle, cave putes
quidquam melius quam epistolae tuae partem ab eo loco :

'cetera labuntur.' Secreto hoc audi : tecum habeto, ne Apellae quidem, liberto tuo, dixeris. Praeter duo nos loquitur isto modo nemo : bene malene videro, sed quidquid est, nostrum est. Urge igitur, nec transversum unguem, quod aiunt, a stilo : is enim est dicendi opifex. Atque equidem aliquantum iam etiam noctis adsumo.

LXV. CURIUS TO CICERO (Fam. vii. 29)

PATRAE, A.U.C. 709 ; B.C. 45 ; AET. CIC. 61

M'. Curius M. Ciceronem laudatis eius erga se beneficiis rogat, ut Ser. Sulpicii se successori commendet.

1. S. V. B. Sum enim χρήσει μὲν tuus, κτήσει δὲ Attici nostri : ergo fructus est tuus, mancipium illius : quod quidem si inter senes coëmptionales venale proscripserit, egerit non multum. At illa nostra praedicatio quanti est, nos, quod simus, quod habeamus, quod homines existimemur, id omne abs te habere ! Qua re, Cicero mi, persevera constanter nos conservare et Sulpicii successori nos de meliore nota commenda, quo facilius tuis praeceptis obtemperare possimus teque ad ver lubentes videre et nostra refigere deportareque tuto possimus. 2. Sed, amice magne, noli hanc epistolam Attico ostendere : siue eum errare et putare me virum bonum esse nec solere duo parietes de eadem fidelia dealbare. Ergo, patrone mi, bene vale Tironemque meum saluta nostris verbis. Dat. a. d. iiii. Kal. Novembr.

LXVI. TO ATTICUS (Att. xiii. 52)

PUTEOLANUM, A.U.C. 709 ; B.C. 45 ; AET. CIC. 61

De Caesaris adventu et quem ad modum se gesserit exponitur.

1. O hospitem mihi gravem, tamen ἀμεταμέλητον: fuit enim periucunde. Sed cum secundis Saturnalibus ad Philippum vesperi venisset, villa ita completa a militibus est, ut vix triclinium ubi cenaturus ipse Caesar esset vacaret : quippe hominum CIↃ CIↃ. Sane sum commotus quid futurum esset postridie, ac mihi Barba Cassius subvenit : custodes dedit. Castra in agro : villa defensa est. Ille tertiis Saturnalibus apud Philippum ad horam VII., nec quemquam admisit : rationes opinor cum Balbo. Inde ambulavit in littore. Post horam VIII. in balneum : tum audivit de Mamurra : vultum non mutavit. Unctus est, accubuit, ἐμετικὴν agebat. Itaque et edit et bibit ἀδεῶς et iucunde : opipare sane et apparate, nec id solum, sed

> ' bene cocto
> Condito, sermone bono, et, si quaeri', libenter.'

2. Praeterea tribus tricliniis accepti οἱ περὶ αὐτὸν valde copiose. Libertis minus lautis servisque nihil defuit. Nam lautiores eleganter accepti. Quid multa? homines visi sumus. Hospes tamen non is, cui diceres : Amabo te, eodem ad me, cum revertere. Semel satis est. Σπουδαῖον οὐδὲν in sermone : φιλόλογα multa. Quid quaeris? Delectatus est et libenter fuit. Puteolis se aiebat unum diem fore, alterum ad Baias. Habes

hospitium sive ἐπισταθμείαν odiosam mihi, dixi, non molestam. Ego paullisper hic, deinde in Tusculanum. Dolabellae villam cum praeteriret, omnis armatorum copia dextra sinistra ad ecum nec usquam alibi. Hoc ex Nicia.

LXVII. TO CURIUS (Fam. vii. 30)

ROME, A.U.C. 710 ; B.C. 44 ; AET. CIC. 62

Cicero Curio scribit quam misere se res publica habeat molesteque fert, quod C. Caesar Caninium ad aliquot horas consulem creaverit: tum de litteris commendaticiis ad Acilium missis significat.

1. Ego vero iam te nec hortor nec rogo, ut domum redeas : quin hinc ipse evolare cupio et aliquo pervenire, *ubi nec Pelopidarum nomen nec facta audiam.* Incredibile est quam turpiter mihi facere videar, qui his rebus intersim. Ne tu videris multo ante providisse quid impenderet tum, cum hinc profugisti. Quamquam haec etiam auditu acerba sunt, tamen audire tolerabilius est quam videre. In campo certe non fuisti, cum II. II. comitiis quaestoriis institutis sella Q. Maximi, quem illi consulem esse dicebant, posita esset, quo mortuo nuntiato sella sublata est. Ille autem, qui comitiis tributis esset auspicatus, centuriata habuit : consulem H. vii. renuntiavit, qui usque ad Kalendas Ian. esset, quae erant futurae mane postridie. Ita Caninio consule scito neminem prandisse. Nihil tamen eo consule mali factum est : fuit enim mirifica vigilantia, qui suo toto consulatu somnum non viderit. 2. Haec tibi ridicula

videntur—non enim ades,—quae si videres, lacrimas non
teneres.   Quid, si cetera scribam?   Sunt enim innumerabilia generis eiusdem, quae quidem ego non ferrem, nisi
me in philosophiae portum contulissem et nisi haberen
socium studiorum meorum Atticum nostrum: cuius
quoniam proprium te esse scribis mancipio et nexo, meum
autem usu et fructu, contentus isto sum.   Id enim est
cuiusque proprium, quo quisque fruitur atque utitur.
Sed haec alias pluribus. 3. Acilius, qui in Graeciam cum
legionibus missus est, maximo meo beneficio est: bis
enim est a me iudicio capitis rebus salvis defensus et est
homo non ingratus meque vehementer observat.   Ad eum
de te diligentissime scripsi eamque epistolam cum ha;
epistola coniunxi, quam ille quo modo acceperit et quid
tibi pollicitus sit velim ad me scribas.

LXVIII. TO TIRO (Fam. xvi. 18)

A.U.C. 710; B.C. 44; AET. CIC. 62

M. Cicero de rebus domesticis scribit ad Tironem eumque
maximo opere hortatur, ut valetudini operam det.

TULLIUS TIRONI SAL.

1. Quid igitur? non sic oportet?   Equidem censeo
sic: addendum etiam 'suo.'   Sed, si placet, invidia
vitetur: quam quidem ego saepe contempsi.   Tibi
διαφόρησιν gaudeo profuisse.   Si vero etiam Tusculanum,
dei boni! quanto mihi illud erit amabilius!   Sed, si me
amas, quod quidem aut facis aut perbelle simulas, quod
tamen in modum procedit, sed utut est, indulge valetu-

dini tuae, cui quidem tu adhuc, dum mihi deservis, ser-
visti non satis. Ea quid postulet non ignoras : πέψιν,
ἀκοπίαν, περίπατον σύμμετρον, τέρψιν, εὐλυσίαν κοιλίας.
Fac bellus revertare : non modo te, sed etiam Tusculanum
nostrum plus amem. 2. Parhedrum excita, ut hortum
ipse conducat : sic holitorem ipsum commovebis. Helico
nequissimus HS cɪɔ. dabat, nullo aprico horto, nullo
emissario, nulla maceria, nulla casa. Iste nos tanta
impensa derideat? Calface hominem, ut ego Mothonem ;
itaque ut ab utro coronas. 3. De Crabra quid agatur, etsi
nunc quidem etiam nimium est aquae, tamen velim scire.
Horologium mittam et libros, si erit sudum. Sed tu
nullosne tecum libellos? an pangis aliquid Sophocleum?
Fac opus appareat. A. Ligurius, Caesaris familiaris,
mortuus est, bonus homo et nobis amicus. Te quando
exspectemus fac ut sciam. Cura te diligenter. Vale.

LXIX. TO ATTICUS (ATT. XIV. 5)

ASTURA, A.U.C. 710 ; B.C. 44 ; AET. CIC. 62

De valetudine Attici, de rebus publicis non bonis.

1. Spero tibi iam esse ut volumus, quoniam quidem
ἠσίτησας, cum leviter commotus esses, sed tamen velim
scire quid agas. Signa bella, quod Calvena moleste fert
suspectum esse se Bruto. Illa signa non bona, si cum
signis legiones veniunt e Gallia. Quid tu illas putas,
quae fuerunt in Hispania, nonne idem postulaturas?
quid, quas Annius transportavit? C. Asinium volui,
sed μνημονικὸν ἁμάρτημα. Ab alcatore φυρμὸς πολύς.

Nam ista quidem Caesaris libertorum coniuratio facile
opprimeretur, si recte saperet Antonius.   2. En ! meam
stultam verecundiam, qui legari noluerim, ante res prolatas, ne deserere viderer hunc rerum tumorem, cui certe
si possem mederi, deesse non deberem.   Sed vides magistratus, si quidem illi magistratus : vides tamen tyranni
satellites in imperiis, vides eiusdem exercitus, vides in
latere veteranos, quae sunt εὐρίπιστα omnia : eos autem,
qui orbis terrae custodes non modo saepti, verum etiam
ἅγιοι esse debebant, tantum modo laudari atque amari,
sed parietibus contineri.   Atque illi quoquo modo beati,
civitas misera.   3. Sed velim scire quid adventus
Octavii, num qui concursus ad eum, num quae νεωτερι-
μοῦ suspicio.   Non puto equidem, sed tamen quidquid
est scire cupio.   Haec scripsi ad te proficiscens Astura
III. Idus.

LXX. TO TIRO (FAM. XVI. 23)

PUTEOLANUM, A.U.C. 710 ; B.C. 44 ; AET. CIC. 62

M. Cicero quum de aliis quibusdam rebus tum de conservandi
Antonii amicitia agit cum Tirone.

1. Tu vero confice professionem, si potes : etsi haec
pecunia ex eo genere est, ut professione non egeat.   Verum
tamen . . . Balbus ad me scripsit tanta se ἐπιφορᾷ
oppressum, ut loqui non posset.   Antonius de lege en ! quid
egerit.   Liceat modo rusticari !   Ad Bithynicum scripsi
2. De Servilio tu videris, qui senectutem non contemnis.
Etsi Atticus noster, quia quondam me commoveri πανικοῖς

intellexit, idem semper putat nec videt quibus praesidiis
philosophiae saeptus sim, et hercle, quod timidus ipse est,
θορυβοποιεῖ. Ego tamen Antonii inveteratam sine ulla
offensione amicitiam retinere sane volo scribamque ad
eum, sed non ante quam te videro. Nec tamen te avoco
a syngrapha : γόνυ κνήμης. Cras exspecto Leptam, ad
cuius rutam puleio mihi tui sermonis utendum est.   Vale.

LXXI. TO ATTICUS (ATT. XIV. 10)

PUTEOLANUM, A.U.C. 710 ; B.C. 44 ; AET. CIC. 62

Queritur de rebus post Caesaris caedem factis et adseculis
Caesaris dominantibus, de adventu Octavii Neapolim, de rebus
privatis ac domesticis, de Q. patris litteris de filio.

1. Itane vero? Hoc meus et tuus Brutus egit ut
Lanuvii esset? ut Trebonius itineribus deviis proficisceretur in provinciam? ut omnia facta, scripta, dicta,
promissa, cogitata Caesaris plus valerent quam si ipse
viveret? Meministine me clamare illo ipso primo Capito-
lino die senatum in Capitolium a praetoribus oportere
vocari? Di immortales! quae tum opera effici potuerunt
laetantibus omnibus bonis, etiam sat bonis, fractis latronibus! Liberalia tu accusas. Quid fieri tum potuit? iam
pridem perieramus. Meministine te clamare causam
perisse, si funere elatus esset? At ille etiam in foro
combustus laudatusque miserabiliter serviquo et egentes
in tecta nostra cum facibus immissi. Quae deinde? ut
audeant dicere, 'tune contra Caesaris nutum?' Haec et
alia ferre non possum. Itaque γῆν πρὸ γῆς cogito. Tua

tamen ὑπηνέμιος.   2. Nausea iamne plane abiit ? Mihi
quidem ex tuis litteris coniectanti ita videbatur.   Redeo
ad Tebassos, Scaevas, Frangones.   Hos tu existimas con-
fidere se illa habituros stantibus nobis ? in quibus plus
virtutis putarunt quam experti sunt.   Pacis isti scilicet
amatores et non latrocinii auctores ?   At ego cum tibi de
Curtilio scripsi Sextilianoque fundo, scripsi de Censorino,
de Messalla, de Planco, de Postumo, de genere toto.
Melius fuit perisse illo interfecto (quod numquam accidisset) quam haec videre.   3. Octavius Neapolim venit XIIII
Kal.   Ibi eum Balbus mane postridie, eodemque die mecum
in Cumano, illum hereditatem aditurum ; sed, ut scribis,
† ῥιξόθεμιν † magnam cum Antonio.   Buthrotia mihi tua
res est, ut debet, eritque curae.   Quod quaeris iamne ad
centena Cluvianum : adventare videtur : scilicet primo
anno LXXX. detersimus.   4. Q. pater ad me gravia de
filio, maxime quod matri nunc indulgeat, cui antea bene
merenti fuerit inimicus.   Ardentes in eum litteras ad me
misit.   Ille autem quid agat si scis nequedum Roma es
profectus, scribas ad me velim, et hercule, si quid aliud.
Vehementer delector tuis litteris.

LXXII. TO ATTICUS (ATT. XIV. 18)

POMPEIANUM, A.U.C. 710 ; B.C. 44 ; AET. CIC. 62.

De Dolabella, de nominibus Albiano et Patulciano, de Montano,
de Servio, de Bruto causaque rei publicae.

1. Saepius me iam agitas, quod rem gestam Dolabellae nimis in caelum videar efferre.   Ego autem, quam-

quam sane probo factum, tamen, ut tanto opere laudarem, adductus sum tuis et unis et alteris litteris. Sed totum se a te abalienavit Dolabella eadem causa, qua me quoque sibi inimicissimum reddidit. O hominem pudentem! Kal. Ian. debuit: adhuc non solvit, praesertim cum se maximo aere alieno Faberii manu liberarit et opem ab Ope petierit. Licet enim iocari, ne me valde conturbatum putes. Atque ego ad eum IIX. Idus litteras dederam bene mane, eodem autem die tuas litteras vesperi acceperam in Pompeiano, sane celeriter, tertio abs te die. Sed, ut ad te eo ipso die scripseram, satis aculeatas ad Dolabellam litteras dedi, quae si nihil profecerint, puto fore ut me praesentem non sustineat. 2. Albianum te confecisse arbitror. De Patulciano nomine, quod mihi suppetiatus es, gratissimum est et simile tuorum omnium. Sed ego Erotem ad ista expedienda factum mihi videbar reliquisse, cuius non sine magna culpa vacillarunt. Sed cum ipso videro. 3. De Montano, ut saepe ad te scripsi, erit tibi tota res curae. Servius proficiscens, quod desperanter tecum locutus est, minime miror, neque ei quidquam in desperatione concedo. 4. Brutus noster, singularis vir, si in senatum non est Kal. Iuniis venturus, quid facturus sit in foro nescio. Sed hoc ipse melius. Ego ex iis, quae parari video, non multum Idibus Martiis profectum iudico. Itaque de Graecia cotidie magis et magis cogito. Nec enim Bruto meo exsilium, ut scribit ipse, meditanti video quid prodesse possim. Leonidae me litterae non satis delectarunt. De Herode tibi adsentior. Saufeii legisse vellem. Ego ex Pompeiano VI. Idus Mai. cogitabam.

ROME, A.U.C. 710 ; B.C. 44 ; AET. CIC. 62

Matius respondet superiori Ciceronis epistolae et purgare se studet propter iniquorum iudicium.

1. Magnam voluptatem ex tuis litteris cepi, quod quam speraram atque optaram habere te de me opinionem cognovi. De qua etsi non dubitabam, tamen, quia maximi aestimabam, ut incorrupta maneret laborabam. Conscius autem mihi eram nihil a me commissum esse quod boni cuiusquam offenderet animum. Eo minus credebam plurimis atque optimis artibus ornato tibi temere quidquam persuaderi potuisse, praesertim in quem mea propensa et perpetua fuisset atque esset benevolentia. Quod quoniam ut volui scio esse, respondebo criminibus, quibus tu pro me, ut par erat tua singulari bonitate et amicitia nostra, saepe restitisti. 2. Nota enim mihi sunt quae in me post Caesaris mortem contulerint. Vitio mihi dant, quod mortem hominis necessarii graviter fero atque eum, quem dilexi, perisse indignor. Aiunt enim patriam amicitiae, non patriae amicitiam praeponendam esse, proinde ac si iam vicerint obitum eius rei publicae fuisse utilem. Sed non agam astute. Fateor me ad istum gradum sapientiae non pervenisse. Neque enim Caesarem in dissensione civili sum secutus, sed amicum, quamquam re offendebar, tamen non deserui : neque bellum umquam civile aut etiam causam dissensionis probavi, quam etiam nascentem exstingui summe studui. Itaque in victoria hominis necessarii

neque honoris neque pecuniae dulcedine sum captus:
quibus praemiis reliqui, minus apud eum quam ego eum
possent, immoderate sunt abusi. Atque etiam res
familiaris mea lege Caesaris deminuta est, cuius beneficio
plerique, qui Caesaris morte laetantur, remanserunt in
civitate. Civibus victis ut parceretur aeque ac pro mea
salute laboravi. 3. Possum igitur, qui omnes voluerim
incolumes, eum, a quo id impetratum est, perisse non
indignari ? cum praesertim iidem homines illi et invidiae
et exitio fuerint ? Plecteris ergo, inquiunt, quoniam
factum nostrum improbare audes. O superbiam inaudi-
tam, alios in facinore gloriari, aliis ne dolere quidem
impunite licere ! At haec etiam servis semper libera
fuerunt, ut timerent, gauderent, dolerent suo potius
quam alterius arbitrio : quae nunc, ut quidem isti
dictitant libertatis auctores, metu nobis extorquere con-
antur. Sed nihil agunt. 4. Nullius umquam periculi
terroribus ab officio aut ab humanitate desciscam ; numquam enim honestam mortem fugiendam, saepe etiam
oppetendam putavi. Sed quid mihi suscensent, si id
opto, ut paeniteat eos sui facti ? Cupio enim Caesaris
mortem omnibus esse acerbam. At debeo pro civili parte
rem publicam velle salvam. Id quidem me cupere, nisi
et ante acta vita et reliqua mea spes tacente me probat,
dicendo vincere non postulo. 5. Qua re maiorem in
modum te rogo, ut rem potiorem oratione ducas, mihique,
si sentis expedire recte fieri, credas nullam communionem
cum improbis esse posse. An, quod adolescens praestiti,
cum etiam errare cum excusatione possem, id nunc aetate
praecipitata commutem ac me ipse retexam ? Non

faciam, neque quod displiceat committam praeterquam
quod hominis mihi coniunctissimi ac viri amplissimi
doleo gravem casum.   Quod si aliter essem animatus,
numquam quod facerem negarem, ne et in peccando im-
probus et in dissimulando timidus ac vanus existimarer.
6. At ludos, quos Caesaris victoriae Caesar adolescens
fecit, curavi.   At id ad privatum officium, non ad statum
rei publicae pertinet.   Quod tamen munus et homiris
amicissimi memoriae atque honoribus praestare etiam
mortui debui et optimae spei adolescenti ac dignissimo
Caesare petenti negare non potui.   7. Veni etiam consulis Antonii domum saepe salutandi causa: ad quem
qui me parum patriae amantem esse existimant rogandi
quidem aliquid aut auferendi causa frequentes ventitare
reperies.   Sed quae haec est adrogantia, quod Caesar
numquam interpellavit quin quibus vellem, atque etiarı
quos ipse non diligebat, tamen iis uterer, eos, qui mihi
amicum eripuerunt, carpendo me efficere conari, ne quos
velim diligam?   8. Sed non vereor ne aut meae vitae
modestia parum valitura sit in posterum contra falsos
rumores aut ne etiam ii, qui me non amant propter meam
in Caesarem constantiam, non malint mei quam sui
similes amicos habere.   Mihi quidem si optata con-
tingent, quod reliquum est vitae, in otio Rhodi degam:
sin casus aliquis interpellarit, ita ero Romae, ut recte
fieri semper cupiam.   Trebatio nostro magnas ago
gratias, quod tuum erga me animum simplicem atque
amicum aperuit, et quod cum, quem semper lubenter
dilexi, quo magis iure colere atque observare deberem,
fecit.   Bene vale et me dilige.

LXXIV. TO ATTICUS (Att. xv. 16)

LUCRINUM, A.U.C. 710; B.C. 44; AET. CIC. 62

De litteris a Cicerone suo ciusque magistris acceptis. Cicero Attico significat se in amoenitate villae suae ad lacum Lucrinum tamen Tusculanum suum desiderare.

1. Tandem a Cicerone tabellarius, et mehercule litterae πεπινωμένως scriptae, quod ipsum προκοπὴν aliquam significat, itemque ceteri praeclara scribunt. Leonides tamen retinet suum illud ADHUC. Summis vero laudibus Herodes. Quid quaeris? Vel verba mihi dari facile patior in hoc meque libenter praebeo credulum. Tu velim, si quid tibi est a Statio scriptum quod pertineat ad me, certiorem me facias. 2. Narro tibi : haec loca venusta sunt, abdita certe et, si quid scribere velis, ab arbitris libera. Sed nescio quo modo οἶκος φίλος. Itaque me referunt pedes in Tusculanum. Et tamen haec ῥωπο-γραφία ripulae videtur habitura celerem satictatem. Equidem etiam pluvias metuo, si prognostica nostra vera sunt. Ranae enim ῥητορεύουσιν. Tu, quaeso, fac sciam ubi Brutum nostrum et quo die videre possim.

LXXV. TO ATTICUS (Att. xv. 15)

LUCRINUM, A.U.C. 710; B.C. 44; AET. CIC. 62

De L. Antonio Buthrotiis molesto, de nummis L. Fadio curandis, de Cleopatra et Hammonio et Sara, de profectione sua per Erotis dispensationem impedita, de Ciceroni suo in annuum sumptum Athenas permutando.

1. L. Antonio male sit ! si quidem Buthrotiis molestus

est. Ego testimonium composui, quod, cum voles, ob-
signabitur. Nummos Arpinatium, si L. Fadius aedilis
petet, vel omnes reddito. Ego ad te alia epistola scripsi
de IIS. cx., quae Statio curarentur. Si ergo petet
Fadius, ei volo reddi, praeter Fadium nemini. Apud
me item puto depositum. Id scripsi ad Erotem ut
redderet. 2. Reginam odi. Id me iure facere sit
sponsor promissorum eius Hammonius, quae quidem
erant φιλόλογα et dignitatis meae, ut vel in contione
dicere auderem. Saran autem, praeterquam quod
nefarium hominem, cognovi praeterea in me contumacem.
Semel cum omnino domi meae vidi. Cum φιλοφρόνως
ex eo quaererem quid opus esset, Atticum se dixit
quaerere. Superbiam autem ipsius reginae cum esset
trans Tiberim in hortis, commemorare sine magno dolore
non possum. Nihil igitur cum istis, nec tam animum
me quam vix stomachum habere arbitrantur. 3. Profectionem meam, ut video, Erotis dispensatio impedit.
Nam cum ex reliquis, quae Nonis Aprilibus fecit, abun-
dare debeam, cogor mutuari, quodque ex istis fructuosis
rebus receptum est, id ego ad illud fanum sepositum
putabam. Sed haec Tironi mandavi, quem ob eam
causam Romam misi. Te nolui impeditum impedire.
4. Cicero noster quo modestior est, eo me magis com-
movet. Ad me enim de hac re nihil scripsit, ad quem
nimirum potissimum debuit. Scripsit hoc autem ad
Tironem, sibi post Kal. Apriles — sic enim annuum
tempus confici—nihil datum esse : tibi pro tua natura
semper placuisse teque existimasse scio id etiam ad dignitatem meam pertinere, eum non modo liberaliter a nobis,

sed etiam ornate cumulateque tractari.   Qua re velim cures
—nec tibi essem molestus, si per alium hoc agere possem
—ut permutetur Athenas quod sit in annuum sumptum ei.
Eros numerabit.   Eius rei causa Tironem misi.   Curabis
igitur et ad me, si quid tibi de eo videbitur, scribes.

LXXVI. TO ATTICUS (ATT. XVI. 3)

POMPEIANUM, A.U.C. 710; B.C. 44; AET. CIC. 62

De Antonio ab Attico convento Tiburi, de libro 'de senectute'
suo et alio συντάγματι per Erotem misso, de Cicerone suo, de
Xenone, de Herode, de Q. filio, tum de discessu suo, de rationibus
suis et re familiari, de Bruto, de Cassio, de Hiera et Blesamio, de
Attica et Pilia.

1. Tu vero sapienter—nunc demum enim rescribo iis
litteris, quas mihi misisti convento Antonio Tiburi—
sapienter igitur, quod manus dedisti quodque etiam ultro
gratias egisti.   Certe enim, ut scribis, deseremur ocius a
re publica quam a re familiari.   Quod vero scribis te
magis et magis delectare 'O Tite, si quid ego,' auges mihi
scribendi alacritatem.   Quod Erotem non sine munusculo
te exspectare dicis, gaudeo non fefellisse eam rem
opinionem tuam, sed tamen idem σύνταγμα misi ad te
retractatius et quidem ἀρχέτυπον ipsum crebris locis inculcatum et refectum.   Hunc tu tralatum in macrocollum
lege arcano convivis tuis, sed, si me amas, hilaris et bene
acceptis, ne in me stomachum erumpant, cum sint tibi
irati. 2. De Cicerone, velim ita sit, ut audimus.   De
Xenone coram cognoscam, quamquam nihil ab eo arbitror

neque indiligenter neque illiberaliter. De Herode faciam ut mandas, et ea, quae scribis, ex Saufeio et e Xenone cognoscam. 3. De Q. filio, gaudeo tibi meas litteras prius a tabellario meo quam ab ipso redditas, quamquam te nihil fefellisset. Verum tamen. . . . Sed exspecto quid ille tecum, quid tu vicissim, nec dubito quin suo more uterque. Sed eas litteras Curium mihi spero redditurum, qui quidem, etsi per se est amabilis a meque diligitur, tamen accedet magnus cumulus commendationis tuae. 4. Litteris tuis satis responsum est: nunc aud, quod, etsi intellego scribi necesse non esse, scribo tamen. Multa me movent in discessu, in primis mehercule, quod diiungor a te: movet etiam navigationis labor alienus non ab aetate solum nostra, verum etiam a dignitate tempusque discessus subabsurdum. Relinquimus enim pacem, ut ad bellum revertamur, quodque temporis in praediolis nostris et belle aedificatis et satis amoenis consumi potuit, in peregrinatione consumimus. Consolantur haec: aut prodcrimus aliquid Ciceroni aut quantum profici possit iudicabimus. Deinde tu iam, ut spero et ut promittis, aderis. Quod quidem si acciderit, omnia nobis erunt meliora. 5. Maxime autem me angit ratio reliquórum meorum: quae quamquam explicata sunt, tamen, quod et Dolabellae nomen in iis est et ex attributione mihi nomina ignota, conturbor, nec me ulla res magis angit ex omnibus. Itaque non mihi videor errasse, quod ad Balbum scripsi apertius, ut, si quid tale accidisset, ut non concurrerent nomina, subveniret, meque tibi etiam mandasse, ut, si quid eius modi accidisset, cum eo communicares: quod facies, si tibi videbitur,

coque magis, si proficisceris in Epirum. 6. Haec ego
conscendens e Pompeiano tribus actuariolis decemscalmis.
Brutus erat in Neside etiam nunc, Neapoli Cassius.
Ecquid amas Deiotarum et non amas Hieram? Qui, ut
Blesamius venit ad me, quum ei praescriptum esset, ne
quid sine Sexti nostri sententia ageret, neque ad illum
neque ad quemquam nostrum rettulit. Atticam nostram
cupio absentem suaviari: ita mihi dulcis salus visa est
per te missa ab illa. Referes igitur ei plurimam itemque
Piliae dicas velim.

LXXVII. ASINIUS POLLIO TO CICERO
(FAM. X. 32)

CORDUBA, A.U.C. 711; B.C. 43; AET. CIC. 63

C. Asinius Pollio de Balbi quaestoris sui flagitiis et de suo in
rem publicam studio exponit.

1. Balbus quaestor magna numerata pecunia, magno
pondere auri, maiore argenti coacto de publicis exactionibus, ne stipendio quidem militibus reddito duxit se a
Gadibus et triduum tempestate retentus ad Calpen Kal.
Iuniis traiecit sese in regnum Bogudis, plane bene peculiatus. His rumoribus utrum Gades referatur an Romam
—ad singulos enim nuntios turpissime consilia mutat—
nondum scio. 2. Sed praeter furta et rapinas et virgis
caesos socios haec quoque fecit, ut ipse gloriari solet,
eadem quae C. Caesar, ludis, quos Gadibus fecit, Heren-
nium Gallum histrionem, summo ludorum die anulo
aureo donatum, in XIV. sessum deduxit:—tot enim fecerat

ordines equestris loci :—quattuorviratum sibi prorogavi: :
comitia biennii biduo habuit, hoc est, renuntiavit quos ei
visum est : exsules reduxit, non horum temporum, sed
illorum, quibus a seditiosis senatus trucidatus aut ex-
pulsus est, Sex. Varo proconsule. 3. Illa vero iam re
Caesaris quidem exemplo, quod ludis practextam de suo
itinere ad L. Lentulum procos. sollicitandum posuit. Et
quidem cum ageretur, flevit memoria rerum gestarum
commotus. Gladiatoribus autem Fadium quemdam, militem Pompeianum, quia, cum depressus in ludum bis
gratis depugnasset, auctorari sese nolebat et ad populun
confugerat, primum Gallos equites immisit in populum—
coniecti enim lapides sunt in eum, cum abriperetur Fadius,
—deinde abstractum defodit in ludo et vivum combussit :
cum quidem pransus, nudis pedibus, tunica soluta,
manibus ad tergum reiectis, inambularet et illi misero
quiritanti : c. r. natus sum, responderet : 'Abi nunc,
populi fidem implora.' Bestiis vero cives Romanos, in
iis circulatorem quendam auctionum, notissimum hominem Hispali, quia deformis erat, obiecit. Cum huiusce
modi portento res mihi fuit. Sed de illo plura coram.
4. Nunc, quod praestat : quid me velitis facere constituite.
Tres legiones firmas habeo, quarum unam, duodetricensi-
mam, cum ad se initio belli arcessisset Antonius hac
pollicitatione, quo die in castra venisset, denarios quin-
genos singulis militibus daturum, in victoria vero eadem
praemia, quae suis legionibus—quorum quis ullam finem
aut modum futurum putabit ?—incitatissimam retinui,
aegre mehercules : nec retinuissem, si uno loco habuissem,
utpote cum singulae quaedam cohortes seditionem fecerint.

Reliquas quoque legiones non destitit litteris atque infinitis pollicitationibus incitare. Nec vero minus Lepidus ursit me et suis et Antonii litteris, ut legionem tricensimam mitterem sibi. 5. Itaque quem exercitum neque vendere ullis praemiis volui nec eorum periculorum metu, quae victoribus illis portendebantur, deminuere, debetis existimare retentum et conservatum rei publicae esse, atque ita credere, quodcumque imperassetis, facturum fuisse, si quod iussistis feci. Nam et provinciam in otio et exercitum in mea potestate tenui : finibus meae provinciae nusquam excessi : militem non modo legionarium, sed ne auxiliarium quidem ullum quoquam misi, et, si quos equites decedentes nactus sum, supplicio adfeci. Quarum rerum fructum satis magnum re publica salva tulisse me putabo. Sed res publica si me satis novisset et maior pars senatus, maiores ex me fructus tulisset. Epistolam, quam Balbo, cum etiam nunc in provincia esset, scripsi, legendam tibi misi : etiam praetextam, si voles legere, Gallum Cornelium, familiarem meum, poscito. VI. Idus Iunias, Corduba.

LXXVIII. TO CASSIUS, IN LAODICEA (FAM. XII. 10)

ROME, A.U.C. 711 ; B.C. 43 ; AET. CIC. 63

M. Cicero Lepidum hostem iudicatum scribit et Cassium cum exercitu in Italia exspectari.

1. Lepidus, tuus adfinis, meus familiaris, pridie Kal. Quinctiles sententiis omnibus hostis a senatu iudicatus est ceterique, qui una cum illo a re publica defecerunt :

quibus tamen ad sanitatem redeundi ante Kal. Septembr.
potestas facta est.   Fortis sane senatus, sed maxime spe
subsidii tui.   Bellum quidem, cum haec scribebam,
sane magnum erat scelere et levitate Lepidi.   Nos de
Dolabella cotidie quae volumus audimus, sed adhuc sine
capite, sine auctore, rumore nuntio.   2. Quod cum ita
esset, tamen litteris tuis, quas Nonis Maiis ex castiis
datas acceperamus, ita persuasum erat civitati ut illu n
iam oppressum omnes arbitrarentur, te autem in Italiam
venire cum exercitu, ut, si haec ex sententia confecta
essent, consilio atque auctoritate tua, sin quid forte
titubatum, ut fit in bello, exercitu tuo niteremur.
Quem quidem ego exercitum quibuscumque potuero rebus
ornabo : cuius rei tum tempus erit, cum quid opis re
publicae laturus is exercitus sit aut quid iam tuleril
notum esse coeperit.   Nam adhuc tantum conatus
audiuntur, optimi illi quidem et praeclarissimi, sed gesta
res exspectatur : quam quidem aut iam esse aliquam aut
appropinquare confido.   3. Tua virtute et magnitudine
animi nihil est nobilius.   Itaque optamus, ut quam
primum te in Italia videamus.   Rem publicam nos
habere arbitrabimur, si vos habebimus.   Praeclare viceramus, nisi spoliatum, inermem, fugientem Lepidus
recepisset Antonium.   Itaque numquam tanto odio
civitati Antonius fuit quanto est Lepidus.   Ille enim ex
turbulenta re publica, hic ex pace et victoria bellum
excitavit.   Huic oppositos consules designatos habemus :
in quibus est magna illa quidem spes, sed anceps cura
propter incertos exitus proeliorum.   4. Persuade tibi
igitur in te et in Bruto tuo esse omnia, vos exspectari,

Brutum quidem iam iamque. Quod si, ut spero, victis hostibus nostris veneritis, tamen auctoritate vestra res publica exsurget et in aliquo statu tolerabili consistet. Sunt enim permulta, quibus erit medendum, etiam si res publica satis esse videbitur sceleribus hostium liberata. Vale.

LXXIX. TO TREBATIUS (Fam. vii. 22)

Cicero cum Trebatio iocatur de controversia quae interciderat de actione furti. Annus quo epistola scripta sit incertus est.

Illuseras heri inter scyphos quod dixeram controversiam esse, possetne heres, quod furtum antea factum esset, furti recte agere. Itaque, etsi domum bene potus seroque redieram, tamen id caput ubi haec controversia est notavi, et descriptum tibi misi, ut scires id, quod tu neminem sensisse dicebas, Sex. Aelium, M'. Manilium, M. Brutum sensisse. Ego tamen Scaevolae et Testae adsentior.

LXXX. TO TIRO (Fam. xvi. 26)

Q. Cicero accusat familiariter Tironem de intermissione litterarum, quas eum etiam sine argumento ad se dare iubet. Annus quo epistola scripta sit incertus est.

1. Verberavi te cogitationis tacito dumtaxat convicio, quod fasciculus alter ad me iam sine tuis litteris perlatus est. Non potes effugere huius culpae poenam te patrono. Marcus est adhibendus: isque diu et multis lucubrationibus commentata oratione vide ut probare

possit te non peccasse. 2. Plane te rogo, sicut olim matrem nostram facere memini, quae lagonas etiam inanes obsignabat, ne dicerentur inanes aliquae fuisse, quae furtim essent exsiccatae, sic tu, etiam si quod scribas non habebis, scribito tamen, ne furtum cessationis quaesivisse videaris. Valde enim mihi semper et vera et dulcia tuis epistolis nuntiantur. Ama nos et vale.

NOTES

This is the first letter of Cicero's extant correspondence.

1. fructu. *Fructu* is not *enjoyment* simply, but *enjoyment with profit.* The latter idea predominates here. 'What a loss I have sustained both in public and in private life.' Lucius was the *cousin* of Cicero. In Fin. v. 1 he expresses the relationship more accurately in calling him *fratrem cognatione patruelem amore germanum.* Lucius (2 Verr. iv. 25) travelled in Sicily with Cicero, to aid him in collecting evidence against Verres. This explains *forensi.*

Nam mihi omnia. 'All the charm that one man's kindly nature may have for another, I felt in him.' *Iucunda* is used predicatively : lit. 'all the things which can come pleasant (we should say *pleasantly* or *with a charm*) to a man from his friend's sweetness of nature.'

humanitate et moribus, 'his kindly disposition' : a very mitigated specimen of the ἓν διὰ δυοῖν so common in the poets and in Tacitus. Cf. Pro Cluent. 111, *mores eius et adrogantiam,* and Att. i. 12, 3, *servatum et eductum,* 'brought out safely.' [Rather 'kindliness and winning ways.' For this emphatic sense of *moribus* cf. Prop. iv. (v.) 11, 86.]

omni . . . ornatissimum, 'graced by every charm of character and principle.' Cf. *summo officio ac virtute virum praeditum,* 2 Verr. i. 135, 'a most obliging and excellent fellow.'

tuique . . . amantem. *Amans* and other participles are often used nearly as subst. ; cf. *homines amantes tui,* Fam. ix. 6, 1 ; *observantem sui,* Rab. Post. 43. If *amantem* were strictly subst. we should require *tuum amantem.*

K

adfinem. Rather loosely used here: properly speaking, Q. Cicero only was the *adfinis* of Atticus, being the husband of Atticus's sister, Pomponia; not even Marcus, the brother of Quintus, still less Lucius the cousin, was *adfinis* to Atticus in strictness of speech. [In other passages a liberal view of *affinitas* is taken, *e.g.* Post red. 11.]

2. **de sorore tua.** For an admirable account of the pettish-ness of Pomponia, see Att. v. 1, 2 (Ep. xxvi.) Cicero appears afterwards to absolve his brother completely from blame in his unhappy domestic relations.

curae fuerit ut. 'She will tell you how concerned I was that Q. should have the proper feelings of a husband towards her.' A subject clause introduced by *ut* is not common after *curae est;* after which the subject clause is usually in the infin. or is introduced by *de*, as *de augenda mea dignitate curae fore*, Att. xi. 6, 3. Cf., however, *curae fore ut omnia restituerentur*, 2 Verr. iv. 73.

eas litteras quibus. 'A letter of a kind to soothe one's brother, to admonish one's junior, and to reprove one who is in the wrong.' The subjunctive is consecutive: if the verbs *placarem*, etc., were in the indicative the meaning would be 'I wrote him that letter in which I soothed,' etc. An admir-able instance of this consecutive subjunctive is to be found in Att. vi. 1, 25 (Ep. xxxv.), where see note.

minorem. Q. was probably about four years younger than M. Cicero—about 34 years of age at the date of this letter.

3. **missione.** Bembus conjectures *intermissione*, and this is accepted by Baiter, who compares Fam. vii. 13, 1, where Cicero uses the phrase *intermissionis epistularum*, but that supplies no reason why we should impugn here *missione* of the mss. The phrase may be rendered exactly, 'You have no right to complain of me as a correspondent': quite similarly in Att. iv. 16, 1, Cicero says, *De epistularum frequentia te nihil accuso*, 'I bring no charge touching your *regularity* as a correspondent,' which is quite as natural a way of speaking as if he had said *infrequentia, irregularity*. So here he might have said *inter-missione*, but did say (quite as correctly) *missione*. Cf. Att. v. 10, 3, *ut meum consilium saepe reprehendam quod non* . . . *emerserim*, where *consilium* really means 'my *want* of prudence.' Cf. Hor. Sat. ii. 4, 85, *haec* . . . *reprehendi iustius illis*, where *haec* and *illis* are both pregnant, 'their *absence* can be more justly found fault with than *the absence* of those things which,' etc. This usage is common in Greek.

4. De Acutiliano negotio. See Att. i. 4, 1, and Att. i. 8, 1. As the latter letter was written in 687 (B.C. 67), the business must have been unfinished at the end of two years. Well might Cicero say *accidit ut contentione nihil opus esset*, 'it so happened that there was no need of any great haste.'

tuo digressu, 'after parting from you'; *tuo* is used instead of the objective gen.; cf. *odio tuo, desiderio tuo*, 'hatred of you, regret for you,' Ter. Phorm. v. 8, 27; Heaut. ii. 3, 66. So Fam. x. 24, 1, *tua observantia*, 'attention to you.' In Att. ii. 13, 1, *tuam epistolam* means 'a letter *to* you.'

confeceram. Perhaps this may be best taken here as the *epistolary pluperfect*. If not writing a letter he would have used the *imperf. conficiebam*, 'I meant to finish the business, but,' etc. In a letter *conficiebam* would mean, 'I am finishing,' so he is forced to use the *pluperf.*, just as in Att. v. 14, *Nunc iter conficiebamus pulverulenta via. Dederam Epheso pridie. Has dedi Trallibus.* See Roby, § 1468. [Cic. seems to me to convey that he actually did carry out the commission given him by Att., which referred to some minor point of the *Acutilianum negotium.* The words *sed accidit* seem to be an apology for not having written earlier to Att.]

duxi. One would at first sight expect *duxissem*, which Malaspina conjectured, and Bosius pretended to have found in one of his fabricated mss. But *duxi* is quite right. Cicero is defending himself from the charge that he neglected to write, so as to escape the trouble of it. 'Seeing that I endured to listen to Acutilius for several days, I did not think it a great task to write you an account of his complaints, when I made so light of listening to them, which was somewhat a bore.' We should rather have expected a word enhancing the meaning of *odiosum* than a preposition which mitigates as *sub.* Cicero affects words compounded of *sub* in this sense.

unas. *Unas litteras,* 'one letter,' there being no ambiguity; but *duae litterae* would be 'two letters of the alphabet.' Two, three letters (epistles), etc., must be expressed by the distributive numerals *binae, trinae*, etc.

5. Quod scribis, etc. 'You write that even if somebody is a little offended with you, my part ought to be to bring about a better feeling: I see what you mean, and I did my best to that end; but he feels the matter very deeply. I did not fail to say all that was needful about your case, but how far I should go in my efforts I thought I should regulate by your wishes, which when you have communicated to me, you will see that I did not care to be more busy than you were yourself, and that on the other hand I shall not be more remiss than you would wish me to be.'

The reference is to Lucceius. He mentions the name plainly afterwards (i. 11, 1, etc. ; i. 14, 7). It is, however, possible that *cuius animus* might be explained as a reference to some general proposition in Att.'s letter. 'I have a right to look to you to mitigate any offence that may be taken.' *Teneo* was inserted by Orelli. It might well have fallen out after *-tere*, the last syllable of *oportere*, and it is idle to suppose that the want of a verb here could be accounted for as a justifiable ellipse. The old commentators defended the ellipse as a *loquendi genus comicum*, and this would have great weight if it could be proved, for we shall find many coincidences between Cicero's letters and the comic drama. It is natural that there should be close resemblances between the language of familiar letter-writing and the language of familiar dialogue.

6. **De Tadiana re.** Tadius had somehow got into his hands the property of an heiress who was still a ward. He had held her property for the two or more years which would give a right to prescriptive ownership. When the property was claimed for the girl by her lawful guardians, Tadius, by the advice of Atticus, pleaded his prescriptive right. Cicero expresses his surprise that Atticus should not know that no prescriptive right can be acquired to the property of a ward under the care of her statutory guardians.

7. **Epiroticam emptionem,** 'your purchase of a place in Epirus (near Buthrotum).' *Emptio* ought properly to mean. 'the act of purchasing,' but it is sometimes (*e.g.* Ep. xvi. 2) used for 'the thing purchased.' The use of the adj. too is somewhat colloquial. In Att. v. 20, 9, Cicero speaks of a letter *for* Epirus as *litterae Epiroticae*. Cf. *Achaico cursu,* 'journey to A.,' Ep. ad Brut. i. 15, 5 ; *Libyco cursu,* 'journey from Libya,' Virg. Aen. vi. 338.

Tusculano. This Tusculan estate of Cicero had formerly belonged to Sulla, and had subsequently passed into the hands of Catulus. About eleven years after this time Cicero offered it for sale (Att. iv. 2, 7), but he seems to have changed his mind, for we find it in his hands at a subsequent period (Att. xii. 41, 1). Mr. Watson in Appendix V to the first part of his Select Letters of Cicero gives a list of Cicero's other estates. They were (1) at Arpinum, which he inherited from his father, and near which his brother Quintus had two estates called Arcanum and Laterium ; (2) at Antium, which he subsequently sold to M. Lepidus; (3) at Formiae; (4) at Pompeii; (5) Cumae; (6) Puteoli; (7) Astura. He had also several *deversoria*, or places where he could put up for a night, *e.g.* at Tarracina, Sinuessa, Cales, Anagnia. Such 'lodges' were indispensable for distinguished persons who would travel in a style befitting their rank at a time when there was hardly anything like hotel accommodation. He also had a house in Rome, on the Carinae, which he made over to his brother Quintus, when he himself after his consulate bought the magnificent house of M. Crassus, on the Palatine, for a sum of nearly £30,000. This was the house which was destroyed by Clodius in the year 697 (57), and for the restoration of which a money grant was made by the senate after Cicero's return from exile, which he complained of as insufficient for the purpose.

8. **articulorum dolores,** 'rheumatism.'

LETTER II. (ATT. I. 7)

Apud matrem. 'Your mother and her household are getting on very well.'

curaturum, 'will see to the payment of.'

HS xxcd. This very sum, 20,400 sesterces (£173 : 8s.), is expressed by quite different symbols in Att. i. 8. It should not surprise us to find such latitude in letters. So the horizontal stroke indicating thousands of sesterces has often to be supplied or not, according to the context. Thus in an English letter if we met the expression 'I gave 100 for a horse,' we should guess it meant £100, not 100 shillings; but if we found 'I gave 1000 for a horse,' we might not feel quite sure whether the word written was *house* or *horse*. This being so, I follow the practice of those editors who do not supply in the text the horizontal stroke (which is not found in the mss.), but leave the symbol as it is found in the mss., adding an explanation, if requisite, in the footnotes. [Cf. the curious story about Tiberius in Suet. Galb. 5 : *sestertium quingenties cum praecipuum inter legatarios habuisset, quia notata non perscripta erat summa, hercle Tiberio ad quingenta revocante, ne haec quidem recepit.*]

conficere, 'secure.'

LETTER III. (ATT. I. 6)

1. Domum Rab. 'Rabirius's house at Neapolis which you had already laid out and completed in your mind's eye, 11'. Fonteius has bought for 130,000 sesterces' (£1100). For the Roman system of reckoning see Roby's Latin Grammar, vol. i. Appendix D, §§ i. ii. viii. pp. 440, 441, 447. *Domi m Rabirianam* implies that it was the family mansion; *domi m Rabirii* would merely express that it was his dwelling.

2. Arpinatibus. The names of the estates of Quintus in Arpinum were *Arcanum* and *Laterium.*

χρηστομαθῆ, 'an adept in *belles lettres*,' ' a man of excellent polite learning,' 'a *savant.*'

Pater nobis d. This is a *locus vexatissimus.* Madvig, Boot, and others read *discessit* on the ground that Cicero would not have been so unfeeling as to announce his father's death in such curt terms. Boot urges that he is deeply moved at the death of his slave, Sositheus (Att. i. 12, 4): we may also notice Cicero's almost exaggerated expressions of grief for Lentulus (Att. iv. 6). But if we read *discessit*, we must also read *pater noster discessit*, 'my father left,' instead of *pater nobis discessit* the ethical dative implying serious loss to oneself; unless indeed, we make a further change, and read *a nobis discessit* and even then it is not probable that Cicero would write 'my father has left' without mentioning whither he went, or why he thought the fact worth recording. But the chief argument against *decessit* is the alleged evidence of Asconius that Cicero's father did not die till the year 690 (B.C. 64). The passage of Asc. is, however, highly suspicious. In enumerating the competitors of Cicero for the consulship, Asc. in his commentary on the Oratio in Toga Candida writes :—'Duos patricios P. Sulp. Galbam, L. Sergium Catilinam ; quattuor plebeios, ex quibus duos nobiles, C. Antonium, L. Cassium Longinum ; duo qui tantum non primi ex suis familiis magistratum adepti erant, Q. Cornificium et C. Licinium Sacerdotem. Solus Cicero ex competitoribus equestri erat loco natus, *atque in petitione patrem amisit.*' Could anything be more abrupt or irrelevant than the words in italics ? I believe the passage of Asc. is unsound. Very possibly Asc. wrote *omisit*, as Mr. Harrison, of St. John's College, Cambridge, has suggested to me. It may have been customary in the *professio* to give the father's name with one's own. Cicero may have excited comment by omitting this customary formality. If then, as I think, we may dismiss the testimony of Asconius, there is no urgent reason for doubting that *decessit* is right, and means 'died.' Yet we may acquit Cicero of want of feeling; thus: let us suppose that he had already communicated the death of his father in a letter to Atticus, now lost; that Atticus in a subsequent letter asked Cicero, 'What did you say was the precise date of your father's death?' and that Cicero here replies *pater nobis decessit* A.D. iv. *Kal. Dec.*, 'the date of my poor (*nobis*) father's death was the fourth day before the kalends.' *Nobis* is itself a tender expression. Cf. *ure mihi*, Prop. iv. 7, 78. Editors do not sufficiently keep before their minds the fact that much that is difficult in these letters arises from the loss of the replies of Atticus. This explanation has been accepted by I. C. G. Boot, the eminent Dutch scholar, in his last edition (1886) of the Letters to Atticus. The question between *discesserat* and *decesserat* rises again in Fam. v. 14, 1, but there *discesserat* has the mss. on its side.

γυμνασιώδη, *objets d'art*, 'articles of *vertu*.' γυμνάσιον was the name given by the Greeks to the places where philosophers gave lectures. Cicero loved to lay out in the neighbourhood of his villas such places for philosophic discussion or for general conversation. These *gymnasia* consisted of a hall with seats called *exedrae*, and a colonnade (*xystus*) or a walk planted with trees for those who preferred to walk during the disquisition or conversation.

LETTER IV. (ATT. I. 2)

1. **L. Iulio Caesare.** 'Julius Caesar and Marcius Figulus having been elected consuls, let me tell you that on the same day I was blessed with a son, and that Terentia is doing well.' Cicero refers to the day on which the result of the election was declared; these men were only *consules designati* until the next year.

salva Terentia. In Ep. xlvii. he expresses this same sentiment by a Greek word, εὐτόκησεν. It is a curious coincidence that while modern physicians write their prescriptions in Latin (or did so till very lately), and largely affect the use of Latin terms in hygienic matters, the Latins in the time of Cicero in the same way affected Greek. In the Letters of Cicero an 'attack' of illness is λῆψις, 'paralysis' is παράλυσις, 'depletion' is ἀφαίρεσις, 'sweating' is διαφόρησις, 'a defluxion of humours' is ἐπιφορά, 'to do Banting' is ἀσιτεῖν or πεινητικὴν facere, 'to be under a *régime* of emetics' is ἐμετικὴν *agere*, 'bile' is χολὴν ἄκρατον, 'a low diet' is λιτότης, to 'feed up' a patient is προσανατρέφειν. In Fam. xvi. 18, 1, Cicero recommends to Tiro to take care of his digestion, not to fatigue himself, but to take regular exercise, to keep his mind amused, and to avoid constipation ; as this is medical advice, Cicero clothes it in Greek in the form of a prescription, πέψιν, ἀκοπίαν, περίπατον σύμμετρον, τέρψιν, εὐλυσίαν κοιλίας. [The physicians and the writers on medicine were Greeks almost to a man.]

meis ad te rationibus. The order of the words is strange, but *hyperbaton* is a feature in the style of these letters : cf. Att. i. 14, 1, *ut huic vix tantulae epistolae tempus habuerim ;* Fam. iii. 9, 3, *tuis incredibiliter studiis . . . delector ;* cf. also At. iv. 17, 3, 4 ; Fam. iii. 7, 4. [The cause here is the great tendency Cic. has to bring pronouns as near together as he can.]

Catilinam . . . defendere. Catiline was now on his trial for his malversation in Africa, and Cicero seems to have entertained the design of defending him. This is put forward by the traducers of Cicero as a proof that he was at this time making advances towards the popular party. But Catiline was not at this time regarded as the leader of the popular party, and if Cicero had defended him he would have been doing nothing at all politically significant. See Or. pro Caelio, 14, in which Cicero says that at one time he did not suspect Catiline. It would have been quite natural that he should now defend Catiline as he afterwards defended Fonteius. His way to distinction depended on his achieving a great position at the Bar, and it would have been very adverse to his ultimate chance of the consulship if he had now refused to undertake important cases. The time came when Cicero could pick and choose his briefs, but it had not yet arrived. As a matter of fact, Cicero did not defend Catiline. This is rendered clear by the fact that in the Oratio in Toga Candida Cicero reproaches his other competitor Antonius with some slight services which he had done him in his candidature for the praetorship. Is it then credible that if Cicero had really defended Catiline he would have failed to twit him with the fact ? And, if he had defended Catiline, could he have said in this speech, 'Miserable man, not to see that by that verdict you were not acquitted, but reserved for a more serious punishment' ? But if Cicero had defended Catiline his act would have been neither immoral nor unprofessional.

summa accusatoris voluntate. He hints that the accuser, P. Clodius, was in collusion with Catiline, and exercised his right of *reiectio*, 'challenging,' against such jurors as were unfavourably disposed to the accused ; such collusion with one's opponent was called *praevaricatio*.

humaniter feremus, 'with resignation,' *i.e.* as part of the 'changes and chances of this mortal life,' ἀνθρωπίνως. Cf. Tusc. ii. 65, *morbos toleranter atque humane ferunt.* The meaning is not 'like a man' (ἀνδρείως). Plautus affects adverbs in *-ter*, even from adj. in *-us, a, um,* such as *saeviter, blanditer ;* the only adverbs in *-ter* in the Letters derived from adjectives of three terminations are *humaniter, inhumaniter* (Q. Fr. iii. 1, 21, but *inhumane,* Off. iii. 30, and 2 Verr. i. 138), *turbulenter,* Fam. ii. 16, 7. Adverbs in *-ter* not from adjectives of three terminations, and peculiar to the Letters, are *desperanter, furenter, immortaliter.*

2. **tuos familiares nobiles.** Perhaps Hortensius, Crassus, and Lucullus, who do not seem to have been very friendly to Cicero. He constantly sneers at them in his subsequent letters. But perhaps he refers to the whole class of the *nobiles* who may have been prejudiced against a *homo novus:* cf. Sallust, Cat. 23, *nobilitas quasi pollui cons. credebat si eum quamvis egregius homo novus adeptus foret.* The latter theory is confirmed by Q. Cic. Comm. pet. 4 ; and the former by Att. i. 19, 6.

LETTER V. (ATT. I. 17)

1. **Magna,** 'a great changeableness of feeling and complete revulsion of sentiment.' Quintus had plainly given ear to some designing traducers of Atticus, as is clear from § 2, *quod erat illi non nullorum artificiis inculcatum.* The quarrel did not arise from the fact that Atticus gave up his idea of going to Asia to meet Quintus ; the words *antea saepe et vehementius post sortitionem provinciae* show that it was prior to Quintus's departure for Asia. However, Cicero fears that this change of plan on the part of Atticus may inflame the quarrel (Att. i. 16, 14), and professes himself (§ 7 of this letter) ready to bear witness that Atticus had given in writing to him his reasons for declining to go to the province ; so that his refusal to accompany Quintus was due to no rupture between them. From § 3 of this letter we gather that the misunderstanding was not due to any bad feeling between Quintus and his wife Pomponia, the

sister of Atticus, though Cicero thinks the good offices of the
latter might have been used to heal the wound. Cicero expressly
says he will not entrust to a letter his theory of the cause of the
quarrel, *facilius possum existimare quam scribere,* and thinks it
has more ramifications than appear, *latius patet quam videtur.*

opinionis incommodae. Cf. in Att. i. 16, 14, *ne quid in
ista re minus commode fiat.*

saucium. This is a favourite expression with Cicero ; cf.
sic nunc neque absolutus neque damnatus Servilius saucius *Pilio
traditur,* Fam. viii. 8, 3 ; and *saucius* is a probable correction
of *atius* of the mss. in Q. Fr. iii. 2, 2, where for *undique
saucius* cf. *undique exclusus,* Cluent. 175.

insedisse governs *animum,* understood. [Rather understand
ei ; for Cic. would hardly use *insedisse* with an accusative.]

2. mollis, 'susceptible,' 'impressionable,' 'sensitive.'

3. sic intellego ut, 'my view is that the breach, even
supposing it was not *caused* by those of your household
might at least have easily been *healed* by them if they had
chosen.'

domesticis. The plural is used to soften down the remark by
making it more vague. He refers to Pomponia. So above,
meos refers to Quintus, *tuis* to Pomponia. Very like this is
that use of the plural which Draeger calls the *pluralis modestiae,*
of which a very good example is *imperatores appellati sumus,*
Att. v. 20, 3. See note on Fam. v. 4, 2 (Ep. xi.)

4. De iis litteris. 'As to his letters from Thessalonica,
and his remarks to certain friends of yours at Rome and on
his journey, I cannot see whether there is any real ground
to justify such language on his part ; but my whole hope of
mitigating this unpleasantness lies in your kindliness.' Boot
follows Orelli in his explanation of the words *ecquid tantum
causae sit*—'I do not see what there is in his letters to justify
such annoyance on your part' ; but this is quite inconsistent
with the next sentence, SED *omnis . . . molestiae,* and Cicero
has already owned in the first words of this letter that Quintus
had shown a very unfriendly spirit in his correspondence with
Atticus.

esse hanc agilitatem, 'that this nimbleness and sensitive-
ness of disposition is generally the sign of a good heart.'

5. voluntatem institutae vitae, 'the paths we chose in
life.'

probitatis. This and the following genitives are *genitivi definitivi,* 'in real glory (which consists in) honesty,' etc. : cf. *Pericles hac laude* dicendi *clarissimus fuit,* Brut. 7 ; exactly similar is Pro Mur. 23, aliis virtutibus *continentiae gravitatis iustitiae fidei ;* so *mercedem gloriae* is 'the reward (which consists) of glory' : Tusc. i. 15 ; Madv. § 286 ; Draeg. Hist. Syn. i. p. 466. Somewhat similar are *vox voluptatis,* 'that word pleasure,' *oppidum Antiochiae,* 'the town Antioch.'

cum a fraterno . . . discessi, 'in affection towards me, after that of my brother and family, I place you first.' Cf. Fam. i. 9, 18 ; vi. 12, 2. Nearly similar is Off. ii. 6, *cum ab hoc discendi genere discesseris. Primas* agrees with *partes* understood.

7. Qua re et illa. 'The rupture between you and Quintus will be healed, and the ties between us which have been so religiously guarded will remain as sacred as ever.' The last words might be more accurately rendered 'will *make good* their former sanctity' : that is, 'I shall be able, with your other friends, to assure Quintus that your declining a place in his retinue is not due to any ill feeling, but is in consequence of a resolution already formed by you and communicated to us. This will heal the quarrel, and will cement our good feeling for you.' [Hardly so : Cic. is rather thinking how the matter will look to outsiders.]

8. ob iudicandum. I have not ventured to read with Klotz *ob rem iudicandam pecuniam accepissent.* Cicero uses *accipere* absolutely in the sense of 'to take offerings or bribes.' Cf. Att. v. 21, 5 ; Q. Fr. i. 1, 13.

in causa non verecunda, 'considering my case was not a very respectable one.' *Non verecunda* is selected as being an expression conveying somewhat less than *impudens,* which he afterwards applied to the same case (Att. ii. 1, 8). Cf. De Or. ii. 361, *habetis sermonem . . . hominis utinam non* impudentis *illud quidem certe, non nimis* verecundi.

9. deliciae, 'piece of coolness (swagger, presumption) on the part of the knights.' Cf. Att. ii. 1, 8, *quid impudentius?* [Rather 'whim,' 'caprice.' Georges quotes from Sen. Rhet. (but without reference), *delicias memoriae,* 'caprices of memory.']

Asiam. *Asiani* of the Med. would mean 'Asiatics' ; *Asiatici* is the word which would be applied to the Equites who farmed the taxes of Asia. But *Asiani* of the M. is probably a corruption of *Asiam,* as Malaspina suggested.

ut induceretur, 'cancelled'; Greek διαγράφειν, 'to draw a pen through' a document.

atque adeo. Mr. Pretor translates, 'I was their leading counsel, and, for the matter of that, their junior, too,' explaining 'senior, if you take into account the service I did then ; junior, if you regard the fact that I did not originate the plea.' But surely this is extremely farfetched. The obvious meaning of the passage is (as Boot takes it) 'I was their leader, or rather the second ; for it was Crassus who urged them to demand the cancelling of the contract.' Boot does not give instances of this usage of *atque adeo*, which Mr. Pretor says 'it would be extremely hard to justify.' Surely he has overlooked Att. xv. 13, 3, *Quod ad te antea atque adeo prius scripsi* (*sic enim mavis*), where Mr. Pretor's rendering 'and what's more' would be nonsense. To this should be added a good example of this use of *atque adeo* in Pis. 41, *tunc etiam atque adeo vos;* and an excellent example from Plautus, which I owe to Prof. A. Palmer—

Cl. Tibi daretur illa? *St.* Mihi enim—Ah non id volui dicere
　Dum mihi volui, huic dixi—*atque adeo* dum mihi cupio—perperam
　Iamdudum hercle fabulor—　　　　　　　　　　　　Cas. ii. 6, 14.

Atque adeo in the corrective sense is also frequently found in the Speeches, *e.g.* 2 Verr. ii. 35, 36, 60, 65 ; iii. 61, 62.

11. cum eo, Lucceius.

cum hoc, Lucceius again : *cum hoc* would seem to refer to Caesar, but this is impossible ; for the agency of Piso would not have been used by Bibulus to secure the co-operation of Caesar, who was on the worst possible terms with Piso at the time (Sal. Cat. 49).

Si exspectare velis. M. omits *si ;* Klotz inserts it after *exspectare,* but it would more easily have fallen out after *tempus.* The meaning is, 'if you mean to remain absent from Rome till you hear from me again (to wait for this fuller letter), let me know.' *Exspectari si velis,* which is sometimes read, would mean, 'if you wish me to stay in Rome till you return thither.' Cicero, we find, visited the country in the beginning of the year. He was desirous of timing his return so as to be at Rome when Atticus arrived there.

modeste of the mss. is absolutely required by the need of an antithesis to *maxime.* Orelli, with Manutius and Lambinus, reads *moleste rogo* = 'I beseech you even to importunity.' The question between *modeste* and *moleste* again arises in Att. ii. 1, 9.

LETTER VI. (ATT. II. 2)

1. **Ciceronem nostrum,** the son of Quintus and Pomponia, who was now ill.

2. **Πελληναίων,** sc. πολιτείαν, 'an account of the constitution' of Pellene,' by Dicaearchus : so Κορινθίων and 'Αθηναίων below.

magnum acervum. The Roman book consisted of strips of papyrus glued together, the last leaf (scheda, scida) being fastened to a stick, round which the whole was rolled, so that the more one had read of a book the more of the papyrus would be unrolled ; and so it would lie on the floor at the feet of the reader, rising into a large heap according as more and more was unrolled from the stick.

It must be remembered that each book of a work formed a separate roll (volumen). If, then, Cic. had read several books of Dic. there would be several volumina together on the floor. Ovid speaks of his Metamorphoses as mutatae ter quinque volumina formae, Trist. i. 1, 117. The meaning of the word umbilicus, as applied to a volumen, is not quite ascertained. The expression itself would seem to point to the extremities of the cylinder round which the paper was rolled. According to Marquardt, when the ancients speak of umbilicus they mean the cylinder itself, the central stick ; when they speak of umbilici they mean the projecting extremities of the central stick, also called cornua. Frontes were the flat surfaces of the rolled paper at top and bottom of the roll ; these were smoothed with pumice stone, and sometimes coloured to produce a pleasant effect. The expression ad umb. adducere, meaning 'to finish the writing of a book,' would seem to show that umbilicus was a 'knob' put into a cavity at each end of the rolled paper for ornament ; which would be natural enough if the central stick was a little shorter than the roll of paper which enveloped it.

Dicaearchi. Dicaearchus of Messene, a Peripatetic, was indeed a remarkable man. His theory of the soul is, to a great extent, in accordance with modern speculations. He held that the soul was a function of the organism, μηδὲν εἶναι αὐτὴν παρὰ τό πως ἔχον σῶμα. A consequence of this was that the βίος πρακτικός was superior to the βίος θεωρητικός (Att. ii. 16, 3). Accordingly his writings were naturally political, accounts of Hellenic constitutions, and such like works. In his τριπολιτικός he sought to show that a mixture of monarchy, aristocracy

and democracy, was the best constitution ; and he found it in
Sparta.   It was probably from this work that Polybius took
(vi. 2-10) the theory that Rome owed her greatness to such an
admixture in her constitution, than which there is, according
to Mommsen (iii. 467), hardly a more foolish speculation.
Dic. was a great favourite of Cic., who calls him *deliciae mene*
(Tusc. i. 77).

Mihi crede.   This is Boot's conjecture for *mihi credes,
leges ; haec doceo, mirabilis vir est,* which is by no means certainly wrong ; *credes* and *leges* might be regarded as 't‍ie
polite imperative,' the future being thus used in Latin as the
opt. with ἄν in Greek.   For *mihi crede* cf. Att. ii. 13, 2, 'tru‍st
me,' 'take my advice.'

Ἡρώδης was afterwards the instructor of Cicero's son, as
seems to be shown by Att. xv. 16 a.

si homo esset, a colloquialism common to Terence and
Cicero.   It here means 'if he had the ordinary sense of a man '
In other passages it sometimes has a moral sense—'if he had
the feelings of a man.'

litteram, γράμμα, a single *letter* of the alphabet.   Cf. in
meis orationibus omnibus litteris, 'in every *letter* of my speeches,'
Att. i. 14, 3.

qui me epistula, 'who has discharged a letter at me (as
a missile), while he has engaged you hand to hand' (as with a
sword).   Herodes seems to have written a memoir of Cicero's consulate, and concerning it to have made some request of Cicero by
letter, and of Atticus personally.   Probably he desired to read
it to them, as Cicero says *audiendum,* 'I should rather have
chosen to be one of the conspirators than the suppressor of the
conspiracy, if I thought I should have to pay such a price for
my distinction as to listen to that fellow.'

3. Lollio . . . vino.   To explain this, or to choose between
vino and *Vinio, lolio* and *Lollio,* we should have the letter of
Atticus to which this is a reply.

Sed heus tu.   'But, I say, don't you observe that the
Kalends of Jan. are approaching, and no Antonius ; that the
jury to try him for extortion is being empanelled ?   Such is the
intelligence sent to me—that Nigidius threatens that he will serve
a summons on any juror who does not attend.'   This law seems
to have been enacted by Cic.   See the very difficult passage, pro
Mur. 47, and Lange, iii. 245.   Antonius was to be prosecuted
by Caelius on his return from Macedonia.   P. Nigidius Figulus

was one of the senators chosen by Cicero to take down the evidence of the informers against Catiline, Or. pro Sulla, 42. Cicero gives a flattering description of him in the beginning of the *Timaeus*. Cf. Mommsen, R. H. iv. 562.

huc. To his Tusculanum, whence this letter was probably written.

apud nos, 'at my *town* house': cf. Att. iv. 5, 3. *Tu 'de via recta in hortos'; videtur commodius ad te,* 'you tell me "come straight to my suburban villa." I think it would be better to go to your town house.'

LETTER VII. (ATT. II. 11)

1. Narro tibi. *Narra* is often used to introduce a rhetorical or ironical question, as in Att. ii. 7, 2, *narra mihi: reges Armenii resalutare non solent?* *Narro* introduces an emphatic statement: cf. Att. xiii. 51, 2, *narro tibi: Quintus cras* (veniet).

die, repeated to show that *quo* does not go with *melius.*

exceptum, 'snapped up': cf. Att. ii. 5, 1.

ponderosam. Cf. Att. i. 13, 1, *qui epistolam paullo graviorem ferre possit nisi eam pellectione relevarit.* There there is a play on the two meanings of *gravis,* 'heavy' (physically) and 'weighty,' 'important.' It is to avoid any such ambiguity that Cicero here uses *ponderosam* (a word not found in his other writings); he wants a heavy, bulky packet, full of the details of affairs at Rome, with Atticus's comments on them.

2. τρηχεἶ', etc. Hom. Od. ix. 27, the description of Ithaca. Arpinum is again connected with Ithaca, de Legg. ii. 3.

Haec igitur. The Med. has *haec igitur, ET cura ut valeas,* *et* being scored out. It seems to me that *et* is sound, and was crossed out by the copyist, who did not understand this sentence, which means 'this is all I have to say except the usual ending, *take care of yourself.*' This not being obvious at first sight, the copyist would score out the *et,* but it is impossible to account for the presence of the *et* except on the theory of its soundness, for it makes the sentence more difficult. [Possibly *haec igitur ego; tu cura.*]

LETTER VIII. (FAM. XIV. 4)

This and the next three letters are written during the period of Cicero's exile ; for the effect of his unhappy position on the style of his writing see Introduction.

1. **Ego.** 'Yes, I *did* send'; the *ego* points to the fact that the clause in which it stands is an answer to a question. Terentia must have asked him why he wrote so seldom, and here we have the answer. Cf. *Ego vero, Servi, vellem ut scribis*, Fam. iv. 6, 1 ; *ego vero Quinto epistolam ad sororem misi*, Att. xiii. 41 ; *de Q. fratre nihil ego te accusavi*, Fam. xiv. 1, 4 ; *quod de domo scribis . . . ego vero*, Fam. xiv. 2, 3 : so ibid., *ego ad quos scribam nescio* is an answer to a suggestion of Terentia, that he should approach his friends by letter.

Quod utinam. 'And would that I had not clung so to life. I should then have seen no sorrow, or at least but little in my life.' Cicero often regrets that he had not destroyed himself, *e.g.* in Att. iii. 3. This use of *quod* is the *connexive* use, as in *quod si* in the next sentence.

si, 'if my present bitter fate is unalterably fixed.' Some edd. would read *sin*, but the opposition is not strong enough to require such a change.

neque di . . . neque homines. Cicero often betrays how lightly he wears his religious beliefs ; here, for instance, he shows much of the spirit of the modern Parisian : his business was with men ; his wife's department was religion. Other features in the character of Cicero which remind us of the modern Frenchman are his hatred of provincial life and his passion for the town (see Att. v. 11, 1 ; Fam. ii. 12, 2), as well as his romantic love for his daughter and indifference to his wife. [Are not the *di* here the *Lares*, with whose worship the women of the household had specially to do ?]

2. **M. Laenium Flaccum.** In Att. v. 21, 10, vi. 1, 6, etc., we meet a M. Laenius Flaccus, to whom Cicero, when governor of Cilicia, refused an appointment as praefectus, on the ground that he carried on a banking business in the province. But this can hardly be the same man (though identified by Klotz in his Index, and Orelli in his Onomasticon Tullianum), for he is invariably mentioned as *Laenius tuus*, as the friend of Atticus, not of Cicero. Now, we must arraign Cicero of great forgetfulness of past favours, if we suppose the Laenius of

whom he speaks so coldly afterwards to have been the man of
whose kindness he here says he will ever have a grateful
recollection. Cicero speaks again most warmly of this Laenius
in Planc. 97, and Sest. 131.

periculum fortunarum et capitis. Cf. Att. iii. 4, *ne et
Sica periret.*

prae, 'in comparison with.'

3. profecti sumus=*proficiscor*, 'I am setting out,' and
petebamus=*petiturus sum.* Both are epistolary tenses, and
look forward to the time when Terentia will read this letter;
so in Att. viii. 3, 7, *reverti Formias*, though he had not yet
left Cales, but would have returned to Formiae before Atticus
received the letter. So *misi*, in Att. iv. 2, 5, means 'I send
herewith'; in Att. v. 15, 3, *faciebam*=*facturus sum;* in v. 17,
1, *habebam*=*habiturus sum*, and in vii. 23, 2, *remittebam*=
remissurus sum. The form *a. d. II. Kal.* which, according to
the Roman way of counting, indicates the same day as *pridie
Kal.* is very unusual. The ms. reading *v. Kal.* must be wrong;
this might easily be a corruption of *II. Kal.*, but hardly of
pridie Kal.

confirmes, 'promote.'

sin, the opposition here is considerably more pointed than
above.

quid Tulliola mea fiet, 'what will become of my dear
Tullia': cf. Att. vi. 1, 14, *quid illo fiet*, 'what will become
of him'; Fam. xiv. 1, 5, *quid puero fiet.*

illius misellae, 'we must devote ourselves to the mainten-
ance of the poor girl's conjugal happiness and of her good name.'
For *serviendum* cf. Att. v. 11, 5. Tullia was married to
Calpurnius Piso, of whom Cicero always speaks in the highest
terms, especially in Brut. 272. Piso refused to go to Pontus
and Bithynia as quaestor, so that he might attend to the affairs
of his exiled father-in-law in Rome, and incurred on Cicero's
behalf the enmity of his kinsman, the consul (Post Red. in
Sen. 38). He died probably about the time of Cicero's restoration. Cicero says (Sest. 68), *Piso ille gener meus cui fructum
pietatis suae neque ex me neque a pop. Romano ferre licuit.*
Tullia's dowry seems not to have been yet paid, and from this
Cicero apprehends danger 'to her married happiness and good
name.'

complexu meo. Cf. *in sinu est neque ego discingor*, Q. Fr.
ii. 11 (13), 1.

L

teneas, 'whether you hold in your hands (still retain) any of my property': cf. Off. ii. 81, *multa dotibus* tenebantur.

4. **De familia liberata.** Terentia had heard that all their slaves had been given their freedom by Cicero. He assures her that she need not be uneasy. 'To your slaves,' he says, 'no promise was made at all, but that you would treat every one as he deserved. Now, Orpheus is so far very well behaved; besides him no one has shown himself particularly deserving. In the case of the others (my own), the arrangement made is this—that if the property is sold by public auction, and *goes out of my hands* (*a nobis abisset*), they should have the position of freedmen of mine, if they could make good their title to that position (against those who might urge that the penalties of confiscation were being thus evaded); but if the property is left in my hands, *i.e.* if I am allowed to buy it in (*si ad nos pertineret*), they should be still my slaves, except a very few (whom I have promised to manumit).'

ea causa est is followed by past tenses, *essent, servirent,* etc., because in *sense* it refers to past time, in referring to the result of an agreement already made.

5. **tempestatem,** 'a favourable wind,' usually with an adj. such as *bona* or *idonea.*

ornamentis, 'my dignities.'

6. **Clodium.** He, as well as Pescennius and Sallustius, was probably a freedman of Cicero.

mecum fore, sc. in Graecia.

quod potes. Some edd. would here read *quoad potes;* but *quod potes* is used in quite the same sense. In proof of this, Hofm. quotes quod *poteris,* Att. x. 2, 2 ; quod eius *facere potueris,* Fam. iii. 2, 2 ; quod eius *facere poteris,* Att. xi. 12, 4. Add Att. ii. 7, 3 ; Fam. v. 8, *fin.* [*Quod potest,* Ov. Trist. iv. 3, 18 ; *quod licet,* v. 3, 58.]

LETTER IX. (Q. FR. I. 3)

1. **Scilicet.** 'Yes, of course, it was you who crushed me. It was your enemies and envy of you that ruined me—and not I who utterly ruined you!' Ironical, of course, as Ter. And. i 2, 14, *id populus curat* scilicet. The sentence is redeemed from

a certain degree of bad taste by the tenderness of *mi frater, mi frater, mi frater.*   The *invidia* referred to is the envy of Hortensius.

fortunas, sc. *eripuit,* taken out of *cripuerit* which follows.

ceciderunt.   'I have met with nothing but what was good and kind from you.'

videre noluerim, 'I not want to see you?' For the subjunct. cf. *ego tibi irascerer* above, and Att. ii. 12, 1, *negent illi,* where the subj. is used in a reply, taking up indignantly a speaker's words.   This usage is peculiar to Cicero's Letters and the comic drama, from which may be quoted as good examples of this idiom, *audi, Ego audiam?* Ter. And. v. 3, 23 ; *non taces, Taceam?* Phorm. v. 8, 95.   See also Att. v. 15, 1 (Ep. xxx.) [Not quite: see some exx. from other writings of Cic. in Draeger, II.² p. 662, and one or two from later writers.   The subj. with *ut* or *ut ne* in a question is essentially the same, and occurs later.]

non eum quem, 'not the brother you mingled your tears with in parting, and who turned back to follow you as you sent him on his way.'   *Prosequi* is the regular word for 'to see off.'

utinam te non solum vitae.   'Would that I had left you behind me to look back on my life, not only finished, but finished with honour.'   The meaning is clear, but the sentence is difficult to render precisely.   Cicero recurs to his oft-expressed wish that he had perished nobly before his humiliation, so that Quintus would have survived his brother, but would not have had his present indignities to look back on.   See Att. iii. 7, 2. The thought is, 'If I had destroyed myself before I left Rome, you would have been able to look back on my life as a finished drama without a single dishonourable episode.'   Ernesti would transpose *vitae* and *dignitatis.*   At first sight this seems plausible,—'Would that I had in you a survivor not only of my honour, but of my existence,'—but had Cicero died before he left Rome, his honour would have been (as he often says) intact ; so if Quintus had been *vitae superstes* he would not have been *dignitatis superstes* in the sense which Ernesti gives to the words. If Cicero had written *utinam te non dignitatis sed vitae superstitem reliquissem,* then we should have the meaning which Ernesti looks for, 'Would that you had survived, not my honour (as is now the case), but my life (as you would have done if I had perished in Rome).'   [*Prius* must be 'before your departure to Asia.'   The words *aut audisses* are very feeble.   Are they

not the marginal comment of some scribe who was not sure
whether to read *vidisses* or *audisses* ?]

2. **scelerate,** 'with wretched, culpable imprudence.' *Scel* is
has often in these letters this mitigated signification ; cf. Att.
iii. 15, 4, *meo non tuo scelere praetermissum est.*

defenderet. This may mean—(1) 'my very death itself
would clearly prove and maintain my affection for you,' as in
Fin. iii. 71 ; or (2) 'might allege in its defence,' as in Fin. ii.
117.

mea vox, 'that my voice should fail to be uplifted when
peril threatened my own family—that voice which so often was
the saving of the merest strangers.'

nam quod. The last six sentences from *Non enim vidisses
. . . praesidio fuisset* must be looked on as parenthetical. *Nam
quod ad te pueri* resumes the train of thought broken off at
immo vero me a te videri nolui, 'The reason I did not meet you
was not that I did not care to see you ; no, but I did not wish
to be seen by you. The fact that my servants arrived without
any letters for you is not to be taken to discredit what I have
said. No, it was my helpless, unstrung condition (I have
already shown that it was not any feeling of irritation)
and the weight of woe that oppressed me.' *Pigritia* is 'listlessness': cf. Tusc. iv. 18.

3. **scripsisse,** 'am writing' ; epistolary perf. = English
present.

Cum enim te desidero, 'When I am parted from you do
I feel the loss only of a *brother* in you ? In losing you, I lose
a brother indeed (and one of well-nigh my own years) in charm
of manner—a son in compliance with me—a parent in judgment.' The reading of M. is *suavitate* prope *fratrem prope
aequalem,* which Ernesti corrected as in the text. Orelli accepts
the reading which Petrarch says he found in his text, *suavitate
prope aequalem ;* and certainly the mention of *fratrem* (in the
reply to *fratrem solum desidero ?*) is to be accounted for only on
the principle that the Letters from exile are badly written. The
aequalis (ὁμῆλιξ, comrade) might well be placed above even a
brother as regards *suavitas,* 'charm of manner,' and the word
fratrem might have been inserted by some copyist who knew
that Quintus was *prope aequalis* with his brother, and misunderstood *aequalis.* To read *suavitate aequalem* would give a
still better sense, and *prope* might have been inserted by a
copyist who thought that *aequalem* implied that Marcus and

Quintus were of the same age, and did not perceive that *aequalis* here is simply ὁμῆλιξ, 'a comrade.' I believe, therefore, that *fratrem* and *prope* are both corrupt, and that the sentence means, 'In you I lose one who is in charm of social intercourse as a comrade, in compliance with my wishes as a son, in the soundness of his advice as a father.'

ferus et ferreus, 'with iron hardness of resolution.' Cf. *quam ferus et vere ferreus ille fuit,* Tibull. i. 10, 2.

reliquias communis calamitatis, 'all that is spared to us by the blow that has prostrated us both': so *reliquias Danaum,* Virg. Aen. i. 30. Cicero uses *reliquias* in a slightly different sense in De Sen. 19, *reliquias avi,* 'the heirloom of a grandfather,' *i.e.* the war with Carthage. [I think that in this passage the meaning of *reliquias* is the same as in Aen. i. 30, 'what your grandfather left unfinished.' The sense 'heir-loom' seems hardly possible.]

4. praesidio, sc. *tibi* (Schütz); but *praesidio* implies action on behalf of another. Cicero would wish Quintus to resist any further hostile acts against himself or his family on the part of those whose malice was not yet sated by his present abject state.

5. si potes, sc. *facere.* The ellipse is common in the Letters, e.g. *quod poteris,* Att. x. 2, 2; *quod potes,* Att. ii. 7, Fam. xiv. 4, 6.

auctoritatis, 'basis,' 'grounds,' 'foundation.'

et aliquid etiam. The order is *et etiam misericordiam nostri aliquid praesidii (tibi) laturam.*

periculo. The prosecution for malversation in his province with which he was threatened by Appius Claudius, son of Clodius.

quam diu tibi opus erit. Cicero seems to have thought of writing a speech for his brother, in defence of his administration.

sustinere, 'to bear up against': cf. Q. Fr. i. 1, 19.

6. genere ipso pecuniae, 'blest in brother, children, wife, fortune—ay, even in the very *nature* of my wealth,' which was won by honourable means, so that he had an unblemished character and unassailable position in society. His wealth seems to have been derived chiefly from the large legacies left by grateful clients, and he did not dissipate his property like many rich men of his day. Manutius ingeniously conjectured *genero,* supposing a reference to Piso, but the order of the words should then be changed, and *pecunia* could hardly be retained. The whole sentence, *ut qui modo . . . diutius possim*, is very loosely constructed : 'It is impossible for me to linger longer than your needs or some trustworthy hope may warrant, in a life so miserable and ignominious, that I (who was once so blest in family, etc., and in rank, character, and reputation as high as ever was any one, be he never so distinguished), even I, may not any longer have the power to lament in my crushed and ruined state the fall of myself and my family.' This, surely, is a sentence which Cicero would never have written in his happier days.

7. **de permutatione.** Quintus had offered to negotiate a bill of exchange for Cicero in Rome. The money would be paid to Cicero at Thessalonica. See Ep. xxx. 2.

quid sceleris. 'I see what a crime I committed when I squandered, to no purpose (probably on bribes to save himself from exile), the money which I got from the treasury on your account, while you are coining your blood and your son's blood to pay your creditors.' This is the money before referred to in Att. ii. 6 *fin.*, and ii. 16 *fin.* There is a difficulty in this sentence which seems not to be noticed by the commentators. After *admiscrim* should stand some word to be the subject of (or to qualify) *dissiparim*. *Qui* would naturally be the word *sentio quid sceleris admiscrim, qui, cum satis facturus sis quibus debes, dissiparim ;* but then *ego* should be omitted. To read *cum, cum satis facturus sis quibus debes, dissiparim* would account for the disappearance of the first *cum*, but would be very cacophonous ; *quod, cum* might be the true reading, but I have followed Wesenberg, who *to some extent* removes the difficulty by suggesting an emphatic *tu* before *de visceribus ;* the same *cum* then governs both *satis facturus sis* and *dissiparim ;* but I do not believe that this is what Cicero wrote. For *ex visceribus,* cf. Pro Dom. 124, *cur ille gurges, helluatus tecum simul reipublicae sanguinem, ad caelum tamen exstruit villam in Tusculano* visceribus aerarii. [Wes.'s cure seems to me very possibly right. *Ego* points to *tu*, which would easily fall out before *cum*.]

M. Antonio. Antonius and Caepio were creditors of Quintus. Cicero had paid them some money before he left Rome.

quantum tu scripseras, 'the amount you mentioned in your letter,' probably ; but, possibly, 'the amount to which you drew on them': cf. Pl. As. ii. 4, 34, *scribit* numos.

desperamur, sc. *ab amicis. Desperare aliquem,* 'to despair of a person,' is a very rare construction, but is found in Cic. Cat. ii. 10 ; Acad. ii. ; Caes. B. C. 7, 3 ; In Pis. 99.

molestiae, 'a prosecution' : cf. Q. Fr. i. 4, 2, *si te satis innocentia tua et misericordia hominum vindicat a molestia.* He advises Quintus to apply for aid to Crassus (the triumvir) and M. Calidius, if prosecuted. M. Calidius, as praetor, next year brought in the bill for Cicero's restoration.

8. **Pomponium.** Hortensius was a friend of Atticus.

ne ille versus, 'lest by some false testimony your author-ship of that epigram be confirmed—that epigram about the Aurelian law which was attributed to you when you were a candidate for the aedileship.' Some epigram on the Aurelian Law, which gave the *iudicia* to the senate, knights, and *tribuni aerarii,* was attributed to Quintus. We do not know what it was ; but we may infer that it was in some way offensive to Hortensius or some of the leading men of the time. Ernesti wrongly under-stands *collatus* as 'applied to,' but cf. Fam. v. 5, 2, quod abs te aiunt falso in me *conferri;* and Fam. vii. 32, 1, omnia omnium dicta in me *conferri.* Hence Cicero was called *scurra consularis.*

tuae preces et tua salus, 'your intercession on my behalf consequent on your acquittal,' for if Quintus was himself under an adverse sentence, he could not, with any effect, plead his brother's cause.

9. **Messallam.** Consul with M. Piso in 693 (B.C. 61).

etiam, 'still,' as before in my case.

10. **Reliqua.** 'More—I swear by my hopes of restoration and of a grave in my fatherland—more my tears do not let me write !' Cf. Att. v. 15, 2, *ita vivam, ut maximos sumptus facio,* 'by my life I am drawing enormously on my own resources.'

LETTER X. (ATT. III. 20)

1. **Quod quidem ita esse.** The words refer to the super-scription of the letter, by the form of which Cicero conveys his knowledge of the fact that the uncle of Atticus had died, adopting Atticus in his will, and leaving him a large fortune (10,000,000 sesterces, according to Nepos, Vit. Att. v. 2). T. Pomponius Atticus now became Q. Caecilius Pomponianus Atticus, his

uncle's name having been Q. Caecilius. In Att. iv. 15, 1, Cicero,
in thanking Atticus for manumitting a slave, Eutychides,
at his request, observed that the new freedman's name will
be T. Caecilius, by a combination of Atticus's old *praenomen*,
Titus, and his (Atticus's) new *nomen* by adoption, Caecilius.
In three other letters, Fam. i. 10, vii. 29, and xvi. 18, the
meaning of the first sentence of the letter depends on the
superscribed address.

animus, 'courage and judgment (on my part); honesty on
the part of my friends.' See Q. Fr. i. 4, 1.

colligere, 'to review in the mind,' 'think over': cf. *cum
. . . maximarum civitatum veteres animo calamitates* colligo,
De Inv. i. 1.

esset, 'what my life would now be, how charming and how
dignified' (what a position).

per fortunas, 'in the name of fortune.' It is strange that
this should be in the plural, in which number *fortunae* means
'circumstances,' whether good or bad. So *per fortunas* should
mean 'I adjure you in the name of our weal or woe.' He uses
the same phrase afterwards (*e.g.* Att. v. 11, 1 ; v. 13, 3), when
not in affliction, but merely as a strong adjuration. But see
Fam. xiv. 1, where he says, *per* miseras *fortunas.* The oath
per fortunas Caesaris gave the early Christians much trouble.

diemque natalem, 'the day of my restoration,' 'my second
birthday.' So he speaks of his restoration as παλιγγενεσία, o·
'second birth' (Att. vi. 6, 4). It was also his daughter's birthday, and the anniversary of the foundation of the colony o·
Brundisium, and of the building of the Temple of Salus. Sest.
131.

praestolari. *Praestolari* is always followed by the *dative*
in Cicero, though in the comic poets it takes the accusative.

2. **ea . . . restituetur**, sc. *domus.* See Fam. xiv. 2, 3,
*quod de domo scribis, hoc est de area, ego vero tum denique mihi
videbor restitutus, si illa nobis erit restituta.*

multas partes, 'have a large share in my restoration.'

3. **accidisse ad animum**, 'that it had ever entered your
mind that I was guilty of any sin of commission or omission
against you.' *Humanitas*, 'generosity.'

Rogatio Sestii. 'The bill of Sestius (for my restoration) is
not drawn up respectfully enough nor carefully enough. The

bill brought in ought expressly to name me, and there should
be a carefully constructed clause about my effects.'

LETTER XI. (FAM. V. 4)

1. collega, Lentulus Spinther.

immutatum, 'turned against me.'

obstrepere, 'obtrude my letters on you,' 'din my letters
into your ears.' [Cf. Att. viii. 1, 4, *ego si somnum capere possem
tam longis te epistolis non obtunderem*; Fam. v. 14, 3.]

2. **orationem,** on the motion of Lentulus for Cicero's recall.

quantum tua fert voluntas. This is to be taken, not
with *ut serves,* but with *peto;* it means, 'I beseech you as
strenuously as I may without offending you.' Otherwise, *fert*
must be changed to *ferat,* or *feret,* which Wes. reads.

tuos mecum serves, 'by aiding me (I beg you) to do a
service to your whole family,' referring to his promise below,
omnibus in rebus me fore in tua potestate.

<u>tuorum.</u> Clodius, whose sister was the widow of the
consul's late brother, Metellus Celer.

Tu tuas inimicitias, 'you have compelled yourself to resign
a private (personal) grudge (see Fam. v. 1) for the sake of the
State. Will you be persuaded to injure the State to make the
spite of another (*i.e.* Clodius) more effective?'

eam vim, referring especially to the violence with which
Clodius foiled the attempt of Jan. 25 in favour of Cicero.

vide ne, 'take care lest afterwards, when you would gladly
recall the opportunity you now have <u>for restoring all your
fellow-citizens to safety and happiness,</u> you may find yourself
unable to do so (as there may not then be one whom you can
even <u>save from utter ruin</u>).' Such is the explanation of Orelli.
The following are his words: *sanissima est ista sententia per-
acuta propter oppositionem verborum reservandi et servandi, sed
varie corrupta a criticis. Hoc dicit:* 'vide ne, cum frustra in
eo labores, ut revoces nunc tempus illud, quo omnes in republica
illaesi atque incolumes reservari etiam tunc poterant, id ipsum
efficere non possis, cum nemo iam omnino erit, qui queat vel
servari *dumtaxat* (id quod minus etiam est quam reservari).'
But this antithesis between *servari* and *reservari* seems to me
to need defence; and, feeling this, most edd. give *servandorum*

for *reservandorum*.   Martyni-Laguna even reads *cum velis revocare ipsum omnium conservatorem* (Ciceronem).   I cannot find a
single passage in Cicero in which *reservare* is used merely as an
intensive of *servare*.   I believe that *reip.* (*reipublicae*) dropped
out before *reservandorum*, and that the sentence means, 'w ien
you wish to recall the opportunity you had of saving the State
from the loss of all her best interests.'   In this sense Cicero
often uses *reservare* : cf. Pro Flac. 106, *nomen clarissimum
reipublicae reservate*, 'save the State from the loss of one so distinguished' ; Sest. 50, *vitam suam* ad reipublicae statum reservavit.   But *reservare* absolutely can only mean in Cicero, ' to
hold over,' 'reserve.'   We have in Prov. Cons. 47, *inimicitias
in aliud tempus* reservare ; but it would be too harsh to construe here, 'when you may wish to recall your present opportunity of at least holding in abeyance all your feuds with me.'
The passage from the Or. pro Flac. just quoted suggests a conjecture which may appear to be rash, but seems to me to derive
considerable confirmation from that passage.   For *omnium reservandorum* read NOMINUM *reip. reservandorum*.   Cicero says,
'when you may wish to recall the opportunity you now have of
saving the State from the loss of a distinguished citizen,' l e
refers to *himself*, and he uses the plural so as to take away
some of the arrogance from the words.   The plural is often
used by Cicero in his letters, though the reference be to a sing e
person, when it is desirable to make the statement vague, either
to avoid arrogance, as in this case, or to avoid offence, as in this
letter (above), where he says, *propter adrogantem crudelitatem
tuorum*, though referring to Clodius alone.   On this theory, in
the words *cum qui servetur non erit*, Cicero hints at his design
to destroy himself if the attempts to restore him should fail.
Draeger calls this plural the *pluralis modestiae* (Historische
Syntax, i. p. 25), and gives as exx., *Moloni dedimus operam*,
Brut. 312 ; *scripsimus . . . tenebamus*, De Div. ii. 3 ; *vide
. . . nos multa conari*, Orat. 105 ; *adolescentuli diximus*, ibid.
107 ; *imperatores appellati sumus*, Att. v. 20, 3.   Cf. *poscimur*,
Hor. Carm. i. 32, 1.   The singular and plural are often found
together, as, *video . . . mea voce . . . nobis*, Catil. i. 22 ; *dis-
suasimus nos. Sed nihil de me*, de Am. 95 ; *viribus nostris
. . . et possim et soleam*, Fam. ii. 11, 1 ; *ardeo . . . cupiditate
ut nomen nostrum*, Fam. v. 12, 1.   A good ex. in poetry is, *Et
flesti et nostros vidisti flentis ocellos*, Ov. Her. v. 45.   Madvig
(Adn. Crit. iii. p. 157) proposes to write : *vide ne tum velis
revocare tempus omnium servandorum cum*, quia *qui servetur
non erit, non possis*.   He says that *si volueris*, not *cum velis*,
would have been used by Cicero to express the meaning usually

assigned to the passage. Mr. Everard of Eton suggests to me to read *cum cui serventur* (sc. *reipublicae*). If *reip.* originally stood in the text the corruption of it would soon have been followed by the alteration of *cui* to *qui*. [I think the interpretation of the passage depends on the idea that unless a reconciliation is effected and Cic. allowed to return, Clodius on the one hand will lose his life in the violent struggles, and Cic. on the other will die in despair. By coming to the rescue Metellus will be doing a service not only to Cic. but to Clodius as well. This is the meaning of *ut tuos mecum serves*, "to secure the safety of those of your own household along with my safety." The words *cum qui servetur non erit* refer to both Cic. and Clodius, and point to the coming extinction of both if reconciliation be delayed. *Omnium* means these two again, because Clodius has been hinted at by the plural *tui*; so the word = *tuorum meique*. The real and only difficulty of the passage lies in the *re* of *reservandorum*. It is an *almost*, but not quite, invariable practice with Cic. to express with *reservare* the *purpose* of the act (by *ad* and acc. or dat.) or the person for whose benefit the act is done (in the dat.) There are some passages which show that it is not absolutely necessary to *express* either purpose or person. But, on the whole, I think you are right in supposing a dat. to have fallen out. Other passages might be quoted in support of *reip.* But I am inclined to suppose that *tibi* (often written in mss. *t¹*) has fallen out after *tempus*. Supplying this, I would render *vide ne . . . possis* thus: "Take care lest, when you may wish to call back again the opportunity of saving yourself the loss of us all, you may find it beyond your power, at a moment when there will be no one left for you to save."]

LETTER XII. (FAM. VII. 26)

1. tuum. Gallus was an Epicurean.

male accipiunt, 'handle roughly.'

alterum. The first *alterum* (= the latter) refers to δυσεντερικὰ πάθη (dysentery); the second *alterum* (= the former) refers to στραγγουρικὰ πάθη (strangury), which was supposed to be the result of sexual incontinence. This passage is generally misunderstood, because it is taken for granted that the first *alterum* must mean 'the former'; but this is not so. See Fam. i. 7, 1, where the first *alterum* = 'the latter,' the second

alterum = 'the former,' the meaning of that passage being:
'You say you are much obliged by my regularity as a correspondent and by my affection for you ; the *latter*, my affect on,
is a bounden duty on my part ; the *former*, my regularity in
correspondence, is a pleasure.' [See letter of Epicurus preserved
by Diog. Laert. x. 22. Cic. translates part of it in Fin. ii. 96.]

Sed visa . . . profuisse. 'The change of scene has done
me good, or perhaps it was the complete holiday I gave myself,
or the fact that the distemper ran its full course and spent
itself.'

2. **commiserim.** 'And strange to say, in case you should
wonder how this came about, and how I incurred this ailment,
it was the Aemilian law, which you would think was for pla in
living, that played me false. For those *gourmets* you wot of,
wishing to popularise the fruits of the earth which are not
under the ban of the sumptuary law, cook mushrooms, pot-
herbs, and every kind of vegetable, in the most charming way
in the world.' For the Lex Aemilia here referred to, see Ge l.
N. A. ii. 24, 12. This passage clearly shows that it is the *Lex
Aemilia* (B.C. 115) which is here referred to, not the *Lex
Licinia* mentioned *ibid.* § 7.

λιτότητα, 'a plain diet'; the Greek word is appropriate to
hygienic matters, see note on Ep. iv. ; λιτός is precisely the appropriate word for a *plain, simple* diet. It was a knowledge of
this fact which led Bentley to what may be held to be the best
conjecture ever made. An epigram of Callimachus begins thus :

τὴν ἁλίην Εὔδημος ἐφ' ἧς ἅλα λιτὸν ἐπελθὼν
χειμῶνας μεγάλων ἐξέφυγεν δανίων.

The old editors changed δανέων to Δαναῶν, and took the
epigram to mean, 'Eudemus dedicates this ship on which, having crossed a smooth sea, he escaped from great storms of the
Danai.' But ἁλίη is not a ship. What are 'storms of the
Danai' ? and if there were storms how came it that the sea
was smooth ? Bentley saw the right answer to these questions : ἁλίη is a *saltcellar*, δανέων is sound and means 'money
borrowed from usurers' ; the corrupt word is ἐπελθὼν, which
should be corrected to ἐπέσθων. Eudemus saved himself from
debt by a life of frugality, and at his death dedicates 'the saltcellar which held the frugal grain of salt, which was the only
relish to his bread, and which saved him from the storms of a
sea of debts.'

Lentulum. P. Cornelius Lentulus Spinther was the son of the consul for this year (57) of the same name, who was active in the restoration of Cicero, and was afterwards proconsul of Cilicia 698. Lentulus, the son, was made augur this year, whence the date of this letter is inferred. He was adopted by Manlius Torquatus into the Manlian *gens*, so that he might become eligible for the augurate. Man. says that it was forbidden by law that there should be two augurs of the same *gens*. Now one of the existing augurs was Faustus Cornelius, son of the dictator Sulla. Hence by his adoption he eluded this statute. The Latin phrase for 'to elude a law' is *fraudem facere legi*. Hence in the words *fraudem fecit* above there is, perhaps, a satirical allusion to the host at whose table Cicero incurred his ailment. The Aemilian law played him false, as his host had played false with another statute. [All the details are in Dio Cassius, xxxix. c. 17, who makes the law apply to every ἱεραρεία, not the οἰωνισταί only.]

consistere, 'to stop'; the word is used in a slightly different sense, though applied to a disease, in Cels. iii. 2, *videndum an morbus increscat an consistat an minuatur*, where *consistat* means *remains unchanged, neither better nor worse.*

[**a beta et a malva.** The prep. shows there is a humorous personification, 'entrapped by Mr. Beet and Mr. Mallow.']

audisses, sc. *me aegrotum esse.* Cp. *cum ita me adflictum videas ut neminem umquam nec videris nec audieris,* Att. iii. 13, 2.

illa, sc. *corpus et vires.* 'I shall soon regain my flesh and strength.'

LETTER XIII. (ATT. IV. 4b)

1. **ad nos,** 'to me here in Antium.' *Ad nos* sometimes means 'to my *town* house,' as distinguished from residences in the country and at the seaside. See Att. iv. 5 *fin.*

design. Tyrannionis . . . librorum. For the double gen. see Att. iv. 1, 2, *fructus tuae suavitatis praeteriti temporis ;* Fam. ix. 8, 2, *superiorum temporum fortuna reipublicae.* There is a triple gen. in Caes. B. G. ii. 17, *eorum dierum consuetudine itineris nostri exercitus.* This refers to his library at Antium, as we learn from Att. iv. 8 a.

duos aliquos, 'a couple'; *aliquos* makes the number

vague : cf. Pl. Men. v. 5, 47, *hos aliquos viginti dies,* 'the next three weeks or so'; *unos sex dies* is 'just one week,' Trin. i. 2, 129; 'a fortnight' is *quindecim dies,* Trin. ii. 4, 1: cf. *quinze jours,* in French.

glutinatoribus, 'for glueing together loose leaves (and) for other purposes.' *Asyndeton,* where there are only two members, is rare ; we have *amici, propinqui,* 2 Verr. i. 125 ; *opilus, viribus,* Tusc. iii. 6 ; so in contracted adjectives used for classification, *publica privata, fanda nefanda, prima postrema,* &c. This *asyndeton* is the rule in referring to colleagues in office —e.g. *Marcio Philippo, P. Lentulo Marcellino consulibus ;* so in judicial language, *dare facere, aequum bonum.*

The duty of the *glutinatores* would be to glue together the separate leaves of parchment of which the newly-written book consisted, so that they might be rolled round the central reed or stick which formed the axis of the cylinder ; they would also have to glue together leaves of old books which had become detached.

indices, strips of papyrus or parchment, on which the title of the book was written in deep red, *coccum* or *minium ;* they were probably attached to the upper one of the two *cornua* or 'knobs,' which projected on both ends below and above the cylindrical roll which formed the book.

Hesych. has σιττύβαι, δερμάτιναι στολαί ; hence *sittybis* has been conjectured here. But the σιττύβαι were quite different from the *indices ;* they were leathern (sometimes canvas) wrappers, into which the rolls were placed for preservation, and are again to be distinguished from the *capsae, scrinia,* which were wooden cases, into which were put the rolls whether covered by the *sittybae (diphtherae, membranae)* or not.

2. adhaerescere, 'if you can stick in such places as this' : the word implies that to stay in a suburban retreat required a voluntary effort of the will. In Att. iv. 8 *a,* Cicero praises Antium, but an expression dropped by him in that letter (§ 2) shows that he was at first bored by the country : 'since Tyrannio has 'arranged my library, the house seems to have got a soul.' Pilia was the newly-married wife of Att.

Medius fidius ne. *Ne* is found with many asseverative particles *medius fidius, edepol, mecastor,* especially in Cicero and the comic poets. It must always be in connexion with a personal pronoun, or the demonstrative *ille, iste, hic,* and their adverbs ; rarely with a *possessive* pron., as *edepol ne meam,* Ter. Hec. v. 3, 1.

λόχον. 'Certes, you have truly bought a fine troop.' It was the habit of wealthy Romans to speculate in troops of gladiators, whom they let out or sold to the aediles for the public games, and to private individuals for other purposes : for instance, we find, Q. Fr. ii. 4, 5, that Att. had sold a gang of roughs to Cato. The reading of the mss. here is *locum*, which is quite unintelligible. Att. had not bought any property near Antium, so far as we know, and the reference here is plainly to the troop of gladiators, of whom Cicero goes on to speak. *Locum* could not mean 'the place where the gladiators were to fight,' for that was always the public amphitheatre, and could not be bought by Att. The usual reading is Ernesti's conj. *ludum ;* but I cannot find that this word ever signifies a troop of gladiators ; it invariably denotes the *school* in which they were trained. Now, it would be absurd that Cicero should congratulate Att. on having secured a good school, or training-place wherein they could train for the forthcoming spectacles. If this is the meaning of the passage, we might as well retain *locum* of the mss. I have accepted the conj. of Bosius : λόχος would be a very natural term for a *troop*, *familia*, of gladiators, and would appear in the mss. as *locum*, if written in Latin characters, as Greek words very often are in the letters. For instance, in this letter σιλλύβους appears as *sillabos* and *syllabos*, and is in some edd. corrupted to *syllabas.*

pugnare mirifice. I hear they are fighting splendidly (*i.e.* in practising for the games).

si . . . esses. 'If you had chosen to hire them out (already), you would have cleared your expenses by the two aedilician spectacles given this year.' Att. could not have wanted the gladiators, except to hire them out or to sell them. We may suppose he did not think they were as yet sufficiently trained. Corradus, who would read *pugnasse*, suggests that Att. had given a *munus* in honour of his uncle, who died the year before. Boot suspects, from the last words of Att. iv. 8 *a*, that the gladiators had not acquitted themselves well, and that the words here should be taken ironically ; but the words of that letter do not justify his view.

liber. Cf. *io, liber ad te venio,* Plin. Ep. iii. 9, 13. *Te liberasses* is the ms. reading. Boot, retaining *liberasses*, would (in pursuance of his theory about the ironical character of the sentence) explain the word as meaning 'you would have given them all their freedom'; that is, they would have fought so badly that they would all now be 'free among the dead.'

LETTER XIV. (FAM. V. 12)

1. **Coram** is generally as here an adverb throughout republican and Augustan Latin, and is used freely as a prep. only by Tacitus. There are only two passages in Cic. where *coram* (acc. to the mss.) is a prep. One is Pis. 12, *mihi vero ipsi coram genero meo*, which is simply emended by Dr. Reid, who inserts *et* before *genero*, thus making *coram* an adverb as usual. The other is Fam. xiii. 6 *a*, 1, *me et coram P. Cuspio tecum locutum esse*, where we should probably read *me et coram cum P. Cuspio et tecum locutum esse*. [There are exx. of the prep. usage in Livy, as in xxxv. 49, 1. Plautus and Terence seem to be the only writers who use the word before Cic. Ennius has not the word, nor Lucilius, nor Catullus, nor (I think) Lucretius. We find an ex. of the prep. use in Hor. A. P. 185, *coram populo Medea trucidet;* also in Sat. i. 4, 74 and 95; Ep. i. 17, 43; I have not noted a certain ex. in Ovid.]

pudor quidam subrusticus, ' a sort of *mauvaise honte.*'

ignoscas, ' pardon my impatience.' Cf. Att. xii. 26, 1, *tuis occupationibus ignosco.*

genus, ' the character of your writings,' *i.e.* ' your success in this branch of literature.' Cf. *generi litterarum mearum*, Fam. xiii. 6 *a*, 3. Cicero had seen a specimen of Lucceius's work, which greatly increased his admiration, and his desire to secure for himself a place in his history.

res nostras, ' the history of my consulship.' Cf. Att. iv. 6, 4.

commemoratio posteritatis. Cf. *mea commemoratione*, Planc. 95. The genitive in connexion with *commemoratio* is usually an objective genitive ; here *posteritatis* is a subjective genitive, ' the praises of future ages.'

vel auct. perfruamur. The meaning of the sentence is that Cicero wishes to enjoy, in his lifetime, that account of his exploits which, if he did not urge Lucceius to haste, might not be published till after his death. Cicero seems to feel sure that the account will be favourable ; but he is not sure whether the commendation which he expects from Lucceius will be the authoritative expression of the historian's real judgment, or a token of friendly feeling on the part of a friend, or, finally, an instance of the sweetness which characterises the whole disposi-

tion of Lucccius. The passage affords an excellent example of
the use of *vel* as distinguished from *aut* and *seu* or *sive*.

2. **coniunctene,** 'to work into the context of your history.'
What Cicero preferred was that Lucccius should publish a
history of his consulate separately.

ad locum, 'to the proper place.' Cf. *epistolae offendunt
non loco redditae*, 'the irregularity of the delivery,' Fam. xi.
16, 1.

qui . . . imponam, 'in imposing.'

3. **leges historiae.** Cicero gives as *leges historiae* De Or. ii.
62, *nihil falsi dicere, nihil veri omittere, nihil gratiae, nihil
simultati dare*.

Herculem. Xen. Mem. ii. 1, 21, where the celebrated story
of the choice of Hercules is told.

eam. For this *epanalepsis* cf. *illud quod . . . id te nunc
etiam atque etiam rogo*, Fam. xiii. 57, 2 ; *lex sumptuaria, quae
videtur λιτότητα attulisse*, ea *mihi fraudi fuit*, Ep. xii. 2.

4. **corpus,** a period of history having an intrinsic unity, ' a
volume.'

habet . . . delectationem. Cf. *suavis laborum est praeteri-
torum memoria*, Fin. ii. 105 ; Cicero's translation of ἀλλ' ἡδύ τοι
σωθέντα μεμνῆσθαι πόνων, Eur. Frag. 131.

5. **cum quadam miseratione,** 'the pathetic charm of the
scene.' Cf. De Sen. 52, *ut quemvis cum admiratione delectent*.

fuga redituque. But Themistocles did not return. Yet
this cannot be a μνημονικὸν ἁμάρτημα of Cicero, though such are
not rare. (In Div. ii. 63 there is a remarkable *lapsus memoriae*,
even *Agamemno* for *Ulixes*.) For Cicero, in other places (*e.g.* Brut.
43 ; Att. ix. 10, 3 ; Lael. 42), dwells on the fact that Themistocles did not return after his exile. It is quite impossible that
in the word *reditu* Cicero refers to the fact that Themistocles
was brought back to Athens after his death, and secretly buried
there, though this is referred to in the passage above quoted
from the *Brutus*. It has therefore been proposed to read
Alcibiadi for *Themistocli*. Perhaps what Cicero really wrote
was, *Themistocli fuga, Coriolani fuga redituque*. But he seems to
be referring here only to Greek notables. In two, however, of the
places quoted above (Att. ix. 10, 3, and Lael. 42) he couples
Themistocles and Coriolanus. If the copyist, having written
Themistocli fuga, happened to raise his eyes from his task, he
would mentally note that he was to resume it after the word

fuga; but if the word *fuga* occurred twice in the passage (the two being separated by only one word), the copyist would very probably go on writing after the second *fuga,* not the fi st. This is such a prolific source of error in copyists that it wo ld be desirable to have a term to denote it. Perhaps *parable sy* would be a more convenient term than *corruptio ex homocte-leuto.* [*Aristidi* would be preferable and nearer to the letters of *Themistocli.*]

6. **sententia . . . ut . . . secernas,** 'if you come to the resolution of separating.'

quasi fabulam, 'a kind of drama.'

quid sis. Cf. *si umquam in dicendo fuimus aliquid,* Att. :v. 2, 2; *quid enim sum,* Att. iii. 15, 2; *ita nihil est,* Att. i. 19, 4. The meaning of the whole passage is : 'you know your own worth ; you are more likely to suspect envy in those who do not admire you, than sycophancy in those who do ; and I am not so stupid as to risk my future fame in the hands of one not fitted for the task—of one not capable of showing his own geni is while praising me.'

7. **gratiae causa,** as a mark of favour to Apelles and Lysippus.

ignotis, 'to strangers.' *Ignotus,* like *notus,* is sometimes active in meaning (*e.g.* 2 Verr. i. 19); while *ignarus* is some-times passive, *mare magnum et ignara lingua commercia pro-hibebant,* Sall. Jug. 18, 6.

perhibendus, 'deserves (honourable) mention.' Cf. Att. :. 1, 4 (Ep. x.) for *perhibere* as a legal term.

in eo genere lab., 'who have taken much pains in (securin ; commemoration of) that kind,' 'whose energies took tha; direction.'

libellus, the Agesilaus of Xenophon.

praeconium. Cf. *bucinatorem,* 'trumpeter,' Fam. xvi. 21, 2.

Sigeum. See Pro Arch. 24.

Hector ille Naevianus. Cf. Fam. xvi. 6, 1. The whole verse is a troch. tetram. cat.—

Laetus sum laudari me abs te, pater, a laudato viro.

8. **scribam ipse de me.** Cicero had written a memoir of his consulship in Greek, and had published it. In Att. i. 19, 10 he also speaks of a poem, and of a Latin memoir of his

consulship. He also wrote a long letter concerning his exploits to Pompeius when in the East. Possibly, however, it was a short history of the consulship, and not merely a letter. If so, it may well be referred to here. Cicero may have kept it by him; and it may have occurred to him that, if he failed with Lucceius, he would now finish and publish it.

praedicent, 'declare.'

9. **illa nos cupiditas.** This is the answer of Cicero : ' If you wonder why I now so earnestly urge my request, after repeated assurances on your part that you were going to write a minute history of the crisis in my career, (I answer) I am consumed by the feeling of impatience of which I spoke in the beginning of my letter, by an eager desire,' etc. The words *illa nos cupiditas* give the answer of Cicero ; we should have expected *scito illam nos cupiditatem incendere;* but this ellipse is common in Cicero. For the meaning of *tempora*, see Fam. i. 9, 23. *Gloriola* is found only here and Fam. vii. 5, 3.

10. **commentarios**, 'notes' which would give Lucceius the *data* for his memoir.

cessabis. The future is a polite imper., ' You will kindly use all diligence, and polish what you have, and believe me yours very sincerely ' ; *nos diliges* is one of the conventional *formulae* for winding up a letter.

LETTER XV. (Att. iv. 9)

1. **censum**, the taking of the census by the newly-elected censors.

vitiandis, *i.e. obnuntiatione eximendis* rendering them disqualified for the transaction of public business by observing the heavens and announcing unfavourable omens. [But *obn.* had been abolished three years before by the law of Clodius. Therefore I rather think the word *vitiandis* is used in a non-technical sense. The tribunes stopped the *census* by continually summoning the people for other purposes. If the censors had gone on the tribunes would have complained (as they do in Livy) *contionem a se avocari* and *se in ordinem cogi*.]

totaque de censura. The *lex Clodia* which was afterwards repealed by Q. Scipio Metellus, consul 52, seriously impaired the censorial power of *notatio*. It enacted that the refusal to allow an ex-magistrate to be adopted into the senate could only

have force if the magistrate was formally accused before tl em
and condemned.   For the political significance of this law, see
Lange, iii. 298.   Cicero thought the tribunes might be disposed
to follow up the attack of Clodius on the censorship.

S. spernens, 'expressing his contempt of Syria (the provi ice
of Crassus), and extolling Spain' (his own province).   Thus is
the passage explained by Boot and all the edd. save Man.,
iactans being read for the obviously corrupt *laetans* of M.   But
Man. gives a quite different meaning to *iactans*, which he
translates *ita exagitans quasi fastidiret*.   This, I think, gives a
far better sense to the passage.   Pompeius wished to display an
ostentatious indifference to provincial governorships, which
others coveted so much.   If *iactans* here means 'extolling,' the
passage lacks all point.   Now, undoubtedly, *iactare* can mean
to 'run down,' 'depreciate,' as Prof. Palmer has shown on Hor.
Sat. ii. 2, 47, where he rightly translates the Lucilian line—

O lapathe ut *iactare* nec es satis cognitus qui sis,

'O sorrel, how thou art *scorned*,' and aptly compares Plaut. Ru i.
ii. 3, 43—

Novi. Neptunus ita solet. Quamvis fastidiosus
Aedilis est; si quae improbae sunt merces, *iactat* omnes.

This meaning of *iacto* is not recognised in L. and S.   But it is
found even in Cic. in Fam. i. 5, 1 ; Div. in Caec. 45. [*Iacta s*
in the Lucilian line had been rightly explained by Madv. :n
Cic. Fin. ii. 24 ; also by Munro, *Journ. of Phil.* vii. 299.]

και τόδε.   Just as Phocylides was in the habit of prefixing
to his gnomic verses 'this too is a gnome of Phocylides,' so
when one speaks of Pompeius one must always add a sort of
refrain, 'as he said,' for Cicero thinks that Pompeius often used
his words only to conceal his thoughts.

componenda, the arrangement of the statues in the theatre
of Pompeius, which was dedicated this year.

2. commendaturum, as a subject for eulogy.

Ciceronem, the son of Q. Cicero.

LETTER XVI. (FAM. VII. 23)

1. Tantum quod . . . veneram, sc. *tantum factum es
quod veneram*, 'I had only just arrived.'   This phrase is com

mon in Cic. Epp. So with negatives, *tantum quod non hominem nominat*, 'he only omits the name,' 2 Verr. i. 116.

nomina se facturum, 'that he will not debit my account till I wish.' Gallus had bought certain statues from Avianius for Cicero. Avianius generously proposed to wait for payment till it should suit Cicero's convenience. Literally, 'that he will enter the debt on whatever day I please.' Interest would begin to run from the day on which the debt was entered : cf. Off. iii. 59. [Because till this was done the contract was formally incomplete.]

Fac, 'Put yourself in my place.'

rogare de die, sc. *solutionis*, 'to ask for credit.'

plus annua, 'to ask for more than a year's credit.'

rata . . . grata, 'not only do I *ratify* your purchase, but I am *gratified* so to do.' This, or 'accepted . . . acceptable,' will reproduce the play on the words.

2. Damasippus. This is the Damasippus mentioned in Hor. Sat. ii. 3. Damasippus had said that he was willing to take the statues off Cicero's hands. Cicero says, 'I hope he will adhere to his offer.' Other characters mentioned by Horace, in common with Cicero, are Tigellius, Craterus, Arrius, Trebatius, the son of Aesopus, Arbuscula, Tarpa. .

quanti . . . tanti. 'In your ignorance of my ways you have bought those four or five statues at a price which I would not give for all the statues in the world.'

genus . . . omnium, 'statues of all kinds.' For the gen. *signorum* (which is the gen. *epexegeticus* of Draeger, Hist. Synt. i. 466), cf. *unum genus est eorum*, Cat. ii. 8 ; *propter eam causam sceleris* (viz. 'crime'), 2 Verr. iv. 51 ; *insidias caedis atque incendiorum*, Cat. ii. 3. Add *proelii dimicationem*, Q. Fr. i. 1, 5 ; *optio eligendi*, Att. iv. 18, 3. For some other curious exx. see Reid on Acad. i. § 6.

erat, '(such a purchase) would have been suitable.' Cf. *et nisi longe alium late iactaret odorem laurus* erat, Virg. Georg. ii. 132 ; *peream male si non optimum erat*, Hor. Sat. ii. 1, 6 ; *et iustum poteras et scribere fortem*, ibid. 16 ; *in patrias artes erudiendus* erat, Ov. Her. i. 112. Prof. Palmer, on Hor. Sat. ii. 1, calls this 'the imperfect of neglected duty.'

pacis auctori, 'the author of peace,' alluding most probably to his feat in crushing Catiline without unsheathing the sword : hence *cedant arma togae* and other such boasts. Others, sup-

posing the reference to be to his attitude as peace-maker betw en
Pompeius and Caesar, place this letter very much later.

duo signa, of two such inauspicious gods as Mars and Saturn.
Mercury, on the other hand, was the god of treasure-trove and
good luck.

3. **trapezophorum.** Starting from the passage in the
Digest, 33, 10, 3, pr. (*suppellectili legata haec continentur:
mensae, trapezophora, delficae, subsellia*, etc.), where the furniture of a house is in a way inventoried, we find mention of three
kinds of tables — *mensae, trapezophora*, and *delphicae*. Now
mensae are large dining-tables, and *delphicae* are round tables on
three legs : for one example, among many, to prove this, take
Procopius de bellis Vandalorum, i. 21, quoted by Marquardt
(iv. 311): ἐν παλατίῳ γὰρ τῷ ἐπὶ Ῥώμης, ἔνθα συνέβαινε στιβάδις
τὰς βασιλέως εἶναι, τρίπους ἐκ παλαιοῦ εἱστήκει, ἐφ' οὗ δὴ τὰς κύλικις
οἱ βασιλέως οἰνοχόοι ἐτίθεντο, Δέλφικα δὲ τὸν τρίποδα καλοῦσι
Ῥωμαῖοι, ἐπεὶ πρῶτον ἐν Δελφοῖς γέγονε.

Turning to *trapezophora*, its derivation is 'table-bearer' ; but
that it can be also used for a 'table' is plain from Pollux,
Onomastic. x. 69, ἔξεστι δὲ τὴν τράπεζαν ἐφ' ᾗ τὰ ἐκπώματα
κατάκειται, τετράπουν τε τράπεζαν εἰπεῖν καὶ μονόπουν καὶ εἴ τς
βούλοιτο φιλοτιμεῖσθαι πρὸς τὴν καινότητα τῆς χρήσεως ('to be ambitious of the elegance of the new style') τραπεζοφόρον, and indeed also from the Digest (*l.c.*), since it is quite impossible that
Paulus should have omitted such a common article of furniture
as the *abacus*, which he has plainly comprehended here under
the term *trapezophora*, for in strictness *trapezophoron* is the
support of the *abacus*.   Now *abacus*, in all its meanings (table
of a pillar, baker's tray, draught-board, calculating-board, wall-
panel, or tile in tesselated pavement), signifies a rectangular
flat surface, with perhaps a rim round it : cf. *coronae mensarum*
in Dig. 34, 2, 19, 14, where the Greek translation gives τὸ
κύκλον τῆς τραπέζης.   In its sense of 'table' *abacus* was supported sometimes by four legs, sometimes by one (see Pollux,
l.c.) ; the legs were usually of marble or ivory (Juv. 11, 122),
but sometimes of bronze (Marquardt, *l.c.*)   The fashioning of
these legs was a distinct branch of sculpture: cf. Juvenal,
3, 203—

> Urceoli sex
> Ornamentum abaci : nec non et parvulus infra
> Cantharus et recubans sub eodem marmore Chiron.

The Chiron was the τραπεζοφόρος.   Examples are also found in
museums of sphinxes and griffins.   The δελφινὶς τράπεζα of
Lucian, Lexiph. 7, probably had a dolphin for the τραπεζοφόρον.

The object of the *abacus* was to expose plate and ornaments
(2 Verr. iv. 35, and indeed *passim:* cf. Mayor on Juv. *l.c.*,
but he does not distinguish sufficiently sharply between the
abacus and the *delphica*, which, though used for the same
purpose, were quite different in shape), and therefore varied
according to the size of the room, just like the cabinets for the
same purpose nowadays in drawing-rooms. Sidonius, 17, 7,
says of them—

> Non tibi gemmatis ponentur prandia mensis,
>   Assyrius murex nec tibi sigma dabit,
> Nec per multiplices abaco splendente *cavernas*
>   Argenti nigri pondera defodiam.

What these *cavernae* were is disputed. E. Guillaume, in
Daremberg and Saglio's Dictionnaire des Antiquités, art.
'Abacus,' gives a picture (fig. 7) of one with *shelves*, which he
thinks the *cavernae* to have been. 'Des vases sont rangés sur
deux tablettes ; d'autres sont placés au-dessous. Les cavités
formées par l'intervalle des tablettes sont peut-être ce qu'un
poète . . . a appelé *cavernae* '; but he goes on : 'à moins que
l'on ne doive entendre par ce mot des casiers fermés, de veri-
tables armoires comme celles qu'on voit sur le devant du meuble
représenté plus haut' (fig. 5). This last is the view of Marquardt, iv. 310, note 6, who refers to a picture of such a one,
given by Stackelberg, Gräber der Hellenen (ii. 42), which is, no
doubt, a regular cupboard with opaque doors. The difficulty I
feel about such a view is that, while no doubt the words of
Sidonius, *defodium*, point to 'cabinets,' not mere tables with
shelves, like our afternoon tea-tables ; yet such cabinets would
require glass doors, to let the ornaments be seen, and, as far as
I can find, there is no proof at all that they had such. That
transparent window-glass did exist is no doubt certain (cf. Lac-
tantius de Officio Dei, 8, 11 : *Et manifestius est mentem esse
quae per oculos ea, quae sunt opposita, transpiciat quasi per
fenestras perlucente vitro aut speculari lapide obductas*) ; but
most Roman window-glass admitted light, though not transparent. Transparent glass was very expensive. On the whole,
however, I am inclined to think that the *abaci* of the wealthy
may have been cabinets, while in poorer establishments they
were open tables, with shelves.

The use of *abaci* came into vogue at Rome after the conquest
of Asia by Manlius Vulso, in 187 B.C. (Liv. 39, 6, 7). But
before this the Romans must have seen them among the Etrus-
cans—of whose *abaci*, of the fourth century B.C., we have some
remains (Guillaume, *l.c.*)—and the Sicilian Greeks.

Exhedra, -ae. Such is the usual form of the word; the diminutive, *exhedrium* (or *cxedrium*), is found here and in C. I. G. 2554, 123, τὸ ἐξέδριον τὸ κατανοτιαῖον. The earliest place I know where the word occurs is Eur. Orest. 1449 ; but the more usual classical Greek term for the building was παστάς: cf. Pollux, vii. 27, παστάδας δ' ὁ Ξενοφῶν ἐκάλεσεν ἃς οἱ νῦν (180 A.L.) ἐξέδρας.

As its derivation seems to show, it was a *sitting-place*—we generally find the occupants sitting (Cic. N. D. 1, 15), seldom reclining (De Orat. iii. 17, *lectulo posito*, points to the proceeding being unusual)—built *out from* some main building (Varro, R. R. 3, iii. 8, uses the word for an aviary), generally from a portico. They were generally open buildings, *perflatilc*, as a Low Latin writer would say : cf. Vitruv. 7, 9, *Apertis vero peristyliis aut cxhedris aut ceteris eiusmodi locis quo Sol et Luna possit splendores suos immittere*. They were often attached to baths, and their semicircular nature may be seen in any ground-plan of Caracalla's baths ; see, *e.g.*, Dict. Antiq. p. 194 ; also to theatres (corresponding to, only perhaps larger than, the splendid foyers in the Parisian and modern London theatres). There was one in the theatre of Pompeius, where Caesar was murdered, τῆς δὲ βουλῆς εἰς τὴν ἐξέδραν προεισελθούσης, etc., Plutarch, Brut. 17.

Their main use was for conversation, disputation, and the delivery of lectures. They corresponded entirely to our lecture-rooms in Universities and in large cities, *e.g.* Strabo, xvii. 8, τῶν δὲ βασιλείων (sc. of Alexandria) ἐστὶ καὶ τὸ Μουσεῖον ἔχον περίπατον καὶ ἐξέδραν καὶ οἶκον μέγαν ἐν ᾧ τὸ συσσίτιον τῶν μετεχόντων τοῦ Μουσείου φιλολόγων ἀνδρῶν ; also Cod. Theod. 15, 1, 53, *Exhedras quae septentrionali videntur adhaerere Porticui* (sc. at Constantinople) *in quibus tantum amplitudinis et decoris esse monstratur ut publicis commodis possint capacitatis et pulcritudinis suae admiratione sufficere supradictorum* (sc. *Professorum seu magistrorum*) *consessibus deputabit* (sc. *Sublimitas Tua*). Each professor had a separate *exhedra*, or lecture-room : see Cod. Theod. 14, 9, 3, *ita ut unicuique loca specialiter deputata adsignari faciat Tua Sublimitas : ne discipuli sibi invicem possint obstrepere, vel magistri : neve linguarum confusio permixta vel vocum aures quorundam aut mentes a studio litterarum avertat*. They were often, too, used for disputations : cf. Vitruv. 5, 2, *Constituuntur in tribus porticibus exhedrae spatiosae, habentes sedes in quibus philosophi Rectores* (qu. *rhetores*) *reliqui qui studiis delectantur sedentes disputare possint*. St. Augustine delivers a lecture in one (Civ. Dei, 22, 8) ; and he also mentions one adjoining a church (*De Gestis cum Emerito Donatistarum*

Episcopo, sub init.), similar to the *capitularia* in the Monasteries (see Gothofred on Cod. Theod. 15, 1, 53).

Exhedrae, or public lecture-rooms, were a very common form of public building, *e.g.* Herod (in Josephus, B. J. 1, 16) Βύβλῳ δὲ τεῖχος καὶ ἐξέδρας τε καὶ στοὰς ἀνέθηκε; and often in Inscriptions (Gruter, lxv. 3 ; clxxii. = Orelli, 3283, where, again, they are joined with *porticus*) we find their builders notifying the erection.

They appear then to have been essentially public ; but examples can be found where the word may mean nothing more than our 'sitting-room,' as opposed to 'bed-room' (*cubiculum*). For example, in a somewhat long title of the Digest (9, 3), where there are copious enactments as regards the liability of people who throw things out of the windows (*De his qui effuderint vel deiecerint*), Ulpian (Law 5) gives us some knowledge of how people lived in lodgings. The passage is interesting, so it may be quoted : *Si vero plures diviso inter se cenaculo* [*i.e.* 'flat' or 'story' ; cf. Plaut. Amph. iii. 1, 3, where Jupiter says he is the fellow *in superiore qui habito cenaculo,* 'who lives in the top story.' *Cenaculum* later came to mean of itself 'an *upper* story,' and quite early had lost its sense of dining-room, as much as our 'drawing-room' has lost its signification] *habitent, actio in eum solum datur, qui inhabitabat eam partem, unde effusum est. Si quis gratuitas habitationes dederit libertis et clientibus vel suis vel uxoris, ipsum eorum nomine teneri Trebatius ait ; quod verum est. Idem erit dicendum et si quis amicis suis modica hospitiola distribuerit. Nam et si quis cenaculariam exercens* ['letting out houses in tenements or flats'] *ipse maximam partem cenaculi* [here = 'upper stories,' τοῦ οἴκου, in the Gk. translation] *habeat solus tenebitur: sed si* [*quis cenaculariam exercens* del. Mommsen] *modicum sibi hospitium retinuerit, residuum locaverit pluribus, omnes tenebuntur quasi in hoc cenaculo habitantes unde deiectum effusumve est. Interdum tamen, quod sine captione actoris fiat* ['if not prejudicial to the plaintiff'] *oportebit praetorem aequitate motum in eum potius dare actionem, ex* cuius *cubiculo vel* exhedra *deiectum est licet plures in eodem cenaculo habitent, quod si ex mediano* [so F. ; *medio cenaculo* other mss. ; ἀπὸ τοῦ μέσου, Gk. trans. ; *maeniano,* Anonym. ap. Dirksen ; Qu. *medio maeniano,* the copyist went on at the wrong *i*] *coenaculi quid deiectum sit, verius est omnes teneri.* Here *exhedra* may mean 'sitting-room' ; but Marquardt is wrong in saying that in Vitruv. 6, 3, 8, and 6, 7, 8, *exhedrae* must mean 'sitting-rooms.'

Still, in Cicero's time, these *exhedrae* in large houses were special rooms for learned discussion. Only the eminent had them, as only the eminent have at the present time private

chapels and private theatres. As is natural to expect, su ch
rooms were adorned with statues (Plut. *l.c.*) and pictures (Cic.
Fam. vii. 23, 3). In our passage, then, I should translate the
diminutive *exhedria*, 'private lecture-room.' [The *exedra* in
the Academy at Athens was not a covered building; cf. F:n.
v. 2 with Diog. Laert. iv. 19, where μουσεῖον is the cover d
lecture-room, ἐξέδρα the open-air recess, for conversation witl a
few pupils.]

Pseudodamasippum. 'I must look out for some woul l-
be Damasippus to sell them to, even at a loss.' Prof. Palm(r,
on Hor. Sat. ii. 3, 16, remarks that Damasippus must ha ·c
been quite at the head of his trade, as he had imitators in it.
Cf. *Cornuto vero pseudo-Catone*, 'a would-be Cato,' Att. i. 14, 5.

4. Crasso. This must be the reading, not *Cassio*, as we read
that he had a sister called *Licinia*. Gallus seems to have
bought or rented a house from Crassus, which was at presei t
occupied by Crassipes and Tullia. Gallus wanted to occupy
the house, but did not wish to cause inconvenience to Tulli ,
who did not desire to move in the absence of her husband wh ׃
was in Spain. *Dexius* must be corrupt. I have not venture l
to print in the text Mr. Purser's ingenious emendation, o ι
account of its apparent boldness; but I believe it has hig ı
probability. He would read *in Hispaniam iam diem undeci·
mum*. The contraction *d.* for *dies* is common, and *d. xi-mur,*
would have easily been corrupted into *Dexius*.

uti non ita multum, 'is not on very good terms with.'

ne vivam, si tibi concedo, 'upon my life, I won't admit.'
Cf. *ita vivam, ut maximos sumptus facio*, Att. v. 15, 2, 'upoı
my life, I am living very extravagantly.'

LETTER XVII. (Fam. vii. 1)

1. ludos. This very interesting and beautiful letter was
written on the occasion of the dedication of Pompeius's theatre
and the temple of Venus Victrix, when Pompeius delighted the
people with spectacles of unusual magnificence, including not
only dramatic and athletic performances in the theatre, but
races and combats with wild beasts (*venationes*) in the circus.
In these were killed five hundred lions and twenty elephants,
according to Pliny. The letter is remarkable, as showing a
refinement very rare in the age of Cicero. It seems to me how-

ever, that the value of the letter from this point of view is
somewhat over-estimated.   It seems clear from § 6, *haec ad te
. . . paeniteret*, that the letter must be regarded rather as a
rhetorical exercise on a theme suggested by his friend, than as
the expression of the writer's own opinion of the question of the
morality of such spectacles as he describes.   Strangely enough,
this particular show seems to have supplied incidents so affecting
as to move even the callous mob of Rome.   Pliny (viii. 7) tells
us that the cries and piteous bearing of the elephants, when
they found escape impossible, touched the people so much that
they rose in a mass and cursed Pompeius, *tanto populi dolore,
ut, oblitus imperatoris ac munificentiae honori suo exquisitae,
flens universus consurgeret dirasque Pompeio imprecaretur.*

modo ut constiterit, 'always provided you made a good
use of your leisure.'   *Constiterit* may come from *consto*, in the
sense of 'to be,' 'exist,' ὑπάρχειν, as in *si ipsa mens constare
potest vacans corpore*, N. D. i. 25 ; or from *consisto*, in the
same sense, *vix binos oratores laudabiles constitisse*, Brut. 333.
[Rather the use of *constare* here is that common in connexion
with mercantile affairs, *e.g.* Flac. 69, *auri ratio constat*.   So
here 'provided that you get a clear profit out of your leisure.']

ex quo tibi † Stabianum † perforasti.   I think *Stabianum*
is certainly corrupt.   *Perforasti Stabianum* is usually explained,
'You have opened a window giving on the Stabian waters of
the Bay.'   But is this a possible meaning of the verb ?   *Perforare*
means—(1) 'to bore through,' a meaning which is clearly impossible here ; (2) 'to make by boring,' and this last signification is common in Cicero : e.g. *duo lumina ab animo ad oculos
perforata*, N. D. iii. 9 ; *viae . . . a sede animi perforatae*, Tusc.
i. 46.   But *perforare Stabianum=perforando patefacere Stabianum* is impossible, as was seen by Boot (Obss. Crit. p. 12).
Under *Stabianum* lurks some direct object of *perforasti*.   Boot
conjectures *tablinum*, 'a balcony.'   I would suggest, to account
for *Stabianum* of the mss., *istud maenianum*.   For *maeniana*,
'timber balconies' thrown out for the purpose of affording
a view, and taking their name from Maenius (cons. B.C.
338), see Reid on Acad. ii. 70.   Either conjecture involves a
violent departure from the mss. ; but a puzzled copyist would
be very likely to suppose a reference to *Stabiae* south of Pompeii,
where the villa of Marius was situated.   Boot would read
sinum for *Misenum*, but on insufficient grounds.   The whole
sentence, *ex quo maenianum perforasti et patefecisti* for *ex quo
maeniano perforato patefecisti*, supplies an example of parataxis
for hypotaxis, not rare in the Letters.   [Most certainly there is

corruption ; but I am not sure that it lies in *Stabianum*. May we not have an ex. of a very common kind of error in mss. when the first part of one word is attached to the last part of the following word ? Cic. may have written *perforando patefecisti*. Cf. Plaut. Mil. 1022, where Ritschl gave *propera expectando* for *properando*. In Acad. ii. § 70, all mss. have *facerent* for *face 'e dicerent ;* in Pro Sull. § 1, all but three give *suspicarentur* for *suspicari viderentur ;* in Phil. vii. § 24, all but one have *conlaudaremus* for *conlaudare debemus*. In Att. x. 4, 1], Orelli with probability conjectures *facere solet* for *faceret*. Hahn and Christ give in Div. i. § 56, *petere dubitanti* for *petenti*. In Balb. § 1, C. F. W. Mueller writes *valere debent* for *valent*. Many other illustrations of the principle are to be found in the texts of almost all authors.]

lectiunculis, 'little dips into books.' This is, I think what Cicero wrote. He had said above (or implied) that the leisure of Marius was not properly employed unless he did something useful. Now, to take little dips into books would be very useful as compared with dozing over bad farces. Kl. conjectured *spectiunculis* for *lectiunculis ;* but would taking 'little peeps ' at the beauties of the Bay of Naples satisfy the condition expressed above, *modo ut tibi constiterit fructus otii tui*? Moreover, *spectarent* is just the word that would *not* be used after *spectiunculis*. But the editors have treated this passage very badly : in the words *neque dubito quin tu* ex *illo cubiculo* ex quo *tibi Stabianum perforasti . . . per eos dies matutina tempora lectiunculis consumpseris*, it seems at first sight that for *ex illo cubiculo* we should certainly read *in illo cubiculo*, and this has been the course adopted by every editor from Lallemand to Baiter. But this is unscientific. If Cicero wrote the easy *in illo cubiculo*, why do all the mss. give us the difficult *ex illo cubiculo*? The fact is, that in *ex illo cubiculo ex quo* we have an example of that *inverse attraction*, which is quite in the manner of Plautus, with whose diction I have already pointed out so many marked parallelisms in the Letters of Cicero : cf., for instance, Pl. Cist. i. 1, 63, *indidem unde oritur facito ut facias stultitiam sepelibilem ;* again, *ego te hodie reddam madidum si vivo probe* tibi quoi *decretum est bibere aquam*, Aul. iii. 6, 39 ; *quid illum facere vis qui*, tibi quoi *divitiae domi maxumae sunt . . . numum nullum habes*, Epid. iii. 1, 8. Hence I would by no means change *ex illo* to *in illo*, with Lallemand. Such a course would be truly 'from the purpose ' of criticism. Either Cicero wrote *ex illo . . . lectiunculis*, or *ex illo . . . spectiunculis ;* certainly not *in illo . . . lectiunculis*.

I believe he wrote *ex illo* . . . *lectiunculis*, and that this
passage supplies another striking instance of the close parallelism
between the diction of the letters of Cicero and of the comic
drama. For a good example of inverse attraction in Greek cf.
βῆναι κεῖθεν ὅθενπερ ἥκει, Soph. O. C. 1226. [*Lectiunculis* I look
on as certainly right, but before it probably *in* dropped out ;
the simple abl. with *consumere* in Cic. is rare and very doubtful.]

comminus. While Marius has a *distant* view of Misenum,
those who left him to come to Rome have a *close* (too close) view
of the farces which Cicero found so tiresome. *Comminus* for
communes is the admirable conjecture of Madv. (Adv. Crit. iii.
158). *Communes* is usually explained 'hackneyed,' 'gewöhn-
liche,' 'alltägliche' (Süpfle). But this is not a meaning which
communis ever bears (*communes loci*, 'common places,' in no
way defends it) ; nor, if it did, would it be suitable here, as
Madv. justly observes. [I am inclined to think *communes*
right after all. Marius has the sole enjoyment of his estate
and his privacy, while those who remained in town looked at
the *mimes*, the spectacle of which was common property. The
contrast is between that which belongs to *one* and that which
belongs to the public generally. I must confess that the
contrast between the distant view of Misenum and the close
view of the *mimi* seems to me forced, frigid, and trivial.]

Sp. Maecius. Tarpa (mentioned by Horace). He was
appointed by Pompeius to be public licenser of plays, like the
Lord Chamberlain amongst ourselves. According to the Schol.
(Comm. Cruq.) on Horace, Tarpa was again appointed to discharge the same functions, as president of a court of five members,
by Octavius.

probavisset, 'if only Tarpa gave his sanction we had to sit
out the play.' The subjunctive is used because *ea* expresses
'the *kind*' of plays which they had to witness. The point of
the antithesis is that Marius could choose his own amusements,
while Cicero and the other spectators of the games were depending on the taste of Tarpa. See Madv. § 379.

2. non tui stomachi, 'not such as you would have
stomached.' This is the genitive which Draeger, Hist. Synt.
i. 461, calls *der Genitiv der Eigenschaft:* cf. *plurimarum
palmarum gladiator*, Rosc. Am. 6 ; *non multi cibi hospitem
accipies, multi ioci*, Fam. ix. 26, 4 ; it is combined with the
qualitative ablative in *multis luminibus ingenii, multae tamen
artis*, Q. Fr. ii. 9, 4.

honoris causa. This phrase is used in two senses : they

had retired from the stage *to preserve their own reputation*
(which they were no longer able to maintain) ; they now came
back to the stage *to do honour to the occasion* (by restoring to
the stage its past ornaments). One might render 'out of respect
for Pompeius they came back to the stage which they had left
out of respect for themselves.'

Aesopus, a celebrated actor of the period.

Si sciens fallo. This was the form of oath *per Iovem
Lapidem*. Sch. remarks that we may hence infer that not
only *palliatae fabulae* but *togatae* were represented on this
occasion ; for in the former there would not have been the
purely Roman *formula*. But may not the players have had to
take some formal oath ? Cicero seems to speak of the words as
if it were well known that all players must use them. Moreover, the *Clyt.* (of Attius) and *Equus Troianus* (of Livius) were
tragedies, *crepidatae*, not *palliatae ;* and in translating a formal
oath from the Greek the regular forms of the Latin oath would
doubtless be used. On the tragedy of the Roman stage cf
Friedländer, ii. 426. [The phrase *si sciens fallo* can hardly
have been restricted to this particular oath ; and it is hardly
likely they would have had to take it in presence of the
spectators.]

creterrarum, another form of *craterarum*, according to
Non. and Paul. ex Fest. 'Bowls' might have formed part
of the spoils in the triumphal procession on the sack of
Troy. Graev. injudiciously conjectured *cetrarum*, 'bucklers,'
'targeteers.'

3. **Protogeni**. Marius's *anagnostes*, or slave, whose duty it
was to read aloud.

quidvis, 'anything, except my speeches' (as Cicero modestly
adds).

senatu vestro, the municipal senate of whatever town
Marius belonged to. Probably, like our town councils and
vestries, these bodies furnished much innocent amusement to
the judicious. *Oscos ludos=fabulas Atellanas*. Cicero says the
town council of Pompeii will supply Marius with plenty of
broad farces like the *fabulae Atellanae*. The allusion seems
rather far-fetched, but the whole letter, it must be remembered,
is a rhetorical exercise.

via Graeca. The *via Graeca* was in very bad repair. Cicero
jestingly says that such is Marius's aversion for the Greeks that
he will not even take the Grecian road to his own villa. About
the *via Graeca* we have no information. A *scala Graeca* was a

ladder with screened sides, but we do not elsewhere read of a *via Graeca*.

glad. contempseris. Graevius conjectures with much probability that this is an allusion to some service which Marius had done to Cicero in defending him against the bravoes of Clodius.

operam et oleum, a proverbial expression for wasted labour. The allusion is to 'midnight oil,' not to the oil used in the training schools: Att. ii. 17, 1 ; xiii. 38, 1 ; Plaut. Poen. i. 2, 119.

venationes, 'fights between men and beasts,' 'wild beast baiting.'

elephantorum dies, 'the elephants' day,' that is, the day for the elephant baiting.

misericordia. See Plin. N. H. viii. 21, who tells us that Pompeius in the dedication of his theatre and the temple of Venus Victrix delighted the people with spectacles on a scale of more than ordinary magnificence. The most interesting feature was, as usual, the *venatio*, or man-and-beast-fight. On that occasion five hundred lions and twenty elephants were killed. It seems that the piteous bearing and terrified trumpeting of the elephants, when they found escape impossible, touched even the callous mob of the circus so much that 'forgetful of the Imperator and of the great munificence of the show they rose up in a body and with streaming eyes cursed Pompeius.' Writing of the same scene Dio Cassius (xxxix. 38) says : ' In five days five hundred lions were used up (ἀναλώθησαν), and eighteen elephants were set to fight with armed soldiers. Some of the elephants were butchered on the spot, but some were left to die of their wounds. Much to the surprise of Pompeius some of them touched the feelings of the spectators. When wounded so badly that they had to give up the fight, they went round the arena, raising their trunks to heaven, and uttering cries so piteous that one fancied they were rational appeals to the gods for vengeance on the treachery by which they were induced to leave their country. The story was that they would not embark to leave Libya until they received a pledge on oath from their drivers that they should not be ill-treated.' We could hardly believe any mob could be so silly, if we did not remember the ridiculous sentiment evoked not long ago by the elephant Jumbo among the lower classes in London.

4. facilem, 'ready' (to let me retire).

artem desinerem. *Desinere artem* is found in Suet. Tib. 6,

36 ; *desinere seditionem* in Gell. ii. 12, 3 ; and this construction
is not rare in the poets. Cf. *orationes a plerisque legi sunt
desitae*, Cic. Brut. 123. [*Not a parallel.* This passage seems
quite as isolated in Cic. as Acad. ii. § 80, where *desinere* is
constructed with abl. Looking to the number of times Cic. uses
desinere, it seems strongly improbable that either passage
should be sound. I would read *arte desisterem* here and *des ste*
in the other place. *Desiste* is now generally read for *desine* in
Ter. Haut. v. 1, 6. Neither Hor. nor Verg. has the acc. (for
in Ecl. v. 19 and ix. 66, *desine plura*, there is an obvious ellipse
of the inf. of a verb of speaking, and similarly in Ecl. viii. 61).
So far as I can make out, there is only one ex. of *desinere* with
acc. in Latin before Cic., *i.e.* Ter. Haut. ii. 3, 64, *mulier telam
desinit*. Ter. uses the verb in about sixteen other places,
either abs. or with inf. I cannot believe the pass. in the Haut.
to be sound. Probably Ter. wrote *nere* (cf. l. 52) and a copyist
added the object *telam*, which then drove out the inf. The
ex. of *desinere* with accus. given in a fragm. of Sall. by the
Lexx. cannot carry much weight. Nor can much stress be laid
on the exx. from Ovid, for Met. vi. 215 quoted by Lexx. is now
altered ; and the interchange of *desine* and *desere* in a good
many other passages must render Ars A. ii. 725 more than
doubtful, to say nothing of the fact that *desere* suits the
context far better. I have not noted any other ex. of *desino*
with acc. either in authors of the age of Ovid or later down to
Sueton. (the passage you quote), where it seems to me that
destituturos is the right reading. There is, I think, strong
reason for doubting whether the constr. *desinere* with acc.
occurs in Latin at all, at least before Fronto. We cannot, of
course, argue that *orationes desitae sunt legi* justifies *desinere
orationes*, any more than *or. coeptae sunt legi* would justify
coepisse orationes. Nor even if we found *orationes desitae sunt*
(without the infinitive) could we say that it made *desinere
orationes* possible. *E.g.*, Cic. says *illa coepta sunt*, but never
coepi aliquid.]

5. **relaxaro . . . exsolvam,** 'remission . . . release.'

6. **relinques,** 'You will not leave at the mercy of a letter
from me any hope you may have of getting enjoyment out of
the games.' Süpfle understands these words to mean, 'You
will come and see me, and so you will not have to depend on
my letters for your entertainment when you will have myself.
But this is a pointless remark, and does not harmonise with
the foregoing sentence. Moreover, such a rendering hardly
takes *aliquam* into account.

LETTER XVIII. (Q. Fr. ii. 9 [11])

1. codicilli. These were tablets made of thin pieces of wood (*codices, caudices*) and covered with wax. Sen., Ep. lv. 11, contrasts *epistulae* (written on paper) with *codicilli*. They were used for any sudden exigency requiring haste, or when *calamus* and *chartae* were not accessible. Sometimes the words of a letter were hastily jotted down with a *stilus* on these *codicilli*, and then given to the *librarius* to copy on *charta* with a *calamus*. It was by *codicilli* that Acidinus (Fam. iv. 12, 2) informed Servius at Athens that Marcellus had died of the wounds inflicted on him by the dagger of Magius Chilo. *Codicilli* were especially useful when an immediate *reply* was required. They corresponded to our reply-postcards. Cicero sent his *codicilli* to Balbus (Fam. vi. 18, 1) when he wanted immediate information about a law. In this case Quintus sent his *codicilli* to his brother, demanding 'in strong language' a reply. *Codicilli* were especially used for writing to those who were near at hand, Sen. *loc. cit.*

alucinari, 'to ramble on' without any consistent train of thought, just as Cicero and his brother chatted to each other when they met.

2. Tenediorum. The people of Tenedos petitioned the Senate for Home Rule, but were refused. Cicero spoke in their behalf.

securi Tenedia. Tenes, the fabled eponym of Tenedos, was the author of a very severe code for the island. Adultery was to be punished by the immediate execution of the adulterer, and this sentence was carried out by order of Tenes in the case of his own son. *Securis Tenedia* is a proverbial expression for any 'short, sharp, and decisive' act or decision.

3. L. Sestii Pansae. Probably a publican, who had made some excessive demands of the Magnetes. The Magnetes of Lydia are called *Magnetes ab Sipylo*, to distinguish them from the Magnetes in Thessaly and in Caria.

neque tibi neque Pomponio. This must refer to some transaction in which Atticus and Quintus were jointly concerned, probably, therefore, affecting in some way the marriage portion of Pomponia.

4. Lucretii . . . artis. This is the celebrated criticism of Cicero on the poem of Lucretius, which had just been published,

N

about four months after the death of the poet. It is the only
place where Cicero mentions Lucretius, and he never quotes
from the poet, though his philosophical works undoubtedly
show acquaintance with the *sex libri de rerum natura*. It has
been observed that it is not the practice of Cicero to quote from
his contemporaries.   He never mentions Catullus, who so
prettily eulogised him in the poem (xlix.) beginning *disert's-
sime Romuli nepotum*.   Cicero twice imitates an expression of
Catullus.   He writes : *oricula infima molliorem*, Q. Fr. ii. 13, 1;
cf. Cat. xxv. 2, *mollior . . . imula oricilla ;* and again, Att.
xvi. 6, 2, he speaks of *ocellos Italiae villulas meas*, which
seems to be a reminiscence of *Peninsularum, Sirmio, insularumque Ocelle*, Cat. xxxi.   But he never mentions the poet, with
whom he was linked as well by political sympathies as by their
common acquaintanceship with Clodia.   Hence it is possible
that the tradition mentioned by St. Jerome that Cicero edited
the poem of Lucretius may be true, in spite of the silence of
Cicero concerning Lucretius.   Cicero had probably some time
during the last four months read (or heard read to him) the *de
rerum natura*, and had sent it to his brother on finishing it.
From a passage in the Pro Sestio, 123, *neque poetae quorum ego
semper ingenia dilexi tempori meo defuerunt*, we may infer that
Cicero made it a practice to read and appreciate the works
of rising poets.   It is very unlikely that Q. Cicero should
have been the editor.   St. Jerome would not have referred to
him as *Cicero*, but as *Q. Cicero*, nor would the friends of Lucretius have been at all likely to submit the poem to Quintus.
The criticism of Quintus, with which Cicero expresses his
accord, was that Lucretius had not only much of the *genius* of
Ennius and Attius, but also much of the *art* of the poets of the
new school, among them even Catullus, who are fashioning
themselves on the model of the Alexandrine poets, especially of
Callimachus and of Euphorion of Chalcis.   This new school
Cicero refers to as the νεώτεροι (Att. vii. 2, 1), and as *hi cantores
Euphorionis* (Tusc. iii. 45).   Their *ars* seemed to Cicero almost
incompatible with the *ingenium* of the old school.   This criticism on Lucretius is not only quite just from Cicero's point of
view, but it is most apt.   Yet the editors from Victorius
to Klotz will not let Cicero say what he thought.   They insert
a *non* either before *multis* or before *multae*, and thus deny him
either *ingenium* or *ars*.   The point of the judgment is that
Lucretius shows the genius of the old school, and (what might
seem to be incompatible with it) the art of the new.   For a full
discussion of this point see Munro's Lucretius, Introd. to
Notes, ii.   The views above given are mainly his.   Dr. Maguire

(Herm. iv. 419) compares for *tamen* Ter. Ad. i. 2, 30, *alieniore aetate post faceret* tamen.

artis. For this gen. see on Fam. vii. 1, 2 (Ep. xvii.)

Sed cum veneris. . . . Some such words as *plura de his poematis dissercmus* are understood.

Virum . . . hominem. 'If you get through Sallust's *Empedoclea* I shall look on you as a being possessed of the resolution of a man, and none of the weaknesses of humanity.' This antithesis between *vir* and *homo* is found elsewhere in Cicero, and must be read in the light shed on the words by the other passages. In Fam. v. 17, 3 Cicero writes to Sestius: 'I feel it my duty to exhort you *ut et hominem te et virum esse meminisses*': and he goes on to explain that by this he means that—(1) Sestius should remember that as a *homo* he is subject to 'the changes and chances of this mortal life,' that he is not exempt from the lot of humanity, and (2) that as a *vir* he is bound to oppose a bold front to fortune. Again, he says of Marius, *tulit dolorem ut vir, et, ut homo, maiorem ferre sine causa necessaria noluit*, Tusc. ii. 53, 'he bore the pain *like a man*, but, *as not being above the weaknesses of humanity*, he did not wish to suffer greater pain without any imperative reason for it.' In antithesis with *vir esse* the meaning of *homo esse* always is 'to be subject to the ordinary weaknesses of humanity'; by itself *homo esse* means—(a) 'to have the feelings or the sense of a man'; cf. Att. ii. 2, 2; (b) 'to have the weaknesses of a mortal,' as *ei moriendum fuit, quoniam homo natus fuerat*, Fam. iv. 5, 4. 'Heroic' and 'human' are the antithetic expressions used by Reid (Arch. 16). Munro would read *lum. ingenii: multae tamen artis esse cum inveneris virum te putabo.* Prof. Nettleship suggests *lum. ingenii: multae tamen* (or *etiam*) *artis ipse dicam, veneris, virium. Virum te putabo*, comparing *fabula nullius veneris sine pondere et arte*, Hor. A. P. 320. [I am convinced that the mss. are right.]

Sallustii. Of this author of a poem on the philosophy of Empedocles nothing is known. [Naturally mentioned along with Lucretius as a philosophic poem, and relating to a poet and philosopher whom Lucretius loved and imitated.]

LETTER XIX. (Q. Fr. ii. 10 [12])

1. Nam. Cicero has no news to tell Quintus, because the meeting of the senate ended abruptly.

pipulo, convicio, 'noisy clamour,' *i.e.* of the senators.
The ms. reading is *populi convicio.* Boot (Obss. Critt. ad M.
T. Ciceronis Epistolas: Amstelodami, 1880) justly observes that
he does not understand how the consul was forced by the
clamour of the people outside to dismiss the senate. He would
read *communi convicio;* but my conjecture is far less rash:
pipulo is a Plautine word, and therefore very likely to be used
by Cicero; it would almost certainly be mistaken by the scribe
for *populo,* which he would naturally change to *populi,* to
obtain a construction. *Asyndeton* is quite a characteristic
feature in the letters of Cicero, even asyndeton between
two words. For two words with asyndeton cf. *patrimonio
fortuna,* Att. xi. 9, 3; *causae meae voluntati meorum,* Att. ii.
13, 1; *querentibus postulantibus,* Att. v. 21, 12; *adsunt
queruntur,* Div. in Caec. 11; *expulerit relegarit,* Sest. 29;
officiis liberalitate, Fam. xiii. 24, 3; *vultu taciturnitate,* Fam.
iii. 8, 2; *gratissimo iucundissimo,* Fam. xiii. 28, 3; *studiis
beneficiis,* Fam. vii. 5, 1. We read in Q. Fr. ii. 1 that the
hired roughs of Clodius, *a graecostasi et gradibus clamorem satis
magnum sustulerunt,* and that the consequence was the breaking
up of the meeting of the senate. But in that case they were
hired by Clodius to do what they did. How could the coldness
of the weather bring the people outside to break up the meeting
of the senate 'with abuse,' *convicio*? But it is quite credible
that the senators themselves should have shouted down every
attempt to put a question to the house with abusive clamour
calling on the consul to dismiss the house. Each senator wished
to go away on account of the cold, but did not wish to leave
behind him a house to pass measures unacceptable to him.
With this passage must be discussed the words at the end of
the letter, *ut summum periculum esset ne Appio suae aedes
urerentur.* Here, again, Boot asks what is the meaning? It
is true that in seasons of great cold there is a greater danger of
conflagrations, because larger fires are kept. But why should
the consul's house be more in peril than houses of other people?
Man. explains by observing that in the house of the consul,
which was frequented by crowds of visitors, and by those who
would escort him home from the senate, a very large fire would
naturally be kept. But such an explanation is manifestly
puerile. This being so, I am disposed to explain the two
passages—the one in the beginning of the letter and the one
at the end—as jocular, or at least covert, allusions to the lack
of interest in public affairs, the inactivity and apathy of the
senate, and the dulness of the business before them. The first
passage would then mean, 'Appius could only get together a

small meeting of the senate, and when it did meet, such was the utter dearth of interest that it ended in noisy clamour for a dismissal of the house.' The sentence at the end would mean, 'The thermometer of public feeling is so near freezing-point that Appius's house runs a great risk of being *frost-bitten*,' that is, utterly deserted by *salutatores* and *deductores*. For examples of *frigus* in the metaphorical sense of 'dulness,' 'apathy,' 'stagnation,' cf. *si Parthi vos nihil calfaciunt nos hic frigore rigescimus*, Fam. viii. 6, 4 ; *Curioni tribunatus conglaciat*, ibid. 3 ; and the synonymous phrase, ibid. 4, *veternus civitatem occupasset;* so also *metuo ne frigeas in hibernis* ('have nothing to do') . . . *quamquam vos istic satis calere* ('are kept pretty busy') *audio*, Fam. vii. 10, 2. Cf. also Ov. Fast. ii. 856, *virque tuo Tereus frigore lactus erit*. *Uri=* 'to be frost-bitten' is common enough ; Cicero uses it in this sense in one passage, where it is as susceptible of misapprehension as it is here, *pernoctant venatores in nive; in montibus* uri *se patiuntur*, Tusc. ii. 40. This explanation, moreover, gives a far more appropriate meaning to *quamquam* in the sentence at the end of the letter. 'I shall give you the news of every day. *Yet* [there is really nothing to tell, for] the thermometer of public interest is so near freezing-point that Appius's house seems likely to be frost-bitten.' It is to be observed that both at the beginning and the end of the letter the mention of *frigus* is introduced to account for the dearth of news. *Frigus* might also be used in the metaphorical sense of *disfavour* (towards Appius): cf. *maiorum ne quis amicus Frigore te feriat*, Hor. Sat. ii. 1, 62 ; *limina frigescant*, Pers. i. 108 ; to which the Dictt. add several examples in Quintilian and Pliny. But this use of *frigus* would not account for *quamquam*, and is not so characteristic of the tone of Cicero's letters. *Infrequentem* is sometimes explained as 'extraordinary.' (See L. S.) [This is certainly right. The first words of the letter lead up to this sense of *frigus*. But I should phrase it a little differently. The senate was called to pass certain measures which no one would have. I still do not feel sure that *populi* is wrong. There are a number of passages (most of them are quoted in the footnotes to Willems's Sénat, ii. pp. 163 *sq.*) which seem to show that the public thronged the doors of the meeting-place (which were left open) and either heard or managed to get to know about what was going on inside. They may have assembled on this occasion to show their disapproval of the measure which the senate had been summoned to consider. Appius was hand in glove with Caesar, Pompey, and Crassus. The contemplated business probably was in the interest of the triumvirate. If *frigus* means the 'chilling frost of popular opposition to the designs of Appius,' the word *urerentur* may well have its natural meaning. 'So unpopular are Appius's plans that he may well have his house burnt about his ears.' This contrast between *frigus* in its non-literal sense and *urerentur* in its literal sense is quite in Cicero's style. The *quamquam* does not seem to me to be out of place. 'I will write to you, if anything is done; but nothing is likely to be done, unless maybe A.'s house is burned.']

2. **Commageno.** Antiochus, King of Commagene, whose capital was Samosata, now *Samsoun*, the birthplace of Lucian. When Syria was made a province, at the end of the Mithridatic war, Antiochus received from Pompeius this little division of the kingdom of Syria.

discusseram, 'pulled to pieces,' that is, 'frustrated,' 'brought to nought.'

blanditur. Appius 'fawns on' Cic. to induce him to abandon that strenuous attitude towards the foreign petitioners which he feared would spoil his market.

sterilem, 'productive of no profit to him.' If Cicero opposed and defeated all the petitions of foreign nations, for the hearing of which Feb. was reserved, there would be no *douceurs* for Appius from successful applicants.

oppidulum. We may infer that Antiochus had two requests to make—that he might be allowed to include or retain in his dominion a certain town on the Euphrates, and that the honour, granted to him in the consulship of Caesar, of wearing a *toga praetexta*, should be confirmed by a decree of the senate.

† **quod . . Zeugmate** †. I have obelised these words. One might read *Zeugma* (inserting *at* before *praeterea*), and render, 'a little village called Zeugma, which had been his, built on the Euphrates'; or else, reading *positum in Euphrati Ζεύγματι*, we could understand Ζεύγμα to mean 'a pier or landing-place' on which some little hamlet was built. One might even retain *Euphrati*, and regard it as the genitive; one would expect to find *Euphrati* beside *Euphratis*, as *Ulixi* and *Ulixei* beside *Ulixis*. Billerbeck would take Ζεύγματι in the sense of 'bridge.' He says that at the site of Bir, or Birtha, there was a bridge over the Euphrates in the time of Alexander, Thapsacus having been before this the customary place of crossing. The town was called *Zeugma*, from the bridge. It would

be natural that the senate should refuse to detach from the
province of Syria a town so situated. [There is good reason to
believe that *Euphrati* is the *only* form of the gen. which Cic.
would have used. Cf. Madv. on Fin. i. § 14 and on v. § 12.
The evidence is of course much more extensive than what is
given in those notes.]

3. **Quod vult.** ' As to his petition for a renewal of the
honours he got in the consulship of Caesar, to save himself the
expense of dyeing his *praetexta* anew every year, I am against
a decree to that effect. Will you, who would not have the
tetrarch of Bostra clothed with the *praetexta*, endure the Commagene in that robe of state?' Such is the explanation of Sch.
and Billerb. There does not appear to be much play of fancy
in the passage. Unless the joke lies in some allusion to the
unknown tetrarch or princeling of Bozra, whom (Cicero says)
the Roman nobles would not endure to see clad in the Roman
robe of state, I see no joke in the passage, except that Cicero
affects to condemn a decree of the senate to refurbish his
robe, to save the King the expense of redyeing it every
year. There would be more humour in the words of Cicero if
renovari could mean, ' to be put on a new footing.' Thus
Cicero would say, ' as regards his petition to have his distinction *put on a new footing* (*i.e.* given to him absolutely without
the necessity of yearly renewal), to save himself the expense of
a yearly redyeing (*i.e.* a yearly embassy to Rome to solicit renewal), I am against such a decree.' The same sense would be
got by reading with Lamb. and Ern.: *quod non vult renovari
honores eosdem*, ' as to his request not to have a renewal of his
distinction on the same terms,' that is, ' not to have it renewed
for a year, but in perpetuity.' This is the reading which
Wieland translates, and is perhaps the most probable solution
of the difficulty, though it is very daring to insert *non*. We
can hardly hope to get any nearer to the meaning without
knowing something of ' the Bozran.' Bostra, the Bozra of
Isaiah, was a considerable town in Arabia Petraea. [It may be
that when Caes. in his consulship gave this man the right of
wearing the *toga praetexta*, he merely gave him the honorary
rank of a Roman magistrate for the year, and his right of
wearing the *toga* would expire with the year, as in the case of
the Roman magistrates. He now begged to have the grant
renewed. The clause *quo minus*, etc., must surely be dependent on *decernendum censeo*, not on *quod vult*, etc., unless
non vult is written. The text may construe thus: I make no
proposal such as would prevent him from furbishing his *toga*

up afresh every year, *i.e.* I am ready to grant him the right of
perpetually wearing the *toga*, which he will naturally furb sh
up afresh and make brilliant with new dye every new year's
day, when the magistrates at Rome assume their *toga praet.*
But will you senators, who could not stand the prince of
Bozra in the *toga praetexta*, allow the prince of Commagene to
wear it ?]

totus est explosus, 'completely, utterly laughed out of
court.'

quo genere = *cuius generis dictis.*

Iovis Hospitalis, Ζεὺς Ξένιος. We must infer that certa'n
Greeks had been instrumental in bringing about a reconcili 1-
tion between Cicero and Appius. If he broke with Appius he
would offend these Greeks, and so the god who 'protec:s
them.' Moreover, *Iupiter Hospitalis* would be the protector of
these strangers in Rome.

4. fugerat me, 'I forgot' ; so *fugit me ratio,* 'I was mi ;-
taken,' in Catull. x. 29. This meaning of *fugere* is very con -
mon in Cicero, and very rare in other writers.

magis optandum. Caesar writes to Balbus that he coul l
see that Balbus had said something about Quintus Cicero i 1
his letter ; that he could not make out the meaning ; that, if
his guess at the meaning was right, it announced a fact which
he (Caesar) might wish, but hardly hope, to be true. Th ;
announcement was probably that Quintus had determined to
transfer his services from Pompeius to Caesar. Nothing could
be more courteous than Caesar's way of receiving this news.

5. Locum. I cannot understand why the editors shoul
agree in changing the ms. *locum* to *iocum.* There is not ₁
particle of evidence that Caesar's letter was playful : the little
extract we have from it here is full of dignified courtesy. The
'passage about his poverty,' *locum illius de sua egestate,* was
no doubt in the same strain. He said with regret that he
could not promise Quintus an El Dorado in his camp. Cicero
advises his brother not to look with disfavour on that passage
—not to let it deter him from joining Caesar—and tells him
that in reply he has let Caesar know how poor they were—how
he (Caesar) 'must not get himself into difficulties through any
reliance on his (Cicero's) resources.'

Quamquam. 'Yet,' though I promise you a regular diary.
See note on *pipulo, convicio,* § 1.

LETTER XX. (Q. Fr. ii. 13 [15a])

1. **Blandenone.** Blandeno is a town near Placentia, not elsewhere mentioned.

refertis, 'overflowing with (lit. crammed with) politeness, affection, and courtesy.'

ista. 'Those tokens of good will on Caesar's part.

2. **currentem,** 'nothing loth.' See Q. Fr. i. 1, 45 ; Att. v. 9, 1 ; vi. 7, 1 ; cf. the Greek σπεύδοντ' ὀτρύνειν.

ego vero, sc. *conferam.* 'Yes ; I will do all I can.' For the emphatic use of *ego* in answer to a question, cf. Fam. xiv. 4, 1.

poëma. Probably the poem *de temporibus suis,* often referred to above.

tuus amor, 'my affection for you' ; so *amori nostro,* 'your love for me' : Fam. v. 12, 3.

3. **isse ad Caesarem.** The point of the joke of Domitius was that the consuls were without power ; Caesar was the source of patronage ; so he says that when his colleague Appius went to Luca two years before to meet Caesar, it was no doubt to get from him some petty office, such as the commission of a *tribunus militum.* [Caesar was in N. Italy as usual in the winter of 55-54, or rather in the early part of 54, the year of Appius's consulship. The visit alluded to was probably paid by Appius then.]

4. **oricula infima molliorem.** This seems to be a reminiscence of an expression of Catullus, xxv. 2, *mollior . . . imula oricilla.* We have another such echo in *ocellos Italiae villulas,* Att. xvi. 6, 2 ; and Catullus xxxi., *Peninsularum, Sirmio, insularumque Ocelle.* But Cicero never mentions Catullus. See on Q. Fr. ii. 9, 4 (Ep. xviii.) 'As soft as the tip of the ear' is here proverbial for extreme gentleness and avoidance of irritability. *Oricula* seems to have more authority than *auricula.*

5. **dictaturae,** of Pompeius : cf. *est nonnullus odor dictaturae,* Att. iv. 16, 11.

senescentis . . . acquiescentis, 'the calm of decrepitude, not of repose.' This seems to me to be in favour of my interpretation of *frigus* in Ep. xix.

τοιαῦθ'. Eur. Suppl. 119.

LETTER XXI. (Q. Fr. iii. 7)

1. et Appia. Something is no doubt lost here. Most ed. disregard the *et* before *Appia*, and print *Romae et maxime App'a*, 'in Rome, and especially on the Appian Way.' But Cicero would hardly have spoken of the *Via Appia* as a part of Rome, and the *et* before *Appia* points to an omission. [I venture to suggest that the only change required is that of *et* to *ex*—a very common corruption. There was a bit of the Appian Way which really was in Rome ; along the first mile of it, between the porta Capena and the old temple of Mars, close to the first milestone, there was a large suburb which seems to have gone by the name of *ad Martis*. See Richter's Topography of Rome in Iwan Mueller, pp. 883 *sq.*, or Jordan's Topogr. ii. pp. 110 *sq.* 'In Rome, and especially in the direction of the Appian Road, in the suburb by the temple of Mars.' This use of *ex* hardly needs illustration, but cf. such things as *e contraria parte*. Even omitting the *et* before *Appia* the passage makes good sense.]

ad Martis, 'near the temple of Mars.'

viget, 'the Homeric theory is still true.' Zeus sends violent rain to punish men for their unjust dealings. This plague of rain is his protest against the acquittal of Gabinius.

cadit . . . in. This may mean—(1) 'is applicable to,' or (2) 'synchronises with' ; rather (1), for the most natural subject for *cadit* is *illud Homeri*, not *alluvies*. But *cadit* has both meanings. The passage is Il. xvi. 385. [*Alluvies* is an improbable word for Cic., nor is the conjecture *proluvies* any more likely. Cic. wrote, I believe, *eluviones*, which he has several times elsewhere.]

2. lychnuchum. Saglio, in his fine article on *candelabrum*, says that wooden *lychnuchi* were the commonest. Cf. Petronius, 95, and Martial, xiv. 44. Others were made of gold, silver, bronze, marble, glass, and clay. *Ligneolus* probably means 'of very thin wood,' which would, of course, enhance the beauty of the *candelabrum*.

Sami. This island belonged to Asia, the province of Quintus, and was no doubt visited by Quintus during his propraetorship.

LETTER XXII. (FAM. VII. 16)

1. Equo Troiano. A play of this name is ascribed both to Livius and to Naevius. The proverb is usually supposed to be *sero sapiunt* because Festus says, *sero sapiunt Phryges proverbium est natum a Troianis qui decimo denique anno velle coeperunt Helenam quaeque cum ea erant rapta reddere.* But according to Festus *sero sapiunt Phryges* is the proverb, and he says nothing about its being a quotation from a play. Here we have expressly a quotation from a play. I believe the words quoted from this play to be *in extremo sero sapiunt*, referring possibly to the Phrygians, but possibly having a general application.

in extremo. The words mean 'when a man comes to extremities it is too late to show the discretion which might have saved him.' The passage is usually printed, *in Equo Troiano scis esse in extremo:* Sero sapiunt. But why should Cicero mention the *part of the play* at which the words occur ? Besides, *sero sapiunt* can hardly be called a sentiment at all, while *in extremo sero sapiunt* is a good proverb. For the words require some further qualification ; they should give some class of men who 'are wise too late,' or some circumstances under which it is too late to be sensible. The proverb, as I understand it, fulfils the last condition, and says that 'when things have come to an extremity it is too late to be wise.' I need not point out that the words as I have given them,

in extrémo séro sápiunt,

form the beginning of a good iambic verse according to old Latin prosody and scansion. [The question may be put the other way. Why should Cic. *not* do here what he does in other places in making quotations, *i.e.* indicate the part of the work where the words come ? The most serious difficulty in the way of your view is, I think, that there is no parallel to this use of *in extremo*, for Sall. Jug. xxiii. 2, *suas fortunas in extremo sitas* will hardly justify this.]

mi vetule. This address is merely playful. He calls Trebatius 'my old fellow,' because he is cautious—has an old head on young shoulders. He congratulates Trebatius on being wise in time, and seeing the folly of the spirit reflected in his earlier letters—a spirit of impatience and discontent, and foolish yearning for Rome.

primas. 'Your earlier letters were couched in a mad-log strain that was silly enough—but then'—you know the rest—you know how you changed your tone.

rabiosulas sat fatuas. No doubt a quotation from some lost play. [*Sat fatuas* has all the appearance of being a gloss on the rare word *rabiosulas*.]

in Britannia, 'in the matter of going to Britain.'

non nimis φιλοθέωρον, 'not too great a sight-seer.'

intectus. It appears from the next letter that there was an insufficient supply of the *sagum* or military cloak, which was also used as a blanket. Cicero alludes to this fact, and says, 'therefore, naturally you don't care to stir abroad.' Then he quotes a verse from some poet which seems to have little point, except in so far as there is a kind of play on *sapere*, 'to be a man of sense,' which meaning it seems to bear in the quotation, and *sapere* as applied especially to jurisconsults, *sapiens* having been the *sobriquet* of Curius, Fabricius, Coruncanius, etc. (Lael. 18). So in another letter he congratulates Trebatius on being in a country where he might seem *aliquid sapere*, that is, where (in the absence of rivalry) he would be at the very top of his profession. But all this is very far-fetched. And it must be remembered that *iniectus*, not *intectus*, is the ms. reading. This would not be of very great importance, were it not that *inicere*, as well as *iniectio, has a juridical sense*, 'to seize on as one's property without a judicial decision,' as in the case of a runaway slave. If *iniectus* could possibly mean 'subjected to this process' we should have a characteristically playful use of a juridical term, 'under arrest'; *inicere manum* takes an accusative of the person arrested, but I will not go so far as to say that this would justify *iniectus* 'arrested': *iniectus* certainly does not bear its ordinary meaning here; it is either a juridical term, or it is unsound, and must give place to some conjecture such as *intectus*. [May not *intectus* come from *intego*? This word is very common (cf. *integumentum*) and Lucr. i. 404 has the participle (which no doubt occurs elsewhere). The jest lies partly in *telum*: 'wisdom is the best offensive weapon; that's why you shirk hard knocks.']

2. Ego. The answer to a question. Trebatius had asked Cicero why he would not accept the invitation of Octavius to dine.

Oro te, quis tu es? Probably a quotation from some poet.

extra iocum. This phrase would seem very doubtful Latin

if we had not Cicero's authority for it; still more apparently canine are *remoto ioco*, 'jesting apart,' in the next letter, and *magna in spe sum*, 'I am in great hopes,' Att. vi. 2, 6. [Still more *in eadem es navi*, 'you are in the same boat,' Fam. ii. 5, 1. And Plaut. Men. *perge in virum*, 'walk into your husband.' Cf. *in aere meo est* = 'is in my debt,' Fam. xv. 14, 1.]

vellem eum, 'a capital fellow surely. Would you had taken him away with you.' Cf. Taming of the Shrew, i. 1, 253—

First Serv. My lord, you nod : you do not mind the play.
Sly. Yes, by Saint Anne, do I. A good matter surely. Comes there any more of it?
Page. My lord, 'tis but begun.
Sly. 'Tis a very excellent piece of work, madam lady : would 'twere done.

[I have often thought that Cic. wrote *bellicosus:* a fighting man who would do well in Gaul ; he had attacked Cic. so persistently.]

3. ecquid, 'at all.'

in Italiam, into winter quarters to Ravenna, which was the nearest point to Rome in the province of Caesar.

more Romano, 'literally.' Sometimes the phrase means 'simply,' 'plainly,' 'without circumlocution,' like *more maiorum*, Att. i. 1, 1. Cf. Fam. vii. 5, 3.

quod negent, 'because, as they say, you do not.' This is the virtual oblique ; for which see Roby, 1722, 1741, 1746.

respondere is a technical word for giving counsel's opinion. Hence the *responsa prudentium*, or opinions of counsel, were an authoritative source of Roman Law. Of course Trebatius does not 'give counsel's opinions' in the camp of Caesar ; but *respondere percontantibus* also means 'to reply to one who asks you a question' ; to fail to do this would show much arrogant reserve. Hence the joke, which, though certainly not of much merit, is repeated afterwards, Fam. i. 10, in writing to L. Valerius, another jurisconsult. [To realise the full force of the jest one must remember that to refuse to give a civil answer to a civil question was regarded by the Romans as a typical act of rudeness. See Acad. ii. § 94, and the passages to which I have referred in my note there. There is really the same jest (an oxymoron) in Att. iv. 18, 3, *multi urbani ne respondent quidem.* No doubt the impression of Tiberius's arrogance was greatly due to his taciturnity when addressed (cf. Suet. Tib 68, *plerumque tacitus*, etc.)]

Samarobrivae. Amiens, the chief town in Gallia Belgica.

LETTER XXIII. (Fam. vii. 11)

1. **tot interregnis.** The whole of this frigid jesting turns on the nature of the office of the *interrex,* for which see Class. Dict. and Merivale, ii. 27. The business of the law courts was intermitted during the *interregnum ;* each *interrex* was chosen only for five days ; on the expiration of five days a new *interrex* was appointed. The jocular counsel which Cicero gives to all defendants in civil actions (*omnibus unde petitur*) is to ask from each *interrex* two of the periods allowed for seeking legal assistance (*binas advocationes*). The defendant could thus postpone his day of trial for an indefinite term. Cicero asks, 'Does not this counsel of mine show that I have profited by my friendship with you in civil procedure ?' [It is hardly to be supposed that the *interregna* stopped the courts entirely ; indeed, the fact that an *interrex* is supposed to listen to an application for *binas advocationes* shows that it was not so. Of course the continuance for six or seven months of *interregna* in this year 53 must have disorganised legal business a good deal.]

2. **signa.** Cicero welcomes in his friend's letters a tendency to be jocular. He says : 'These signs (*signa*) of reviving spirits in you are better than the statues (*signa*) in my Tusculanum.' The play is on the two meanings of *signa,* 'signs' and 'statues.' I do not see how the play could be reproduced in English. We learn from Fam. vii. 23 that Fadius Gallus had bought for Cicero some statues (*signa*), for which Cicero did not at all care. He probably refers here to this unlucky purchase. He says : 'I like the look of your last letter, with its bantering tone, far better than I like the look of those statues which Fadius Gallus bought for me.' He had perhaps already told Trebatius how he was disappointed with the purchases of Fadius Gallus.

consuli. Cicero welcomes the sportive tone of his friend's letter, but he wants to know what is the source of his pleasant state of mind. 'You tell me,' he writes, 'that Caesar has consulted your judgment : I had far rather he had consulted your interests. If you think the latter is so (or that there is any chance of it), don't shirk the campaigning : stay on. I can console myself for my separation from you by the prospect of your advancement. But if it (your advancement) is all in the clouds, come back to me. Something must turn up here some time ; or, if not, I declare I think one hour's talk between us will be worth all the Samarobrivas in the world.' We have frequently met the plural thus used in the case of persons, as,

for instance, *omnes Catilinas Acidinos postea reddidit*, Att. iv. 3,
'He made every ruffian like Catiline seem thenceforth as respectable as an Acidinus.' Exactly parallel to *omnes Samarobrivae*, 'every town such as Samarobriva,' is *Lucerias horrent*,
'they are terribly afraid of another Luceria' (where it was
reported that plans for proscription were being hatched).
Att. viii. 11, 4 ; 16, 2. [Prob. an error for *Luceriadas*, like
'Ιλιὰς κακῶν in Att. viii. 11, 3.]

si cito te rettuleris. His final advice is : 'If you come
back soon there will be no comment ; but if you are long away,
and to no purpose, I fear Laberius will introduce you into a
farce. He will get his points from our friend Valerius, the
jurisconsult, and he will have in you a splendid character—the
lawyer in Britain.' Valerius is the jurisconsult to whom Cicero
has already written, and who is mentioned again, Fam. iii. 1, 3.
Laberius, the celebrated writer of *mimi*, is another of those
persons who are mentioned alike in Horace's Satires and Cicero's
Letters.

LETTER XXIV. (FAM. VII. 12)

1. O castra praeclara! 'What a wonderful military camp
that must be of yours' ; for the hardships of a military camp
were not likely to engender Epicurean principles. In consideration of the next clause, this seems a better sense than to interpret : 'That is a fine camp to take your stand in,' *i.e.* 'a fine
philosophical system to range yourself as a supporter of.'

Tarentum. For the charms of this the chief of winter
resorts compare the well-known passage in Horace, Odes, ii. 6,
Ille terrarum, etc. ; also Seneca, Tranquil. Animi, 2, 13 ; add
Friedländer, ii. 96.

Iam tum, 'Even then, when you were holding the same
tenets as my friend Selius, I did not approve of you.' Klotz
reads *Selius* for *Zeius, Scius*, etc. of the mss., without giving
reasons. Perhaps the reasons are as follows :—This is plainly
a reference to some philosophical views which were more akin
to Cicero's own tenets than the Epicurean, but yet did not
wholly please him. In point of ethics, it may have been the
New Academy ; their doctrine, that probability, not certainty,
is all that mankind can arrive at, deprives morals of that firm
foundation and immutability which Cicero desired. Let me
quote at length a passage from the De Legibus : *Sibi autem*

*indulgentes et corpori deservientes atque omnia quae sequan'ur
in vita, quaeque fugiant voluptatibus et doloribus ponderan es,
etiam si vera dicunt (nihil enim opus est hoc loco litibus) in
hortulis suis iubeamus dicere, atque etiam ab omni societue
reipublicae cuius partem nec norunt ullam nec umquam nesse
voluerunt, paullisper facessant, rogemus. Perturbatricem aut m
harum omnium rerum Academiam, hanc ab Arcesila et Carneu de
recentem, exoremus ut sileat. Nam si invaserit in haec, quae
satis scite nobis instructa et composita videtur, nimias elet
ruinas. Quam quidem ego placare cupio, submovere non aud'o,*
De Legg. i. 39. Here Epicurean ethics are wholly condemne l ;
Academic ethics condemned indeed, but in a less degree. Now,
if we compare Acad. 2, 11, *nam aderant familiares n ei*
(Lucullus is speaking) *docti homines P. et C. Selii et Tetrilius
Rogus qui se illa audivisse Romae de Philone et ab ipso duos libros
dicerent descripsisse,* we see that two members of the Selian
family were followers of Philo ; and however reactionary the se
'two books' may have been, there is little doubt that 'n
the public lectures which Cicero heard Philo gave expression
to that brilliant and negative criticism that he had inherited
from Carneades, leaving reactionary doctrines for private conversation and his written books' (Reid, Acad. Introd. p. 60).

2. **Sed quonam modo.** Cicero goes on to rally Trebatius is
to how his occupation will be gone if he becomes an Epicurean.
The Epicureans held that 'in the sphere of morals individual
feeling must be made the standard, and individual well-being
the object of all human activity' (Zeller, Stoics, Epicureans,
and Sceptics, Eng. Trans. p. 445, and the references), and that
'pleasure is the only unconditional good' (*ibid.* p. 446). How
then will Trebatius be able to use the legal formula in actions
against trustees about honest dealing amongst honest men ? for
the honest man (*bonus*) is he who regards the fair claims of
others beside himself. And similarly, how will Trebatius see to
the fair division of a joint property ? Further, if Trebatius is
a Fetialis, how will he be able to swear by Jupiter, the stone,
and ask this fine old god to cast him forth from his fatherland
if he perjures himself, seeing that the Epicureans *know* all
about the gods—how that they were 'perfectly free from care
and trouble, and absolutely regardless of the world' (Zeller,
p. 441), in fact, 'a society of Epicurean philosophers' (*ibid.*
p. 442), to whom caring for others outside their own circle, and
mixing in civil society or in political life was regarded as a necessary evil, and only to be practised 'as far as it is necessary for
the philosopher's own safety' (Zeller, p. 463 ; cf. the sixth κυρια

δόξα in Diog. Laert. x. 142). What, then, will become of the poor inhabitants of Ulubrae, if Trebatius ceases to be their *patronus*, and to lend them his disinterested aid ?

formula fiduciae. If a man transferred his property to another, on condition that it should be restored to him, this contract was called *Fiducia*. If the trustee refused to surrender it, he was liable to an *actio fiduciae*, which was an *actio bonae fidei*. In the *actiones stricti iuris* the praetor expressed in precise, curt, and strict terms (*directum asperum simplex*, Rosc. Com. 11) the matter submitted to the judge, whose authority was thus circumscribed. In the *actiones bonae fidei* (Top. 66, an important passage) more indulgence and latitude (*mite moderatum*) was given by the formula of the praetor, and the whole circumstances of the case were taken into consideration, in order to come to an equitable decision. The terms in the formula were *Quantum aequius melius, id dari*, or *ut inter bonos bene agier oportet*, or *ex fide bona :* Gaius, iv. 47, 50, 62, and Poste on § 45.

Quis enim bonus est, qui. *Bonus* is wanting in MII. Manutius had already added *bonus*, but after *est*. Orelli wished to omit *est*, which might readily have got inserted after *enim* by dittographia, and to understand *bonus* out of *bonos*. This is no doubt hard ; so we had better acquiesce in Wesenberg's reading, which inserts *bonus* before *est*. Words often are dropped out, owing to the proximity of a similar word.

communi dividundo. This was an action for dividing the property of partners. It was one of the three actions—*familiae erciscundae*, 'for dividing a family inheritance,' and *finium regundorum* being the other two—which the judge 'adjudicated.' See Justinian, Instit. iv. 17, 5, and Sandars *ad loc.* and Introd. § 103 ; also a clear article by Mr. Moyle in Dict. Antiqq. p. 513. Cicero seems to imply (of course with but a bare semblance of accuracy) that the individualistic hedonism, as it is called, of the Epicureans cannot coexist with any sort of partnership.

Iovem lapidem iurare. For *iurare* with the simple acc. see Virg. Aen. 12, 197, *Haec eadem, Aenea, terram mare sidera iuro ;* also Juv. 3, 144, *iures licet et Samothracum et nostrorum aras.* This oath was in accordance with 'a very old Roman rite' (Apul. De deo Socrat. 5). The *locus classicus* is Polybius, iii. 25, of the treaty with Carthage, 475 (= B.C. 279): τὸν δὲ ὅρκον ὀμνύειν ἔδει τοιοῦτον, ἐπὶ μὲν τῶν πρώτων συνθηκῶν Καρχηδονίους μὲν τοὺς θεοὺς τοὺς πατρῴους Ῥωμαίους δὲ Δία λίθον κατά τι

O

παλαιὸν ἔθος, ἐπὶ δὲ τούτων τὸν ῎Αρην καὶ τὸν 'Εννάλιον.   ἔστι δὲ
τὸ Δία λίθον τοιοῦτον.   λαβὼν εἰς τὴν χεῖρα λίθον ὁ ποιούμενος τὰ
ὅρκια περὶ τῶν συνθηκῶν, ἐπειδὰν ὁμόσῃ δημοσίᾳ πίστει λέγει τάδε.
'εὐορκοῦντι μὲν ποιεῖν τἀγαθά· εἰ δ' ἄλλως διανοηθείην τι ἢ πρήξ-
αιμι πάντων τῶν ἄλλων σῳζομένων ἐν ταῖς ἰδίαις πατρίσιν, ἐν τοῖς
ἰδίοις νόμοις ἐπὶ τῶν ἰδίων βίων ἱερῶν τάφων, ἐγὼ μόνος ἐκπέσο.μι
οὕτως ὡς ὅδε λίθος νῦν.'   καὶ ταῦτ' εἰπὼν ῥίπτει τὸν λίθον ἐκ
τῆς χειρός.   The stone was a flint, symbolical, no doubt,
of the thunderbolt.   We may compare 'the all-dread:d
thunder - *stone*' in Cymbeline, and hear Chapman speak
out loud and bold, when he renders εἴπερ μοι καὶ μοῖρα Δ ὸς
πληγέντι κεραυνῷ κεῖσθαι ὁμοῦ νεκύεσσι μεθ' αἵματι καὶ κονίῃσιν
(Il. 15, 117) by 'though I sink beneath the fate of being
shot to hell by Jove's fell thunder-*stone*,' a translation n ot
altogether unworthy of Homer.   This stone was one of the
symbols used by the Fetiales, which, with the *sceptrum*, used ·o
be kept in the temple of Jupiter Feretrius ; cf. Fest. p. 92 :
*Feretrius Iupiter . . . ex cuius templo sumebant sceptrum p r
quod iurarent et lapidem silicem quo foedus ferirent.*   The *sceptrum* was the peculiar mark of Jupiter ; and so the Fetial s
became on the occasion of the solemnity symbolically a Jupiter ;
cf. Servius on Aen. 12, 206 (*Audiat haec genitor qui foeder i
fulmine sancit*), where he says : *Ut autem sceptrum adhibeatur
ad foedera haec ratio est quia maiores semper simulacrum Iovis
adhibebant : quod cum taediosum esset—inventum est ut sceptrum
tenentes quasi imaginem simulacri redderent Iovis.   Sceptrum
enim ipsius est proprium.*   Grimm (Deutsche Mythologie, pp.
163-4, ed. 1844) tells of the flint of the German god Donar, and the
Miölnir, or hammer, of Thor.   'Hammer' is connected philo
logically with ἄκμων (Curt. G. E. No. 3), which itself means ι
thunderbolt (χάλκεος ἄκμων οὐρανόθεν κατιών, Hesiod, Theog.
722).   Compare generally on Jupiter Lapis Preller, Röm. Myth.
p. 220, and Marquardt, iii. 408-9, who agree more or less with
the above.   Another interpretation is, however, given by
Rudorff (Röm. Feldmesser, ii. 242), viz., that Jupiter Lapis is
the god who watches over boundary stones (*termini silicei*) ;
and Jupiter (according to the Etruscan Vegoia Arruns Veltym-
nus) as this guardian pours down many and varied woes on
those who remove their neighbour's landmarks (Grom. Vet.
350, 18 sqq.)   But this is not in accord with the definite and
official explanation of Polybius.   Mr. Strachan Davidson,
Selections from Polybius, p. 73, makes a good case for the
theory that *Iovem lapidem* means *Iovem et lapidem* on the
analogy of such expressions as *Patres conscripti = Patres et
conscripti.*   [Juppiter was no doubt regarded as in some way

dwelling in the stone. Cf. Robertson Smith's *Religion of the Semites* and Frazer's *Golden Bough* for similar ideas.]

scias, 'know all about how,' not merely think—a hit at the dogmatism of the Epicureans.

Ulubrano. In CIL. x. 6489 (= Or. 123) we find a *duovir et quaestor reip.* at Ulubrae, and in 6490 (= Or. 121, 4942) a *praef. iuri dicundo.* Ulubrae was accordingly a *municipium.* But it was proverbial for a poor and deserted town. Hor. Epp. 1, 11, 29 : *Quod petis hic est est Ulubris animus si te non deficit acquus ;* Juv. 10, 102 : *pannosus vacuis aedilis Ulubris.* Trebatius was *patronus* of the town. These *patroni* were influential Romans, selected by the *decuriones,* who used to lend assistance and protection to the town at Rome. The townsmen then were their *clientes.* The *patroni* were put first in the list of the senate (see the album of Canusium, CIL. ix. 338). For full information on the *patroni* and their origin, see Marquardt, i. 188, and Mommsen's splendid note on the Lex Colon. Juliae Genetivae in Eph. Epig. ii. 146.

πολιτεύεσθαι. This word does not occur in the κυρία δόξα on the subject.

adsentari, 'to humour.' On no account must we translate it 'assent to,' which is *adsentiri.* See a learned note by Mr. Reid on Academ. 2, 45.

LETTER XXV. (Fam. vii. 13)

1. arbitrare. The reading of M., accepted by all the editors, is *arbitrarere.* But it seems to me that this is probably wrong. *Arbitrarere* was, by one of the commonest of errors, assimilated to the mood of *viderere.* Now the Codex Turonensis has *arbitrare,* which seems to me to be more probably right. It is true that the Codex Turonensis, in giving *arbitrare,* naturally makes the same kind of mistake as M. and gives *videre* for *viderere,* while Cicero, in my judgment, wrote *viderere . . . arbitrare.* For what satisfactory meaning could be got out of *arbitrarere ?* 'Did you think me so unreasonable as to be annoyed with you because you seemed to me wanting in firmness, and too impatient to leave Gaul, *and because you supposed it was for that reason that I was so long without writing ?*' For what reason ? Because Trebatius seemed to Cicero wanting in firmness, and impatient ? But would Cicero be annoyed with Trebatius

because Trebatius mistook the reason why Cicero did not write ?
It seems to me far more natural that Cicero should say, 'Did
you think me so unreasonable as to be annoyed with you
because I thought you weak and impatient, *and do you suppose
that was the reason of my long silence?*' It will be observed
that the present is found afterwards in *insimulas, accipio,* and
that there is really .as good authority for *arbitrare* as for
arbitrarere. [I have always thought that *arbitrarere* depended
on *ut,* not on *quod. Existimasti ut arbitrarere* is no doubt
pleonastic, but very many close parallels might be quoted from
Cicero.]

Neque alia ulla, 'There was no other reason for my silence,
save my ignorance of your whereabouts.' That is, the only
reason for his silence was his ignorance of Trebatius's address ;
the uneasiness which showed itself in the early letters of Trebatius distressed Cicero, but did not prevent his writing. *Ulla*
is omitted by two early editions : perhaps what Cicero wrote
was *ulla,* not *alia ulla.* But *alia ulla* is quite intelligible in
the sense in which I have explained it. [*Alia* is certainly
sound.]

Hic . . . accipis? An indignant question : for the use of
hic in such cases cf. *hic tu . . . miraris?* Fam. v. 15, 4 ;
hic . . . commemorat? Phil. viii. 11. Wes. ingeniously proves
that such passages should be treated as questions, by pointing
to Sall. Cat. 52, 11, where, if there were no question, *aliquis*
would have been used instead of *quisquam.* [Not all ; in many
a fact is strongly stated.]

satisfactionem, the regular Latin word for 'an apology.'

Audi, Testa mi. For the use of *nomen, praenomen* and *cognomen* in familiar communications see note on Fam. vii. 32, :
(Ep. xxxiii.)

gloria, 'desire of distinction,' ' ambition,' as often in Cicero
and the comic drama.

inaurari, 'gilded'; that is, 'enriched.' Cf. Hor. Ep. i.
12, 9, *fortunae rivus inauret.*

utrumque est, that is, if you. are being gilded by Caesar,
as well as consulted.

2. illud, 'your former impatience'; hoc, 'your present con-
tentment.'

artificium, 'profession.' Cicero says he fears Trebatius will
not make much by his profession among the Gauls,

> Because the good old rule
> Sufficeth them, the simple plan,
> That they should take who have the power,
> And they should keep who can.

The quotation which Cicero uses to convey this sentiment is from Ennius, Annales, 275 (Vahlen). The whole fragment which describes the uselessness of the arts of peace in time of war runs thus—

> Pellitur e medio sapientia, vi geritur res,
> Spernitur orator bonus, horridus miles amatur,
> Haud doctis dictis certantes sed maledictis
> Miscent inter sese inimicitiam agitantes.
> Non ex iure manum consertum sed magi' ferro
> Rem repetunt regnumque petunt, vadunt solida vi.

In this fragment *sapientia* seems to be used in the sense which it often bears in the letters to Trebatius, 'the art of the juris-consult.' Observe the unelided *-ām* in *inimiciam*. The con-struction of *manum consertum* is strange. *Consertum* is the supine of *conserere*, depending on *eunt* or *vocant*, taken out of *repetunt*, and governing *manum*. *Ex iure* means 'in accord-ance with legal rights of a citizen.' *Manum conserere* has a double sense—(1) 'to make a legal claim to property,' (2) 'to join battle.' The fragment is again quoted (there more fully) in Pro Murena, 30.

et tu soles. Wes. first saw that this must be taken in close connexion with what goes before. I have followed him in putting a comma, instead of a full stop, after *repetunt*, and in omitting the mark of interrogation inserted by all other edd. after *adhiberi*. The meaning is : 'There is no place for a juris-consult in the camp of Caesar, where they may keep who can, and where you, a jurist, are actually *employed* (*adhibere*) to commit violence' [in battle against the enemy, instead of being *consulted* (*adhiberi*) in cases of assault and battery]. There is a play on two senses of the word *adhiberi*. [There is a jest on *vim facere*, to do actual violence in battle, as compared with *vim facere*, the legal phrase for asserting a right (quite peaceably) to a bit of land.]

exceptionem in interdicto. The *interdictum* was a pro-visional decree of the praetor, chiefly in the case of disputed possession. There were three kinds of interdict, *adipiscendae*, *retinendae*, and *recuperandae possessionis*. This is probably an interdict *retinendae poss.* The formula in this case runs : "Uti eas aedes quibus de agitur, *nec vi nec clam nec precario alter ab* *altero possidetis,* quominus ita possideatis vim fieri veto." The words in italics would constitute the *exceptio.* There are, however, to me two difficulties, in reference to this interdict—(1) I cannot find in the Digest at all the exact expression QUO 'U PRIOR VI NON VENERIS ; (2) nor any provision about *armed* violence (*vi hominibus armatis*), which was different from the ordinary *vis.* There is a strong objection to making this an interdict *recuperandae poss.,* for in this case, when armed force had been used, we are distinctly told that no *exceptiones* are tolerated (Gaius, iv. 155, and Poste). This point also clearly appears in the Caecina, § 63. Cicero says: 'You have no reason to fear the *exceptio ;* I warrant you never made a forcible entry.' *Quo non veneris = in quam possessionem non veneris = si in eam possessionem non veneris.* The correlative to *quo* would be found in many *formulae* in the words *eo restituas,* which are common in *formulae.* See, for a passage very similar to this, Fam. xv. 16, 3. It will be seen that the words of Cicero do not exactly fall in with any of the three common types of interdict. Perhaps he tripped in his law here. He can hardly have deliberately jumbled together two kinds of interdict, *reti- nendae* and *recuperandae possessionis,* as a joke, in the spirit in which he writes, *satisne tibi videor abs te ius civile didiciss ,* Fam. vii. 11, 1. I here add the view of Mr. Roby given in Classical Review, vol. i. p. 66. His authority will be generally held to be decisive on the question ; but I thought it as well to state the difficulties which had occurred to me.

'Trebatius, the lawyer, is attending Caesar in his camp in Gaul, and Cicero chaffs him on his position. "I am only afraid that your professional craft is of little good to you, for, I am told, where you are (to quote Ennius) 'men don't join issue in due course of law, but effect a recovery sword in hand,' and actually *you* are now called in to use force ! Well, there is no ground for much fear of your being troubled with the plea of having been the first to come with a force of armed men, for I know you are not forward in attack."

'Trebatius, if dispossessed of some land by armed violence would apply to the practor for an interdict which would state the issue in some such words as these, addressed to his opponent : *Unde tu C. Trebatium ui hominibus armatis deiecisti eo C. Trebatium restituas.* If, however, Trebatius had himself previously turned out his opponent by the like means, the opponent would urge the practor to insert in the formula after "*deiecisti*" *quo ille prior ui hominibus armatis non uenerit,* and the practor would naturally consent. The matter would then be referred to a judge to decide with these instructions.

If the judge found that Trebatius had been ejected by armed force and had not himself been the aggressor by the same means, the injunction would be made final, and the defendant probably be condemned in damages : if his prior aggression were proved or his dispossession not proved, the injunction would drop and in some cases the plaintiff would pay a forfeit (cf. Gai. iv. 141, 161-165).

'There is, I think, no doubt that the interdict referred to is *de ui armata* (which in the Digest is consolidated with that *de ui*, Dig. xliii. 16). Prof. Tyrrell erroneously takes it to be the interdict *uti possidetis*, and naturally finds difficulties. He has been misled by the language of Cic. Caecin. 22, § 63, and Gai. iv. 155, whence he infers that no *exceptiones* were allowed when armed force had been used. It is not necessary to assume in either passage that such a plea as we have here was in question. But that such a plea was allowable is, I think, clear (1) from this passage itself ; (2) from the analogy of the interdict "*de ui*" (cf. Cic. Caecin. § 92) ; (3) from the reason of the thing, supported by the language of the Digest.

'The use of armed violence in matters of ejectment was rightly held to be so contrary to the dignity of legal procedure as to require peremptory prohibition. Accordingly a person who had himself acquired possession from his opponent by force (*ui*, not *ui armata*) or by stealth or by sufferance was yet entitled to immediate restoration, if his opponent ejected him by armed force. Obviously the same principle applies against him, if he has himself used armed force. His own armed violence disentitles him from claiming the peremptory protection of the law, on the same principle on which armed violence disentitles his opponent from pleading the wrongful possession of the former. Indeed the two acts may well have been successive events in one day's struggle. If Trebatius (in the supposed case) had brought a body of armed men to dispossess his opponent, he could not be aggrieved by his opponent's resorting to the same means to dispossess him in turn. *Eum qui cum armis uenit, possumus armis repellere, sed hoc confestim, non ex interuallo ; dummodo sciamus non solum resistere permissum ne deiciatur, sed, et si deiectus quis fuerit, eundem deicere non ex interuallo sed ex continenti.* (Ulpian in Dig. xliii. § 16, l. 3, § 9 ; and cf. l. 1, §§ 27, 28.)'

I add the comment of Dr. Reid. [The statements in Cic. Caec. are not to be relied on. He may not have said anything false, but he has certainly concealed matters which make his account of the law as it stood in his time utterly untrustworthy. And the law had changed so much between his time and that of the

writers quoted in Dig. that they do not help us to make good
Cicero's deficiencies so much as we could wish.   The fact that
there is no mention elsewhere of the *exceptio quo tu prior*, etc.,
is not surprising.   The rays of light we get on the *exceptiones*
are few and scattered.   Many must have existed which are
never quoted at all in extant literature.   I think the procedure in Cic.'s time as to *vis armata* was not always the same
When a plaintiff asked redress of the praetor, the pr. might
issue an interdict without hearing the other side ; or he might
insist on hearing the other side.   In the latter case there
would be an opportunity for the defendant to bar the plaintiff
by getting the judge to insert such an *exceptio* as *quo tu prior*,
etc.   If the plaintiff had been the first to use force, he would
naturally lose when the *facts* came to be investigated as they
had to be.   If the defendant thought he had a good enough
case to resist the plaintiff, he always pleaded that he had
obeyed the interdict, meaning thereby that he had obeyed it
so far as the law required him to obey it, *i.e.* not at all.   The
plaintiff joined issue on this statement, and the final verdict
went by the *law* of the matter generally.   The interdict practically was only a way of leading up to a trial on the merits.
It would make little or no difference in the end whether *exceptiones* were inserted in the interdict *de vi armata* or not.
The defendant could ultimately get cognisance taken of any
points he had to urge.   Cic. in Caec. only says *ut solet* of the
practice of issuing the interdict *de vi armata* without any
exceptiones.   I think that if that had been the *universal*
practice, he would have made a good deal more of it in the
speech than he does.]

de vestris cautionibus.   There are two kinds of *cautio*—
the moral quality of *caution, wariness*, and the legal act of
going security for another.   Trebatius is very familiar with
cautiones in the latter sense ; 'but,' says Cicero, 'there are
other kinds of *cautio*, and I advise you to beware of the Treviri ;
I hear they are a parlous folk.'   Then, when he has called the
Treviri 'parlous' *capitales*, he plays on the name of the *tres
viri capitales*, who had charge of prisons and executions in
Rome—'I don't want you to have anything to do with the *III
viri capitales* ; I had rather they were the masters of the mint
that you were associating with.'   The allusion is to the *III
viri auro argento aeri flando feriundo*, called in inscriptions
III V. A. A. A. F. F., 'the three commissioners for the
casting and stamping of gold, silver, and copper coinage.'
Broadly, he means : 'I wish you had less of the hardships of

campaigning, and a better prospect of making your fortune,' which is, indeed, the burden of most of his letters to Trebatius. These commissioners were also called *III viri monetales*. One might take off the play on words somehow thus :—Avoid the Treviri. I hear they do great execution, like their namesakes in Rome: now I don't want to hear about executions in connexion with you, unless it might be the execution of a deed of gift in your favour from Caesar.

LETTER XXVI. (ATT. V. 1)

Cicero was now on his way to his province, Cilicia.

1. **Ego vero,** 'Yes, I *did* see': for the emphatic *ego* see on Ep. viii. 1.

mei in eo. The usual reading is *et meo sum ipse testis.* But Cicero almost always has a genitive after *testis*, the other constructions used by him being *de* with abl., *in* with abl., and *in* with accus. The Codex Ravennas (R.) gives *in eo*, words which may have ousted *mei*, and given rise to *meo*. For the confusion between *m* and *in*, cf. *Esses sin* for *esses me*, Att. i. 10, 6 ; *in hercle* for *mehercle*, Att. i. 12, 3 ; *in alam* for *malam*, Att. i. 19, 2.

ut ne. *Ut ne* in final sentences, as here, is common in Cicero and Latin comedy. It is also found in Varro, Phaedrus, Suetonius, and the writer of the Bellum Africanum, but not in Sallust, Livy (except in xxxiv. 17, 8), or Caesar (except in B. C. iii. 56, 1). *Ut ne* in sentences dependent on a foregoing verb or noun is often found in the comic drama and in Cicero, both in positive sentences, as Fam. ii. 7, 4, *peto . . . ut ne,* and in negative, as *caveamus . . . ut ne quod in nobis insigne vitium fuisse dicatur,* Q. Fr. i. 1, 38, but is very rare elsewhere. Draeger, Hist. Syn. §§ 411, 542, 2. The meaning is 'that no new (further) term of provincial government be assigned to me by the senate.'

plus sit annuum. 'In descriptions of size, age, etc., *plus amplius minus* are used without change of case (as adverbs), and the noun of size, etc., if not put in the ablative, is subjoined in the proper case with or without *quam*': Roby, § 1273. Of the omission of *quam*, as here, good examples are : *me non amplius novem annos nato,* Nep. 23, 2 ; *boves minores trimos,* Varr. R. R. 1, 20 ; *nix minus quattuor pedes alta,* Liv. xxi. 61, 10.

2. Annio Saturnino. Probably a freedman of T. Annius Milo.

satis des, 'guarantee the purchaser against loss by flaws in his title' to some property which Cicero was selling ; or, if Cicero was now buying some property, *satis des* must mean 'give security for the payment of the sum agreed on as the price.' The former meaning seems better suited to the sub-sequent phrase *satisdatio secundum mancipium*. He recommends Atticus to use the *satisdatio* employed in the case of the sale of the Mennian estate, adding, 'or perhaps I should rather call it the Atilian property.' Cicero probably refers to a former sale by him of some farms which he had bough; belonging to the estate of Mennius, who, he afterwards re members, had previously disposed of the lands to Atilius, so that Atilius was really the seller of the farms to Cicero. [Rather *veluti . . . vel* = 'for example . . . or,' *i.e.* first one example is given and then another.]

Oppio. The agent of Caesar, to whom Cicero owed 800,000 sesterces.

aperuisti. This verb is explained in the Dictt. as meaning 'to declare one's willingness to pay.' But this sense is not even alleged to be found elsewhere, and it is very hard to see how *aperire dccc.* could mean 'to declare one's willingness to pay' that sum of money. The same is said to be the meaning of *exposuisti*, 'you said the money was at his disposal,' Att. v. 4, 3. But there M. reads *de* dccc., which makes the meaning easy. Hence here, too, I have added *de:* for *aperire de*, 'to explain,' cf. Herenn. ii. 50 ; and *aperire de* dccc. is a very natural expression for 'to explain the details of a transaction' about 800,000 sesterces. *De* would have easily fallen out. Cicero goes on to say, 'I would willingly borrow to pay this debt (*versura facta solvi volo*) rather than keep Caesar waiting until the last penny due to me is gotten in.'

3. transversum versiculum, 'the crossing' of your letter, written along the margin of the page.

admones de sorore. We may gather from the words at the end of § 4, *haec . . . monendi*, that Atticus had asked Cicero to give his brother Quintus some advice about his demeanour towards Pomponia.

Arpinas, sc. *praedium*.

dies, sc. *festus*. Arcanum was *en fête*, so Quintus thought it was incumbent on him to stay there and entertain his tenants.

He suggested to Pomponia that she should invite the women, while he should summon the men.

ascivero. 'In some few instances the meaning of the *futurum exactum* approaches that of the *futurum simplex* in signifying what will happen *while something else takes place*, or *what will soon be done:* Cic. Att. v. 1, 3'; Madv. § 340, Obs. 4. The ms. here gives *ego vero ascivero pueros.* Probably *vero* is a mistake for *viros.* But what lurks under *pueros?* Possibly we should read *ego viros ascivero porro*, 'I shall ask the men in due course' (when you have given your invitation to the women). This would illustrate a slightly different employment of the future perfect, which is sometimes used when a thing is postponed to another time, as *quae causa fuerit mox videro*, Fin. i. 35. For the position of *porro* cf. Hand. Turs. ii. p. 266, who remarks that the placing of adverbs at the end of the sentence is characteristic of the *sermo popularis*, and quotes *quo evasurust denique*, Plaut. Trin. 938 (iv. 2, 93), and *in nervom erumpat denique*, Ter. Phorm. 325 (ii. 2, 11). We find *tamen* last word of a sentence in Att. i. 17, 10, and *nunc* in Fam. xiii. 1, 1. [It may be doubted whether *asciscere aliquem* is possible for inviting a person to an entertainment. *Accivero* is possible (Wes. after Lamb.) But Gronovius's *accepero* is, I believe, right, and *pueros* has arisen from a dittogr. of *-pero*.]

animo ac voltu, 'the feeling which prompted the words and the expression of countenance which accompanied them.'

Ego . . . hospita, 'I am treated as a stranger in this house'; cf. *peregrinum atque hospitem*, Att. vi. 3, 4. [Is not the sense 'I am mistress of this house,' *i.e.* I don't mean to have you interfering with the invitation arrangements? The fault about Statius seems to be that he had received his orders from his master, not from his mistress.]

ex eo, 'all because Statius had gone on before us to see to dinner.' *Videre* in the sense of to 'see to, provide, look after,' is common enough in Cicero and the comic drama, *e.g.* Ter. Heaut. iii. 1, 50 (459), *aliud lenius sodes vide.* Perhaps this, too, is the right explanation of the verb in Juv. xiii. 57, *licet ipse videret plura domi fraga.* Munro conjectured *tu vides* for *tu bibes* in Hor. Carm. i. 20, 10, where *vides*, 'thou providest,' certainly supplies the required sense. ὁρᾶν has the same meaning in ὅρη δίφρον, Εὐνόα, αὐτᾷ, Theocr. xv. 2.

4. sic absurde et aspere, 'with such uncalled-for acrimony.' This use of *sic* to express intensity with verbs and adjectives is found chiefly in Cicero and the comic writers;

ita, tam, adeo, are far more usual in this sense. This is another objection to the otherwise suspicious reading, *sic raro scrib's,* in Hor. Sat. ii. 3, 1. For *absurde,* cf. *epistolarum absurde et inusitate scriptarum,* 'letters written in uncalled-for and eccentric fashion,' Q. Fr. i. 2, 9.

Dissimulavi dolens, 'Though I felt her conduct deeply, I did not let my feelings be seen.' *Dissimulavi* is used absolutely. *Dissimulavi dolens* would not be a correct alternative form of expression for *dissimulavi dolorem.*

de mensa misit. When Pomponia refused to take her seat at table (*discumbere*), Quintus sent her some food from the table (*de mensa misit*), which she refused.

5. extrudas, 'make my lieutenant Pomptinus leave Rome and come to me.' Cicero's other *legati* were his brother Quintus, M. Anneius, L. Tullius, and Q. Volusius. We know nothing of Anneius and Tullius. Pomptinus was an old friend of Cicero; he had been a praetor during Cicero's consulate, and Cicero had proved his vigour and energy in the repressing of the Catilinarian conspiracy. We read of his being balked of his triumph (Q. Fr. iii. 4, 6; Att. iv. 18, 4). Sallust calls him *homo militaris* (Cat. 45), and Cicero no doubt trusted to him and to his brother Quintus to compensate for his own want of experience in military affairs.

me ad te scripsisse, 'I wish you would tell him I wrote to you about him.' Cicero wishes Atticus to repeat to Torquatus the warm expressions he has just used about him.

LETTER XXVII. (Fam. viii. 1)

1. decedenti, 'leaving town': cf. Fam. viii. 10, 5. Except in these passages of Caelius I do not know of any place where *decedere* is used absolutely in this sense. It is therefore uncertain whether we should consider this a peculiar usage of Caelius or alter to *discedenti.* [However, as *decedere* is used abs. of 'leaving a province,' there seems to be nothing unnatural in the use here.]

data opera. A somewhat rare (and apparently later) form of the more usual *dedita opera* = 'intentionally.' 'I deliberately procured a man to describe *everything* so very fully, that I fear his efforts in this direction may seem to you rather long-winded.' The expression is careless. Fully expressed it should be : 'I got a man to describe everything, and he did so in such great detail that,' etc.   For *data opera* Becher compares Dig. 29, 5, 1, 37, *dicendum est parci eis debere nisi si ipsi sibi vulnera ista fecerunt data opera ne punirentur;* also 4, 7, 1 pr.; 9, 2, 9, 4 ; Plin. Epp. vii. 12, 6.   For *argutus* in the sense of 'very detailed,' almost 'garrulous,' see Att. vi. 5, 1, *velim obvias mihi litteras quam argutissimas de omnibus rebus crebro mittas.* [There is no other ex. of *data opera* in Cic., and I do not know of any ex. before Cic.]

meum hoc officium, 'not to stigmatise as supercilious the way I have fulfilled this duty in that I have deputed,' etc.

ad litteras scribendas . . . pigerrimo, 'a wretchedly bad correspondent.'

tuae memoriae, 'to memories of you.'

volumen, 'packet'; **misi**, 'herewith send,' epistolary perfect.

quoius.   For this archaic form we have the evidence of M. which reads *quo ius*, and H. which reads *quid ius*, errors which would easily arise from the rare archaism *quoius*, but not from the common form *cuius*. Caelius affects archaism. Cf. Fam. viii. 2, 1 ; 2, 8 ; 12, 2.

non modo . . . sed.   Without *etiam* or *modo* cf. Fam. v. 16, 1 ; Q. Fr. ii. 3, 2 ; Mil. 66 ; Off. i. 99.   It is not true, as it is sometimes stated, that when *etiam* is omitted there is a descent from a more extensive to a less extensive idea : cf. (besides the passages quoted above) Fam. i. 6, 1, *non solum interfuit sed praefuit* ; Draeger, ii. 103.

animadvertere, 'to look over them.'

fabulae, 'gossip.'

ne molestiam, 'lest I should spend money in boring you.'

2. operarii, 'clerks.'

spes sit.   All mss. read *est*, which must be altered to *sit*. Note *spes* used in the neutral sense of 'expectation entertained about it.'

nulla magno opere exspectatio est, 'interest is not very keen on any topic.'   For *magno opere* in negative sentences cf. Liv. i. 17, 1 ; iii. 26, 3 ; Att. iv. 16, 6.

comitiis Transpadanorum.   See Att. v. 2 *fin.*, 'there is a rumour that the Transpadane Gauls have been directed to create

quattuorviri.' These were municipal officers; so the meaning
is that these Gauls were being encouraged to seek the *civitas*.
They now had the *ius Latii*. This was a favourite project of
Caesar's. [Att. iv. 17, 2. The rumour rather was that ~~Cic~~ was
going to treat them as Roman citizens. He had already
enrolled many in his legions.]

Cumarum tenus caluerunt, 'kept up their heat only as
far as Cumae.' [*Tenus* with gen. is poetical, and post-Augustan,
outside Cael.; Cic. Arat.; Virg. Lucr. Plin. N. II.; Quint. Apul.;
cf. prepositional use of *fine*.]

ne tenuissimam quidem auditionem, 'not even the
slightest whisper.' This is the regular word for 'hearsay' (cf
Nägelsbach, p. 181, for such words in -*io*).

de successione Galliarum, that Caesar should give up his
provinces on March 1, 49. This was the persistent demand
of the republican party in their proceedings to bring matters to
a crisis with Caesar.

expressit, 'wrung from people those criticisms about himself which had been made when we were in Rome,' viz. that he
had no energy: cf. Fam. viii. 10, 3, *Nosti Marcellum quam
tardus et parum efficax sit* (Hofm.) The subjunctive is often
used with *cum* after *tum, nunc*, etc., where we should rather
have expected the indicative: cf. Att. v. 11, 7, *tum videlicet
datas cum ego me non belle haberem;* Fam. xiii. 16, 1, *Apollonium
iam tum equidem cum ille viveret et magis faciebam et probabam;*
and Draeger, ii. 576. *Expressit* could hardly mean '*reproduced*'
in the sense of '*justified*.' [But *exprimere* often means 'to
give vivid expression to,' 'to embody in a conspicuous shape,'
and this sense seems well in place here and more likely than
the other. Cf. *e.g.* Tusc. iv. § 62.]

3. **Pompeium,** who was at Tarentum.

solet . . . cupiat, 'for his wont is to think one thing
and say another, and not to have sufficient adroitness to conceal
his aims.' It is rare to find *aliud . . . et;* yet cf. Caecin. 57,
Off. ii. 61, and Draeger, ii. 29. On the insincerity of Pompeius
see Att. iv. 9 (Ep. xv); Q. Fr. iii. 8, 4, *velit nolit scire difficile est.*

4. **Quod ad Caesarem,** sc. *attinet.* For this omission
Hofmann refers to 2 Verr. i. 116, *quod id ad praetorem uter
possessor sit*, De Orat. ii. 139, and Att. i. 13, 6; Dig. 41, 1,
3, 1.

belli, 'pleasant,' 'nice.' There is always a slight touch of
colloquialism about this word.

susurratores, 'croakers,' or 'whispering messengers.'

equitem. The collective use of *eques* for 'the cavalry' is not Ciceronian. Hofmann thinks that Caelius here intends a joke, taking *equitem* in the sense of 'a single horseman.' [Not in Caesar either, though I think one or two exx. occur in Bell. Af. and Hisp.]

vapulasse. This word is never used by Cicero of troops being beaten, but is sometimes so used in Livy. It, too, is somewhat colloquial, 'were thrashed.' [A very rare word in Cic. Does it occur except in Att. ii. 14, 1?]

Bellovaci. They lived about the modern Beauvais. The modern names of French towns are derived partly from names of clans (especially in the north), partly from the names of cities; in Spain and Britain wholly from the names of cities: cf. Merivale, iv. 132.

neque iactantur, 'nor are these, uncertain as they are, yet generally talked about.' This use of *iactari* without any sense of 'boasting' attached is common in Livy, i. 50, 2; x. 46, 16: cf. Caes. B. G. i. 18, 1. For another much less common use of *iactari* see note on Ep. xv.

palam secreto, 'as an open secret.' Compare perhaps *aperte tecte,* 'with obvious guardedness,' Att. i. 14, 4: if we are not to take that 'openly *or* covertly,' as Hofmann does, comparing for the asyndeton *serius ocius.* There is no *certain* intelligence of the disaster, and no prevalent talk about the mere reports which have arrived: amongst some few they are talked about as an open secret, but Domitius makes a wonderful mystery about them. [I agree with Hofm.]

cum manus ad os apposuit, the gesture of one telling a secret. Understand some such words as *tum demum narrat.* [This has generally been taken to refer to L. Dom. Ahenobarbus, consul in 54 B.C. But he and his nephew Cn. were Pompeians, and one does not see why they should have gone about speaking of the disaster with bated breath. If *manus ad os app.* means this, the passage must rather refer to the Caesarian Cn. Dom. Calvinus, consul in 53. But would not *manum* be expected? And may not *manus* convey just the opposite, *i.e.* he makes a speaking trumpet of his hands and roars out the news? *At Domitius* seems to introduce a contrast to *secreto.*]

5. **subrostrani,** idlers about the *rostra:* cf. *subbasilicani,* Plaut. Capt. iv. 2, 35; *columnarii,* Fam. viii. 9, 5.

illorum. So the mss. Wesenberg reads (Em. Alt. p. 18)

ipsorum, in opposition to *te*. More probably we should read *illorum ipsorum*.

Q. Pompeio, sc. *Rufo*. He was a violent opponent of Milo s, and accordingly an enemy of Cicero's also, against whom he excited great odium on the occasion of the trial of Milo. He was accused *de vi*, on account of his harangues to the people on the occasion when they burned Clodius's body in the Senate-house, and in so doing burned down the Basilica Porcia. Pompeius did not support him on the trial as he ought to have done (Momms. R. II. iv. 326).

iam πεινητικὴν facere, sc. *τέχνην*. This is perhaps the most reasonable emendation of the corrupt reading of the mss. *embeneticam*. It may mean 'is doing Banting.' It is true that Caelius does not much affect Greek words, but Greek was the regular language for the prescriptions of physicians. See note on Ep. iv. However, there may be an allusion to the saying of Pompeius to Marcellinus, when the latter attacked the former, that it was owing to him that Marcellinus had become ἐμετικὸς ἐκ πεινητικοῦ (Plutarch, Pomp. 51 *fin*.) No reader of Plutarch needs to be reminded how often he relates sayings, stating in addition that they were uttered in Greek, even ἀνερρίφθω κύβος (Plut. Pomp. 60). The retort on Marcellinus was doubtless on the lips of every one, and in allusion to it perhaps Caelius says of Rufus πεινητικὴν *facere*, that he is now in the most abject state of poverty and starving. An annotator, thinking of *esurire* and the Roman practice of vomiting (cf. Att. xiii. 52, 1, ἐμετικὴν *agebat*), put ἐμε above πεινη, and the two ran together.

esurire. So the mss. There is no necessity to read *esurici*.

et hoc . . . optavi, 'and I prayed that at the cost of this lie we might get rid of whatever danger hung over you.' For abl. instrum. after *defungi* see Livy, ii. 35, 3, *adeo infensa erat coorta plebs, ut unius poena defungendum esset patribus*.

Plancus tuus, 'your friend, Plancus': irony, for T. Munatius Plancus was an associate of Q. Pompeius, and a bitter enemy of Cicero. At the trial of this Plancus, Pompeius, in violation of his own laws, appeared as a *laudator*, or witness to the character of Plancus; yet Plancus was condemned. His brother, L. Plancus, was a lieutenant of Caesar's in Gaul.

nec beatus, 'neither rich nor even well-to-do.'

πολιτικοί. *Politici* is not a Latin word. Nägelsbach (p. 22) shows that wherever the idea 'political' occurs in Latin it is expressed by a periphrasis, *civilis et popularis*, some combination

with *respublica* or the like. In De Orat. iii. 109 it is expressly
used as a Greek term. I have accordingly printed it in Greek
characters. The books referred to are the six books De Republica,
begun in 54 ; also, probably, the De Legibus, written in 52.

omnibus vigent, 'are popular with all parties' : cf. *gregal-
ibus illis, quibus te plaudente vigebamus, amissis*, Fam. vii. 33, 1.

LETTER XXVIII. (ATT. v. 9)

1. Sybota, a group of small islands between Corcyra and
the mainland.

muneribus. Gifts of food and wine which Areus and
Eutychides, freedmen of Atticus at Corcyra, heaped on Cicero
by direction of Atticus.

Saliarem in modum, 'like Aldermen.'

pedibus, 'by land.'

qui . . . navigassemus, 'as we had had a wretched
passage.'

decorum, an amusing instance of Roman *gravitas*.

currentem, 'nothing loth.' See note on Ep. xx. § 2, and
cf. σπεύδοντ' ὀτρύνειν in Greek.

extraordinarium. So called because Cicero held his present
office long after his consulship, not immediately after, as was
usual.

praestabimus, 'guarantee (answer for) my own behaviour.'

2. suo statu. *In* is not used in this phrase ; so the common expression *in statu quo* is wrong.

ne quid novi, 'new term of provincial government.'

intercaletur, 'not have any intercalary days added,' which
was at the discretion of the *Pontifices*.

Annum . . . teneto, 'be firm on the subject of my year,'
i.e. 'stick to (insist on) only a single year of provincial government for me ; do not allow any renewal of my tenure.'

3. cotidie. This seems irregular for *in dies pluris facio*, but
there is a slight difference in meaning between (*a*) *cotidie pluris
facio*, 'there is not a day but I feel an increased sense of his
worth,' that is, 'a stronger sense than I once had,' and (*b*) *in
dies pluris facio*, 'I value him more and more every day,' 'my
sense of his worth increases each day.' In Att. v. 7, 1, Cic.

P

contrasts these two expressions, *cotidie, vel potius in dies singulos breviores litteras ad te mitto,* 'I find myself day after day send-ing you shorter letters (than I used), or rather, my letters are becoming shorter every day'; he goes on—*cotidie enim magis sus-picor,* 'for there is not a day but I feel an increased suspicion,' etc. Cf. *cotidie magis in his studiis conquiesco,* Att. i. 20, 7 ; *cotidie demitigamur,* Att. i. 13, 3.

LETTER XXIX. (ATT. v. 12)

1. **Negotium**, 'A piece of business,' like Greek ἔργον : sometimes it is used like Greek χρῆμα, as Teucris is called *lentum negotium,* 'a slow coach,' Att. i. 12, 1 : cf. also Att. v. 18, 4 ; Q. Fr. ii. 11, 4.

Zostera. Zoster was a promontory of Attica, with a town and harbour, now C. Lombarda.

Ceo = Κέω, the accus. of Κέως, according to the so-called Attic declension.

Iam nosti, 'you know by this time (*iam*) what the open (unscreened) Rhodian boats are like.' There is no need to change *iam* to *nam,* for the sentence does not explain why they went quicker than they wished ; the effect of the Rhodian vessels is the opposite, to make them go slower, not quicker, as we see in next letter.

ἄκρα Γυρέων pura. The absurd reading accepted here by all the edd., without even an *obelus,* is ἀκρωτηρίων οὔρια, which is supposed to mean 'such signs of fair weather as may be given by pennants on flagstaffs and at mastheads,' *signa secunda tempestatis ex vexillis in fastigiis domorum ac navium.* The reading in the text, which has never before appeared in any ed. of the letters, was admirably restored by L. Dindorf from a fragment of Archilochus (54 Bergk)—

> Γλαῦχ', ὅρα, βαθὺς γὰρ ἤδη κύμασιν ταράσσεται
> πόντος, ἀμφὶ δ' ἄκρα Γυρίων ὀρθὸν ἵσταται νέφος
> σῆμα χειμῶνος· κιχάνει δ' ἐξ ἀελπτίης φόβος.

The fragment is quoted by Plut. de Superstit. c. 8, and by Theophr. de Signis Tempest. 3, 8. So the heights on the pro-montory of Gyrae afforded a recognised, almost proverbial, weather-gauge, and nothing is more natural than that Cicero, who knew the works of Archilochus well, and who was now close to Paros, the birthplace of the poet, should refer to this passage, finding himself in the neighbourhood of the very place. Dio Chrysost., Or. vii. p. 222 R., mentions a similar weather-presage drawn from the clouds round the peaks of Euboea, βουλοίμην δ' ἂν ἔγωγε καὶ μετὰ πέντε ἡμέρας λῆξαι τὸν ἄνεμον· ἀλλὰ οὐ ῥᾴδιον, εἶπεν, ὅταν οὕτω πιεσθῇ τὰ ἄκρα τῆς Εὐβοίας ὑπὸ τῶν νεφῶν ὥς γε νῦν κατειλημμένα ὁρᾷς. So Cicero says here, '<u>I don't mean</u> to stir from Delos until I see all the peaks of <u>Gyrae clear</u>.' The promontory of Gyrae is the south point of Tenos, due north of Paros, with a large expanse of open sea to the north; heavy clouds round the peaks of Gyrae would threaten bad weather from the north, the most dangerous point. The reading in the text is far nearer to the ms. reading, ακρατηρεων iura, than the vulgar reading, ἀκρωτηρίων οὔρια, which is mere nonsense, and which would never have established itself at all but for the general belief in the fictitious codices of Bosius, in which he declared it was to be found.

2. a te. I have thus corrected ad te, which makes the passage quite unintelligible, as was seen by Madvig, who reads Ad Messallam (Adv. Crit. iii. 175), and omits ad te. He justly points out that Cicero would not inform Atticus that he had written to him about Messalla. The state of the case was :—Atticus had informed Cicero that Messalla had been acquitted on the charge of ambitus brought against him, and he had advised Cicero to write to Messalla. Cicero answers that he did so at once, 'and, moreover—this was my own idea —I wrote also to Hortensius,' Messalla's uncle, who had defended him. A te ut audivi de Messalla is good epistolary Latin for the more formal phrase ut litteris a te acceptis audivi. A much greater laxity will be noticed in the note in the next section on cui rei fugerat me rescribere. The insertion of ad cum after dedi litteras would make the sentence clearer, but the words are not indispensable. Atticus would understand whom he referred to. We read in Fam. viii. 4, 1, a letter written shortly after this, that immediately after his acquittal Messalla was tried again (under the lex Licinia de sodalitiis) and found guilty. If the present letter contained the latter announcement as well as the former, συνηγωνίων refers to the condemnation. But even if only the acquittal was announced he might say, 'I sympathised greatly with Hortensius for the anxiety which the defence of his nephew must have cost him, and the marks of disapprobation with which Hortensius was received in the theatre.'

πολιτικώτερον, 'more on public topics.' [Rather 'more worthy of a man with an insight into politics,' which Cic.

jestingly says he must have got from reading the De Republica and De Legibus.]

gravissimus. This word seems here to mean 'very tire-some,' with a play on the ordinary meaning of the adjective. [Possibly with an allusion to his obesity; cf. Caec. (of P. Caesenius), *auctoritate non tam gravi quam corpore.* No doubt the man was a *quidnunc* also.]

habemus, 'the consuls will have been made': Lehmann, p. 89, defends *habemus,* the reading of M., by saying that the present is sometimes used for the future to indicate the certainty of the occurrence of a thing; so we might say, 'I am there,' in the sense of 'I will certainly go there.' So here, 'by the time you read this the consuls are made.' He compares Att. i. 20, 6, *simul atque hoc nostrum legerunt . . . retardantur,* which I do not think is at all parallel. In Att. v. 17, 1, *habebam,* which, according to epistolary usage, takes the place of *habeo,* assumes also the faculty of the present to stand for the future when certainty is to be expressed : *paucis diebus* habebam *certos homines=paucis diebus habiturus sum.* So in Att. v. 7, *proficiscebar=profecturus sum;* Att. v. 20, 5, *recipiebam=recepturus sum;* Att. vii. 23, 2, *remittebam=remissurus sum; faciebam=facturus sum,* next letter.

3. **Cui rei fugerat me rescribere.** 'I forgot to answer one thing in your letter—about the brickwork. I beg you, without any qualification (*plane*), to show your usual attentiveness to my affairs, and about the aqueduct to show the same, if anything can be done about it.' *Fugerat* is 'I forgot': cf. *fugit me ratio,* Catull. 10, 29. *Rei rescribere,* 'to answer a point in a letter,' would seem to be bad Latin if we had not Cicero as authority for it: it arose out of the other not quite accurate usage, 'I answered your letter,' instead of 'I answered you,' or 'I answered what you asked me in your letter,' *antemeridianis tuis litteris heri statim rescripsi, nunc respondeo vespertinis,* Att. xiii. 23, 1. [Is it not possible that *rescribere* may have its mercantile sense here? 'As to a matter in respect to which I forgot to make payment, I certainly beg you to see to it,' *i.e.* to provide the money.] The *aqua* seems to have been the *Aqua Crabra,* which perhaps he thought of bringing into Tusculanum (cf. Fam. xvi. 18, 3). Philippus was the contractor, as we learn from the end of the next letter. [Cf. *de aqua nostra Tusculana,* Balb. § 45. In Att. xv. 26, 4, I believe *Tusculano capite* should be read for *Tulliano.* The mention of Cascellius (compared with Balb. 45) shows that the

reference is to water. *Capite* could not be used of a sum of money without reference to interest.]

LETTER XXX. (ATT. V. 15)

1. **Ex hoc die,** 'Count the beginning of my year from that date.' Cicero finds that he has arrived within the borders of his province one day earlier than he had expected; and he wishes this to be carefully recorded, lest his hated government should be prolonged even by twenty-four hours. We might render 'put a nick in the post for the beginning of my year.' The literal meaning is 'move on the peg'; Att. had to start with Aug. 1 and move on the peg each day one hole in something like a cribbage board. *Commovere* is more usual in the sense of 'to take in hand,' 'put in motion'; but we have *movere* in the phrase *quieta non movere*, 'to leave well alone.' The same idea is expressed by the words παράπηγμα ἐνιαύσιον commoveto in the letter preceding this in the complete collection. The phrase is said to take its rise from an old custom whereby the Pontifex Maximus on the Ides of Sept. struck a nail into the wall of the temple of Juppiter Opt. Max. to keep count of the years. Cf. *mea si commovi sacra,* Plaut. Pseud. 110 ; *nummus commovetur,* 'put into circulation,' Cic. Font. 11. Laodicea was in Cicero's province, which included not only Cilicia, but Pamphylia, Pisidia, Isauria, the island of Cyprus, and three διοικήσεις, Cibyra, Apamea, and Synnada, which usually belonged to Asia, and were only under the governor of Cilicia for a short time. It was only between 56 and 50 that these assize-districts were added to Cilicia, and it is not known for what reason. After 49 they were again under the proconsul of Asia, Fam. xiii. 67.

habeat . . . cesset? 'You will ask, has that intellectual dash, which you know so well, no scope for its exercise, and has my mental energy ceased to be rich in produce ? Just so ! To think of *my* seat of justice being here, while Plotius has his in Rome !' Plotius was *praetor urbanus* this year. For this use of the subjunctive cf. *negent illi,* Att. ii. 12, 1, where the subj. is used as taking up indignantly another's words, and see note on Ep. ix. § 1, *videre noluerim :* cf. also Att. vi. 3, 2. Slightly different is *exercitum tu habeas,* Att. vii. 9, 4, where the subj. is merely exclamatory, like the accus. and infin. here, *ius L. me dicere !* For *quippe* cf. Att. xv. 21, 3, *nullas a te* xi. Kal. *Quippe* ('of course not'), *quid enim iam novi ?* So Mil. 47 and Att. vi. 3, 1.

noster amicus. On the whole it seems most probable that he refers to Caesar. Boot thinks he refers to C. Cassius, who had gone with Crassus to Syria, and after the defeat and deatl of Crassus had gained successes against the Parthians before the arrival of Bibulus. But there is no reason to suppose that Cassius was at all well provided with troops. On the con· trary, Fam. xv. 1, 5 would rather seem to show that he was weak.

exilium, ‘the nominal command of two skeleton legions.’ *Exiles* is opposed to *plenae*, the word applied to a legion or troop which is up to its full strength, *tres cohortes . . . plenissimae,* Fam. iii. 6, 5.

Denique, ‘And, to crown all, it is not an army, or anything I have been complaining of, that I want. It is the world, the forum, the city, my home, all of you.’ *Lucem* is ‘public life,’ ‘the world,’ ‘a conspicuous position.’ See Sen. 12, and Reid’s note there.

2. Ita vivam ut, ‘Upon my life I am living very extravagantly’: cf. Fam. vii. 23, 4, *ne vivam si tibi concedo,* ‘upon my life I won’t admit.’

permutavi. Att. had given him a draft on some bank in Asia, probably a draft on Laodicea or Ephesus. Cic. says he fears he will have to borrow money to pay it.

non refrico. ‘I avoid opening the wounds which Appius has inflicted on the province, but then they are palpable, and they can’t be concealed.’ Appius was his predecessor.

3. faciebam = *facturus sum:* cf. note on *habebam* in last letter, § 2.

Moeragenes, a robber chief, with whom a runaway slave belonging to Att. had taken refuge. He says he is going to try conclusions with Moeragenes in a pitched battle for the *fugitivus.*

clitellae, ‘panniers on an ox,’ a proverb quoted in the words *non nostrum, inquit, onus; bos clitellas* by Quintil. v. 11, 21. Ammianus Marcellinus, xvi. 5, 10, quotes the proverb as here, *vetus illud proverbium* clitellae . . . onus *Platonem crebro nominans exclamabat.* I have given the passage in the form in which it is cited by Ammianus. It forms a trochaic *septenarius.* It is usually printed as prose, the *sunt* being placed before *impositae.*

sim annuus. Cf. *ut simus annui,* Att. v. 13, 3 ; *ut annui* *essemus*, 17, 5. *Annuus* in these passages means 'lasting only for a year,' and this seems to be the meaning of the word in Plaut. Asin. v. 2, 36 (877), *non edepol conduci possum vita uxoris annua*, 'by the death of my wife within the year.' So in Att. vi. 3, 2, *sumptus annuus* means 'supplies *only* for a year'; and in Att. vi. 2, 7, *triduum quatriduumve* means 'for *only* three or four days.'

Adsis. This use of the subj. for imper. is common in the letters, *e.g.* Att. i. 17, 11, *cures;* Fam. ix. 26, 1, *vivas;* xiv. 4, 3, *confirmes . . . adiuves.*

epistolam. I have accepted here the admirable emendation of Gronovius, *epistolam sciebam* for *plura scribebam*. He points out that the customary abbreviation for *epistolam* was *eplā*, which would easily be misunderstood and corrupted into *plura*. The fact that *redditum iri* is certainly the ms. reading makes *sciebam* a necessary correction. The *sed* of the following clause is altogether in favour of the conjecture of Gron. : 'I know this letter will take a long time to reach you, *but* I know well the person to whom I am entrusting it, so you will ultimately receive it.' He adds : 'Now *you* will have plenty of people to carry your letters to me. You can give your letters to the farmers of the pasture tax and port dues, who will give them to the publicans' letter-carriers, who will deliver them to me.' [Especially as *plura* would be written *pl'a* in some mss.]

portus is the gen. sing., *portus* being used for *portoria* here : cf. Att. xi. 10, 1, *operas in portu et scriptura Asiae pro magistro dedit*, 'he was deputy collector of the pasture tax and port dues of Asia.'

LETTER XXXI. (FAM. VIII. 5)

1. animi, locative case. This is a construction mostly found in the comic drama and in epistolary style : see examples in Roby, § 1321. This usage of *pendere animi* occurs as late as Petron. 113 ; and Apuleius has *recreari animi* (Met. ii. 11), but he affects archaisms, especially those of the comic stage.

hoc more moderari. It is best to adhere to the mss. with Lehmann. The custom alluded to is that of regarding the most trifling military successes as being sufficient to entitle commanders to obtain triumphs and *supplicationes*. Becher (p. 19) reads *hoc more* REM *moderari possemus ;* but there is no necessity to add *rem:* cf. Att. vi. 3, 9, *moderabor ita ne quid eum offendam,* 'I shall manage so that I do not offend him' which shows that *moderari* can be used absolutely. Klotz and Baiter, after Bengel, read *hoc modo rem moderari.*

quantum gloriae triumphoque opus esset, 'as much as is required for a success and for a triumph.' For this sense of *gloria,* used as we might speak of an artist having a success with his picture at an exhibition, cf. Juv. vii. 81, *tenuique Saleio Gloria quantalibet quid erit si gloria tantum?* It would be more usual to write *ad gloriam* after *opus esset.* Boot (p. 17) omits *que* after *triumpho,* transposing it to *periculosam,* and takes *gloriae* as a. genitive. This certainly makes excellent sense.

illam, 'that dangerous and decisive engagement which you allude to,' or 'which we all fear'; some such reference must be understood: cf. note to De Petit. Cons. § 18, Corr. of Cic. Ep. xii.

ducit rationem, 'takes into account this point.'

2. **non video.** Strictly the negative goes with *futuram.* The idiom is common to most languages: cf. οὐ φημί, *nego.* The meaning is, 'I don't imagine any successor will be appointed.'

moretur. Ernesti and most edd. alter to *moremur.* But there is no real objection to the passive use of a deponent, especially in a writer like Caelius, who affects archaisms (Becher, pp. 7, 16); and it is only by degrees that the passive meaning entirely disappears from deponent verbs. Thus we find in Draeger's list (§ 91, 8) *abuti* in Varro, *dilargiri* in Gracchus, *morari* in Ennius, Naevius, and Pacuvius, used passively. In Plautus we have *adipisco, amplecto, contemplo, cuncto, frustro, intermino, potio. Sortita* is pass. in a legal document in Att. iv. 17, 3. This passive use of deponents is often found in the Digest; but legal language is of an archaic nature.

3. **incili,** 'stuck in the ditch.' This is the brilliant emendation of Manutius for *incilicia* of the mss. The word means a 'drain,' derived from *incidilis,* 'what is cut into.' We apply the term 'cutting' to rising ground cut through, not to level ground cut down into. According to Festus *incilia* are *fossae quae in viis fiunt ad deducendam aquam:* cf. Cato, R. R. 155, 1. *Incile est autem,* says Ulpian (Dig. xliii. 21, 1, 5), *locus depressus ad latus fluminis ex eo dictus quod incidatur: inciditur enim vel lapis vel terra unde primum aqua ex flumine agi possit.* The word 'cut' is used exactly in Ulpian's sense. This emendation, which is accepted by all the editors, has

quite superseded Turnebus's proposal, *cilicio*, which was used, he supposes by Caelius, because through such a cloth liquors were sometimes strained.

Hoc si praeterito anno. In a learned note Lehmann (pp. 38, 39) defends this, the reading of the mss. He shows that as violent *hyperbata* as that of *si* here may be found even in Cicero, *e.g.* Att. iv. 17, 4, *quo ego haec die scripsi;* Att. i. 14, 1, *ut huic vix tantulae epistolae tempus habuerim.* The present passage means 'when this year has passed, if Curio, as tribune, and the same old business about the provinces come on the stage, you cannot fail to see,' etc. This I take to be the metaphor rather than that of entering on a magistracy: cf. Att. i. 18, 2, *introitus fuit in causam fabulae Clodianae.* Wesenberg reads *hoc* SIC *praeterito anno Curio tribunus* ERIT *et eadem actio de provinciis introibit: quam,* etc., on grounds which might perhaps be valid if the letter had been written by Cicero. Note *praeterire* used passively. It almost always, when used in the passive, is applied to a candidate's defeat at elections.

in sua causa. I have added *in*, which might easily have fallen out after *qui*. The sense is, 'when their own interest is at stake they care no whit for the state.' Now *sua causa* can only mean 'for their sake,' a sense foreign to the passage. For this usage of *in* cf. Att. v. 12, *fin., quod in tua re faceres.*

hoc, sc. *omnia impedire,* the possibility of obstruction.

sperent. This emendation of Orelli's is adopted by most editors. The mss. *superet* is explained by Ernesti as an artificial expression for 'is easy for.' He reads *Caesari, qui . . . curet.* Kahnt's certain conjecture, *Caesar iique qui,* has been adopted in the text.

LETTER XXXII. (ATT. v. 20)

1. Saturnalibus. The *Saturnalia* were at this time cele-brated Dec. 17-19: the first day of the *Saturnalia* is here indicated ; the siege therefore began on October 21. It must be remembered that before the Roman Calendar was reformed by Caesar in 45 the number of days in the month were : in March, May, July, October, 31 ; in Feb. 28 ; in all the rest 29. Remembering this, and allowing for inclusive reckoning, we find that the 57th day before Dec. 17 is Oct. 21.

Qui, malum ! 'Who the mischief!' a phrase redolent of the comic stage.

Quid faciam ? 'What am I to do ? (is it my fault that yo 1 never heard of Pindenissus before ?) Could I have transformed Cilicia into an Aetolia or Macedonia ?' (Could I have mad ? Cilicia as familiar to you as Aetolia and Macedonia ?) Cf. *omne ? Catilinas Acidinos postea reddidit*, Att. iv. 3, 3, ' He made ever' Catiline seem henceforth an Acidinus,' that is, ' as respectable as Acidinus,' see Leg. Agr. ii. 64.

hoc exercitu, 'with such an army': abl. of attendan : circumstances like *hac infirmitate*, Att. v. 18, 1. *Hic=in ho loco*, 'in such a place as this.' Such ablatives are *modal*, not absolute, with ellipse of the deficient participle of *esse*. Good exx. are *hac iuventute=cum talis sit iuventus*, Att. x. 11, 3 *praesertim hoc genero=cum talis sit gener meus*, Att. xi. 14, 2 ; *tirone et collecticio exercitu*, 'with an army of raw recruits,' Fam. vii. 3, 2 ; *cuius dubia fortuna*, 'considering the insecurity of his position,' Fam. xiii. 19, 2 ; *omni statu omnique populo*, 'whatever may be my position or the popular feeling,' Att. xi. 24, 1.

ἐν ἐπιτομῇ, '*tout court*.'

† que erant † No satisfactory emendation of these words has been proposed.

revellimus, 'took the sting out of': the metaphor is from plucking out a thorn. He means that his unexpected affability made them forget their wrongs. The *quadriennium* refers to the rule of Appius and his predecessor.

3. in aquarum divortio, 'by its watershed'; lit. 'at the point where its streams run different ways': see Fam. ii. 10, 2, where he says that Mount Amanus belongs partly to the province of Bibulus and partly to his own, *divisus aquarum divortiis*, where perhaps we should read *divisus in aquarum divortiis*, or *divisis aquarum divortiis*.

Scis . . . πολέμου, 'You know there are such words as *panic* and *war's uncertainties*.' If this reading is right, and is to be punctuated as in the text, the only meaning is that Cicero accounts for his leaving Amanus by the fear that his men might take alarm, or that the tide of his success might turn. But it seems unnatural that he should assign such a reason, or indeed any reason, for leaving Mount Amanus, where he had no further business. Sch. would transpose the words to follow *cum graves de Parthis nuntii venirent* above,

§ 2. It would be a less bold step to transpose them to stand after the almost immediately subsequent words, *animus accessit . . . iniectus est.* Some edd., supposing some such word as *Interim* to have fallen out after *discessimus*, would read *Interim —scis enim . . . πολέμου—rumore*, etc. Then the words *Scis . . . πολέμου* account for the confidence of Cassius and the discouragement of the Parthians. κοινά would seem a more natural word than κενά. The allusion would be to Homer's (Il. xviii. 309) ξυνὸς Ἐνυάλιος, καί τε κτανέοντα κατέκτα. [The fault seems to me to lie in the *enim;* but for that the words might well be taken with what comes after. *Enim* may be an error for *autem.* The two words are very frequently confused. Cf. Att. viii. 3, 6, Boot, and the reference to Wunder. κενά carries on the idea of πανικά better. If a Roman defeat had followed, κοινά would be more in place.]

4. **appell. hac inani**, the title of *Imperator.*

loreolam in must. The *mustaceum* was the Roman wedding-cake. It was made on bay leaves. Hence 'to look for a bay leaf in a wedding-cake' is to look for a thing where it is very easily found. When Appius had plucked his laurel from the Amanus it would be very little credit to him. But we find that he failed to pluck it.

nobilem sui generis. This is always understood to mean, as Boot explains it, *non illustri loco natum sed qui sua virtute inclaruit.* But is *nobilem sui generis* possible Latin for 'not of noble birth, but ennobled by his own qualities'? The words might mean 'noble in his own class' of centurions, that is, 'a noble fellow,' one of nature's noblemen, though of course not noble in the technical sense, or 'a man of distinction in his own rank of life.' But why should Cicero state this fact here amid his sneers at Bibulus? On the other hand, there is no reason why an ancestor of Asinius Dento should not have held a curule office—no reason, therefore, why Asinius should not be *nobilis.* The position of a *centurio primi pili* was a distinguished one. Is it not quite possible that Cicero here falls a victim to his besetting sin of punning on names? *Asinium* lends itself to an obvious play on the word *asinus.* 'He lost,' says Cicero, 'a noble *of his own kidney*, like himself if you can judge by his name, in *Asinius* Dento.' It will be remembered that Cicero applies the word *asinum* to himself in Att. iv. 5, 3. My rendering involves the more normal use of *sui*, though of course *sui* might refer to Dento. It is hardly too much to say that Cicero cannot resist a pun on a name. [May not the words mean 'famous in his own rank,' *i.e.* among the class of men who follow the military career ? For the gen. after *nobilis* cf. Sull. 29, *omnes boni omnium generum*; and for *sui* N. D. i. 77, *sui generis belua.*]

plagam odiosam, 'a galling, mortifying reverse.'

5. Nos ad Pindenissum. Some such words as *adduximus exercitum* must be understood; they are supplied in Fam. xv. 4, 10.

omnium memoria. The phrase found in Cicero is either *omni mem.* or *hominum mem.* But there seems no reason against *omnium mem.* found in Sull. 82. The whole sentence is a careless one, 'the town in Eleutherocilicia best fortified for war of which history bears record in these parts': cf. *iisdem in armis fui*, Lig. 9; *est tua toga omnium armis felicior*, Fam. xii. 13, 1; Fam. xv. 4, 10. [There is a difference between *omni mem.* and *omnium mem.*; the former is 'within memory however far back'; the latter 'within memory of all the people there.']

incolumi exercitu, 'without any disaster, though many were wounded.' It is bad criticism to insert *non* here: cf. Fam. xv. 4, 10.

Hilara . . . concessimus, 'We had a pleasant Saturnalia, which the troops enjoyed as well, for I gave them all the booty except the prisoners.'

Sat. tertiis. The third day of the Sat., Dec. 19.

res, 'the sum realised,' viz. by the sale of the captives. [The stop, I think, should be placed at *tribunali*, not at *scribebam*. The slaves were sold at the tribunal. Plut. describes Sulla as selling his booty ἐπὶ βήματος καθεζόμενος (c. 33).]

dabam, 'I am making over the army to Q. to take into winter quarters in the more disturbed part of the province, while I am returning myself to Laodicea.' As in English, so in Lat., the present (which is here represented by the epistolary imperfect) has sometimes, as here, the force of a future: see on Att. v. 12, 2, Ep. xxix.

6. Ligurino μώμῳ, 'my Ligurian *moqueur.*' It is most probable that he thus describes P. Aelius Ligur, who took a bitter part against him at the time of his exile, and of whom he often speaks very severely, *e.g. Ligur iste additamentum inimicorum meorum*, Sest. 68; *ille novitius Ligur*, Pro Dom. 47; *quisquilias seditionis Clodianae*, Sest. 74. This Ligur had no doubt essayed sarcasm without much skill, hence Cicero, with a play on his name, calls him *Ligurinus :* he describes the Ligures as *montani duri atque agrestes*, De Leg. Agr. ii. 95. He alludes slightingly to them in a similar passage, Cluent. 72.   Momus was not the god of laughter and fun, as with us, but presided over carping criticism and taunts (see Hes. Th. 214 ; Plat. Rep. 487).   So Cicero means, 'I will not leave room for objection even from the most carping critic.'   Hortensius has been supposed to be here alluded to, but without reason. There is, however, much to dispose one to believe the reference to be to Cato.   We should then suppose that this Ligur called Cato Μῶμος, 'the god of carping criticism,' and that Cato is here referred to as 'Ligur's Momus.'   It is to Cato that Cicero constantly refers as the universal moral referee, *e.g.* Att. vi. 1, 7, 13 ; vi. 2, 8, etc.

moriar, si . . . elegantius, 'as I live the punctiliousness of my rectitude could not be surpassed.'   We have had *ita vivam ut . . . facio*, Att. v. 15, 2, Ep. xxx.; *ne vivam si concedo*, Fam. vii. 23, 4, Ep. xvi.

continentiam. *Continentia*, ἐγκράτεια, implies a conquest achieved over a desire, and is therefore οὐκ ἄνευ λύπης ; but Cicero feels the greatest pleasure in his 'self-restraint,' so he finds the word inapplicable.   Aristotle (Nic. Eth. ii. 3, 1) makes this very pleasure in the act the test of the existence of the moral quality.   *Abstinentia* would not necessarily imply a desire overcome.   The opp. to *continentia* is *libido*.   The word he prefers to apply to his own case instead of *continentia* is *integritas*, which of course implies no struggle with a counter-desire.   *Elegantia* and *integritas* are coupled together in Att. vi. 2, 8.

Fuit tanti, 'For this feeling of satisfaction it was worth while' (to undergo the tedium of provincial life).

noram . . . sciebam.   A good example of the different use of these two verbs.

πεφυσίωμαι, '*entêté* with myself.'   πεφῦσίωμαι is fr. φῦσιοῦσθαι, 'to be puffed up.'   The word is found in 1 Cor. iv. 6.

haec λαμπρά, 'this is a score for me,' or 'meantime I have made a *coup* in this.'   Greek terms may often (but by no means always) be rendered by analogous French expressions or by slang phrases.   [*Haec* λαμπρὰ refers to what comes after.   'These are my successes.']

Ἐν παρόδῳ, 'In my progress through my province.'   So

again in Att. v. 21, 2, I believe that ἐν παρόδῳ should stand fɔr *transitam*, which arose from *in transitu*, a gloss on ἐν παρόδῳ.

quod . . . praebui, 'by refusing to receive not only their bribes but their visits.'

pīlum, 'the value of a hair': cf. *ne pilo quidem minus ꞃ.ιe amabo,* Q. Fr. ii. 15 (16), 5 ; *ne ullum pilum viri boni habeꞏe dicatur,* Rosc. Com. 20. Supply some such word as *abstuli* or *sustuli.*

ablectum . . . excitavi. Cicero 'encouraged' Brutu ꞓ, who was 'cast down' at the prospect of losing the money l e had lent to Ariobarzanes.

quam tu, sc. *amas ;* **quam te,** sc. *amo,* 'whom I love ɩ s much as you do, I had almost said, as much as I do you.'

7. Nunc . . . parabam. For the conjunction of the epistolary imperfect with an adverb denoting *present* time, cꞏ. *cogitabat . . . nunc,* Att. v. 16, 4 ; *erat . . . etiam nunc,* Attꞏ. xvi. 3, 6 ; *nunc Romae erat,* Q. Fr. iii. 1, 4.

Uberiores erunt, 'richer in detail.'

est totum, 'the result of the first of March is everything.' On that day the new consuls were to bring before the senat⟩ the subject of the provinces. If Caesar refused to give up hiꞩ province, Cicero feared that the senate would not let Pompeiu⟩ leave Rome. Cicero hoped that Pompeius would be sent out tɔ finish the Parthian war when his own year of office shoulɖ expire.

8. a.d. xv. Kal. Ian. denique, 'only on the 17th of Dec.' *Denique* goes with the date as with adverbs of time, *nunc, tun. denique.*

Nam, 'Unsafe, *for* I did not receive the letters sent by thɩ same route by the hands of Laenius's messengers.'

decrevit. To consider the question of sending a successoɩ to Caesar.

salvi sumus, 'my case is won,' that is, 'I shall be safe from a prorogation of my term of provincial government.' For thiꞇ use of the present to indicate the certain future see on *habemus consules,* Att. v. 12, 2, Ep. xxix.

Incendio, metaphorically used ; Plaetorius was condemned for extortion ; Seius, who shared the plunder, was tried on the charge *quo ea pecunia pervenerit,* and was compelled to pay part of the fine. [Does not *ambustus* generally imply that a man has escaped on trial 'by the skin of his teeth'?]

Q. Cassio, brother of C. Cassius, and a friend of Atticus.

9. non modo negotii. See Planc. 66, where this sentiment is quoted from the Origines of Cato.

in officio est, 'N. is working well for me.'

meus Alexis, 'Tiro, who is my Alexis,' who stands to me as A. to you: cf. *Alixen imaginem Tironis*, Att. xii. 10; cf. also Att. iv. 8*a*, 1, where a topographical relation is strangely expressed. Cicero asks why does not Alexis write to him as Tiro does to Atticus.

Phemio. A musical slave of Atticus, named from Hom. Od. i. 154. That Atticus was in the habit of purchasing musical slaves is clear from Att. iv. 16, 7 (13). κέρας is a horn for blowing.

LETTER XXXIII. (FAM. VII. 32)

Volumnius was a wealthy Roman knight, best known by his agnomen Eutrapelus, and as patron and lover of his freedwoman, the actress Cytheris. Cicero in Ep. liv. gives an account of a dinner-party where he met Volumnius and Cytheris. Volumnius was influential with Antonius, whose *praefectus fabrum* he was (Nep. Att. 12). Accordingly we find Cicero sometimes on friendly terms with him, as here, and asking his good offices (Att. xv. 8, 1), sometimes speaking of him with contempt (Phil. xiii. 3). Volumnius was saved by Atticus when the partisans of Antonius were in danger (Nep. *l.c.*), and in turn was able to do the like service for Atticus (*ibid.* 10).

1. sine praenomine familiariter. There being no postal arrangements whatever in the time of Cicero, it was necessary either to employ private messengers, or to avail oneself of the services of the *tabellarii* of the *publicani*, who were constantly travelling between Rome and the provinces.

The outside address was brief. In Att. viii. 5, 2, Cicero speaks of a packet with the superscription *M'. Curio*, and in a fresco at Pompeii there is a letter directed *M. Lucretio*.

The letter began with simple greeting, *M. Cicero s. d. (salutem dicit) M. Caelio*, or *s. p. d.* = *salutem plurimam dicit*, and it seems that in a very frequent or familiar correspondence even

this form was dispensed with. *Cicero Attico Sal.*, as a heading
to each letter to Atticus, is probably not genuine, for Cicero
never uses the name *Attice* in the body of a letter until we
come to the year B.C. 50 (Att. vi. 1, 20). *Mi Pomponi* is the
nearly invariable form of address, even after the year B.C.
65, before which he must have received his surname Atticus ;
therefore it is not probable that this surname was used all along
by Cicero in the headings of his letters and nowhere else.

It has been observed that Cicero very rarely introduces the
names of his correspondents into his letters.   In the whole
of the sixteen books to Atticus, containing 397 letters, he apostrophises his friend by name only twenty-two times.   Such
apostrophes are very much more frequent in the Brutine correspondence ; there are twenty-three in the first book of eighteen
letters.   This is one of the arguments against the authenticity
of the Brutine correspondence.

Cicero occasionally calls Atticus *mi Attice* (vi. 1, 20 ; xiv.
12, 1) ; sometimes, but very rarely, *mi Tite* (ix. 6, 5) and *mi
T. Pomponi* (iv. 2, 5).   In dedicating the De Senectute to him
he writes O TITE ; but in this passage he is quoting from
Ennius.   Cicero addresses Trebatius as *mi Trebati, mi Testa,
Testa mi*, and in one place as *mi vetule* (Fam. vii. 16, 1).   He
calls him *C. Trebati* in Top. i. 1, as he is dedicating his work
to Trebatius ; but to address his friend thus in a letter would
be stiff and formal.   The omission of the *praenomen* was a mark
of close intimacy in the time of Cicero, as is distinctly proved in
this letter by the words *quod sine praenomine familiariter, ut
debebas, ad me epistolam misisti, primum addubitavi num te
Volumnio senatore esset, quocum mihi est magnus usus.*   Compare also Fam. xvi. 18, 1, where Cicero addresses a letter to
Tiro with the greeting *Tullius Tironi Sal.*, and Tiro seems to
have taken exception to the form as unsuited to their respective
positions.   Words which indicated close familiarity were scarcely
suitable between Cicero and a manumitted slave.   Cicero in
reply suggests even a more familiar form of address—*Quid
etiam ?   non sic oportet ?   equidem censeo sic : addendum etiam
Suo ?*   But he adds, *sed si placet invidia vitetur.*   The omission
of the *praenomen* would have provoked unfavourable comment.
This is probably the real interpretation of Hor. Sat. ii. 5, 32
Quinte, puta, aut Publi, gaudent praenomine molles Auriculae.
Punctilious Romans wished to be addressed with distant and
formal respect.   The places which Orelli cites in support of his
view, which is the contradictory of mine (as he holds, without
evidence, that the use of the *praenomen* was a mark of intimacy),
are not relevant.   The passage from the De Pet. Cons. has no

reference to the *praenomen* as distinguished from the *nomen* or *cognomen ;* and that quoted from Fam. i. 9, 19 is utterly irrelevant, for Cicero does not even hint that it was by calling Clodius Publius that the senators sought to flatter him ; the point of the passage is wholly and solely that Clodius and Vatinius both had the praenomen Publius. Again, it seems to be very far-fetched to explain the Horatian passage by supposing that the poet is thinking especially of the freedman Dama, who would be proud of the *praenomen* which he received on his manumission. The context appears hardly to warrant this supposition. Now my explanation is very simple, and is quite in keeping with the passages in Cicero. [It seems probable that the address *by one name only* was the familiar style. In choosing one of these for the outside of a letter it was, of course, necessary to choose the *nomen*.]

εὐτραπελία, 'graceful raillery.' Aristotle, Rhet. ii. 12, 16, defines it as πεπαιδευμένη ὕβρις, *esprit railleur et malin.* St. Paul warns the Ephesians against it (v. 14), where the E. V. translates the word 'jesting.'

salinarum, 'my Attic salt mines,' jestingly for ' my stores of *sales*, Attic salt, witticisms, *bons mots.*'

Sestiana. P. Sestius, whom Cicero defended, though a man of eminent respectability and varied virtues (Sest. 6), did not possess much grace of style or liveliness of wit. The severe cold which Catullus caught from the speech read by Sestius at a dinner-party, in consequence of which Catullus had to go to the country for change of air, forms a melancholy page of history (Catull. 44). Pompeius on another occasion (Att. vii. 17, 2) had to address a public letter to L. Caesar, and got Sestius to write it—a proceeding on which Cicero is very severe, for whereas Pompeius had an admirable style, Sestius on this occasion out-Sestiused himself (*nihil unquam legi scriptum* σηστιωδέστερον).

2. **faex**, 'scum.'

ἀκύθηρον, lit. 'without charm' (like ἀναφρόδιτος), *fade, banale.*

venustum, 'charming.'

pugna . . . **mea non esse**, 'insist, an you love me, unless a smart *double entendre*, a tasteful hyperbole, a good pun, a jocular παρὰ προσδοκίαν, unless everything else is *secundum artem*, and pointed according to the rules discussed by me in the second book De Oratore, under the character of Antonius

Q

on the subject of jokes, maintain, even unto the laying of money thereon, that they are not mine.' παράγραμμα, usually called *paronomasia*, is exemplified in Ter. Andr. i. 3, 13, *inceptio est amentium haud amantium.* The section on jokes in De Orato 'e ii. is really handled by Caesar (C. Julius Caesar Strabo Vopiscus). It is a mere μνημονικὸν ἁμάρτημα on Cicero's part to ascribe t to Antonius.

ut sacramento contendas. The translation given above perhaps goes near hitting the spirit of the passage, lit. 'insist so that you are willing to go to law.' The *actio sacramenti* was the most ancient of the actions at law. After some formalities, each party 'challenged his adversary to deposit a certain sum, which the loser of the cause was to forfeit to the Treasury of the people, to be applied to the expenses of the sacrifices' (Sandars's Justinian, p. lxiv.) This stake was called *sacra mentum.* [Still in use in Cic.'s time in the centumviral court. An owner of an estate might proceed as owner *dominus*, or as *possessor ;* in the former case he would go to the centumvirs, in the latter to the practor, for an interdict. Cic. alludes here to both courses.]

Trahantur per me pedibus omnes rei. Cf. Att. iv. 18, 2, 'for all I care litigants may go to perdition' (as they will do in consequence of the dreadful decadence of legal oratory you tell me of). 'I care not a jot about that. It is in brilliancy in conversation that I am really interested to maintain our supremacy. Do get an interdict. You are the only rival I fear ; the rest I despise. Think you I am laughing at you ? Well *now* I fancy you are not far wrong.' The whole passage applies 'graceful raillery' to the 'graceful railler,' for what he seems to think the be-all and the end-all for which a man should strive is—to be *urbanus.* For *urbanitas*, a witty and cultivated style of conversation, see Quintilian, vi. 3, 102-112. The definition of the *urbanus* given there is (§ 105) *cuius multa benedicta responsaque erunt, et qui in sermonibus circulis conviviis, item in concionibus, omni denique loco ridicule commodeque dicet.*

amabo, 'I pry'thee,' a word belonging to the language of conversation.

interdictis, an order of the practor having reference to a special case, though there was always an under-idea of public interest in the grant, of protecting the public peace, or the like. Interdicts were chiefly used in cases of possession or quasi-possession, and mostly were prohibitory (Justinian, Instit. iv. 15).

3. Illa. There must be some word or words lost here possibly referring to indiscreet actions or expressions on Curio's part; or the lost word may apply to the position in the epistle of the expression in question, e.g. *illa extrema*, or the like.

ei cupio. Cf. Plancus in Fam. x. 4, 4. [A variation on *eius causa cupio.*]

non videor nimium laborare, 'I do not think I am too anxious.'

LETTER XXXIV. (FAM. IX. 25)

1. Cineae. Both Pyrrhus and his minister Cineas wrote treatises on military service (Aelian Tact. 1).

hoc amplius, 'more than this, I am thinking of having some ships.'

ullam armaturam. This is a joke. Running away by sea is the best means of fighting the Parthian horsemen.

Παιδείαν Κύρου. Of the Cyropaedia Cicero says, Q. Fr. i. 1, 23, *Cyrus ille a Xenophonte non ad historiae fidem scriptus sed ad effigiem iusti imperii.* This ideal government Cicero, who had read and re-read it, has now exemplified in practice (*explicavi*). For *explicare* in this sense cf. De Orat. iii. 103, *nam ipsa ad ornandum praecepta quae dantur ciusmodi sunt ut ea quamvis vitiosissimus orator explicare possit.*

contriveram, 'had well thumbed.'

2. ades ad imperandum, 'attend to orders': cf. Sall. Jug. 62, 8, *cum ipse ad imperandum Tisidium vocaretur,* 'attend to orders,' *i.e.* to your commander giving you orders—an old military expression. It is best not to take *imperandum* passively: see Kritz on Sall. *l.c.*, and Roby, ii. pref. lxiii.-lxvii.

3. percussus est, 'he got a severe blow by a shocking letter.'

proscriptum esse, 'was advertised for sale': cf. Off. iii. 66.

eo progressum esse, 'has taken this hasty step.'

Auctoritate . . . gratia, 'We want you to command, to advise, to even ask it as a favour.'

iudiciis turpibus conflictari, 'to be brought to ruin by a disgraceful lawsuit'; disgraceful, as between brothers.

Pollionem, probably Asinius Pollio.

tam perscribere. *Tam . . . quam* are correlative: literally the words mean, 'I cannot write with an emphasis as strong as will be my obligation.'

LETTER XXXV. (ATT. VI. 1, 17-26)

17. **ὦ πραγμάτων,** 'O what a tangle of topics!'

nihil habuit aliud. I have given this passage as it stands in M., only transposing CENS. and Cos. The words *per te* can hardly be right, as it does not seem probable that Atticus would have set up a statue of a person in no way connected with him. It is possible, as Boot urges, that Atticus, who took on him the arranging of the statues in Pompey's theatre, might have erected a statue of Scipio Nasica on the Capitol; but it is far more likely that this should have been the work of a descendant of Scipio. I have therefore accepted the conjecture of Jordan (Eph. Epigr. iii. 65), who proposes to read here *ad Opis Opiferae* (sc. *aedem*) at the temple of *Ops Opifera*. The more important point involved in the transposition of CENS. and Cos. must be defended at some length.

We have it on the authority of Macrobius, Saturn. 2, 4, that in the De Rep. Cicero makes Laelius regret that there was no public statue of Scipio Nasica Serapion, the slayer of Tib. Gracchus. Now Q. Caecilius Metellus Scipio, the great-grandson of Serapion, had placed in the Capitol, near the Temple of Ops, a statue of his great-grandfather, as he supposed; and accordingly he drew Atticus's attention to what he regarded as an error made by Cicero. But, argues Cicero, it was Metellus Scipio himself who made the mistake, for the statue which he had placed in the Capitol, supposing it to be a statue of his great-grandfather Serapion, was really a statue of another person, which he might have known, had he remembered that Serapion had never been a Censor.

So far all is plain; but it is evident that for the argument it is essential that Cicero should go on to prove that the statue erroneously supposed by Scipio Metellus to be the statue of his ancestor was really the statue of a man who *had been* a Censor. Now, according to M., which gives CENS. first and Cos. after, Cicero does indeed go on to state that the statue placed in the Capitol by Scipio Metellus was the statue of one who had been a Censor, for it bore the inscription CENS.; but why does he say this statue had *no other inscription but* CENS., and why does he introduce at all the mention of the other statue near the Hercules of Polycles? The solution of the difficulty is, in my mind, this—CENS. *and* Cos. *should change places.* This transposition I have accordingly made in the text. The copyist of M. saw that the argument required that the statue supposed by Scipio Metellus to be that of his ancestor should be shown to be that of one who had been a Censor, and so was in a hurry to introduce CENS., not much troubling himself about the logical analysis of the whole sentence. Copyists do not, as a rule, go beyond the first step in any process of thought. Now if Cos. be put in the first place, and CENS. after, the whole argument may be thus paraphrased : 'Is it possible that Scipio Metellus is not aware that his great-grandfather was never Censor? It is true, indeed, that the statue placed by him near the temple of Ops, and supposed by him to be the statue of his ancestor, had no inscription on it but Cos., showing that it was the statue of a person who had been Consul. [This indeed would not have shown the statue not to have been the statue of Scrapion, who was Consul.] *But* another statue standing near the Hercules of Polycles had the inscription CENS.; and it can be proved that it commemorates the same person as the statue placed by Metellus near the temple of Ops. That the two statues are statues of the same man is proved by the *pose,* the dress, the ring, in fine, the whole work.'

Both are statues of the same man ; therefore, as the statue near Polycles's Hercules had the inscription CENS., the man commemorated by the two statues must have been a Censor ; but Scipio Nasica Serapion had never been a Censor ; therefore Scipio Metellus has made a mistake about his own great-grandfather, and the remark put by Cicero into the mouth of Laelius has not been shown to be incorrect.

Both are, in Cicero's opinion, statues of Scipio Africanus Minor, who was not only consul, *but censor* with Mummius in 142 (see Att. xvi. 13c, 2, *videor mihi audisse P. Africano L. Mummio censoribus*).

Cicero then goes on to say that when he saw the statue of Africanus with the name of Scrapion written under it, he thought it was a mistake on the part of the sculptor, but he now sees it was Metellus Scipio who made the error.

Orelli was not aware that X and Y are figments of Bosius. He is not therefore conscious that in introducing the readings of X and Y—Cos. in both places, and *item* for *autem*—he has foisted on Cicero the (in this case, stupid) conjecture of the generally clever but never very scrupulous Frenchman.

Boot, in his first edition, read CENS. in both places, and gave *item* for *autem*. This is—(1) a greater change than that which I propose ; (2) it renders otiose the statement that the first-mentioned statue had inscribed on it *nothing else but* CENS.; (3) the establishing of the identity of the person commemorated by the two statues, a point much dwelt on by Cicero, is in this case superfluous ; for if the statue placed in the Capitol by Metellus Scipio had the inscription CENS., the proof was already complete that it could not be a statue of Serapion, who never was Censor. Boot now (ed. 2) reads Cos. in both places. But if we read Cos. in both places, it is evident that the whole logical *nexus* of the passage disappears. [Are not three statues mentioned ?—(*a*) one *Ad Opis* with an old inscription, of which only CENS. was legible; (*b*) one *Ad* Πολυκλ. *Herculem*, which was undoubtedly a statue of Africanus, and is mentioned in order to identify the person for whom (*a*) was intended ; this statue probably had a long inscription on it, and Cic. only mentions Cos. because it was set up when Africanus was consul ; then (*c*) an equestrian statue, copied from (*a*), but with a fresh inscription setting forth that it was Serapio. The *turma equestrium statuarum* must have been copies and adaptations. The practice of setting up new statues to heroes of bygone times, and especially equestrian statues, is often mentioned.

It is curious that the *anulus* should be used as a mark of identification. I suppose it was not the common gold ring, but a signet ring. For *turma equestrium statuarum* cf. the interesting passage in Velleius, i. c. 11 ; and the jest of the elder Scipio in De Orat. ii. § 262. The phrase *statuae equestres inauratae* occurs elsewhere in Cic.

This supposition makes *per te* easier.]

in Serapionis subscriptione, 'with the name of Serapion under it.'

18. illud de Flavio. In § 8 of this letter Cicero refers to a mistaken criticism of Att., who supposed that Cicero in his De Rep. implies that Cn. Flavius, who first published the *fasti*, lived before the decemvirs.

belle ἠπόρησας, 'that was a nice point you raised against me.'

τὸν τῆς ἀρχαίας, sc. κωμῳδίας.

iacet, 'is Theophrastus therefore put out of court?' *Iacet* is a forensic term, as in *iacent suis testibus*, Mil. 47.

19. HS XXDC. We gather from various covert allusions

to this transaction in Att. vi. — 4, 3 ; 5, 2 ; 7, 1 — that Philotimus, the steward of Terentia, had dealt in a questionable way with a sum of money arising out of the sale of the goods of Milo.

20. mi Attice. This is the first time that Cicero addresses his friend as *Attice ;* therefore the heading *Cicero Attico Sal.*, usually prefixed to the letters to Atticus throughout, is certainly not genuine.

τί λοιπόν ; 'what have I still to tell you?' This phrase would imply that what followed was not very important ; yet Atticus beseeches him to look after his staff, and watch what goes on.   Hence Cicero asks, 'Have you heard a whisper about any of them?' adding, 'Yet it cannot be so ; *pas de tout ;* it could not have escaped my notice, and will not. But your earnest admonition perplexed me somewhat.' For *quid de quo* compare *quid ne quo*, my conjecture, in Att. iv. 17, 1, Corr. of Cic. cxlix. *Inaudire* is properly to 'overhear,' and so often indicates eavesdropping : see on Plaut. Mil. Glor. ii. 2, 57 (212). *Etsi* is often used like ἀλλὰ γάρ, and refers to a sentence understood.

21. De M. Octavio. See Att. v. 21, 5. Caelius had requested Cic. to try to get some panthers for him from Cibyra for the purposes of the aedilic show to which Caelius was about to treat the populace of Rome. Octavius, his colleague, had asked Atticus whether he thought Cic. could procure some panthers for him too. Att. had answered that he thought not, and Cic. thanks him (Att. v. 21, 5) for giving this reply. Caelius seems to have been somewhat offended because Cic. did not like to order a general panther hunt in his province, so that Caelius might put himself in the running for the consulship, on gaining which he would again look to the provinces to reimburse himself for the expenses of his candidature. Cic. (Fam. ii. 11, 2) writes to Caelius : 'I am doing my best through the public *shikarees*, but tigers are very scarce. Indeed,' he adds jestingly, 'those that are to the fore think it very hard that they should be the only creatures oppressed under my rule, and have resolved to leave my province and emigrate to Caria.'

et a civitatibus. The reading in the text may possibly be right, though the correction of *a* to *de* before *civitatibus* would make the passage easier. But it would be hard to account for the corruption. If *a civitatibus* is what Cicero wrote, the meaning is, 'I received a carefully written letter from Caelius, asking to be supplied with panthers for his show, and enclosing copies of letters from the different *civitates* in Cilicia offering contributions.' The first *alterum* refers to the *latter* point (as often : see Fam. vii. 26, 1 ; i. 7, 1), with which Cicero deals, by expressing his regret that the fame of the purity of his administration had not found its way to Rome ; warning Caelius that he could not allow, nor Caelius accept, any subscription of money from the province ; and impressing on Caelius the greater necessity for circumspection in his case, as he (Caelius) had signalised himself by the severity with which he had prosecuted provincial malfeasance. Then he turns to the first point, and says it would not be respectable to have a public panther-hunt in his province. Boot has clearly shown that the reference cannot be to Fam. viii. 9, as Man. supposed. The offer made by the province to Caelius was a money vote for his games, such as we read of in Q. Fr. i. 1, 26. [? *Ad civitates; ad* and *a* are often confused. The abl. would follow the change to *a*. Caelius sends Cicero a letter about the panthers, and encloses letters for him to send on to the *civitates*.]

22. Lepta. Cicero's *praefectus fabrum :* see Att. v. 17, 2.

iam pridem. I agree with Boot, who brackets these words. Cicero distinctly says above, Att. v. 19, 2, that he had never seen her : he now writes, 'Your daughter's politeness in sending her love to me was the greater because she was sending it to one whom she had never seen.'

Litt. datarum dies, 'The date of your letter pleasantly reminded me of the celebrated oath I took' (for which see Fam. v. 2, 7). *Pridie Kal. Ianuar.* is in apposition with *dies ;* it would have been more normal if he had written *qui fuit*, as in Att. iv. 1, 5, *postridie in senatu qui fuit dies Nonarum Septembrium.* We have a parallel to the construction used in this passage in Fam. xvi. 3, 1, *is dies fuit Nonae.* The Latin reads, however, as if something more than a mere date was referred to ; perhaps Att. had used some half-humorous historical era, as Cic. did when he dated his letter (Att. v. 13) 'on the 560th day after the battle of Bovillae,' that being the name which he gives to the fray in which Clodius lost his life.

Magnus praetextatus. 'A Pompeius in a *toga praetexta*.' Pompeius would be *Magnus paludatus.* My friend and colleague, Rev. T. T. Gray, acutely suggests that in the well-known passage *stat magni nominis umbra* we should write *Magni.* Pompeius is called *Magnus* in the letters, very frequently, and elsewhere, *e.g.* in Catull. lv. 6, *in Magni simul ambulatione ;* Mart. xi. 5, 11, *cum Caesare Magnus amabit ;* so all through Lucan.

23. ἀναντιφώνητον, 'unanswered.'

Bene mehercule potuit. It is quite useless to put forward any of the theories formed as to the meaning of this passage. We may, however, arrive at a negative result, that it is idle to supply *vendere* after *potuit*, or *se ibi oblectare* after *solet enim cum suo tibicine*.

αἰδεσθεν. These are the words applied to the chieftains of the Greeks on hearing the challenge of Hector to single combat, Il. vii. 93. The words do not seem very applicable to the present context as it is usually understood, which seems to imply that these embarrassed Roman nobles were ashamed (why?) to refuse the aid of Caesar, and were afraid to accept it, lest it should compromise them in the approaching struggle. Perhaps they were ashamed to display that distrust of Caesar's offer which might be inferred from a refusal. Cicero's quotations from the poets often have only a very slight relevancy to the topic illustrated. In fact it is quite a modern law that a quotation should exactly suit the thing to which it is applied—should 'go on all fours,' as the saying is. The loose applicability of the quotations of Greek writers, especially Aristotle, from Homer has often been noticed. Perhaps, however, the commentators have been hasty in postulating an allusion to Caesar in this passage. The verse might have been quoted by Cicero with the meaning, 'They are ashamed to repudiate (their debts), and are afraid to face them (take them on their shoulders).'

restituendo. Memmius was still at Athens, whither he had retired on being exiled in 52.

24. sunt collata, 'have been assigned in a body to the month of March' to be then definitely arranged.

25. suos nummos. Pompeius must have lent Caesar a large sum of money, so that he might look on Caesar's money as his own. The following words present some difficulty. As they stand, we must suppose that Pompeius was opposed to the great expenditure which Caesar was making on the building of a house near the sacred grove of Diana, called *Nemus*, in the neighbourhood of Aricia. Suet., Jul. 46, tells us that when this villa had been completed at great expense, Caesar had it pulled down 'because it did not altogether suit his taste' (*quia non tota ad animum ei responderat*). The sentence would then mean, 'Pompeius thinks you money-lenders (in "wringing the 50 talents out of Caesar") have got into your clutches (gobbled up, *comedisse*) a large sum of money which was in effect his, and that it will not have the good effect of cooling

Caesar's mania for building—in fact he will be all the more eager to carry his projects out.' A good sense would thus emerge, but the expression is not satisfactory; we should rather have expected some such words as *Caesarem tamen in Nemore aedificando nihilo indiligentiorem fore.* So unsatisfactory is the expression that I am strongly disposed to accept Boot's suggestion, and read *nec Caesarem . . . diligentiorem fore.* The word *diligens* would then bear the meaning 'economical,' not uncommon in Cicero, and the train of thought would run thus : If the parting with this large sum made Caesar more economical in his building projects, then Pompeius would be satisfied ; but he feared that it would not have that effect. The theory adopted by Boot, and most commentators, that Pompeius, as son-in-law, looked on Caesar's money as being virtually his own, seems improbable, especially as Julia had been some years dead.

Curio legem. The *lex viaria* of Curio, referred to Fam. viii. 6, 5, is supposed from this passage to have imposed a heavy tax for keeping the roads in repair on such as kept equipages larger than ordinary. But, as Boot remarks, Cicero would then have written *pro quibus* instead of *pro qua* (sc. *familia*). It is safer to suppose that Cicero refers to a sumptuary law of Curio, which levied a tax on the rich, proportioned to the extent of their establishment (*familia*). [Lange assumes a proposed *lex Scribonia de itineribus*, setting limits to the paraphernalia to be taken on a journey—distinct from the *lex viaria.*]

ad Magnum. I think *Pompeium* is a gloss. There is a similar gloss in Att. viii. 6, 3, *Hoc tamen spero Magnum [nomen imperatoris] fore magnum in adventu terrorem.* [The insertion of *Pompeium* seems not unnatural after the mention of the other Pompeius just before.]

C. Vennonius. It was supposed that the property of Vindullus, who died intestate and childless, would go to his patron Pompeius. C. Vennonius came to take an inventory of the goods of the deceased, and among the rest he found some property of Vedius, which he had left at the house of Vindullus on setting out to visit Cicero. Among the belongings of Vedius, deposited for safe keeping with his friend the deceased Vindullus, were found portrait models of some Roman ladies. This compromised these ladies, for Vedius was a notorious *roué*. Among the models was one of Junia, half-sister of Brutus and wife of Lepidus (her sister was the wife of Cassius). Neither Brutus nor Lepidus took any notice of the matter, and Brutus still kept up his intimacy with Vedius. Cicero, by

a most delicate use of language, in telling the tale, introduces
a play on each name merely by using the subjunctive instead
of the indicative : 'among which was a portrait of the sister
of your friend Brutus—a brute part indeed to keep up the man's
acquaintance—and wife of Lepidus—gay fellow indeed to take
the matter so coolly.' I have followed Wesenberg in inserting
uxoris, because though *Iunia Lepidi* might well mean 'Junia
the wife of Lepidus,' yet it is clear that the ellipse of *uxoris*
would be impossible in the present passage.   Perhaps, however,
we should rather supply a Greek term, which would account
better for the dropping out of the word ; perhaps ἀλόχου *illius
lepidi*.   The Greek words used for 'wife' in Att. vi. 4 are δάμαρ
and ξυνάορος ; but in the latter passage, while C. and M. give
συναόρου, other mss. have ἀλόχου ; so that it seems far from
improbable that Cicero here wrote ἀλόχου.

Hamlet makes a play on *Brutus* similar to that of Cic. here :
'*Polonius.* I did enact Julius Caesar.   I was killed in the
Capitol ; Brutus killed me.   *Hamlet.* It was a brute part of
him to kill so capital a calf there' (iii. 2).   If the subjunctive
were replaced by the indicative the whole play on words would
disappear, and the meaning would be 'sister of Brutus who is his
acquaintance, and wife of Lepidus, who takes the matter coolly.'

παριστορῆσαι, 'to ask *en passant*.'

belle curiosi, 'we both are nice gossips.'

26. πρόπυλον.   An inscription discovered in 1860 (Corp.
Inscr. Lat. I. p. 181) no doubt refers to this very porch.   It
is thus quoted by Boot : Ap. Claudius *Ap. F. Pulcher propylum
Cer*eri et Proserpin*ae cos. vovit* imp*erator.* coepit Pulcher.
Claud*ius et Rex Mar*cius fecerunt.

ipsas Athenas.   The material city : see Att. v. 10, 5.

falsas inscriptiones.   We learn from Plut. Ant. 60 that
there were statues of Eumenes and Attalus at Athens which
bore the inscription of *Antonius.*

mysteria, the festival of the Bona Dea, as in Att. v. 21, 14 ;
Cic. wishes to be informed on what day that festival falls.
This reminds him of Clodius, and hence he dates his letter by
the number of days since the fray in which he lost his life,
which he sportively calls *the battle of Leuctra*, as he had already
called it the *battle of Bovillae* (Att. v. 13, 1).   Clodius was slain
on Jan. 18, 52 ; the date of this letter therefore is Feb. 23,
50, reckoning of course according to the pre-Julian calendar,
and inclusively after the Roman fashion.

quo modo hiemaris, 'how you have passed the winter.'

LETTER XXXVI. (ATT. VI. 4)

1. Mescinius. See Att. vi. 3, 1, where he speaks of this quaestor Mescinius as 'a dissolute fribble—light-fingered too.'

Caelio. C. Caelius Caldus, mentioned again in the next letter, § 3, is not to be confounded with the celebrated M. Caelius Rufus, whose correspondence with Cic. is so interesting. Cic. left C. Caelius Caldus in command of his province. To h m is addressed Fam. ii. 19. In Att. vi. 6, 3 he writes of him as 'a mere lad, rather a noodle, and without any weight or firmness of will.' But in Fam. ii. 15 he defends his choice by reminding the other Caelius that he was leaving behind him one who, though a mere lad, was yet a quaestor and a *nobilis*. Cic. did not hesitate to commit a province larger than Ireland to a 'young noodle, if a noble.' Yet his provincial career has always been considered most praiseworthy, so favourably did it compare with the conduct of his predecessors.

discessus, 'separation,' as in Tusc. i. 71 ; 'departure' s the far more usual meaning.

2. condicione. Tullia's proposed marriage with Dolabella.

honore. The *supplicatio* which he expected to be voted i 1 his honour.

3. τῆς δάμαρτὸς . . . ἐξασφάλισαι. 'My wife's freedman (Philotimus) seemed to me the other day, from some remark which he casually dropped, to have cooked his accounts in the matter of the sale of the goods of the Crotoniate tyrannicide I am afraid you may not have observed what has been going on : take the matter into *your own hands only* and secure the residue.' The Crotoniate tyrannicide is Milo, who slew Clodius, and bore the same name as the celebrated athlete of Crotona. For εἰς δήπου has been suggested Οἰδίπου ; but see Att. vi. 9, 2, where exactly the same meaning is conveyed by the curious adverbial superlative αὐτότατα. Terentia seems to have availed herself of the relation in which she stood to Philotimus to appropriate some of the money raised from the sale of Milo's effects. I have inserted οὐ, which is necessary for the sense after μή τι. It would have easily fallen out after the foregoing μή. The copyist of these letters hardly knew any Greek, as may be perceived by any one who consults the critical notes of any edition.

volent obviae, 'fly to meet me' : cf. *tum vero omnis actas*

currere obvii, Liv. xxvii. 51, 1 ; the nom. as secondary predicate is rare ; we have accus. in Att. v. 20, 1, *num potui Ciliciam
Aetoliam reddere ;* abl. in Att. i. 14, 6, *utimur . . . Cornuto
. . . pseudocatone ;* the dat. is common after *licet, necesse
est,* etc.

LETTER XXXVII. (ATT. VI. 5)

1. **domi,** 'at Rome.' This is an excellent example of the
fact first pointed out by Lehmann, pp. 73, 74, that in the
letters *domus* often means Rome : cf. *ego me . . . exiturum
puto aut in Tusculanum aut domum,* Att. xii. 42, 3 ; *domum
et ad me in Formianum,* 'the packet was brought first to Rome,
then forwarded to me at Formiae,' Att. ii. 13, 1 ; *Dolabellam
spero domi esse,* 'at Rome,' Att. xv. i.*a*, 2 ; and see Corr. of Cic.
vol. ii. p. 20. In this sense I supply *domi* in Att. vi. 8, 5, Ep.
xxxviii. Cicero here means that though Atticus would actually
be nearer to him if he were in Greece than in Rome, yet his
friend seems further parted from him when absent from the
Urbs.

quam argutissimas, 'long long letters.'

τῆς ξυναόρου, 'my spouse's freedman seemed to me, by ever
and anon stammering and showing confusion in his interviews
and talks, to have done a bit of cooking of the accounts *in re*
the sale of the Crotoniate's assets.'

2. **ἐξ ἄστεως,** 'on leaving the city of the seven hills he
delivered an account of two debts to Camillus, amounting to 24
and 48 minae, and he set himself down as accountable for 24
minae from the sale of the Crotoniate's estate, and 48 from the
property in the Chersonese ; [he further set down] that he had
come in for 640 + 640 minae in legacies, and that not a penny
had been paid up, all being due on the 1st of the 2nd month ;
that Milo's freedman, the namesake of Conon's father (Timotheus), had been utterly negligent. Now (addressing Atticus)
I want you, best of all, to see that the whole sum is secured ;
next, not even to overlook the interest calculated from the
aforesaid date. During the days I had to put up with his
presence I was greatly alarmed ; for he came to me to recon-
noitre, and with some little hope ; when he saw it was all up
he went away without any explanation, adding, "I yield :

'twere shame to tarry long,"

and he reproached me with the hackneyed saw "needs must."'

I have printed ἀπὸ τῆς προεκκειμένης. ἡμέρας ὅσας for ἀπὸ τῆς προεκκειμένης ἡμέρας. ὅσας. We must either do this or repeat ἡμέρας, for the ellipse of ἡμέρας with ὅσας would be intolerable, while the ellipse of ἡμέρας with προεκκ. is quite normal, as in ἡ προθεσμία and many such expressions. The Homeric verse (Il. ii. 298) is of course the familiar αἰσχρόν τοι δηρόν τε μένειν κενεόν τε νέεσθαι. The proverb τὰ μὲν διδόμενα is found in Plat. Gorg. 499 C (thus embedded in the text), καὶ ὡς ἔοικεν ἀνάγκη μοι κατὰ τὸν παλαιὸν λόγον τὸ παρὸν εὖ ποιεῖν καὶ τοῦτο δέχεσθαι τὸ διδόμενον παρὰ σοῦ. Olympiodorus gives the proverb as τὰ ἐκ τῆς τύχης διδόμενα κόσμει ('make the best of'), and tells us it is said τῶν κυβευόντων. The proverb would then mean 'make the best of a bad business.' We have κοσμεῖν 'to make the best of' in the proverb already more than once quoted by Cicero, Σπάρταν ἔλαχες ταύταν κόσμει. [τὰ μὲν διδόμ. 'take what you can get.' The expression occurs again in Att. xv. 17, 2; cf. the similar *quod das accepero*, Acad. ii. § 68; *accipio quod dant*, Fin. ii. § 82.]

3. emeritum. See Att. vi. 2, 6, *annuae mihi operae a.a. III. Kal. Sextil. emerentur*, 'on July 30 I have served my time.' See on Ep. xxxii. § 1, for the method of computing dates before the reformation of the calendar by Caesar.

maerore suo. Two of his sons were slain in a mutiny of the soldiers of Gabinius in Egypt: cf. Caes. B. C. iii. 10, 6. Bibulus, with rare magnanimity, refused to take any vengeance for their deaths.

nostra robora. 'The main strength of Cicero's army in Cilicia was its non-Roman element; but in the main the practice of using provincial troops almost to the exclusion of Italian did not establish itself before the Empire': Arnold, Rom. Prov. Admin. p. 27.

Caldus. C. Caelius Caldus: see last letter, § 1.

4. iocari. See Att. v. 5, 1, where Cicero intimates what he thinks ought to be the main ingredients of a letter—commissions, news, bantering. The fact that he looks on a letter as a natural vehicle for bantering causes most of the difficulties in the correspondence. It is hard to interpret jokes without full data, especially when a writer 'jokes wi' deeficulty,' as a candid Scot is reported to have said of himself—a remark, it must be allowed, fairly applicable to Cicero, as he appears in his letters.

LETTER XXXVIII. (ATT. VI. 8)

1. opportunitate Piliae, 'the opportuneness of Pilia,' a careless way of writing 'the opportuneness of Pilia's meeting with you.' Atticus had mentioned to Cicero some circumstance which made his meeting with his wife especially opportune. [*Opportunitate:* rather Pilia, going to meet Atticus on his arrival and naturally not knowing exactly when to expect him, just came in the nick of time. *Tranquillitates:* cf. νηνεμίαι, Plat. Theaet.]

2. meros terrores. Cf. *mera monstra*, Att. iv. 7, 1 ; *merum bellum*, ix. 13, 8 ; *merus est φυράτης*, vii. 1, 9.

cum illo . . . facere, 'are on his (Caesar's) side.'

designatos. This word qualifies not only *praetores* but *tribunum pl.* and *consulem.*

3. patruo sororis tuae filii. Cicero thus jocularly describes *himself;* his brother Quintus being the husband of Pomponia, the sister of Atticus, Cicero was uncle to the son of Pomponia. In the same vein, writing to Atticus, he refers to the son of Quintus as *avi tui pronepos* (Att. xvi. 14, 4), and to his own son as *patris mei nepotem.* In Att. v. 19, 3, using the same phrase as here, he alludes to one who had unsuccessfully competed for office with 'the uncle of your sister's son,' that is himself. There the allusion is supposed to be to C. Hirrus, who was an unsuccessful competitor against Cicero for the augurate (as afterwards against Caelius for the curule aedileship). In this letter the allusion is generally supposed to be to Cato. But it has been shown to be highly probable in a learned tract by Dr. L. Moll, Berlin 1883, that the allusion in both letters is to M. Calidius, an orator who failed in his candidature for the consulship of 50, and again of 49, and who had expressed an unfavourable opinion about Cicero's forensic style; of whom, therefore, Cicero might naturally say that he was 'in the habit of vaunting himself over him,' or that he 'had pitted himself against him.'

a quibus. C. Claudius Marcellus and L. Lentulus Crus. Cicero did not think highly of these successful rivals of Calidius, of whom he writes slightingly in Att. vii. 20, 1.

4. ipsos, 'precisely,' opp. to *aliquos.* The open Rhodian vessel which he used caused a loss of exactly 20 days *etiam* (in addition to the delay caused by the violence of the trade winds).

This great loss of time can hardly have been due altogether to
the slow sailing of the Rhodian vessels.   From what follows it
appears that Cicero would not put to sea in these unscreened
vessels unless the weather was very favourable.   'Yet,' he adds,
'we are making all the way we can.'

tranquillitates, 'we have to look out for fine days on
account of the nature of our vessels.'   This word ought in
plur. to mean 'calms': cf. *me mirificae tranquillitates adhuc
tenuerunt*, Att. x. 18, 1 ; 'fair weather' is better expressed by
some such term as *felicitas navigandi* above, but sing. *tran-
quillitas* is not rare in this sense.   Hence, perhaps, we should
here read *tranquillitatem* ; however, the plur. might perhaps be
used to indicate that Cicero lay in wait for fair weather *at each
successive place* where he put in.

5. **De raudusculo Puteolano.**   This probably refers to the
repayment of a debt to Vestorius of Puteoli.

domi, 'at Rome.'   See on Att. vi. 5, 1, Ep. xxxvii.   There
is clearly an allusion to the consulship of Bibulus and Caesar,
when Bibulus did not leave his house for eight months.   It has
been proposed to insert *olim* or *consul*, but *domi*, which I
suggest, is far more probable, both as being a frequent word
for *Romae* in the letters, and as being a word which would very
easily fall out before *domo*.   [I should prefer *modo domo ; modo*
is often used to cover considerable spaces of time.   *Porta*, the
gate of the camp.]

αἰσχρὸν σιωπᾶν, βαρβάρους δ' ἐᾶν λέγειν, Eur. Philoct. Frag.
8.   Cicero says he would not be eager for a triumph were it not
that Bibulus, whose exploits were very trifling, was straining
every nerve to secure a triumph for himself.

qui properarem, 'for one who is in a hurry, as I am.'

verbis, 'in my name,' 'from me.'   A good example of the
meaning of *meis verbis* is in Att. xvi. 11, 8, *meis verbis suavium
des volo*.   In Att. v. 11, 7 *Piliam meis verbis consolere* should
be explained in the same way, not 'in words such as I would
use,' which would not be expressed by *meis verbis*.   Cicero there
asks Atticus to assure Pilia (wife of Atticus) *in his name* that
things are not so bad as she thinks.   He only requests Atticus
to conceal from Pilia that he had opened her letter to Quintus
condoling with him on the ill-humour of Pomponia, and had
thus discovered how much Pilia was distressed by the estrange-
ment between Quintus and her sister-in-law.

LETTER XXXIX. (ATT. vi. 9)

1. **in Piraeea.** See Att. vii. 3, 10, where he discusses the Latinity of this expression.

σύγχυσιν **litterularum**, 'again, when I opened the letter, I was startled at the illegibility of the handwriting, for your writing is generally most excellent and legible.'

quod ita scripseras. Here is a somewhat carelessly expressed sentence. The meaning is that he had at first reason to infer that Atticus was in bad health from the shortness of the letter and the badness of the writing, and that on reading the letter he had Atticus's own word for it. This, it will be seen, is not very clearly expressed : 'On my first sight of the letter, before I broke the seal, I was surprised at its shortness, then, on opening it, at the badness of the writing, and, finally, I discovered from your own statement therein that you were suffering from fever when you arrived at Rome.'

Ille . . . incommode, 'He said that such was your impression of the case and his own, and such were the accounts he received at home from your people, that nothing serious could be the matter'; *ita . . . ut* must often be carefully rendered. See Correspondence of Cicero, I², p. 65. For *esse* with adv. see *ibid.* I², 70, 71.

Id videbatur, 'What seemed to confirm this view was the expression you used in the end of the letter that you had a *slight attack* of fever when you wrote.'

te amavi, 'I was greatly pleased with you.' I have inserted *te*, which has been corrupted into *cl* in M.—a very common mistake. M. gives *clamavi*, which Victorius corrected to *amavi*, Orelli to *exclamavi*, and Klotz to *adamavi*. Cicero would not use *amavi* or *adamavi* absolutely, nor would he make them take as object the clause *quod—scripsisses* : cf. *amavi amorem tuum*, Fam. ix. 16, 1 ; *in Atilii negotio te amavi*, Fam. xiii. 62 ; *volo ames meam constantiam*, Att. ii. 10 ; *Alexidis manum amabam*, Att. vii. 2, 3. [Is it so certain that *clamavi* is wrong ? Cf. Div. ii. § 50, *clamoremque maiorem cum admiratione ;* De Or. i. § 152, *clamores et admirationes ;* Parad. § 37, *admirantem, clamores tollentem ;* Orat. § 135, *exclamatio . . . admirationes.*]

2. τοῦ φυρατοῦ, 'Keep, an you love me, keep your very ownest eye on the *philotimousness* of the Unready Reckoner ; and as to this legacy from Precius—which is indeed a great sorrow to me,

for I loved Precius—don't let him put so much as a finger on :t,
small as it is.' Αὐτότατα is an adv. formed from αὐτόταιος
ipsissimus [cf. Plaut. Trin. iv. 2, 146 (888)], which is found :n
Aristoph. Plut. 83 ; αὐτότερος αὐτῷ is in Epicharm. Fr. 2, and it
is probably from him, whom he often quotes, that Cicero he·e
takes αὐτότατα.   Similarly we have Δαναώτατος, Ar. Fr. 25ℓ ;
ἑταιρότατος, Plat. Gorg. 487 D ; Phaed. 89 E.   Philotimus is
called φυρατῆς because he is said above (Ep. xxxvii.) πεφυρι-
κέναι τὰς ψήφους.   As Cicero seems to think he *cooked* his
accounts, we might in the same vein call Philotimus 'tl e
professed cook,' or the *chef* or *cordon bleu*.   For the abstract
subst. coined from a proper name cf. *Lentulitas, Appieta*ℓ,
Fam. iii. 7, 5.   *Dices* means 'kindly tell him ': see note on Plau :.
Mil. ii. 4, 42 (395).

κενὸν . . . ἄτυφον, 'You will see that I shall not show ι
spirit of silly vanity in trying to get it, nor a spirit of insensi-
bility in refusing it.'   The word ἄτυφος in classical Greek means
modest ; here it has the meaning of ἀναίσθητος, 'phlegmatic,' Ar.
Eth. Nic. ii. 7, 3.   *Lentitudo* is the nearest Latin to ἀναισθησία,
Q. Fr. i. 38.   [κενὸν . . . ἄτυφον : he will be οὖτ' εὐτυχῶν περι-
χαρής, οὖτ' ἀτυχῶν περίλυπος.   The *nec* before ἄτυφον seems to
me an error for *et ;* ἄτυφον will then bear its ordinary sense.]

3. **Adeon,** 'Did you think I so utterly failed to read betweei
the lines of your letter when you spoke of your *philosophic
doubts ;* you could not have hesitated to approve of my choice
of my brother [as my successor in the province] if there had
been a single point in favour of his appointment, knowing as we
do what a fine fellow he is.   No ! I took your *philosophic
doubt* for a *dogmatic rejection* (your *scepticism* for *dogmatism*)
in the matter.'   For ἐπέχειν see Att. vi. 6, 3 ; and especially
xiii. 21, 3, where he objects to *inhibere* as a rendering of
ἐπέχειν on the ground that *inhibere* is a term used in rowing,
and means to 'back water' and move in an opposite direction,
whereas ἐπέχειν is to hold oneself *balancé* between two opinions,
so we should need a word implying no motion at all in the
boat, this way or that, if we were to borrow a term from
rowing to translate ἐπέχειν.

τοὐμὸν ὄνειρον, 'You're telling me what I know already.'
Perhaps there is an allusion to this proverb in *Palaestrionis
somnium narratur*, Pl. Mil. ii. 4, 33 (386).   [ἐπιχρον. ἐπ. I find
these words hard.   In what sense does Cic. call A.'s downright
statement about Q. the younger an ἐπιχρονία ἐποχή ? Should
ἐπιχρονίᾳ be read and taken with *dubitatione*, so that ἐποχὴ
tua is a sarcastic reference to what is stated above, that Atticus's

ἐποχή is equivalent to ἀθέτησις? Or should *liberavi* be read, and *tua de dubitatione* (see M.) be taken as a gloss on ἐπιχρονίᾳ ἐποχῇ? Something is wrong.]

5. id est, de Dolabella, ' or rather I should say'; see Reid Acad. i. § 6, *si Epicurum id est si Democritum.*

praevideo. This verb occurs here only in good mss. of Cic. [It is almost certainly an error for *provideo.* The contractions for *prae* and *pro* are very similar, and *praevideo* is elsewhere given wrongly by inferior mss. against *provideo* of the better class. Cic. probably wrote *in summis fore periculis;* the omission of the infin. is hardly tolerable.]

referaturne, 'Will the matter be brought before the Senate?' The censors Appius Claudius Pulcher and L. Calpurnius Piso had affixed a limit in their edict to the amount to be spent by private persons on works of art. This required the confirmation of the Senate to become law. [I think the explanation usually given is very unsatisfactory. Such a proclamation of the censor could have no legal effect, whether with or without the sanction of the Senate. It could only stand as a moral exhortation. Only the *comitia* could make it practical. All sorts of things were indeed brought before the Senate, and the mere issue of such an edict might cause sufficient indignation to induce the consuls or tribunes to consult the Senate about it. But the words *de modo agri* in Fam. viii. 14, 4, indicate *contemplated legislation,* which would be a serious matter for the wealthier classes. The word *agere* there also points to this conclusion, and away from the supposition of an *edict.*]

legiones quattuor, sc. *ducturus erat.* This rumour turned out to be false. See Introd. for ellipse.

statio, 'my quarters'; he used a military term because he is still *cum imperio.* Cicero's year of office expired on July 30, 50; he did not actually enter Rome, though he was often near the city, until the end of the year 47, because he would then have been obliged to lay down his *imperium,* and thus resign his claim to a triumph. [*Arce . . . statio:* rather a jocular reference to the dangers at Rome as compared with his safety on the Acropolis.]

LETTER XL. (FAM. XVI. 9)

1. Cassiopen. A town in the north of Corcyra, with a temple to Jupiter Cassius (Plin. H. N. iv. 52). It was one of the stations on the Greek coast, from which the crossing was often made to Brundisium : cf. Gell. xix. 1, 1 ; Suet. Nero, 22 ; Dig. xiv. 1, 1, 12, *quaedam enim naves onerariae quaedam* ἐμβατηγοὶ *sunt : et plerosque mandare scio, ne vectores recipiant, et sic, ut certa regione et certo mari negotietur, ut ecce sunt naves quae Brundisium a Cassiopa vel a Dyrrhacio vectores traiiciunt ad onera inhabiles.*

cupide, 'eagerly.' Cf. Att. ii. 1, 1.

2. Hydruntem.   Otranto ; also called Hydruntum, Liv. xxxvi. 21, 5.

ludibundi, 'gaily' ; sometimes used of what one expects to be irksome, but finds to be child's play : cf. 2 Verr. iii. 156, *Si Volteium habebis omnia ludibundus conficies.* [*Ludibundi* reminds one of the undergraduate slang phrase 'to romp in,' *i e.* to do a thing with the greatest ease.]

3. Symphoniam, 'musical party.' The Romans had among their various kinds of slaves *symphoniaci pueri*, Mil. 55 ; Div. in Caec. 55.   They used to sing in concert during dinner : cf. Becker-Göll, Gallus, ii. 147, iii. 373.

ne in quartam hebdomada incideres, 'lest on that very day you should be attacked by (lit. *synchronise with,* cf. Att. ix. 4, 3) the fourth weekly attack' (of fever).   Every seventh day Tiro appears to have been liable to an attack ; the oftener he had an attack the more the fever would get into his system, and the harder it would be to throw it off ; Tiro should then have been more careful to avoid getting a fourth attack.   But when Lyso, at whose house he was staying, gave a large musical party, Tiro did not like (that is the force of *pudori*) to fail to put in an appearance.   The ancients considered every seventh day a *dies* κρίσιμος in fever.   [Pliny mentions fevers with periods of 1, 1½, 3, 4 days, but not 7 ; he says, curiously (xxviii. § 23), *cur impares numeros ad omnia vehementiores credimus, idque in febribus dierum observatione intellegitur.*   Cf. Celsus, iii. 16, *quartana neminem iugulat*—he does not mention the seventh day fever.   Lidd. and Sc. quote ἑβδομαῖος πυρετὸς from Hippocrates.]

misi, 'am sending orders to' : cf. *scripsi*, Fam. xvi. 4, 2 'I am writing,' and *reliqui*, 'I am leaving,' below.

honos haberetur, 'that a complimentary present be made'. cf. Dig. xxxvii. 5, 3, 2, *nec enim quaerimus cui adquiratur sea cui honos habitus sit.*

me cui iussisset curaturum, 'that I shall pay any one

he orders,' *i.e.* that instead of Cicero's sending the money by bill of exchange to Patrae, Curius will delegate Cicero to some creditor whom Curius may have in Rome, or to some bank with which he may have an account, and Cicero will pay over the money to the creditor or bank specified.

reliqui, 'am leaving.' For *ecum*, 'horse,' which M. gives, H. has *metum*, with *medicum* written above it.

Kalend. Ian. When the new consuls, L. Lentulus Crus and C. Claudius Marcellus, both violently opposed to Caesar, would enter on their office.

4. mare magnum, 'a stormy bit of sea': cf. Lucr. ii, 1, and 553 ; or it may be simply 'a great tract of sea.'

navicularius, 'shipowner,' who, intent on his gains, would press for no delay.

stiteris. This use of *sisto* is very common in the comic drama: see Dictt. It also occurs Att. iii. 25 ; x. 16, 6.

Vale et salve. *Et* has been added by Wesenberg (Em. Alt. 56), who compares Fam. xvi. 4, 4.

LETTER XLI. (ATT. VII. 17)

Cicero was still uncertain whether he would join Pompeius, or remain longer in the neighbourhood of Rome.

1. sunt. This must refer to the general effect of the letters of Att. on Cic. We should rather have expected *fuerunt*, and then the reference would be to certain letters recently received from Att. But he often expresses this sentiment generally. See Ep. lxxi. 4.

[**peteremus**, 'we should now be making for Spain.' When it first occurred to people that Pompeius would leave Italy, they naturally inferred that he would go to Spain. Cic. assumes all through this letter that he will share P.'s fortunes, whatever they may be. Cic. now expected a war in Italy. *Cum fuga quaeri videbatur* means 'when P. thought of flying.' Cic. now believes P. to have abandoned the design of leaving Italy.]

Sexto. Sextus Peducaeus was an intimate friend of Cicero's, as also was his father, who was governor of Sicily as propraetor B.C. 76-74. They are both mentioned frequently in Cicero's correspondence, especially the son, to whom the reference is in this passage.

de urbanis praediis detraxit, 'depreciated city property.'
Pompeius in abandoning the city and leaving it exposed to an
attack by Caesar, who might follow the Sullan precedent of
proscription and confiscation, took a step likely to depreciate
property in the neighbourhood of Rome, and thus inflict an
injury on Atticus and Peducaeus. The reading of M., *praesidiis*,
is certainly an error; these words are very frequently confounded by the copyists. Cic. is careful to point out that what
he says is not serious.

2. **L. Caesar.** L. Julius Caesar, son of the L. Julius Caesar
who was consul in 64, and who is often mentioned in the correspondence, was at this time carrying communications between
Pompeius and Caesar.

proponerentur, 'with a view to the widest circulation';
lit. 'with a view to being placarded on the public hoardings.'
The expression is a strong one, but signifies no more than the
succeeding phrase, *quae in omnium manus venturae essent.*
[Cf. Att. viii. 2, 1, *in publico proponat velim.*]

σηστιωδέστερον, 'more Sestian,' that is, 'more characteristc
of Sestius,' whose style was proverbially frigid. Catullus (xliv)
tells us how he once endured the infliction of hearing Sestius
read a speech of his own composition, an experience which was
followed by such a severe cold (*gravedo*) and cough (*tussis*) that
he was obliged to retire to his Tiburtine farm and lie up till he
recovered. This is the same Sestius who befriended Cic. in his
exile, and whom Cic. defended in the celebrated extant speech
B.C. 56.

quis enim tu es. Cic. here apostrophises Caesar, who demanded as a condition of his laying down arms that Pompeius
should retire to his province and disband his army. Render,
'who are you to say?' and for this use of the consecutive subjunctive see Roby, ii. 1678 sqq. This usage is common in
Plautus; a good example is Capt. 568—

> *Ty.* Tu enim repertu's Philocratem *qui superes* veriverbio,
> *Ar.* Pol ego ut rem video tu inventu's vera vanitudine
>   *Qui convincas.*

impetrasset, 'had carried his point and stood for the consulship in his absence.'

3. **ab illo.** Caesar is often referred to simply as *ille.* In
the next line but one *ei* of course also refers to Caesar.

ex dierum ratione. Cic. calculated that the day on which

Caesar asked Trebatius to write to him must have been the very day on which Caesar had first heard that Pompeius and the consuls had left the city.

4. qui mihi nihil scripsisset, 'because he had not written to me himself.'

neque . . . suscepisse. Cic. does not appear to have ever made any attempt to raise troops for Pompeius, but *neque negotium suscepisse* is not strictly true. He expressly writes *Capuam sumpsimus*, Fam. xvi. 11, 4, and he often speaks of a commission he held to watch the coast, Capua being his head-quarters (Att. vii. 11, 5). He appears, however, to have resigned it almost immediately (Att. viii. 11, D, 5). [*Suscepisse* may very well mean that Cic. had not 'taken up' or actually 'entered on' the *negotium*, which is clearly the case, as he first went to Capua on Feb. 5.]

ὑπεκθέμενος. He might just as well have written *transportando*, the word which he used at the beginning of the letter ; but Cic. frequently uses Greek words even when he has a Latin synonym ready to his hand. These Greek words are a fruitful source of the corruption of the text in the correspondence of Cicero. The Greek word here of course means more than the Latin would have expressed, 'getting them out of harm's way.'

otium. The mss. have *sin autem etiam indutiae*, which has been corrected to *sin pax aut etiam indutiae*. But *otium aut* would easily have been corrupted into the *autem* of the mss. The word is used in Att. vii. 18, 2 : *O! vix ullo otio compensandam turpitudinem.* I have adopted Mr. Purser's suggestion in restoring *otium* here. [*Sin autem etiam indutiae :* I think these words are right ; 'on the other hand, if there is going to be even so much as a truce, I will seize the opportunity of seeing you.' *Etiam* often has a sense like this, and can be rendered in this way or by 'merely,' as in Prov. Cons. § 38.]

5. scripseram ut manerent, 'I had told them by letter to remain in Rome.'

LETTER XLII. (ATT. VII. 20)

1. Pacem desperavi. Cf. *remp. desperaverint*, Fam. xii. 14, 3. Cic. in his letters is prone to give a direct object to a verb which usually is followed by a preposition, e.g. *pacem hortari*,

Att. vii. 14, 3, on the analogy of *idem te hortor*, Q. Fr. i. 3, 4 ; so *suadere* takes a direct object of the thing in Fam. vii. 3, 2, *desperans victoriam primum coepi suadere pacem.* Caelius writes *gaudere gaudium*, Fam. viii. 2, 1, and *gaudere dolorem*, Fam. viii. 14, 1.

bellum nullum, 'the military operations on our side are nil.' This is a much stronger expression than *non administrant* would have been, and may be compared with such colloquial expressions as *nullus renit*, 'not a bit of him came,' Att. xi. 24, 4 ; *nullus discedere*, 'not to move an inch,' Att. xv. 22, 1 ; *nullus tu quidem domum*, 'don't stir a foot to visit him,' Att. xv. 29, 1.

Cave . . . consulibus, 'Don't imagine that there is anything which concerns our present consuls less than the war.' This seems more probably right than the other possible rendering, according to which *consulibus* is not dative but ablative after *minoris:* 'don't imagine that anything could be more worthless than our present consuls.' The consuls were C. Claudius Marcellus and L. Cornelius Lentulus Crus.

quorum ergo, 'on account of whom, in the hope of hearing something I came to Capua in heavy rain.' The mss. read *ego*, not *ergo*, and that reading might well be retained, and explained on the analogy of Plautine usage which we have so often found a safe rule for the diction of the letters. We have a parallel to this use of two genitives (one being a gerund) dependent on a noun, *quorum spe audiendi* instead of *quorum audiendorum* (or *quos audiendi*) *spe*, in Plaut. Capt. 846, *nominandi istorum tibi erit magis quam edundi copia.* Moreover in Cic. himself we have *causa . . . corum quae secundum naturam sunt adipiscendi*, Fin. v. 19 ; *facultas detur . . . agrorum suis latronibus condonandi*, Phil. v. 6. Other passages, too, very probably afford instances of this usage, as, for instance, *studium illius aeternitatis imitandi*, Tusc. v. 70, where the reading has been impugned ; *quarum potiendi spe*, Fin. i. 60, where *quarum* may, of course, be governed by *potiendi* (where see Madv.) The fact, however, that *audiendi* has in this sentence an object *aliquid*, and that another gen. follows, makes it slightly different from the other examples cited above, and induces me to follow Bosius in changing *ego* to *ergo*. [It seems hardly possible that *quorum ergo* can be right. *Ergo* with gen. only occurs in Cic. in quotations from or imitations of the language of statutes : thus four times in De Leg. ; also Att. iii. 23, § 2 ; and De Opt. gen. dic. § 19.

Nor is it easy to believe that Cic. wrote *quorum ego spe audiendi aliquid* for *de quibus*, etc.   Most probably a substantive in the abl. has dropped out on which *quorum* depended, such as *vocatu.*]

ad Nonas. C., the ms. which Cratander used, is said by him to have the reading *illi autem adhuc, id est Nonis, nondum venerant;* which reading may be right, for this letter was written on the morning of the 5th, as is shown by the use of *hodie* in § 2, and we read at the end of the letter that the consuls are to arrive 'on their appointed 5th.'   Boot, seeing that some statement of the time at which the consuls were expected would naturally find a place in the sentence, proposed to read *Nonis* for *inanes.*   It seems to me better to suppose that *ad Nonas* fell out before *inanes*, and that C. preserves a part of the right tradition by introducing the Nones, but in the wrong place.   Cic. heard the report that they were expected 'by February 5th,' and that they were without equipment or preparation of any kind, 'bare and bootless.'

Appianarum. This is a most probable correction of the ms. reading *Attianarum*, which cannot be right.   P. Attius of whom we read (Att. vii. 13 *b*, 2) as being at Cingulum seems not to have been in command of any *legiones*, and the *cohortes* with which he held Auximum had surrendered to Caesar (Caes. B. C. i. 13).   The only other Attii who appear in the narrative of Caesar are Attius Varus (*ibid.* 31) and Attius Paelignus (*ibid.* 18, and Cic. Att. viii. 4, 3), who plainly cannot be referred to in this passage.   Lipsius with great probability emended the word to *Appianarum.*   The reference would then be to the legions which were taken from Caesar under the pretence that they were to be employed against the Parthians, and were unfairly made over to Pompeius.   The name of the lieutenant who marched them from Gaul was Appius.   Plutarch (Pomp. 57) tells us that Appius commanded on the march from Gaul 'the force which Pompeius lent to Caesar,' ἣν ἔχρησε Πομπήιος Καίσαρι στρατιάν.

illum, sc. Caesarem.

2. Ego . . . ago. 'Now, were the scene Italy, *It is but Death that comes at last*—on that point I am not asking your counsel—but if the issue is to be decided out of Italy, what am I to do?'   The whole verse, of which according to his habitual practice he quotes but a couple of words, is from a lost play of Diphilus, and runs—

κἂν ἀποθανεῖν δίῃ με θανοῖμ' ἑκουσίως.

So we often quote but a few words of a proverbial expression, 'Needs must——' or 'When thieves fall out——.' Cf. Hamlet, iii. 2, 358, 'While the grass grows,—the proverb is something musty.' *Consulere*, with a double accus. of the person and of the thing, is found only in the comic drama (Pl. Men. 687); that is no reason why we should suspect the usage here, but rather why we should expect it; the accus. of the person is of course quite regular, and the accus. of the thing is not very rare, e.g. *consulere quiddam*, Pl. Most. 1083; *rem delatam consulere*, Liv. ii. 28; *consulendis rebus*, Cic. Divin. i. 3. So that it is a mere chance that the double accus. is not more frequently forthcoming. [*Te id consulo:* the fact that the accus. *rei* is a neut. pron. makes the constr. much less strange than it would otherwise be, and the passage is not very unlike two others, viz. Div. ii. § 10, and Mil. § 16.]

coniungendi. On the apparently *passive* use of the gerund see Roby, ii. pref. lxiv.-lxvii. The exx. collected there under class *c* especially illustrate the present passage, because here the gerund may be regarded as rather reflexive than passive; among the best of the exx. are *signo recipiendi dato*, Caes. B. C. iii. 46; *lusus exercendique causa*, Liv. v. 27; *vix spatium instruendi fuit*, Liv. xxxi. 21; *potestatem defendendi*, Cic. Mil. 11. See Reid, Acad. ii. 101.

Phalarimne an Pisistratum. Phalaris was typical of the worst kind of tyrant, Pisistratus of the best. In Att. vii. 12, 2, Cic. uses the word φαλαρισμόν, which we might perhaps render 'Napoleonism,' to indicate autocratic power misused. 'Caesarism' is now beginning to be used very much in this sense, though Caesar himself gave no justification for it. It seems to be accepted as a more manageable word than 'Czarism.'

calere. This is not nearly so strong an expression as 'to be in hot water.' It means little more than 'to have one's hands full,' 'to have plenty of business of one's own to occupy one.' Hence Boot's *carere* (sc. *consilio*) is not required.

LETTER XLIII. (ATT. VIII. 4)

1. **Dionysius,** a literary slave of Cicero's, whom he manumitted, and to whom he entrusted the education of his son and nephew. Cic. had before this (Att. vii. 7, 1) expressed himself as not quite satisfied with the manners of Dionysius, but sub-

sequently withdrew his condemnation. Cic. writes about him
with much consideration in Att. vii. 18, 3, where he says that
he thinks Dionysius ought to accompany him in his flight if
he should fly from Rome ; 'but,' he adds, 'we must not expect
too much from a Greek,' and, 'if I am obliged to send for him
(which I hope I may not be) you must see that we consult his
convenience in every way.' It appears from this letter and the
next that Dion. flatly refused to remain an inmate of the house
of Cic. during this unhappy crisis, but afterwards became
alarmed and apologised. Cic. courteously dismissed him, as we
learn from Att. viii. 10. His conduct seems to have been most
ungrateful after this. In Att. ix. 12, 2, Cic. writes : 'I hate
him, and always shall. I wish I could make him smart for his
conduct.' In Att. x. 16, 1, we read that Dion. apologised to
Cicero, and the latter accorded him pardon grudgingly ; writing
to Att., 'I hope you may preserve his friendship. When I
utter this wish I am wishing for the permanence of your prosperity. The two will coincide.' Yet he writes (Att. xiii. 2, 3):
'D. writes me a long letter telling how he feels his long separation from his pupils. I fancy it will be longer. Yet I am
sorry for it. I miss him greatly.' The Dionysius who, having
for several years carried on peculations as librarian to Cic.,
finally absconded to escape punishment, was a slave, and is not
to be confounded with the Dion. of this letter.

tuus. Att. constantly undertook the defence of the ungrateful Greek. [Does *noster* mean here 'our common friend,'
or is it the equivalent of *meus?* See my note on Acad. i. § 1,
and Fam. i. 9, 24, *Lentuli tui nostrique;* but *ibid.* ii. 16, 5,
Dolabellam meum vel potius nostrum.]

veritus. This is the only place out of Latin comedy where
vereri takes the genitive. The constr. is ascribed by Nonius to
Accius and Pacuvius. Their precedent, however, would not
justify us in ascribing the constr. to Cicero, the diction of
whose letters conforms not to the extreme archaism of Accius
and Pacuvius, but to the more modern colloquialism of Plautus
and Terence. However, Ter. (Phorm. 971) has the gen. with
vereri—

> Neque huius sis veritus feminae primariae,
> quin novo modo ei faceres contumeliam.

Boot denies the applicability of this passage by making *feminae*
the dative after *faceres contumeliam*, and taking *huius sis veritus*
to mean 'did not care that (a snap of your fingers) for.' But
the natural constr. is rightly recognised by grammarians, *e.g.*

Roby, 1328. [The probabilities seem to me to be heavily against the genuineness of *testimonii tui veritus*. Some word on which *testimonii* depended has most likely dropped out. Possibly *verba* has been lost before *veritus*.]

motum, 'the shock' which his fortunes have suffered. The word *gubernabimus* is carelessly added as if he had written *quas quamvis motas* before. A man might write with a natural metaphor 'I shall guide my shipwrecked fortunes' into safety, but not 'I shall guide the shipwreck of my fortunes' into port. [*Motum:* is not this rather 'the onward course'? Cic. seems to say that he will divert the attack of this *fortuna* by skilful piloting before it leads to shipwreck. *Gubernare fortunam* occurs in Vell. ii. 127, 2 (or rather *ad gubernandam f.*) It is not necessary to regard *cuius fortunae* as identical with the *adverse* fortune just mentioned ; rather here it is the personified fortune. Cf. Att. x. 4, 4, *ne fortunam quidem ipsam qua illi florentissima nos duriore conflictati videmur.*]

ad ceteros. These words are usually taken with *commendatio*, but we should have rather expected *ad alios* or *ad omnes*. If taken with *contempti* they could only mean 'as compared with others' introduced by me to my friends, and that sentiment would not have been so expressed, though this use of *ad* is common enough in Plautus, e.g. *ad summos bellatores*, Trin. 753, and in Cic. with *nihil*, e.g. *nihil ad Persium* De Or. ii. 25 (where see Wilkins's note). If we accepted Boot's suggestion to read *apud*, that word would more naturally go with *contempti*, 'despicable *in the minds of* others,' though commended by me. [*Ad ceteros:* it is hard to divorce *ad* from *commendatio*. *Ceteri* is often used where *omnes* would at first sight be expected, because a limitation of the reference to a particular set of people is assumed though not stated explicitly. To take only one example, cf. Off. ii. § 37, *admiratione autem afficiuntur ei qui anteire ceteris virtute putantur*, i.e. the rest *of those among whom they live*. So here *ceteros*=the rest of the people (besides myself) whom Dion. desired to approach. But *contempti cuiusdam hominis* has all the appearance of being one of those exclamations with which copyists sometimes relieved their feelings, writing them on the margin.]

cuiusdam, 'a despicable kind of fellow.' *Quidam* slightly mitigates the force of the adj. or part. with which it is joined, like τις with adjectives in Greek and πως with adverbs.

subdoceri, 'secretly taught.' Cic. says that he preferred to face the reproaches of his brother Quintus and all his friends rather than give up eulogising Dion., and that rather than dismiss him for his incompetency as a teacher, he chose that his boys should be taught on the sly by himself. Possibly, however, the *sub-* indicates that Cic. was ready to take on himself the duties of an '*under* master,' ὑποδιδάσκαλος, to correct the deficiencies in the teaching of the boys' ostensible instructor.

Dicaearchum aut Aristoxenum. These philosophers are again mentioned together in Att. xiii. 32, 2. [*Dic.* and *Aristox.* constantly go together because of the similarity of their views about the soul; *e.g.* Tusc. i. 41. With this cf. Att. ix. 12, 2, where Cic. says he had treated Dion. with more distinction than Scipio showed to Panaetius.]

2. **memoria bona.** 'But you, his constant defender, will urge *he has a good memory.* He will find that I have a better.' The great merit of Dion. was the retentiveness of his memory. Cic. bitterly says he will find that his is better still, that is, he will never forget the ingratitude of Dionysius.

ita . . . ut, 'in a tone which I never used to any one in declining to take up his case.'

numquam . . . praecidit, 'never was client so low, so mean, so plainly guilty, or so completely a stranger to myself, that I gave him as abrupt a refusal as his flat, unceremonious, unqualified *No*.' The elliptic use of *tam*, which I have endeavoured to express by a paraphrase, is here complicated by the fact that it is followed by the regular and normal use of *tam* before *praecise*. After *humili* we must understand some such words as *quam qui humillimus*. The nearest literal translation, then, of *tam humili* would be 'ever so humble,' and this would be a suitable rendering as being itself a loose expression incapable of exact analysis, since the correct form seems to have been 'never so,' as in 'and heareth not the voice of the charmer, charm he never so wisely.'

praecise, ἀποτόμως. *Praecidit = praecise negavit*, Att. x. 16, 1.

in quo vitio nihil mali non inest. Cf. *ingratum si dixeris omnia dixti*, a familiar quotation of which I am not able to find the source.

3. **navem.** He had vessels in readiness at Caieta and Brundisium, Att. viii. 3, 6.

Gnaeum . . . desertum. The mss. have *Gnaeum ire Brundisium desertum*. Hence it is most probable that Cic. wrote

Gnacum ire Brundisium, iri Domitium desertum, and that the general likeness between *ire Brundisium* and *iri Domitium* caused the latter words to drop out. Still more naturally, if the archetype had *Brundisium ire* the words *Domitium iri* wou d have dropped out, the copyist raising his eyes after writing *i e,* and then, by an oversight, going on with the word after *iri*—a case of the common source of error in mss. called *corruptio ex homoeoteleuto.* This letter was written on Feb. 21 ; Domitius surrendered that very day. [Rather *Domitium desertum,* merely 'that he has turned his back on Dom.' With Antonius at Sulmo and P. on the march to Brund. Cic. would hardly say that Dom. was *going* to be deserted.]

LETTER XLIV. (ATT. VIII. 5)

1. Etsi. 'Yet (he might have come on his own mere motion and uninfluenced by you, for) he usually gets sorry after his tantrums.' Lit. 'it is accustomed to repent him,' *paeniter* being of course impersonal.

cerritior. This is the excellent conjecture of Bosius fo *certior* of the mss. *Certus* usually means 'safe' of a messenger : it also means 'firm,' 'determined,' Att. x. 11, 3. But here a word suitable to *furiose fecit* is evidently required ; such a word exactly is *cerritior,* and it is rare enough to be easily ousted by such a common word as *certior.*

a tertio miliario timuisse, 'after he had passed the third mile-stone,' that is, 'as soon as he had got well out of the city and its suburbs.' He was apparently resolved to leave the city and betake himself to some place where Cic. could not even communicate with him. But when he had passed the third mile-stone he 'became alarmed, took fright,' and went back again to Rome. For *tum cum isse,* which really has no meaning, I read *timuisse,* which would closely resemble *tm̄ cū isse* in the mss. For *timuisse* used absolutely 'to take alarm,' cf. Att. ix. 5, 3, *at ipsi tum se timuisse dicunt* (a passage which suggests that we ought perhaps here too to read *tum timuisse*) ; and *ab altera te ipsum nunquam timuisse certo scio,* Fam. vi. 1, 2. For *a* in the sense of 'after leaving' cf. *a Peducaeo,* Att. xii. 51, 1 ; so in Fam. x. 8, 2, *ab ea vita* is 'after such a life.'

πολλὰ . . . θυμήναντα. We do not know the source of this verse, but it doubtless comes from some Alexandrine poet. It probably suggested well-known passages to Virgil (A. xii.

104) and to Catullus (lxiv. 111), *nequicquam vanis iactantem cornua ventis.* It reminds us of the Euripidean ἐς κέρας θυμούμενοι (Bacch. 743), and may be rendered—

> When he had wreaked the fury of his horns
> On the void air in vain.

Cic. then goes on to explain the *sense* in which he quotes the verse, which is, 'after he had uttered many idle curses, which,' he adds, 'I hope will come home to roost, as the proverb has it.' *Cum dixisset,* the reading of the mss., is quite right and quite indispensable. Edd. make a great mistake in changing it to *eum dixisse.*

en. I have restored this word, which is demanded by the construction. Btr. inserts *o,* but *en* would have fallen out more easily before *m.* So in Att. xiv. 5, 2, I would restore *en meam stultitiam.* His placableness of disposition was shown by recalling the furious letter which he had written to Dionysius. [It must be allowed, I think, that Cic. used the accus. of exclamation without either *en* or *o.* The exx. are too numerous to be all due to the chances of mss. I would therefore not alter either this passage or Att. xiv. 5, 2, or Att. xv. 3, 2, *praeclaros XIV. ordines!*]

a pedibus meis, 'from personal attendance on myself,' which shows that Cic. had even to submit to personal inconvenience in recalling his angry missive. Body-servants in close attendance on their masters were said *a pedibus stare.* We have *a legatorum pedibus abduxerit* in Deiot. 2, and *circum pedes* in 2 Verr. i. 92. Victorius changed *meis* to *meum,* and supposed *servum a pedibus* to mean 'a valet,' but this designation of the duties of slaves by the prep. *a* is post-Ciceronian. [Are there exx. of *a pedibus stare?* Suet. has *ad pedes stare, ante pedes stare.* I think the text corrupt, and that Cic. wrote *ab aedibus,* which being written *abedibus* would almost inevitably pass to *a pedibus,* the phrase *servus a pedibus* being such a familiar one later on.]

2. de re Corfiniensi. I have inserted *de re* on the suggestion of Mr. Purser, who points out that it probably got out of its place and gave rise to the corrupt reading *des M'. Curio.* The regular prep. after *exspectatio* is *de;* cf. *exspectatione de Pompeio,* Att. iii. 14, 1. *Exspectatio Corfiniensis* for 'anticipations of what is going on in Corfinium' seems strange Latin; for some account of how things were going on at Corfinium see Att. viii. 3, 7. [I suppose it is the fact that *exspectatio* is a word describ-

ing the feelings of the mind, which makes this expression look
different from a hundred others, such as *pulsatio Putcolana;*
but I think it is hardly possible to set limits to the usage
whereby an adjective is substituted for a noun dependent on a
preposition. The best collection of examples is in a pamphlet,
"Ueber den Gebrauch des adjectivischen Attributs, etc.," by
Wichert (Berlin, Weidmann, 1875).]

velim. On this word depend *cures, commendes, roges,* with
the common ellipse of *ut* in each case.

LETTER XLV. (ATT. IX. 2)

1. **die tuo,** 'the day of your attack,' 'the day on which the
intermittent fever occurs': ὑπὸ τὴν λῆψιν is 'just as the attack
was coming on.' Cf. *sub.*

eam ipsam brevem. We have large quotations from this
short letter in Att. ix. 10, 8.

ita si, 'only if.'

2. **adesse,** sc. *in senatu.*

xxviratu. In the year 59 Cic. had offended both Caesar
and Pompeius by refusing a place among the twenty commissioners appointed under the Julian law for the division of the
Campanian land.

3. **ἀπαρρησίαστον,** 'his expostulation is estopped' because
he is now of opinion that Cicero's forecast of the whole situation
was more accurate than his own. Cic. had seen that the municipal towns could not hold out against Caesar, that men would
not answer the call of Pompeius to arms, that peace on any
terms was preferable to war, that the public funds were not
safe in the treasury, and that Picenum should be occupied by
Pompeius.

cum potuero. Caesar not now stopping the way to Brundisium.

iure, 'he will be justly hostile to me if I refuse to join him
when there is nothing to prevent me.' Boot corrected *tum* of
the mss. to *iure.*

τίς δ' . . . ὤν, quoted by Plut. as from Eur.

ἀσμενιστὸν, 'acceptable'; this is a verbal adj. in the positive
degree from ἀσμενίζω, and should be accented as in text, not

ἀσμένιστον, which is usually, but wrongly, taken as a superlative of ἄσμενος ; for in the first place the word could then only mean 'very glad,' not 'very welcome,' which latter sense the passage demands ; and secondly, the superl. of ἄσμενος used by Cic. is ἀσμεναίτατος. See Att. xiii. 22, 1, where ἀσμεναίτατα means, as it ought to mean, 'most gladly.'

temperatius. This, not *temperantius*, is the right reading, for *temperate* is often used by Cic., *temperanter* never. The difference between the two words would be infinitesimal in a ms., the *n* being indicated only by a horizontal stroke over the *a*, which was often omitted.

hic, Caesar.

Vetant. This is the certain correction by Boot of the ms. *vita.* The influences which forbid him to adopt any but a desperate course are—'his character, his previous history, the nature of the enterprise on which he has embarked, the material strength or even the moral firmness of the Pompeian party.' *Ante facta* is probably an allusion to the complicity of Caesar in the Catilinarian conspiracy (see Correspondence of Cicero, vol. i. pp. 17-19), which is more clearly recognised in a subsequent letter (Att. x. 8, 8), *non est committendum ut iis pareamus quos contra me senatus, ne quid resp. detrimenti caperet, armavit.* (Observe the strange ambiguity introduced into this sentence by the anastrophe of *contra*, a figure which Cic. affects ; cf. *quem contra* = 'against whom,' Mur. 9 ; 2 Verr. v. 153.) Boot does not seem justified in giving to *constantia* the bad sense of 'obstinacy': I cannot find that Cic. ever uses the word except in a good sense. Indeed, it is contrasted with 'obstinacy' in Mur. 31, *quae enim* pertinacia *quibusdam, eadem aliis* constantia *videri potest.* In this passage, however, I believe that both *vires* and *constantia*, though bearing their natural meaning, are used ironically by Cicero, who does not in his letters seriously ascribe either material or moral strength to the partisans of Pompeius. Lehmann (Quaestiones Tullianae, p. 111) suggests that we should read *vetant vita mores*, etc., and suppose *vetant* to have been lost from the text of the mss. through its similarity to *vita*, which followed it in the archetype. He compares *quid acta tua vita . . . flagitet*, Fam. iv. 13, 4 ; *et vita et fortuna tua . . . invitet*, Phil. x. 3 ; *mores ipsius et vita*, Sull. 71 ; *usus vita mores civitas ipsa respuit*, Mur. 74.

4. currens ad illum, 'hurrying to join Caesar.'

eripiebat . . . persequebatur, 'he talked of Caesar's

s

wresting the Spains from Pompeius, occupying Asia, and pursuing Pompeius into Greece.' This use of the verb is very rare in Latin, but not so unusual in Greek, *e.g.* σὺ δ' ᾖσθα Οηβῶν . . . ἄναξ, Eur. Herc. Fur. 462, means 'you (he used to say) are king of Thebes'; πλουτεῖς ἐν οὐ πλουτοῦσι, 'you talk of yourself as an heiress among beggars,' Andr. 211. So Ar. Thesm. 616, τί καρδαμίζεις = 'cross me no cresses,' *i.e.* 'don't talk to me about cresses'; Vesp. 652, μὴ πατέριζε, 'father me no fathers.' Not unlike is *voto . . . mittit in hortos,* Pers. ii. 36, for 'she prays that he may come to those pleasure-grounds.'

quicumque sunt, 'whatever they are.' He will not allow that they deserve the name *boni,* which he generally applies to the Pompeian party. This shows that he is using language ironically above when he speaks of their *vires* and *constantia.*

LETTER XLVI. (ATT. x. 17)

At this time Cicero was desirous of leaving Italy, but was not at all sure that his attempt to embark would not be resisted by Caesar. He reposed great hopes in the apparent cordiality of Hortensius, who held a command under Caesar; but we find from what he says in the next letter that his hopes were ill founded.

1. **Pridie Idus.** 'On the 14th of May Hortensius called on me just as I had finished my letter to you. I only hope the rest of his conduct towards me will be of a piece with his present demeanour. You would hardly believe he could have gushed so. I mean to take advantage of it.' *Vellem cetera cius* is highly elliptical, but not more so than is characteristic of Cicero's epistolary style. The same sentiment is again expressed below. Cic. fears the amiability of Hortensius is too great to last. And so it proved. The Greek word corresponds to a slang expression with us. In the same way in the correspondence we find ἄμορφον, 'bad form'; ἐπίτηκτα, 'veneering'; ἐξοχή, 'a lead'; ὀξύπεινος, 'peckish'; ἐξακανθίζειν, 'to pick holes.' [*Vellem cetera = scripta essent:* 'I would rather he had confined himself entirely to writing.']

aperuissem. This is the reading of the mss. which many edd. retain; '*foedo mendo,*' says Wes., 'because Cic. never uses the subjunctive when one thing is simply said to have occurred before another.' True; but this passage does not say simply that Cic. before opening the letter told Serapion how kindly Att. had already written about him. No; 'prior to opening the letter,' and deliberately so, was Cicero's statement about Att. If he had waited till he had opened the letter which Serapion brought, the latter would not have believed that Att. had already recommended him; so 'as a preliminary to opening' the letter of recommendation, Cic. told Ser. how kindly Att. had already written and spoken. The subj. is quite requisite to express that thought. Then 'after skimming the letter,' says Cic., 'I entered on the whole matter in the fullest detail,' telling Serapion all that Att. had written in his praise. [*Aperuissem.* I entirely agree.]

stricta. The reading of the mss. is *scripta*, which is clearly wrong. Most edd. read *lecta*, which of course gives a very good sense; but why was it superseded by *scripta?* The corrupt word must have been some rare one which the copyists did not understand, and some word far more like *scripta* than *lecta* is. Such a word we have in *stricta*, which nowhere else is used in the sense of 'to skim,' or 'hastily read.' But *strictim attingere, legere, scribere,* etc., are common enough expressions, and *stringere cautes* is 'to graze the cliffs'; *stringere* is also 'to treat a subject concisely,' and *strictus* is 'concise.' These senses come so near to that ascribed to the word here that I think we are justified in supposing that Cic. in a familiar letter used the word in this sense, and that, being misunderstood by the copyists, it gave place to the very common word *scripta* of the mss. [*Stricta.* I think this passage is one of many where confusion has been caused by the contraction *apta* for *aperta*, which I think to be the original reading.]

quin . . . puto, 'nay, even I think I will make use of his vessel and take him as my fellow-passenger.' Cic. seems to have contemplated taking Serapion as a tutor for his boys, and as a successor to Dionysius.

2. Crebro refricat, 'My sore eyes give me annoyance from time to time—no very great annoyance indeed, but enough to make writing inconvenient.'

3. perturbatum, 'boisterous,' 'tempestuous.'

Inde si ἀκραὲς erit, 'then if a brisk breeze for sailing springs up (and thus I am enabled to sail), I only pray that Hortensius may maintain his present amiability (and assist me); since so far nothing could be more courteous than his demeanour.' It is possible, however, that there is a certain humorousness in the passage: 'if the wind proves fair, I only hope the temper

of Hortensius will be like it.' The word ἀκραές is the conjecture
of Bosius for *cras* of the mss. The very word for the wind
that Cic. wanted is ἀκραής, which is always used in Homer for
a 'brisk, steady' breeze, enabling a man to start on a voyage.
Hitherto the wind was boisterous and squally, chopping and
changing, all of which is implied in *perturbatum*. The very
opposite kind of weather to that indicated by ἀκραής is a calm;
and that was the weather which it was his lot to meet: see
next letter where he complains of the *mirificae tranquillitates*.
He hoped to be enabled to sail by the connivance of Hortensius,
who held a command under Caesar, and who might have made
himself very disagreeable to Cicero, but who so far was all that
could be desired. It turned out, however, that his 'gush' was
all humbug (*infantia*), as we read in the next letter. I have
accepted *inde*, Dr. Reid's correction of the ms. reading *d*.
One might say that the *aequinoctium* was *perturbatum*, but one
could not call it ἀκραές, which could only be used of a wind.
Erit is impersonal.

4. diplomate. This word generally refers (1) to a state
letter of recommendation given to a person travelling in the
provinces; (2) to a document drawn up by a magistrate,
securing to the holder some favour or privilege, especially to
soldiers. Here the reference seems to be to 'a pass or passport;'
which Caesar himself issued permitting persons to leave Italy;
or to return to Rome from abroad (Fam. vi. 12, 3). Cic. seen s
to have said something implying that Att. had procured such a
passport, and Att. seems to have resented this, as if Cic. had
thought him capable of a crime. It seems Att. had secured a
passport for the young Ciceros, which led Cic. to suppose he
would use one himself; moreover, Cic. was under the impression
that such a document was indispensable for those who wished
to leave Italy or to re-enter Rome.

LETTER XLVII. (ATT. x. 18)

1. xiiii. Kal. Iun., May 19. Before the reformation of the
calendar by Caesar, B.C. 45, March, May, July, October had
each thirty-one days, Feb. twenty-eight, and the rest twenty-
nine. Therefore May 19 is fourteen days before June 1, reckoning inclusively after the Roman fashion. Att. xii. 21, written
in the spring of 45, is the first letter written after the reformation of the calendar. In it and the subsequent letters

we must calculate our dates on the principle that the Roman months contain the same number of days as they do now.

ἑπταμηνιαῖον, 'a seven-months' child.' For this and *εὐτόκησε* cf. note on Ep. iv. 1 concerning the use of Greek terms in medicine and hygiene.

est quod gaudeam, 'I have reason to be glad.'

Quod natum. It is the habit of Cic. to use the neuter gender with reference not only to the unborn, but to the newly born, infant.

Nam illa Hortensiana. Cic., in telling Att. that he is under surveillance, adds that all his hopes founded on the amiability of Hortensius have been dissipated, 'all the gush of Hortensius turns out to be mere moonshine.' The word *infantia* is very probably corrupt; whether we take it as the nom. sing. of the subst. or the nom. plur. of the adj. it is not a suitable word. It ought to indicate, as it does elsewhere in the writings of Cic., 'a want of eloquence,' 'incapability of expressing oneself,' but here it must bear the much later meaning of 'folly,' 'drivelling.' The force of *nam* is this : 'the calms are a worse obstacle to me than the surveillance to which I am subjected, (I am under surveillance), for the gush of Hortensius turns out to be all nonsense.' Att. might have judged from the previous letter of Cic. that the surveillance of Hortensius was a mere form, if Cic. had not here put him in possession of the real facts of the case. [For *fuere infantia* I would read *fuerunt* (the other form is highly improbable in Cic.) *fatua ;* if *fatua* were accidentally written *fantua, infantia* would result, like *temperantius* above for *temperatius.* A subject for *depravatus est* seems to have dropped out ; probably the name of a letter-carrier who had allowed Salvius (freedman of Hort.?) to open Cic.'s letters and betray Cic.'s designs to Hortensius. This supposition seems necessary to account for Cic.'s resolve to say no more about his plans.]

Ita fiet, 'So it will be found to be'; cf. *quiescet,* Juv. i. 126, and Mayor's note there. The most common example of this use of the fut. is *sic erit,* 'you will find it to be so,' which is frequent in the comic drama, so that we need not regard with suspicion a similar usage in the letters of Cicero. Cf. *incrunt,* 'there will be found to be in the purse,' Plaut. As. 727 ; *conveniet,* 'you'll find it right,' Ter. Phorm. 53.

Κωρυκαῖοι, a general term for 'spies,' 'eaves-droppers,' borrowed from the name of a seafaring folk who lived on the promontory of Corycus in Pamphylia, and earned a livelihood by gathering information for the pirates who infested the coasts of Asia Minor.

2. nec . . . cursu, 'do not count on any letters from me unless I reach my destination, or possibly get a chance of communicating with you from shipboard.'

tarda et spissa, 'everything so far goes so slowly and heavily.' *Spissa* contains a metaphor drawn from a heavy muddy road.

sequimur, 'Formiae is my present destination'; cf. Virg. Aen. iv. 361, *Italiam non sponte sequor.*

non probamus de Melita, 'to judge from your talk w th Balbus, my project of going to Melita does not meet the views of Caesar'; lit. 'we do not approve, commend, to Caesar.'

Egi gratias. De altero, 'I thanked him (for his good will). As regards the other point (his suspicion that I was seeking an opportunity to join Pompeius), I put myself right with him.' Cic. may have possibly written *de altero* twice, which would be a little clearer, but the text as it stands in t ms. is quite accurate enough for the demands of the epistola y style.

3. infeliciorem, sc. *nosti, vidisti.*

conficior venisse, 'I am tortured (by the thought) that the time has come when I can no longer act with either boldness or discretion.' For the infinitive as oblique predicate with its subject in the accusative, the whole expression forming the object after a verb, see Roby, ii. 1351, 1352. A good parallel example is Att. xi. 17, 1, *incredibili sum dolore affectus tale ingenium in tam misera fortuna versari.*

LETTER XLVIII. (ATT. XI. 1)

In the interval between the last letter and this Cicero left Italy (June 11) and crossed over to Dyrrachium, with his brother, his son, and his nephew, to join Pompeius. Caesar had now made himself master of Spain, become dictator, and defeated Pompeius at Pharsalia, during which engagement Cic. was at Dyrrachium. Cic. returned to Brundisium at the end of November, 48. The following letter was written from Epirus.

1. signatum, 'sealed,' not 'signed.' The practice of sealing among the Romans was merely for security. It was not, as with us, an element in the due execution of a document (Roby, Classical Review, vol. i. p. 69).

qui eas dispensavit, Philotimus.

existimationis, 'my credit.' Cf. *ut bonum nomen existimor*, Fam. v. 6, 2. 'Credit' is more usually *fides*, as below, § 2.

2. **cistophoro**, an Asiatic coin, so called from the device stamped on it, the sacred *cista* of Dionysus half open, with a snake creeping out of it. The value of the *cistophorus* was probably about three *denarii*.

permutatione, 'by negotiating a bill of exchange to that amount.'

credens ei, sc. Philotimo.

LETTER XLIX. (FAM. IX. 16)

1. **amavi amorem tuum**, 'I was charmed with your affection for me.' See on Ep. xxxix. 1.

Silius, probably the propraetor of Bithynia in 50 (Fam. xiii. 61). He doubtless brought some message which made Cic. uneasy with regard to the feelings which Caesar entertained towards him.

bis quidem, 'twice indeed in exactly the same terms.' Paetus sent two copies of the same letter by different messengers to make sure of his warning reaching Cic.

2. **sed tamen**, 'but, however that may be, whatever can be wrought or effected to win and get a fund of good-will with those friends of yours (*Caesarianos*), that I have sought to accomplish by most earnest efforts ; and successfully too, as I think : for I am so esteemed and respected by all those who are intimates of Caesar that I think I may say they actually love me.' For *sed tamen* resumptive see Reid on Acad. ii. 17. *Diligere* is weaker than *amare ;* cf. ad Brut. i. 1, 1, *Clodius valde me diligit, vel, ut ἐμφατικώτερον dicam, valde me amat.*

Tametsi. This is Cratander's excellent correction of *nam etsi* of the mss.

perspici. This passage, among others, shows that *perspicere* is the regular word for the trying of friendship like gold : cf.

Catull. c. 6, *perspecta est igni tum unica amicitia,* according to Prof. A. Palmer's certain restoration of the poet's text.

3. **praestari,** ' to be guaranteed.'

nihil loqui. Supply from the preceding clause *arbitror nunc esse meum.*

4. **notandis . . . legendi,** ' by marking the different styles of poetry and habitually studying them.' For *notare,* ' to mark clearly,' cf. Fam. vii. 2, 1, *equidem sperabam ita no ata me reliquisse genera dictorum meorum ut cognosci sua sponte possent,* ' I hoped that my *bons mots* had such a characteristic *genre* of their own.' Caesar was making a collection of *bons mots* or witty apophthegms. Cic. had a great reputation for wit ; *habitus est nimius risus adfectator,* says Quintilian, vi. 3 3.

actis, ' the news of the day.' Cf. *res urbanas actaque omnia,* Fam. x. 28, 3.

audiendum, here curiously used in a different sense from the immediately preceding *audiat,* ' if he hears anything el e, he does not give ear (pay attention) to it.'

Oenomao tuo nihil utor, ' I have no use for your quotation from the Oenomaus of Accius, tho' it came in so pat.' Paetus had quoted some verses from that play on the wisdom of avoid-ing the making of enemies. *Loco* is ' their *proper* place,' a meaning which *locus* often has, and hence *apponere loco* is ' o quote appositely.'

5. **posse,** sc. *invideri.* Cf. Phil. ii. 5, *cum tu occideres. Fac potuisse* (sc. *te eum occidere*).

praestare, ' to guarantee,' as above ; here it means t) ' guarantee (the absence of) what is blameworthy,' ' to b answerable for one's own innocence.' So *consilium,* Att. v. 10, 3, really means ' my *want of* forethought ' ; Att. iv. 16, 1 *epistolarum frequentia* means ' *want of* regularity as a corre spondent ' ; and in Hor. Sat. ii. 4, 85, *haec . . . reprehend. iustius illis,* the meaning is ' *the absence of* these can be con-demned more fairly than *the absence of* those.'

Reliquum est, ne quid. Wesenberg (Em. Alt. 29) would insert *ut* before *ne ;* but Reid (Lael. 42) has shown that *ne* and *ut ne* are used indiscriminately by Cic. in short final sentences.

6. **fluctum a saxo frangi.** Wesenberg marks this as a quotation ; it does not, however, seem to be a quotation, but rather an adaptation by Cic. of an image of Accius to express a thought of his own. Oenomaus, it appears, in the play of Accius

so called, was alarmed at an oracle which told him to beware of
Pelops. The latter tried to reassure him, that he was going to
act fairly, that he wanted to marry Hippodameia, not to injure
Oenomaus, but, says Oenomaus,

> Saxum id facit angustitatem, et sub eo saxo exuberans
> Scatebra fluviae radit rupem ;

that is, as the waves by their perpetual action wear away a
rock, so does this suspicion beset him and wear him away.
Paetus must have used the image of Accius to indicate the
ceaseless and silent working of envy which he feared might
finally ruin Cic. Cic. explains at length how he cannot be
exposed to jealous hatred, and finally accepts the simile but
transfers it to the action of fortune, 'let the waves of chance
beat as they will against the strong man, they beat as idly as
the tide against a cliff.' The term is Cicero's own, and is not
at all likely to have ever stood in the play of Accius.

Athenis vel Syracusis, *e.g.* Socrates at Athens under the
Thirty, and Plato at Syracuse under Dionysius.

7. secundum. 'You have brought on as an afterpiece to
the Oenomaus of Accius, not an Atellane comedy, as the fashion
used to be, but a farce, as is the *mode* now.' Since the time of
Sulla the mime had more and more superseded the Atellane
comedy as an afterpiece. The *mimus* was much looser and
coarser than the *Atellana*. See Dict. of Ant. s.v. *mimus*, and
for *fabulae Atellanae* Mommsen, bk. iii. ch. 14.

Quem tu mihi pompilum, 'What is this pilot-fish you
talk to me of, this thunny-dinner, this dish of stock-fish and
cheese ?' *Pompilum* and *thunnarium* are the corrections suggested by Rutilius for *popilium* and *denarium* of the mss.
Denarium, indeed, might be retained. Paetus may have said
that he would entertain Cic. at the cost of a *denarius*, and Cic.
might write in joke, 'What is this penny-dinner you offer
me ?'

Hirtium et Dolabellam. These were well-known *gourmets;*
they were learning the art of speaking with Cic., and were, he
says, imparting to him the art of the *bon vivant* in return.

`      bonam copiam eiures,` 'your pleading insolvency to me is
no use.'

quaesticulis, 'it (your property) obliged you to be somewhat
careful about small gains.' *Quaesticulis*, the reading of the
mss., is rightly retained by Hofm. [*Quaesticulis*. I cannot
remember an ex. of *attentus* with dat. in prose. Usually it is

used by itself, without any further constr., but sometimes with *in* and abl. or *ad* and acc.   In Hor. there is of course a cat. (*attentus quaesitis*).]

non est quod, 'there is no reason why.'   It is quite neces- sary to insert the words *est quod* with Wesenberg ; *non sis* would be a solecism for *ne fueris ;* even if with C. F. Müller we read *non eo sis censeo animo*, the proper particle would be *ne.*   Paetus had sustained some pecuniary loss, which the jocular tone of the allusions shows not to have been seriou s; probably he had been obliged to accept an *aestimatio* instead of full payment from some debtors.   [May not *non eo sis consilio ut* mean 'you would never think it necessary to'?]

aestimationem, 'valuation,' *i.e.* property made over to or e on a valuation, hence here much the same as 'composition.' The abstract *emptio*, 'purchase,' is used in the same way for 'the thing purchased.'   According to one of Caesar's laws about debt, creditors were obliged to take in payment the lands of their debtors, the value of the lands being estimated by the price which they would have fetched before the war.   By this law all creditors lost about a fourth of the money claimed by them.   Lands made over to their creditors by debtors at a valuation were called *aestimationes.*

levior ab amico, 'such a blow comes less heavily from a friend than a debtor.'

8. **eas . . . ut,** 'the sort of dinner where there would be quantities of things left untouched.'

temperius, 'earlier'; the more luxurious the Roman dinners were, the earlier they began ; hence *tempestiva convivia* means 'grand (smart) dinner-parties,' Att. ix. 1, 3.

matris tuae, 'a dinner like your mother's,' that is, old- fashioned and frugal.

polypum miniati Iovis similem, 'a polypus cooked as red as the ruddled Jupiter.'   Pliny, H. N. xxxiii. § 112, tells us that Verrius adduces unimpeachable authority for the fact that on festal days it was once the custom to paint the statue of Jupiter vermilion.   The polypus was not naturally red, but assumed that colour when cooked with a coarse red sauce.

mea nova lautitia, 'my late conversion to smartness.'

promulside, 'the first course,' consisting of eggs, olives, salt-fish, sausages (*lucanicis*), and such like savoury *hors d'œuvre* taken to whet the appetite.   The drink was generally mead (*mulsum*), whence the name. It was also called *gustus* and *gustatio*. Cic. says he has abolished the 'antepast' because he found it 'took the vigour out of' his appetite.

9. **superiora illa lusimus,** 'what I said above was only in fun.'

10. **villa Seliciana,** a villa at Naples belonging to the banker Selicius which Paetus told Cic. not to buy.

Salis . . . parum, 'We have had enough joking, too little sober sense.' This is his excuse for putting in a remark about business at the end of a letter chiefly devoted to jokes. The mss. read *sannonum*, and many editors give *sannionum*. These words could only mean 'there is much material for jesting, but few jokers' (or rather 'clowns'), *i.e.* few with the heart to joke. The words would with this reading better follow the verb *lusimus.* Hofm. suggested *sanorum*, showing that Cic. thus uses the neuter plural of adjectives by adducing Or. ii. 111, 262. I prefer the comparative, both as suiting the sense better and as being nearer to the reading of the mss., which present *sannonum* or *sanniorum.*

LETTER L. (FAM. IX. 18)

1. **ob viam,** to meet Caesar.

eadem, sc. *viâ,* or *operâ.* *Via* might easily be taken out of *ob viam,* but *eadem opera* is very common in the comic drama, in the sense of 'as part of the same act (transaction),' 'while I am about it.' 'You might as well whistle jigs to a milestone' would be expressed by *una* (sc. *operâ*) in Plautus.

plenissimas suavitatis, 'most charming.'

ludum aperuisse. Who would have said that *ludum aperire* was good Latin for 'opening a school,' were it not that we have here Ciceronian warrant for it ?

sublatis iudiciis, a Ciceronian exaggeration of the fact that trials were not as regularly conducted as they used to be. For the irregularity of legal procedure during the civil war see Mommsen, R. H. iv. 325, 485.

regno forensi, 'my primacy at the bar.'

2. **Id cuius modi sit,** 'the value of this protection I do not know.'

in lectulo. Cic. is perhaps alluding to the illness fiom which he was suffering while the battle of Pharsalia was being fought (Plut. Cic. 39).

Lentulus tuus. It is uncertain whether this is the Lentulus who was consul in 49, and was put to death in prison by Ptolemy (Caes. B. C. iii. 104), or P. Lentulus Spinther, to whom Cic. addressed the letters in Fam. i. We do not know what was the end of the latter, but he was dead in 43 when Cic. delivered Phil. xiii. 29.

Scipio. Metellus Scipio, father-in-law of Pompeius, endeavoured to escape to Sicily after the battle of Thapsus, but was overpowered by Sittius, and (probably) destroyed himself. Afranius met his death at the hands of the forces of Sittius (Bell. Afr. 95, 96).

foede, 'miserably,' not 'disgracefully.'

istuc quidem licebit, sc. *ire* or *me conferre.*

id quod agimus, 'and that is what I am now aiming at.'

3. Ergo hoc primum, 'This, then, is my first advantage,' namely, that I am trying to act in a conciliatory manner towards the victors. 'There follows another,' namely, that my health is improving.

intermissis exercitationibus, sc. *declamandi.* The Romans practised declamation to supply the place of that physical exercise for which we have recourse to field sports and out-of-door pursuits of various kinds. Cf. Phil. ii. 42.

facultas . . . exaruisset, 'the founts of my inspiration would have run dry.'

Hateriano iure. Haterius seems to have been an advocate who was staying with Paetus at this time. Cic. cannot refrain from his well-worn play on the double meaning of *ius*, 'legal procedure' and 'sauce.' He had made the same joke twenty-four years before, 1 Verr. i. 121.

προλεγομένας, sc. θέσεις, 'principles and axioms' (of the art of cookery) ; the expression was also applied to the principles of rhetoric and law. Perhaps 'institutes' would be a fit rendering.

sus Minervam, sc. *docebo;* 'tho' it is a case of teaching one's grandmother.' For the proverb see De Orat. ii. 233 ; Acad. i. 18 ; ὖς ποτ' Ἀθηναίαν ἔριν ἤρισε, Theocr. v. 23 ; the shorter form ἡ ὖς τὴν Ἀθηνᾶν is found in Plut. Demosth. 11.

4. Sed quo modo, videro, 'But as to the ways and means (of your getting the instruction), I shall see to that.' [*Quo modo videro:* very unsatisfactory. Perhaps we should read *quoquo modo, te videro.* 'There is of course no need for you to take lessons from me in what you know very well already; but whatever be the pretext, I shall have the advantage of seeing you.']

aestimationes. See on last letter, § 7.

item istic, at Naples. The meaning is, 'I hope your friends too at Naples are as hard up, so that they may not be able to entertain you well, and so keep you there.' Wes. reads *item istic.* The reading of the mss. is *idem istuc.*

cantherium comedisti, 'you have eaten your pack-horse,' that is, you have thrown away on dinners the money which would have kept your pack-horse.

hypodidascalo, *privat-docent.*

proxima, 'next to mine.'

pulvinus sequetur, 'a cushion will come in due time.'

LETTER LI. (ATT. XII. 6)

1. Caelio. Caelius was a banker; Cic. refers to him Att. xii. 5, 2.

lacuna, 'flaw,' 'defect' in the gold; the word is sometimes used by Cic. to indicate more generally 'loss,' e.g. *lacunam rei familiaris explere,* 2 Verr. ii. 138. The Latin for a 'dimple' is *lacuna.*

ista non novi, 'I am not versed in such matters.'

collubo, 'exchange,' 'agio.' Cic. says 'the exchange will involve loss enough; if to this is to be added loss arising from the inferior quality of the material of the coin——' and then breaks off with an aposiopesis, which he says is characteristic of the style of the rhetorician Hegesias, who introduced the Asiatic school of rhetoric, and who was commended by Varro. For Hegesias of Magnesia see Mommsen, iv. p. 567. Mommsen makes him responsible for 'the vulgarism of Asia Minor,' which was a reaction from the classicism which had hitherto prevailed in the higher language of conversation, and consequently also in literature. Hegesias and his school rebelled 'against the orthodox Atticism, and demanded full currency

for the language of life without distinction, whether the word
or phrase originated in Attica, or in Caria and Phrygia.'
The prevailing characteristic of the style of Hegesias was its
'abruptness.'

2. **Tyrannionem.** Tyrannio had written a book on accents,
περὶ προσῳδιῶν, which Cic. was annoyed to find that Atticus
had read without waiting for him to read it with him. Cic.
had more than once put off his perusal of the work until
Atticus should be with him. He says Att. can only atone for
his error now by sending him the book.

πάντα φιλειδήμονα. This is a very probable correction of
φιλόδημον of the mss. which used to be explained by supposing
that Cic. writes to Att. 'I like every man to be patriotic,' and
so I am glad to find that you, *Atticus*, admire the work of this
Greek, Tyrannio. But this is very forced, and the corrected
reading gives a natural sentiment, and one often expressed or
hinted at by Cic. 'I like every man to have a taste for knowledge' (of all sorts). I should prefer to read παντοφιλειδήμονα, a
word which would have been very likely to undergo corruption.
He likes a man to desire knowledge *of all sorts*, even of such
minute studies as the doctrine of accentuation. Reading πάντα
φιλειδήμονα we are obliged to supply in thought a word or words
expressing 'of all sorts,' which is conveyed by παντοφιλειδήμονα.
He often quotes the Greek sentiment, γλυκύτερον οὐδὲν ἢ πάντ'
εἰδέναι.

tua sunt eius modi omnia, 'the whole bent of your mind
is for subtle speculations.'

quo uno, 'you desire knowledge, which is the only *pabulum*
of the mind.' This is a good example of the difference between
the indicative and subjunctive ; with *alatur* the meaning would
be 'you want to know by what the mind is fed.'

quid ex ista acuta et gravi, 'what in that *acute and grave*
treatise has any bearing on the *ultimate principle* of conduct ?'
The epithets chosen contain a play on the 'acute and grave'
accents, which were the subject of the treatise ; Cic. had projected at this time the De Finibus, a treatise on the τέλος, the
summum bonum or ultimate principle of conduct ; no doubt
he had unfolded his project to Atticus in a lost letter, and now
observes that this particular study is not germane to its scope.

Sed longa oratio. I cannot understand this passage at all,
except on the hypothesis that a sentence has fallen out in
which Cic. wrote to Att. about his projected De Finibus, and

probably asked Att. to give his judgment on some scheme of
the future work. The missing sentence may have ended with
the word τέλος, and so may have fallen a victim to that common source of omissions in mss. called *corruptio ex homoeoteleuto.*
He breaks off with the reflection, 'It would take a long time
to develop to you my scheme, and you are busy, probably on
my affairs.'

asso sole. In his Brutus Cic. introduced Atticus as one of
the interlocutors in the discussion about distinguished orators
held *in pratulo propter Platonis statuam* (Brut. 24). Att. had
a far higher opinion of that treatise than Cic. himself entertained. Now if we may assume that Cic. thought of giving
Att. a place among the speakers in the De Finibus he might
very well have written here words which would playfully
express the sentiment that he would put into the mouth of
Att. in the projected dialogue far more ornate and elegant
language than that with which he had furnished him in the
Brutus. He calls the whole dialogue 'a basking' (*sole*) because
it was held *in pratulo*, and he writes, 'Instead of that dry
basking in the meadow we shall call on you for one full of
unguents and all sorts of brilliancy.' Then he returns to the
subject of Tyrannio's book on accents. He did introduce Att.
into De Fin. v., but did not give him much to say. In Att.
xiii. 12, 3, he calls the De Fin. περὶ τελῶν σύνταξιν, and writes,
Bruto ut tibi placuit despondimus. Perhaps Att. requested
Cic. not to give him an important place among the characters
in the dialogue. [τέλος. I feel sure there is no allusion to the
De Finibus. The word τέλος is to be explained by *tua sunt
eius modi omnia: scire enim vis.* The τέλος of Atticus is to
obtain knowledge. But is any real knowledge to be gained
from a work on so trivial a subject as that of accentuation? It
would take long to discuss the point, as Att. is so delighted
with Tyrannio's book. The sentence *Et pro isto . . . repetemus*
is to be explained by the one preceding. Its general drift is,
'I shall be getting a much greater boon from you (in the great
attention you are giving to my affairs; cf. the last sentence of
Att. xii. 5, 2, *te quidem . . . ignota*) than the boon I conferred
on you (in giving you a place in my Brutus).' *Repetemus* = I
shall be claiming in return.]

abusus es. *Abuti* is much the same as *uti* in many passages of Cic.; in others of course it means 'to use ill,' 'to
abuse.'

3. Chremes . . . tibi. Ter. Heaut. i. 1. 23.

Aristophanem . . . pro Eupoli. See Orator, 29, and
Sandys's note there. The verses which Cic. wrongly ascribed
to Eupolis were verses in the Acharnians of Aristoph.—

> ἐντεῦθεν ὀργῇ Περικλέης Οὐλύμπιος
> ἤστραπτ᾽ ἐβρόντα ξυνεκύκα τὴν Ἑλλάδα.

The mistake of Cic. arose from the fact that Eupolis also often
called Pericles 'the Olympian' or Zeus (ὁ σχινοκέφαλος Ζεύ).
In Brut. 39 and 59 Cic. refers to two celebrated eulogies of
Eupolis on Pericles, that ' he alone of all the speakers left his
sting in his hearers,' and that 'persuasion sat upon his lips.'

4. quaeso. Att. must have used this word too often, and
thus incurred the bantering of Caesar. The word itself is often
used by Cic.

εὐπινές, 'quaint,' almost as we would say 'a classicism.'

dubitationem. This refers to the case of the Buthrotians
who were in danger of confiscation, but owed their preservation
to the good offices of Att. with Caesar. Cic. says the tone of
Caesar to Att. was such as to leave no doubt in his mind that
everything would go as Att. wished.

tam diu, sc. *febri laborare.*

horrore, 'shivering.'

LETTER LII. (FAM. IX. 19)

1. malitia, 'so you won't give up your tricks, no matter
what I say (*tamen*).' For *malitia* in the sense of the *esprit
malin,* and so generally 'shrewdness,' cf. Att. xv. 26, 4. So
also Plancus, Fam. x. 21, 3, *non malus homo.* The word
malitia ought in this sense to be brought to the aid of a
corrupt passage in Att. xiii. 22, 4, where for *a quibus sine te
opprimi militia est. Alteris* I would read *a quibus sine tua
opprimi malitia! Est alteris,* etc., 'to think of my being pounced
on by them without your shrewdness to help me! There is in
the other letter,' etc. *Nisi tua malitia adfuisset* (Att. xv. 26,
4) is exactly parallel to *sine tua malitia.*

Tenuiculo apparatu, 'A very poor spread.'

reges, a sneer at the Caesarians, who have abolished the
free state.

Nescis . . . venisse, 'You don't know that I fished all the

news out of him, by reason of the fact that he had come straight
from the gate to my door. I am not surprised at his not going
to his own door, but at his not going to his own dear.' The
play of fancy which Cicero expresses by the omission of the
prep. we must reproduce less neatly by a play on words.
Venit domum suam is good Latin for 'he came home' but 'he
came to his own (girl)' demands a prep. Cic. makes insinua-
tions against the sobriety of Balbus in another letter to Paetus
(Fam. ix. 17, 1). Some edd. change *suam* of the mss. to
suum, by which they understand *Caesarem*, 'his patron.' [*Recta
enim*, etc.: *enim* is probably a corruption of *eum*; the two words
are frequently confused.]

tribus primis verbis, 'the first three words I spoke to
him.' But *tertio quoque verbo* means 'at every second word.'

libentius, sc. *fuisse*.

2. verbis ... opsonio, 'conversation ... catering.' 'If it
was your conversation which made Balbus enjoy himself so
much, I must try not to be too hard to please; if it was your
catering, pray remember that I, the eloquent, have as good a
right to be considered as a *stammerer*.' Cic. puns on the
meaning of Balbus, to which is opposed *disertus*, the adj.
which is applied to him by Catullus in the poem beginning
Disertissime Romuli nepotum.

non committam, 'I shall take good care that you shall
not say I have given you insufficient notice.'

LETTER LIII. (FAM. IX. 20)

1. scurram velitem, 'that I like a light-armed wit-slinger
have received a fusillade of raillery from you.' There is a perfect
volley of jokes here. The *scurra* or parasite who was invited to
dinner for his light and ready jests on everybody and everything
(Plin. Ep. ix. 17, 2) is likened to a light-armed soldier who
could move quickly about and direct his sling or bow at any
point while lightly skirmishing with the enemy; we should
more naturally take the metaphor from a light-weight in the
prize-ring. These parasites seem to have been made the butt
of a good deal of horse-play, such as having pots and other
utensils broken about their heads (Plaut. Capt. i. 1. 20, iii.
1. 12). They were often, no doubt, pelted not only with raillery
(*malis*) but with material missiles such as apples (*malis*), which,

T

forming part of every *cena*, would furnish convenient projectiles
to be used against the *scurra*.   It may be, too, as some of the
commentators have suggested, that Paetus had sent Cic. a
present of apples, or promised him some particularly fine ones for
second course.   We may feel pretty sure that Cic. here introduces a play on *malis* in its two senses.

ista loca, Paetus's villa near Naples.

non hospitem, sed contubernalem, 'not as a guest, but as
one of your family circle.'

promulside.   See on Ep. xlix. 8 : 'what a gastronomic hero
you will find me now !   Not the poor creature whom you used
to put *hors de combat* with a mere appetiser.'

ad ovum, 'I bring an unimpaired appetite to the eggs.'
The *ova* were the beginning of the regular dinner.   Cic. says
he does not destroy his appetite by the *promulsis*.   'Roast
veal' seems here to have marked the end of the *cena* proper
before the *mensae secundae* or *dessert*.   In the celebrated dinner
on the inauguration of a Lentulus as Flamen of Mars, the menu
of which is preserved by Macrobius (Sat. iii. 13, 11 ff.), the last
course before *dessert* was roast fowl (*altilem assum*).   The word
for ' courses ' is *fercula*.

insolentiam, 'extravagance.'   In Rosc. Am. 23 *insolens* is
opp. to *egentissimus*, and in Phil. ix. 13 Cic. contrasts *maiorum
continentiam* with *huius sacculi insolentiam*.   With *ad hanc
insolentiam* we must understand some verb like *venimus, nos
contulimus*, taken out of *nos coniecimus*.

lautitiam, 'elegant, refined *ménage*.'

in sumptum habebas, 'when you had money to spend.'

praedia.   Paetus had been obliged to accept in lieu of money
from his debtors lands valued at their price before the war ; see
on *aestimationem*, Ep. xlix. 7.

2. ὀψιμαθεῖς.   Horace's *seri studiorum*, those who learn
late in life what should be acquired earlier.   Cic. was an
' overgrown pupil ' in the art of dining.

sportellae, ' fruit-baskets.'

artolagani, ' omelettes,' cakes made of meal, wine, pepper,
milk, and oil or lard.

ἐξοχῆς.   This is my conjecture for *ex artis* of the mss
Wesenberg would read *exquisitae artis*.   This is better than
Ernesti's *iam etiam artis*.   But I feel sure that *ex* represents

some Greek word which the copyist could not read, such as ἐξοχῆς, 'a leading position,' a word which Cic. uses in Att. iv. 15, 6. The copyist would have written down *ex* and then inserted the obvious conjecture *artis*, forgetting to erase his unsuccessful attempt at ἐξοχῆς. The notion required is rather that of 'a leading position' than of 'refined art.' A man might require *exquisita ars* to order a good dinner, but he must have 'a leading (acknowledged) position' as a *bon vivant* before he ventures to invite well-known *gourmets* to his table.

munditia . . . elegantia, 'refinement . . . taste.'

ius. Here curiously we do not seem to have the usual play on *ius*. Hirtius was celebrated for his 'sauce.'

3. salutatio defluxit, 'when the stream of morning visitors has flowed by.'

audiunt, 'interview' we would now say. *Audire* is the regular word for attending lectures, but this cannot be the meaning here. The *victores* or triumphant Caesarians would be glad to hear what Cic. had to say.

eluxi, 'I have done my mourning for my country.' *Elugere* is the proper word for 'to be in mourning' for a dead friend or relative, and the perf. expresses that the term of mourning is completed. [*Elugere* naturally = 'to be mourning thoroughly for'; but the word is very rare.]

LETTER LIV. (Fam. ix. 26)

1. Accubueram . . . exaravi, 'I have just taken my place at table at three o'clock, and I am dashing off a copy of this letter in my note-book.' The tenses are epistolary. Cic. would afterwards copy the letter on to *chartae*. Cf. *haec cum essem in senatu exaravi*, Fam. xii. 20. It is not necessary to insert *litterarum*, as Klotz does ; *iis* stands for *iis litteris* in Fam. xi. 14, 3. For *codicilli* see on Ep. xviii. 1.

supra . . . infra. Cic. occupied the middle seat on one of the dinner couches ; see Hor. Sat. ii. 8, 20, and Palmer's note and diagram there.

exhilaratam, 'has become so gay.'

philosophum audis, 'you who are having lessons from a philosopher,' Dion the Epicurean.

Angar? 'Am I to distress, to torture myself?' M^2. gives *excruciemne*, but the use of the interrogative particle with the second question and not the first would be very strange; moreover H. confirms the omission of the *-ne* by M^1.

quem ad finem? 'how long?'

minimum mihi est in cena, 'I set very little store by my dinner, the one subject of inquiry you set before Philosopher Dion.' This is explained below.

2. **Cytheris,** an actress, mistress of Volumnius and afterwards of M. Antonius (Mayor on Phil. ii. 20 and 58). Some comm. see an allusion to her in the word ἀκύθηρον (Ep. xxxiii. 2), but this is not probable.

accubuit, *quia meretrix: honestae mulieres sedebant,* Man.

quem aspectabant. Ribbeck places this among the fragments of doubtful authority; others refer it to the Telamo of Ennius. The line before this is *hicine est ille Telamo modo quem gloria ad caelum extulit.*

Aristippus, the head of the Cyrenaic school. He held that the bodily pleasure of the moment (μονόχρονος ἡδονή) was the *summum bonum*, and that εὐδαιμονία was the sum of pleasurable moments.

Habeo non habeor, ἔχω οὐκ ἔχομαι. Cic. says it is better in Greek because *habeor* does not mean 'I cling to,' as ἔχομαι does. The Greek expression is something like or 'among them but not of them.' The Latin is quite different, *habeor* being distinctly passive. An equivalent in English would take some such form as 'She is my mistress, but I am her master.' All relations sat lightly on Aristippus (Hor. Epp. i. 17, 23).

a Laide. These words can hardly have proceeded from Cic., who would certainly have written *habeo Laida, non habeor ab illa.* Lais was a celebrated courtesan of Corinth. Diogenes Laertius (ii. 84) tells us that Aristippus dedicated to her two of his works.

interpretabere, 'you will give a rendering of it.' So Cic. recognises that his *habeo non habeor* is, as I have said, no translation of the Greek, but another (and an inferior) *mot*, into which the word *habeo* enters.

in solum. On De Nat. Deor. i. 65 Prof. Mayor translates 'turns up, is brought on the *tapis*,' adding that the origin of the phrase is doubtful. Man. thinks it refers to chance-grown weeds (*solum* = ground); but Prof. Mayor, suggesting that *solum* would refer rather to what comes from above than from below, would connect it with the legal *res soli;* Dr. Reid thinks the phrase may mean what meets the foot (*solum*), comparing τὰ ἐν ποσί and like expressions.

3. **baro.** It appears that the 'pedant' Dion (a term which seems to have been often applied to Epicureans) desired to know whether any one had a knotty point (ζήτημα) to propose for solution, and put his general challenge of the company in the form of a question 'whether any one was looking for anything' (that is, any solution of a speculative difficulty). Paetus irreverently replied that he 'had been looking for his dinner since morning.' The *baro*, 'pedant,' thought that the question would be something deep, such as 'whether there is a plurality of worlds.' 'But,' says Cic., ' *what is such a question to you?* Now who would think of saying *what is dinner to you?* especially to a well-known *gourmand* such as you are?' Thus Cic. shows that the thing which Paetus was 'looking for' was really a more rational object of pursuit than the abstract problems which the pedant was prepared to solve. The reading of M. is *at hercule cena non quid ad te tibi praesertim.* Wes. would read *non est neglegenda* or *non parvi est*, but my correction of the ms. seems to me more in the tone of the letter and more likely to have incurred corruption. Some such word as *dicet* must be understood before ' *cena num quid ad te ?* ' and that understood verb is followed by *tibi.* [*Baro:* rather 'dull dog'; so in Fin. ii. 76, *nos barones stupemus;* Div. ii. 144. Lucilius has *barones et rustici.* In Pers. v. 138 *baro* is 'stupid fellow.' The *barcalae* of Petron. 67 is probably an error for *barunculi.*]

4. **vivitur,** 'this is the way my life goes.'

intra legem, 'within the law, and indeed well within it.' This was the sumptuary law of Caesar passed in 46 which *inter alia* restricted the liberty of buying certain dainties. A strict watch was kept on the markets, and sometimes dishes which had been already set on the table were removed by order of Caesar. The *Lex Sumptuaria* of Ep. xii. 2 was the Aemilian law of 115.

cibi . . . loci. Genitives of belonging (*Eigenschaft*): cf. *plurimarum palmarum gladiator*, Rosc. Am. 6; *ludi . . . non tui stomachi*, Fam. vii. 1, 2 (Ep. xvii). Draeger, Hist. Synt. i. p. 461.

LETTER LV. (ATT. XII. 11)

Male de Seio. This was the usual formula for expressing sorrow at the death of a friend. The word *beatulus* was
applied by their friends to the recently dead ; we say 'poor so-
and-so,' but the Romans, who said *beatulus*, and the Greeks,
who said ὁ μακαρίτης, were more euphemistical. Cf. Catulls's
o factum male on the death of Lesbia's sparrow.

ad nos pertinent, 'which concerns me more nearly,' as
being a thing which I may avoid and is not a necessary evil
like death : namely, 'the question what I am to do about the
senate, am I to attend it or no ?'

multo, sc. *magis ad nos pertinent.*

Postumiam Sulpicii, sc. *uxorem.* She seems to have been
a highly energetic woman, and was now busying herself about
some new marriage which she wished to recommend to Cicero ;
probably she desired that the daughter of Pompeius should be
the successor to the divorced Terentia. We find that he is not
disposed to entertain that proposal. As to the other candidate
for Cicero's hand we are left without any knowledge, but it is
amusing to find the sexagenarian orator and philosopher writing
'I never saw anything uglier than she is,' yet expressing himself as prepared still to consider the question. He subsequently
married Publilia for her dowry. He does not seem to have felt
any affection for her, and he divorced her because he thought
she lacked due sympathy with him for the loss of his beloved
daughter Tullia.

adsum, a nice use of the present for the future.

hilaritatem, 'the excellence of her spirits.'

commotiunculis, 'slight indisposition' ; we have *leviter
commotus* in the same sense in Ep. lxix. 1.

LETTER LVI. (FAM. XV. 17)

1. **Praeposteros,** 'unnatural,' doing just the opposite to
what they should do ; their duty being to bring letters, they
bring none, but clamour for letters to take away with them.
Praeposterus always contains the notion of *inversion*, and hence
is by no means conterminous with our 'preposterous.' *Prae-*

pestera is applied by Cic. to a letter which came to him before another one which was written earlier and delivered earlier to the carrier.

Sed tamen. This is the usual *epanalepsis* which these conjunctions convey. Having said 'they give me no concern,' he adds, 'and yet (they do annoy me because) they clamour for letters on leaving me, but bring none on their arrival.'

id ipsum facerent, i.e. *flagitarent litteras.*

petasati, 'with their travelling caps on'; see Plaut. Amph. prol. 143, and Palmer's note. We would rather say, 'they come booted and spurred.'

ignosces, 'you will kindly excuse,' the fut. standing for a polite form of imperative.

2. Sullam. He speaks in the same tone on the death of Sulla in Fam. ix. 10, 3. This is the man whom he defended in the Pro Sulla. He was a great buyer of the confiscated estates of Caesar's enemies ; hence *verentem ne hasta refrixisset.* [*Combustum:* there is probably a jest here. He was not merely *ambustus,* owing to his trial, but *combustus. Pro tua sapientia,* 'such is your philosophy.']

πρόσωπον πόλεως, 'a prominent personage,' 'a well-known figure' in Rome. [Cf. *personam civitatis gerere,* Off. i. 124.]

Mindius Marcellus. He and Attius the perfumer rejoiced at his death, as he used to bid against them (*adversarium*) at the auctions of the confiscated estates.

3. paludatus, 'in military uniform.' This must have been a preliminary journey, for he did not leave Rome to take up his province of Cisalpine Gaul from Brutus till March (Att. xii. 17; xii. 19, 3).

nuper. This is an allusion to the fact that Cassius had recently become an Epicurean, and so was bound to oppose the Stoic doctrine that right was to be pursued for its own sake and apart from consequences—a doctrine which the general admiration of Pansa's conduct seemed to confirm.

4. εἰ ἀκενόσπουδος fueris, 'if you keep clear of idle pursuits.' Cic. warns his friend as an Epicurean not to trouble himself about such vain pursuits as the restoration of the commonwealth.

LETTER LVII. (FAM. XV. 16)

1. Puto te iam suppudere, ' I fancy that you must be a little ashamed of yourself by this time, now that this thi·d letter is upon you without a scrap, without a word, from you.' *Scida* is properly 'a leaf,' from *scindo ;* the Greek σχέδη w·s probably a late corruption of the Latin word, *nec summa potes ·n scida* (al. *scheda*) *teneri*, Mart. iv. 91, 4. *Littera* is properly 'a letter of the alphabet.' Notice the ellipse of *misisti* or *scripsisti.*

ternas. The distributive numeral is used because the word understood is *litteras*, which, being plural with singular meau - ing, takes the distributive not the ordinal numerals. *Tris litteras* would mean 'three letters of the alphabet.'

κατ' εἰδώλων φαντασίας, ' by the presentation of images t· the eyes.' The Epicurean theory of vision was that minute bu; material copies of the object of sight passed into the eyes ; th· rival Platonic view being that there was an emission of rays from the eyes. Cic. discusses these theories in a jocular passage in Att. ii. 3, reminding one of the quasi-philosophic scene in the Vicar of Wakefield, where the Squire applies the maieutic method of dialectic to Moses. The Epicurean theory is in that letter more accurately described as the theory κατ' εἰδώλων ἐμπτώσεις. The word φαντασία rather belongs to the Stoical vocabulary. For a full account of ancient theories of vision see Grote's Plato, vol. iii. p. 265, note.

διανοητικὰς φαντασίας, ' mental pictures.'

spectris Catianis. The translation of εἴδωλα by *spectra* appears to have had a comical tinge (Fam. xv. 19, 1). Catius the Insubrian was an Epicurean writer who had recently died. He treated his subject superficially, but in a fairly readable manner (Quintil. x. 1, 124). That this is not the Catius of Hor. Sat. ii. 4 is wellnigh certain ; see Palmer's Introd. to that Satire.

ille Gargettius. Epicurus, who belonged to the deme Gargettus, north-west of Athens.

2. animus qui possit, ' how the mind could be impinged upon by the *idola*, I cannot see.' Cicero's objections to the Epicurean theory of mental images are these :—granting that actual sensation is caused by *idola* impinging on the eye, how is it that the mind can be affected by just those images by which it wishes to be affected—that just those *idola* come which we want. I read *quae velis incurrunt*, inasmuch as *quae* for *cum* seems demanded by the argument (neither word is found in the mss.), and *incurrunt* is the most proper word to convey the sense needed here, and has the authority of H. and its family, while M. gives *occurrunt*, which is usually changed to *accurrunt*.

The impressions derived from the *idola* or *spectra* in a mental picture are too delicate to affect the senses but can act on the mind. Our power of calling up a mental image, the difficulty here suggested by Cic., is a real difficulty, and is by the Epicurean school either ignored or met by an unjustified assumption of a power of initiation in the atoms such as Lucretius is obliged to assume. If Epicurus and Lucretius had hit on the theory of latent mental modifications they might at least have thrown on their opponents the burden of disproof.

haeres in medullis. Cf. *in medullis populi Romani ac visceribus haerebat*, Phil. i. 36.

pectus. This is where the intellect resides, according to the Epicureans.

3. postulabimus . . . restituare, 'we shall make an application that you be restored to that system (Stoicism) from which you have been ousted by force of arms (the influence of Caesar).' Cic. says he will get an interdict of the praetor to restore Cassius to Stoicism. The word αἵρεσις, from which comes our *heresy*, was especially applied to sects and systems of philosophy, without conveying, as *heresy* does, a deviation from an established form of belief.

nuntium remisisti, 'you have repudiated your true spouse, Virtue.' The message was *res tibi habeas* (or *habeto*) *tuas*, or *tuas res tibi agito*. Cf. XII. Tables, *Si vir ab uxore divertit res suas sibi habere iubeto eique claveis adimito*.

in integro, 'the matter will be open to us still,' 'we are not estopped by any Statute of Limitations.'

LETTER LVIII. (ATT. XII. 12)

1. De dote. Cic. had divorced Terentia, and it is probable that he here speaks of the obligation under which he lay to restore to her the marriage portion which she had brought to him. The words *turpe est rem impeditam iacere* are in favour of this view. But we must infer from Att. xvi. 15, 5, a letter

written a year after this one, that Terentia had not been paid
even then, though Cicero's son had made the generous proposal
that the sum due to her should be deducted from his own
allowance while studying at Athens.   It is possible also that
the words *de dote* refer to Tullia's dower, which Dolabella was
bound to refund to her.   We read in Ep. xlvii. that on May 19
in the year 49 Tullia had given birth to a seven-months' child.
In a letter written in the following year (Att. xi. 6, 4) Cic.
expresses alarm at her state of health.   She subsequently had a
quarrel with Dolabella, and Cic. recommended a divorce (Att.
xi. 23, 3).   This quarrel seems to have blown over, but subsequently Dolabella divorced her.   She was then again with
child (Fam. vi. 18, 5), and Cic. in that letter speaks about the
difficulty of getting her marriage portion from Dolabella.   She
died early in 45, probably in February, and we read in this
letter and many of those written about this time how deeply
Cic. felt her loss, and how anxious he was to pay a token of
respect to her memory by dedicating to her a sort of shrine
This act he describes as an ἀποθέωσις of his daughter, and per
haps nothing in the whole correspondence of Cicero presents a
more marked contrast to the religious feelings of the present
day.   If the reference in *de dote* is to the dower which Dolabella
was bound to refund, the words *turpe est rem impeditam iacere*
do not seem quite so suitable, but are by no means out of place.
It was a slur on him and Atticus as business men that the
matter should not be settled.

tanto magis perpurga, sc. *quanto difficilius est.*   Att.
had dwelt on the difficulty of coming to a settlement.   *Perpurga* is a stronger expression than *explica* or *expedi* for winding up a business transaction.

delegandi.   *Delegare* is to defray a debt by giving a draft
on another, and thus to impose on one's creditor the difficulty
of enforcing payment.   Balbus seems to have proposed this
method of payment, which Cic. calls 'high-handed' (*regia*), to
Cicero if the *dos* in question was Terentia's, to Dolabella if it
was Tullia's.

Insula Arpinas, a portion of Arpinum, which was sur-
rounded by a loop of the river Fibrenus before it falls into the
Liris (De Legg. ii. 6).   Cic. says, 'It would be a perfect site for
the deification, but I fear its out-of-the-way position would
seem to diminish the token of respect' paid to the memory of
the dead.

in hortis, some pleasure-ground in the neighbourhood of
Rome.

tamen, 'in any case,' as often.

2. **μεθαρμόσομαι,** 'I shall remodel.' Att. had asked Cic. to give the statement of the Epicurean view in the De Finibus to some friend of his, who had asked him to make interest with Cic. to procure him this honour. Cic. grants his request, but adds, 'In future I shall remodel my practice with regard to the persons in my dialogues. You would be surprised how some people covet a place among the interlocutors. I will have recourse only to the ancients. This causes no heart-burnings.' Cf. Juv. i. 170—

> Experiar, quid concedatur in illos,
> Quorum Flaminia tegitur cinis atque Latina.

ut eliciam, 'to write with a view of drawing replies from you'; *ut eliciam* follows *mittere* closely; if it went with *institui* it should of course in strict sequence be *elicerem;* but *institui elicere* practically is the same as *missurus sum.*

LETTER LIX. (ATT. XII. 32)

1. **Publilia.** Cic. was now married to Publilia. He writes to his friend Plancius (Fam. iv. 14, 3) that he married her only to repair his shattered fortunes by means of her ample dower. He divorced her not long after this time, we are told, because she did not seem to feel the death of Tullia. He seems to have had some trouble about refunding her dower to her brother Publilius (Att. xiii. 34 and 47 *b*, 2). Even now he refuses to see her in his affliction.

videretur. So Klotz and Wesenberg for *loqueretur* of the mss.

mi etiam gravius esse. M. has *me etiam gravius esse,* and many edd. preserve this reading, adding *affectum.* But Orelli's change of *me* to *mi* is far simpler. *Graviter est mihi* is a very good phrase for 'it goes ill with me,' that is, 'I am in great distress of mind'; cf. *fuit periucunde,* 'I enjoyed myself greatly,' Ep. lxvi. 1, and note there. The mss. often give *mi* for *mihi* in the letters. It seems to have been a habitual form in familiar communication.

non illius esse. Publilia had written the letter at her mother's dictation. She would not come when Cic. forbade her, but she might have done so if Cic. had left the letter unanswered. But he says in the next sentence that he thinks 'they will come'; who are 'they'? Plainly, I should say, the brother Publilius and the mother. Hence I have changed *illae* to *illi*, understanding that word to mean the other two, Publilius and the mother, the pronoun according to rule following the masculine gender. 'If the subjects connected are of different gender, the adjective is regulated in gender by the nearest substantive if the singular is used. If on the contrary the plural is employed, then the gender *in the case of living beings* is masculine, as *uxor mea et filius mortui sunt*,' Madv. § 214, *a*, *b*. *Uxor mea et filius* would be referred to by a masculine pronoun, *illi*. So 'a brother and a sister' are called *fratres*.

una vitatio. See Reid on Acad. ii. 51.

avolem. This word has been inserted by Madvig. It would have easily fallen out before *nollem*.

ut scribis. Att. had probably recommended gentleness in the treatment of Publilia in a former letter. We need no suppose that he had discussed this very incident with Cic. before, for in that case Cic. would not now have written in such detail.

2. Ciceroni velim hoc proponas. 'I wish you would make this suggestion to my son—that is, if you think it fair—that in this sojourn of his at Athens he should keep his expenses within the sum which the rents of my property in the Argiletum and the Aventine will yield; he would have been quite satisfied with that allowance if he had rented a house in Rome, as he had intended. And further, I should be obliged if you would so arrange that out of these rents I may be able to supply him with what is necessary.' The *Argiletum* was the booksellers' street in Rome. Martial directs thither a friend who asked him for a copy of his book. 'No doubt,' he writes, 'you often go down the Argiletum,' *Argi nempe soles subire letum*, i. 118, 9. The *tmesis* is nearly as bad as the Ennian *cere comminuit brum* for *comminuit cerebrum*, for the *Argiletum* no doubt meant 'Clay St.' and was derived from *argilla*, and had no reference whatever to the 'death of Argus.'

Praestabo, 'I will guarantee that none of the other young Romans who are going to study at Athens will have a better allowance.'

quanti. This is the genitive of price.

ut sint qui ad diem solvant, 'you must see that the tenants shall be persons who shall pay their rent punctually.'

instrumenti, 'outfit.'

iumento, 'an equipage.'

animadvertes, 'you will see to be the case.' The ms. gives *animadvertis*, but this must be corrected to *animadvertes* or *animadvertisti*. The former seems the easier remedy.

LETTER LX. (FAM. IV. 5)

1. sane quam. This coupling of *quam* with adverbs is very common in the letters.

pro eo ac debui, 'I deplored it as bitterly as I was bound.'

istic. In Italy, where Cic. was.

genus hoc consolationis, 'consolation of every kind,' 'consolation in the abstract,' 'consolation *per se*'; this is a common use of *genus*. In Fam. v. 12, 1 *genus tuorum scriptorum* means 'your work as a whole,' and in Fam. vii. 23, 2 *genus omnium signorum* means 'all the statues in the world.'

conferi. Cic. uses *confici*. Another correspondent, Balbus (Att. viii. 15 *a*, 3), agrees with Sulpicius in writing *conferi*.

brevi. Cf. Fam. i. 19, 13, *tantum dicam brevi*. Some such word as *opera* is understood, so that *brevi* means 'briefly'; so Fam. vi. 6, 1, *brevi gratulabimur*. [Rather the neut. adj. is turned into a noun, without any idea of a special noun being left out; so *proclivi*, *ex facili*, etc.]

quod perspicias. *Quod*, as stating the real reason, should be followed by the indicative, but *forsitan* justifies the subjunctive.

2. intestinus, 'private,' 'personal.'

callere, 'to be callous.' In Cic. this word means 'to be thoroughly conversant with.' *Concallescere* is 'to be callous.' [I think *callere* means 'to be wise' or 'to be sensible.']

3. cedo. I have corrected *credo* to *cedo*. The mss. give *an illius vicem, credo, doles*, where *an* and *credo* cannot stand together. Hofm. changes *an* to *at*. Munro would correct *credo* to *Cicero*. Far better in my mind is the change of *credo* to *cedo*, which often means 'tell me' in the comic drama and in Cic., both in his letters and in his other works. *Cedo* is used *exactly* as here, 'pray,' parenthetically, by Cato ap. Quintil. ix. 2, 21, *cedo, si vos . . . quid aliud fecissetis.* Cf. Ter. Andr. iv. 4, 24. The copyist would have been much less likely to write *an* by error for *at* than to corrupt to *credo* a word like *cedo,* 'pray,' which might puzzle any one who was not a fairly go od scholar.

illius vicem, 'for her sake.' Cf. *nostram vicem,* 'for our sake,' Fam. i. 9, 2; Liv. xxxiv. 32.

et tu veneris. The *et* is probably corrupt, and shou'd either be omitted or corrected to *ut.* If Sulpicius wro:e the sentence as it stands, he wrote a slipshod sentenc', for while the *et . . . et* should connect both *veneris* and *incidimus* with *necesse est,* the difference in mood shows that this 's not so, but that *et . . . incidimus* is parenthetical. See, hov ever, the masterly notes of Reid on Acad. ii. 69 and ii. 12, where he shows that *et* is often displaced from its logical position by a natural laxity. See also note on *ne aut,* Ep. lxxiii. § 8.

res . . . spes, 'present enjoyment and hope of future.' Watson well compares *neque solum spe sed certare,* Fam. xii. 25, 2.

credo, 'of course,' ironical; another reason for regarding *credo* above as corrupt, for there the irony would have been simply brutal. *Credo* parenthetic is not, however, always ironical.

ordinatim, 'in their due course.' He refers to the quaestorship, aedileship, and consulate, which were held in that order, *magistratus quorum certus ordo est,* Leg. Agr. ii. 24.

nisi, 'only this is worse.' This elliptico-adversative use of *nisi* is very common in the comic drama. See note on Plaut. Mil. Glor. 24. There is a good ex. of it in Att. xi. 23, 1, *nisi illud quidem mutari . . . non video posse.*

4. regiones circumcirca = *quae circumcirca sunt.* Cf. *discessu tum meo,* 'by my then departure,' Pis. 21; *deorum saepe praesentiae,* 'the frequent appearances of the gods,' N. D. ii. 166; so even when place or time is indicated by a periphrasis, *et tot locis sessiones,* De Or. ii. 20; *Carbonis eodem illo die mors,* Phil. viii. 13. It is sentences like these which show us the great loss which the Latin language sustained in having no article. This fine passage is alluded to by Byron in a familiar stanza of great beauty, Childe Harold, iv. 44. Melmoth, in his translation of the letters ad Fam., compares the reflections of Addison in Westminster Abbey, *Spectator,* vol. i. No. 26:—
'When I see kings lying by those who deposed them; when I

consider rival wits placed side by side, or the holy men that divided the world with their contests and disputes, I reflect with sorrow and astonishment on the little competitions, factions, and debates of mankind.   When I read the several dates of the tombs, of some that died yesterday, and some six hundred years ago, I consider that great day when we shall all of us be contemporaries, and make our appearance together.'

Megara.   Megara was destroyed by Demetrius Poliorcetes in 307 B.C. ; Piraeus in the Mithridatic War, 86 ; Corinth by Mummius, 146.

Hem ! nos homunculi, 'Ah ! we poor mortals.'   *Homullus* and *homuncio* are other forms of the diminutive.

oppidûm cadavera, 'corpses of towns,' a very strange expression, for which Mr. Watson compares the much less bold *sepulta patria*, Catil. iv. 11.   *Oppidum* for *oppidorum* is also strange.   [*Corpus reipublicae* is found Pis. 25 ; Phil. viii. 15.]

Visne tu.   We should rather have expected *vis tu*, which conveys an earnest exhortation, than *visne tu* or *vin'tu*, which merely asks a question, as Bentley showed.   Perhaps, however, the less strong form of adjuration is suitable to a man apostrophising himself.

Hoc idem.   The order of words seems to me decidedly in favour of regarding *idem* as the accus. neut. rather than the nom. masc.

de imperio.   This does not mean that the boundaries of the empire have been contracted, but that it has in the recent civil war lost *prestige* and moral influence.

in animula, 'the loss of the poor little life of a poor weak woman.'   Where we say *loss of* the Latins said *loss in;* cf. Fam. x. 28, 3, *magnum damnum factum est in Servio.*

homo, ' a mortal '; cf. *ut eam nemo hominem appellare possit,* Cluent. 199.

5. tua persona, 'your position,' 'the aspect which you present to the world.'

adolescentibus primariis.   C. Calpurnius Piso, Furius Crassipes, and P. Cornelius Dolabella.   Of these, Piso was by far the best.   She was divorced by Dolabella and probably by Crassipes.   She seems to have had most affection and admiration for Dolabella, who was quite the worst of her husbands.   It was probably her grief for her divorce from him which prevented her rallying from the childbirth which cost her her life.

perfunctam, 'experienced,' used both of good and bad experiences. Cf. Ad Brut. i. 12, 2.

quod . . . possitis, 'what quarrel on that score could you or she have with fortune ?'

imitari, depending on *velis,* taken out of *noli.* The mss. have *neque imitare,* but Latinity demands *neve imitare* or *neque imitatus sis.* Hofm., who, however, reads *neque imitare* (I suppose because he thinks Sulpicius *capable de tout*), gives an excellent parallel for the construction which I ascribe to *imitari.* It is Fam. xii. 30, 1, *noli mihi impudens esse nec mihi molestiam exhibere.* So, again, N. D. i. 17, *noli existimes me adiutorem huic venisse sed auditorem.*

6. longinquitas temporis. Cf. Soph. Electr. 179, χρόνος γὰρ εὐμαρὴς θεός, 'time is a comfortable god.' Sulpicius urges Cic. not, like an ordinary person, to await the healing influences of time, but, as a philosopher, to 'go to meet' that comfort which it must at last bring. For *occurrere* in this sense cf. Q. Fr. i. 1, 4, where Cic. tells his brother that he should not only not shirk business but even *court* it (*occurras*).

inferis, ' if the dead have any consciousness '—a sad *if.* This passage has been referred to by the late Archbishop Whately to show that belief in a life to come, though nominally professed, cannot be regarded as practically forming any part of the creed of the Romans of Cicero's time. Cic. acknowledges that the letter of Sulpicius embraces every source of consolation which the case admitted ; yet there is in it no allusion what ever to the comfort which would have been afforded by a belief in the happiness of Tullia in another state. The expression in the letter which even contemplates the possibility of the permanence of consciousness after death is not used with the view of ascribing happiness to Tullia, but only of estimating what might be her judgment about her father's obstinate perseverance in his grief ; and the words used do not seem to suggest that Sulpicius himself believed that consciousness would survive death. In a letter written to Torquatus within a few months of this Cic. speaks of death, if it should befall him in the troubles and tumults of the period, as *sine ullo sensu* (Fam. vi. 4, 4). It deserves, however, to be noticed that when Cic., to beguile his grief, devoted himself to philosophical studies, one of the first results (about a year later) was the first book of the Tusc. Disp., in which he has collected whatever his learning or reflections could contribute to throw light on the condition of the soul after death. The received philosophical opinion on the subject seems to have been expressed by Seneca, when he terms the belief in the immortality of the soul a beautiful dream (*bellum somnium*), and describes its adherents as asserting rather than proving a most acceptable doctrine (Ep. 102). Friedländer (*Sittengeschichte Roms*, iii.) has treated with his wonted mastery the whole question of the relation of a belief in a future life to ancient Roman speculation and conduct.

hoc facere, sc. *dolere*.

huic rei serviendum, 'we must stoop even to such a consideration as this' (which follows).

aliorum, sc. *Caesarianorum;* possibly 'other supporters of the Republic.'

provincia.   Macedonia with Achaia.

LETTER LXI. (FAM. IV. 6)

1. Ego vero, 'Yes, indeed, I wish you had been with me.' *Ego vero* points as usual to a question which has been asked, and introduces the answer.

aeque dolendo, 'by your perfect sympathy.'

aliquantum acquievi, 'I felt a little more calm.'

quam . . . fore, 'and the pleasure which he thought you would feel at such an evidence of sympathy with my grief.'

iucundiora . . . gratiora.   *Gratus* may be applied to that which one welcomes and approves of, *iucundus* being reserved for that which produces an actual emotion of delight, (amor tuus) *gratus et optatus, dicerem iucundus nisi id verbum in omne tempus perdidissem*, Fam. v. 15, 1 ; *ista veritas, etiam si iucunda non est, mihi tamen grata est*, Att. iii. 24, 2.   *Scilicet* means 'of course,' because Cicero's recent loss precluded emotions of actual delight.

Q. Maximus . . . M. Cato.   The persons referred to as having sustained a loss similar to his own, but at a time when their great position in the state afforded much to console them, are Q. Fabius Maximus, the cunctator in the second Punic war ; L. Aemilius Paullus, who defeated Perseus at Pydna in 168 ; C. Sulpicius Gallus, consul 166 ; and M. Cato the censor. Gallus is called *vester*, as belonging to the *gens Sulpicia*.   The story of the death of the two sons of Paullus just at the time of his triumph is pathetically told by Velleius, i. 10.

U

2. frangerem iam ipse me, 'when I crushed down my sorrow.' Cf. *ita flectebar animo atque frangebar ut iam ex memoria insidias deponerem,* Sull. 18.

habebam quo confugerem, ' I had a refuge and a rest ng-place, one in whose sweet society I could lay aside all my cares and griefs.'

consanuisse . . . recrudescunt, 'the old wounds, that seemed to have got well, broke out afresh.' *Consanesco* is found only in the letters of Cic.

Non enim . . . foro, 'All is changed : then, when I came back depressed from public affairs, a home welcomed me to give me comfort ; but now I cannot fly from my house of mourn ng for refuge to the state, and borrow comfort from its happiness. No : I shrink from private and public life alike.' For *maestum a,* ' coming back sad from,' Watson excellently compares *rec ns a volnere Dido,* Virg. Aen. vi. 450.

domo absum. It is wellnigh certain that *a* must have fallen out before *domo.* See Reid on Acad. i. § 2.

3. Maius . . . ratio. H. and T. give this reading, which is certainly right, 'No philosophical system can bring me greater comfort than your kindly intercourse and conversation.' From the corrupt reading of M., *maior mihi ratio mihi adferre,* has been educed the vulgate reading, *maior enim levatio mihi adferri,* et .

quamquam, ' I have my hopes, however,' because the earnestness of the appeal just uttered might seem to imply that his early meeting with Sulpicius was a matter of doubt.

amicissimi. Sulpicius held his province by the gift of Caesar.

magnae . . . quiescendi, ' it is a matter for careful consideration what plan I shall pursue ; I do not mean what plan of action, but what mode of passing that retirement which Caesar kindly grants me.'

LETTER LXII. (ATT. XII. 45)

1. Ego . . . absolvi. We learn from other passages that the two treatises here referred to, the Academica and the De Finibus, were written at Astura. Yet it is clear that the rest of the letter was not written at Astura, but probably at Tusculanum. Hence edd. have proposed to regard the first section of this letter as the end of the one immediately preceding it. Reid, Acad. p. 30 (ed. 1885), argues that συντάγματα here refers to the Acad. as he first wrote it in two books.

2. 'Ακηδία, 'listlessness,' what Cic. elsewhere calls *pigritia*.

refricant, sc. *me ;* the word is always transitive, a reflexive pronoun being easily supplied in the places where the verb is apparently intransitive, as here and in Att. x. 17, 2 (Ep. xlvi.), *crebro refricat lippitudo.*

3. **Eum . . . Salutis.** The temple of Quirinus on the Quirinal Hill, dedicated by L. Papirius Cursor on the defeat of the Samnites, was burned down in the year 49. Caesar restored it, and this year his statue was erected there with the inscription, *Deo Invicto.* There was also a temple to *Salus* on the same hill. Cic. here bitterly says that he would rather see Caesar 'enshrined with' (occupant of the same temple with) Quirinus than Salus. Romulus was torn to pieces just before he was acknowledged as a god. In Att. xiii. 28, 3, he calls Caesar *Quirini contubernalem.*

Hirtium. The work is called by the name of the writer, just as we now speak of our *Cicero* or *Horace*, and as Juvenal wrote of *Flaccus* and *Maro.* This was a tirade against Cato (Att. xii. 40, 1), and as it was dedicated to Caesar it is spoken of as *epistolam* in Att. xii. 41, 4. He says the effect of the *brochure* will be to reflect credit on the literary ability of Hirtius, but discredit on the scheme of blackening the character of Cato.

LETTER LXIII. (Fam. vii. 24)

M. Fadius Gallus, who is not to be confounded with the T. Fadius Gallus to whom Fam. vii. 27 is addressed, is frequently recommended by Cic. to many of his friends, and is mentioned (Att. viii. 12, 1) as a close friend of Att. as well as of Cic. He appears to have been very anxious that Cic. should not lose the favour of the Sardinian musician Tigellius, who was very influential with Caesar.

1. **vestigia.** Some verb like *sunt* or *apparent* or *vidi* or *animadverti* must be understood, but there is no reason why we should introduce it into the text, as many edd. do.

vel, 'for instance, just now in the case of Tigellius.' For Tigellius see Palmer on Hor. Sat. i. 2, 3.

Ciplus. The story about Cipius was that he was in the habit of pretending to be asleep, lest he should find himself forced to condemn anything in the conduct of his wife, but that on one occasion, when a slave taking advantage of his apparent slumber was making away with a stolen cup, he suddenly started up with the words, 'I am not asleep to every one,' and recovered his stolen property. So Cic. here says, 'As Cipius declared there are cases in which he would not play the sleeper, so there are cases in which I will not play the slave, and I will not endure the insolence of this Sardinian singer.' Cf. *doctus spectare lacunar*, said of a husband, Juv. i. 56, and Mayor's note on that passage.

regnare. Cic. often had to bear this reproach during and after his consulship ; see for instance Att. i. 16, 10 ; Su ll. 21, 48. [This is the very reproach Cic. brought against Hortensius in the Div. in Caecil.]

non tam ab ullis, sc. *observabar*.

Id ego . . . praeconio, 'I regard it as a clear gain no longer to have to endure this fellow, who is more noisome than his noisome birthplace, one, moreover, who (as I take it) has been by this time quite knocked down as a cheap lot by the scazon ic hammer of Calvus.' Sardinia was proverbially unhealthy. *Addicere* is the technical term for knocking down a lot at an auction to the highest bidder. The setting forth of the qualities of the goods offered for auction was called *praeconium*, and the auctioneer was *praeco*. The allusion here is to the biting scazons which Calvus wrote against Tigellius, of which the first line has been preserved—

> *Sardi Tigelli putidum caput venit,*
> 'For sale Tigellius the Sardinian oaf.

The meaning is : Any little vestige of character he ever had, he has lost since he became the subject of the lampoon of Calvus. Hippōnax was the Greek writer of scazons who lampooned the brothers Bupalus and Athenis, two sculptors of Chios who had caricatured his ugliness.

2. quid suscenseat, 'what he is angry at.'

Phameae, grandfather of Tigellius.

P. Sestio, accused under the Pompeian law of 53 for *ambitus*. This case, it appears, must have been tried before 49 the year in which Phamea died.

in consilium iri, 'the jury had to consider their verdict in the case of P. Sestius'; the jury were said *ire in consilium*, and the president *mittere iudices in consilium*.

unctorem. The Greek form *aliptes* or *alipta* is commoner than the Latin ; see Fam. i. 9, 15.

Sardos venales. After the conquest of Sardinia by Ti. Sempronius Gracchus in 177, Sardinian slaves became a drug in the market. They were of a very poor physique, owing no doubt to the unhealthiness of their native climate. The form of the proverb was—

> *Sardi venales: alius alio nequior,*
> 'A job-lot of Sardinians, one worse than the other.'

salaconis, 'snob,' 'swaggerer.'

iniquitatem, 'unfairness,' 'unreasonableness.'

Catonem tuum. Cf. Mommsen, R. H. iv. 449, on the literature of *Catos* by the republicans : 'The republican opposition borrowed from Cato its whole attitude, stately, transcendental in its doctrine, pretentiously rigid, hopeless, and faithful to death ; and accordingly it began even immediately after his death to revere as a saint the man who in his lifetime was often its laughing-stock and its scandal.' We find Brutus, Cicero, and Gallus writing *Catos,* and Caesar and Hirtius countering with *anti - Catos.* The subject could be easily handled in rhetorical fashion from either point of view.

LETTER LXIV. (FAM. VII. 25)

1. **conscissam.** This probably refers to the last letter, in which Cic. had written severely about Tigellius. Fadius Gallus had torn it up, through fear lest it might compromise Cicero, for Tigellius enjoyed great influence with Caesar. Cic. assures him that he has a copy. From this we may infer that Cic. kept copies of some (perhaps most) of his letters, and this accounts for the very considerable correspondence which Tiro was able to collect.

ne si istum. The reading of the mss. is *vereri nisi istum habuerimus;* now *vereri* must be followed by *ne*, so it is pretty certain that for *nisi* should stand *ne si*. The sense then will demand after *istum* some word like *iratum* or *infestum*, or rather *infensum* (since *infestum habere* means in Cic. *infestare*, 'to keep in a state of turbulence'; see Att. ix. 19, 3 ; 16, 3).

For the meaning is 'you seem to me to be afraid that if we offend Tigellius we may have to laugh on the wrong side of our mouths.' More probably, however, some Greek word such as σκῶμμα has here been lost. A very apt phrase would have been *ne si istum ἀνὰ στόμα habuerimus*, 'lest if we say our say about this fellow'; and if ἀνὰ στόμα had been written in Roman characters, as Greek words often are in these letters, *anastoma* would have been likely enough to fall out before *istum*. Of course *istum* might also be taken as referring to Caesar, but in that case too we must assume that a word has fallen out, unless we read *ne nisi istum habuerimus*, and give to *habuerimus* the strange meaning of 'have on our side.' But Cic. would not so have expressed that thought. Whether we refer *istum* to Caesar or Tigellius, the allusion in either case is to an enmity incurred by provoking the Sardinian, as is shown by γέλωτα σαρδόνιον.

γέλωτα σαρδόνιον. So Ernesti for σαρδάνιον of the mss., rightly as I think, for γέλωτα σαρδάνιον means the 'sneer of triumphant malice,' which is plainly out of place here. Now σαρδόνιον, which alludes to the fabled Sardinian herb which poisoned those who tasted it, twisting their features into a convulsive grin, is quite appropriate in reference to the *Sardinian* Tigellius. 'To laugh on the wrong side of the mouth' is a phrase which (in Ireland at least) expresses a laugh which is the sign of pain, not pleasure. We might of course preserve σαρδάνιον of the mss., and give to it, not the Homeric meaning, but a meaning derived from a *Volks-Etymologie* connecting the word with *Sardus* and forcing on it an allusion to the fabled Sardinian herb.

manum de tabula, sc. *tolle*. 'But, I say, hands off the slate, sir; the schoolmaster is here, sooner than we expected him,' *i.e.* Caesar is returning from Spain. *Tabula*, translated 'a slate' for convenience, was rather a tablet of wood or metal covered with wax, for doing writing lessons or arithmetic on; see Palmer on Hor. Sat. i. 6, 74. *Tabula (litteraria)* was the regular word for the exercise-book of children, Varro, R. R. iii. 5, 10. The evident allusion to a schoolmaster gives verisimilitude to the explanation of the early commentators (which, however, is only a guess) that Roman schoolboys used to scribble on their tablets during the absence of the schoolmaster, and that *manum de tabula* was the form of call to 'Attention!' which announced his presence. Pliny, H. N. xxxv. 80, uses the phrase in a different sense when he tells us that Apelles used to say that he *manum de tabula sciret tollere*, that is, that he knew at what point to stop further elaborating his pictures.   It is possible, therefore, that Cic. here means 'you must put no more touches to your *Cato;* now is the time to publish it, since Caesar has returned from Spain.'   It does not seem that this kind of composition entailed any serious risk of offending Caesar ; but if the apprehension expressed in the next words is serious (which I do not believe it to be), we might suppose *manum de tabula* to mean 'you must stop writing *Catos* now.'

catonium.   This is the conjecture of Salmasius (universally but erroneously ascribed to Ernesti) for *catomum* of the mss. The question is, is there a word *catomum* or *catomium* meaning 'a whip' or 'a whipping-place'?   Preller, R. M. 454, note 1, quotes *catomum ergastulum* as a gloss in Isidore, and there are similar glosses in Ducange.   Then the analogy of *catomidiare,* 'to lay on the shoulders of another to be flogged,' goes for something, but not much.   Again Aulus Gellius, Noctes, xvi. 7, 4, quotes *catomum* as used by the mime writer Laberius.   The verse quoted by him demands the form *catomium,* for *catomum* violates the metre.   The verse is—

> Tóllat bona fidé vos Orcus núdas in catómium,

a trochaic septenarius.   Here 'a whipping-place' seems suitable enough, and *catomium* might be a word formed comically from κατ' ὤμων ; but the mention of *Orcus* is decidedly in favour of the slight change which makes the word *catonium.*   The chief objection to *catonium* is the want of analogy for such a formation from κάτω ; it certainly suits the play on words in the Latin better, though *catomium* lends itself better to an English rendering.   Reading *catomium* we might translate 'I am afraid he will give us Catonians the cat'; with *catonium* we might render 'I am afraid he will send us Catonians to join our hero below.'

2. transversum unguem, sc. *discesseris,* 'a nail's breadth.' This and *digitum transversum* are common enough in Cic. and the comic drama.

a stilo, 'from the pen,' that is, 'from the practice of writing.'

dicendi opifex, 'writing is the artificer of oratory.'   This is a favourite maxim of Cicero's ; see De Or. i. 150, 257 ; iii. 190 ; Brut. 95.   It is quite possible that Cic. here urges his friend to further work on his Cato, thus showing that the fears expressed in this letter are not serious.   But as the expression which he admires is quoted as *epistolae tuae partem,* it is possible that he is urging his friend to attention to style in all his writings, even in his letters ; a precept which Cic. certainly carried out himself.   It is to be remembered, however, that Cic. calls the Anti-Cato of Hirtius *epistola* (Att. xii. 41, 4), so he may here so describe the Cato of Gallus.   If he is referring to letters, we have here an interesting expression of his own consciousness of his superiority to his correspondents as a letter-writer.

aliquantum noctis adsumo.   The Romans seldom worked at night.   Cic. says that Sulpicius in his province may keep up his reading by devoting the night to it.   The phrase is almost proverbial for intense industry : cf. *noctem addens operi*, Vi g. Aen. viii. 411 ; *nox parandis operibus adsumpta*, Tac. H. ii. 21.

LETTER LXV. (FAM. VII. 29)

1. **S. V. B.** = *si vales bene* (est).

χρήσει.   The opp. of χρῆσις and κτῆσις is very common in Greek, especially in the Politics and Ethics of Aristotle.

fructus, put simply for *usus fructus ;* cf. Cicero's reply to this letter, Ep. lxvii.   The *fructus* includes the *usus*, but not the *usus* the *fructus ;* cf. Munro on Lucr. iii. 971—

> Vitaque mancipio nulli datur, omnibus usu.

mancipium = *dominium* here.

senes coëmptionales.   At slave-sales old and worthless slaves were often put up, not individually, but in a lot ; hence the word here means 'a cheap job lot' ; so in Plaut. Bacch. iv. 4, 52, where see Ussing.   There is no reference to the *senes qui ad coemptiones faciendas interimendorum sacrorum causa reperti sunt*, Mur. 27, where see Mr. Heitland's note.

proscripserit, 'advertise for sale.'

egerit non multum, 'he won't do much good,' that is, 'he will not make much profit,' almost a slang expression here.

At . . . habere.   'But that constant asseveration on my part —namely, that all I am, all I have, all my reputation as a member of society, is solely due to you—how that enhances my value !'   Curius is pointing out that though his real value is very small, and therefore κτήσει or as a *mancipium* he is almost worthless, yet the fact that he is able to boast the refining in-fluences of Cicero's society and advice is of such importance that χρήσει or as a *fructus*, as a useful instrument, he is of a high value. This effusiveness seems quite excessive to us, but Cic. says of him *est quam facile diligas αὐτόχθων in homine urbanitas*, Att. vii. 2, 3. On *homines* see Ep. xviii. 4. [Cf. Liv. vi. 14, (*se*) *videre lucem forum civium ora M. Manli opera; omnium parentium beneficia ab illo se habere; . . . quodcunque sibi cum patria, penatibus publicis ac privatis, iuris fuerit, id cum uno homine esse.* Possibly among the many services Cic. had done to Curius (Fam. xiii. 50, 1) had been a successful defence in a law court.]

de meliore nota, 'give me an introductory letter of a superior brand,' a metaphor drawn from wines ; cf. Hor. Carm. ii. 3, 8, *interiore nota Falerni.*

refigere, 'to break up my establishment.' This too is a phrase partaking of the nature of slang ; we might render *déménager.*

deportare, ' to fetch *home.*'

2. amice magne, 'powerful,' 'influential,' the sense which Verrall rightly ascribes to μέγας φίλος in the Medea.

duo parietes. 'To whitewash two walls from the same pot' stands between our proverbs 'to kill two birds with one stone' and 'to blow hot and cold,' or 'to run with the hare and hunt with the hounds.' It is said of one who pretends to be altogether devoted to one person, while at the same time offering his services to another.

nostris verbis, ' in my name.'

LETTER LXVI. (ATT. XIII. 52)

1. O . . . ἀμεταμέλητον. I have introduced the slight change suggested by Boot into the reading of the mss., which is *O hospitem mihi tam gravem ἀμεταμέλητον.* This would naturally mean 'O how little reason I have to regret the visit of my so formidable guest,' and *O* and *tam* suit very ill together. Now 'O what a formidable guest, yet I have no reason to regret his visit' gives an excellent sense, and *tam* and *tamen* are constantly confounded. Boot, who in his text gives the reading of the mss., strangely proposes to get rid of the incompatibility of *O* and *tam* by omitting *O* and governing *hospitem* by ἀμετ., a construction which would be possible only if there were such a verb as ἀμεταμελεῖν. [*Mihi tam gravem* may be parenthetic,

the words *O hospitem* ἀμ. going closely together : 'to think that I have nothing to be sorry for about a guest so burdensome to me !']

fuit enim periucunde, 'for he enjoyed himself greatly'; cf. *libenter fuit*, § 2 ; *ut familiariter essem et libenter*, Att. xvi. 7, 1 ; *Antonio volo peius esse*, Att. xv. 3, 2 ; *mi gravius esse*, Ep. lix. 1.

Sed, 'however,' announces the beginning of the detailed description of the incident first briefly characterised by an exclamation.

secundis Sat., December 18.   The *Saturnalia*, originally lasting one day, afterwards extended over three ; they began fourteen days before the kalends of January, namely December 17.   After the reformation of the calendar by Julius Caesar, December 17 was of course sixteen days before the kalends of January ; the day for the beginning of the Saturnalia remained unchanged.   Macrob. i. 10, 2.

L. Philippus, consul 56, stepfather of Octavian.   He had a villa near Puteoli, which must have been a large one to hold two thousand men.

completa a militibus.   This is a stronger expression than the more usual *completa militibus*.   It indicates that all the rooms were thronged by soldiers ; hence 'there was hardly a room to spare for Caesar to dine in.'

commotus quid, 'I was made anxious (by the doubt) what would befall me the next day.'   Caesar had intimated his intention of visiting Cic. the following day, and Cic. did not know what he would do with the two thousand armed men.

Barba Cassius subvenit.   Barba Cassius (a friend of Caesar and Antonius, Phil. xiii. 3) came to his assistance by compelling the soldiers to encamp in the open country and setting a guard over Cicero's villa to prevent their entering it.   For the *constructio praegnans* in *commotus quid futurum esset*, Hofm. compares *earum exemplum nobis legit si quid videretur*, 'to see if anything should occur to me,' Att. xvi. 4, 1.

ad horam vii., 'till about twelve.'   See Dict. Ant. s.v. *hora* (art. by A. S. Wilkins).

rationes . . . cum Balbo, sc. *subducebat ;* Balbus was his treasurer.

audivit de Mamurra.   Mamurra was Caesar's *praefectus fabrum* in Gaul, and was assailed in two bitter epigrams of

Catullus (29 and 57). We do not know what news was conveyed concerning Mamurra, certainly not the news of Catullus's
lampoons, which were written some years before this time.

vultum non mutavit. *Vultum* is found only in Z., not in
M. It seems required, and suggests that the intelligence may
have been the death of Mamurra. Boot ingeniously suggests
that the true reading might be *non mutivit*, ' he did not say a
word.'

ἐμετικήν. This means 'he was undergoing a course of
emetics,' as is shown by the deviation from the tense of the
two preceding verbs. See by all means Munro, *Elucidations*,
pp. 92-95, on the question whether this practice of *vomitus* implied
a gluttonous disposition.

ἀδεῶς, because the emetics would relieve him from the consequences of excess.

bene cocto . . . libenter. This passage must be read by
the light of De Fin. ii. 25, where Cic. distinguishes between
bene cenare and *libenter cenare.* The former, 'a good dinner,'
implies the latter, 'a pleasant dinner,' but a man may have 'a
pleasant dinner' even though he had not 'a good dinner.'
Here the dinner was not only expensive and elaborate, but was
good and *pleasant. Bene cocto condito* (the *et* being omitted
after the fashion of archaic Latin) indicates that the dinner was
good; then he adds that 'the talk was agreeable, and in a word
(*si quaeris = quid quaeris* below) the dinner was *pleasant.*' It
is a mistake to make *cocto condito* agree with *sermone;* the participles agree with some such word as *cibo* or *apparatu* understood, or possibly supplied in an unquoted portion of the original
verse of Lucilius.

2. **tribus tricliniis.** Cic. divides Caesar and his retinue
(οἱ περὶ αὐτὸν) into three classes, each class being entertained in
a separate room. The three classes were (1) Caesar himself and
the *liberti lautiores;* (2) the *liberti minus lauti;* (3) the *servi.*
The first were received with elegance (*eleganter*), the second and
third with abundance (*nihil defuit*).

homines, 'a social figure'; see on Ep. xviii. 4. However,
here the meaning would rather seem to be 'we were quite
friendly together'; Caesar did not 'assume the god.'

Amabo . . . revertere. Peerlkamp says this is an iambic
line taken from some comic poet; and he would read *ehodum*
(comparing Ter. Andr. i. 2, 13) for *eodem.* If so, there must be
hiatus after *eodem* (which is quite possible), and *revertere* must

be the present used for the future, 'when you are on your way back'; this too is possible, cf. Virg. G. i. 209, (Libra ubi) *medium luci atque umbris iam* dividit *orbem Exercete viri tauros*, and Madvig, 339, obs. 1. But *chodum* after *amabo te* is surplusage, and the future *revertēre* is more natural ; this form of the future second pers. sing. is often used by Cic., e.g. *consequēre*, Ep. xxiii. 3. It is more likely that the words are Cicero's, 'my dear fellow, come back here and dine with me on your return.' *Eodem* = '*to* this same place.'

Σπουδαῖον . . . multa, 'no serious (political), but much literary, talk.'

ad Baias, 'in the neighbourhood of Baiae.'

Habes . . . molestam, 'Now you have the whole story of his visit—or perhaps I should call it his *billeting* on me—which gave me disquietude, as I have told you, but really was not disagreeable.' The Latin word for ἐπισταθμεία is *deductio*.

dextra sinistra ad ecum, sc. *se praestabat;* 'the whole guard paraded under arms round Caesar, who was on horse back, and this they did nowhere else.' This was a special token of honour to Dolabella.

Hoc ex Nicia, sc. *audivi*. This Nicias, a grammarian of Cos, was a friend both of Cicero and of Dolabella.

LETTER LXVII. (FAM. VII. 30)

1. **Ego vero.** These words, as usual, point to a question asked which is here answered.

ubi . . . audiam, a favourite quotation of Cicero's from the Pelops of Accius. Sometimes it is represented only by the words *ubi nec Pelopidarum.* In Att. xv. 11, 3 it is *ubi nec Pel. facta neque famam audiam.* Hence Ribbeck gives the verse as *ubi nec Pel. nomen nec facta aut famam audiam*, a trochaic septenarius.

Ne, a particle of asseveration, formerly written *nae.*

comitiis quaestoriis institutis. Caesar at this time took care to superintend the elections, and, as he did not return from Spain till September or October, and then celebrated a triumph and gave shows to the people, the elections usually held in the summer were delayed till December. Though a chair was placed for the consul, it must be remembered that it was Caesar and not the consul who presided (Momm. St. R. iii. 909, note 1). The quaestors as well as the tribunes and aediles were elected at the *comitia tributa.*

Q. Maximus. In 45 Caesar was for nine months consul without a colleague. On his return from Spain he resigned, and had Q. Maximus elected. Hence the latter is called *trimestris consul* (Suet. Jul. 80). For *quem illi dicebant* cf. Att. xvi. 4, 1, *ad consules sive quo alio nomine sunt.*

Ille . . . habuit. Caesar (*ille*) had taken the auspices for the *comitia tributa*, for the business of the day was the election of quaestors. Mommsen (St. R. i. 95, note 6) says that the signs required of the gods were not different for the different *comitia*, but that in asking for signs it was notified to the gods what the particular *comitia* were and the object for which they were summoned.

consulem, C. Caninius Rebilus.

mane postridie. The *civil* day amongst the Romans dated from midnight to midnight, and all children born in that interval were said to be born on the same day ; the *natural* day was from sunrise to sunset.

neminem prandisse. For other jokes made by Cic. on this incident see Macrobius, ii. 3, 6 ; vii. 3, 10.

viderit. Cf. Ter. Heaut. iii. 1, 82, *somnum hercle ego hac nocte* ('last night') *oculis non vidi meis.*

2. mancipio et nexo. This is an allusion to the beginning of Curius's letter, Ep. lxv., to which this is the answer. Wordsworth (Frag. pp. 522, 523) well explains the difference between these two terms as follows : *mancipatio* is the ceremony of the conveyance of what alone was considered property, *res mancipi*, in early times, viz. land and ἔμψυχα ὄργανα such as slaves and cattle. It was effected *per aes et libram* in the presence of witnesses, all full-grown Roman citizens representing the five classes of the Servian constitution, and a *libripens* whose function theoretically was to weigh the uncoined bars of copper (Gaius, i. 119). Now while *mancipatio* is a conveyance or transfer, *nexum* is a bond or contract. The two seem to have originated in the same process, since *nexum* is defined as *omne quod geritur per aes et libram.* Gradually *mancipium* was restricted to actual transfer, while *nexum* was used to express an incomplete conveyance. Persons who had not carried out their share of the supposed conveyance (*e.g.* debtors) were called *nexi.* For further details see Gaius, iii. 174.

3. maximo meo beneficio est. This strange ablative of quality is also found in Phil. viii. 18. In both places Wesenberg would supply *usus*. In our passage Cratander has supplied *affectus*. It is certainly a much stranger abl. than *magna gloria esse*, and the like, quoted by Madv. 272, obs. 2, or even tl an Q. Fr. iii. 3, 4, *summo studio rhetoris*, which is now correc ed to *summe studiosus*. [I would insert *ibi* after *beneficio*, comparing Ad Quir. § 17, *in eo me loco, in quo vestris beneficiis fueram . . . reposuistis.*]

salvis rebus, 'successfully,' or 'without loss,' lit. 'his fortunes being safe.' This has been interpreted to mean 'when the republic still existed,' but then an adjective signifying 'public' would have been required with *rebus*.

LETTER LXVIII. (FAM. XVI. 18)

1. Quid . . . suo. See the long note on Ep. xxxiii. , where this and other passages bearing on the use of the *praenomen* are treated. Cic. here omits his *praenomen*, which might be thought too familiar in addressing a freedman. Such preliminary greetings as *Tullius Tironi Sal.* are prefixed to the letters in the mss., and this and a few other letters (see note on Ep. x. 1) show that certain words were sometimes at least superscribed, inasmuch as the first words of the letter refer to them. Yet we find *Cicero Attico Sal.* prefixed in the mss. to all the letters to Att., though we know that Cic. for the first time calls him *Attice* in a letter (Att. vi. 1, 20) written in 50. This makes one look on all the superscriptions as of doubtful authority, and I have not printed them except when they were necessary to elucidate an allusion in the letter, as here.

διαφόρησιν, 'perspiration,' 'sweating.' *Diaphoretic* is now a common medical term.

Tusculanum, sc. *profuerit*, 'if the air of Tusculum has the same good effect, heavens ! how that will enhance my affection for the place.'

quod tamen in modum, 'though I know your health is improving to some extent, but improving or not, I beseech you to take care of it ; you have not been paying sufficient attention to it while devoting yourself to me.' *In modum* is certainly a strange expression for 'to a certain degree,' '*modice*,' but it does not appear to me to transcend the possibilities of the familiar style or *volksprache* which characterises these letters. The insertion of an adjective is not good criticism, and such an adjective as *mirum* (Lamb.) or *incredibilem* (Wes.) seems to me to injure the sense. These admonitions to Tiro to take care of his health seem to have been either uncalled for or very accurately attended to, for we are told that Tiro reached the age of 100 years. [*In modum:* with this passage should be compared Verr. ii. 4, § 20, *haec tibi laudatio procedat in numerum* (Lucr. has *in numerum procedere*, iv. 788), where edd. rightly compare *in numerum ludere, brachia tollere, exsultare, pulsare acra*, etc. *In modum procedit* is a phrase of exactly the same type, and may be similarly illustrated. Cf. Catullus, lxi. 38, '*agite, in modum | dicite, O Hymenaee Hymen.*' There is hardly an expression in which *numerus* occurs to which one cannot find a parallel with *modus*. Somewhat similar is *tabulae in ordinem confectae*, Qu. Rosc. § 7, *i.e.* 'so as to keep the *right* arrangement.'

But I would refer *quod* not to Tiro's health, but regard it as equivalent to *simulare* understood from *simulas:* 'If you care for me, as indeed you either do, or make a very nice pretence of it, which pretence, however, I must say answers your wishes (*i.e.* produces the same effect on me as the reality would do), well then (*sed* resumptive), however that is, take care of your health, etc.' I don't see how the clause *quod . . . procedit* can be anticipative of *indulge valetudini tuae.*]

πέψιν . . . κοιλίας, a kind of prescription, and therefore written in Greek ; see on Ep. iv. 1. For τέρψιν, which appears as τρψιν in the mss., some edd. read τρῖψιν, 'massage'; but who does not recognise the characteristic tendency of medical advisers to tell their patients to keep their mind amused, while at the same time prescribing a *régime* which renders all enjoyment or amusement a mere impossibility ?

2. **Parhedrum . . . Mothonem.** As far as we can understand the circumstances alluded to in this section they are as follows : Cicero had let the flower and vegetable garden of his Tusculan villa to a market-gardener when in a very incomplete condition, without any spot for growing choice flowers, without drains or a wall for training fruit trees to, or a lodge for the gardener. Cic. had added all these improvements, and wished to raise the rent. The 'ruffian Helico' (another market-gardener apparently) had offered nearly as much as the rent now demanded, and that before any of these improvements were made ; 'is he (the present tenant) to be allowed to scoff at a raised rent after all the expense I have gone to ?' Cic. could

of course have evicted his tenant, who seems to have adopted
the modern view of his obligations, and while refusing his rent
to have 'kept a grip of the land'; but he preferred not to do
so until at least he had secured another.   One Parhedrus seems
to have been looking after the place, and Cic. tells Tiro to 'stir
him up' (*excita, calface*) to make an offer, 'thus,' he writes,
'you will smarten up' (*commovebis*) the gardener; and these
were the tactics which Cic. pursued successfully with Motho in
another similar transaction. [*Hellico*. Possibly *heluo* or *heluo*
is the right reading.   Cf. Leg. Agr. i. § 2, where Baiter's ms.
denoted by F. has *hellico* for the word.   I should then take
dabat = 'used to give,' *i.e.* before I made all these improvements,
for which I have charged him so little.]

aprico horto, a spot in the garden especially laid out so as
to catch as much sun as possible.   It would be used, as green-
houses with us, for growing choice flowers.   Schütz thinks the
words must be corrupt, and conjectures *nullo apiario nul'a
cohorte* or *nulla avium cohorte.*

itaque . . . coronas, 'and so arrange as to close with whichever of them will supply me with flowers.'   Thus I have endeavoured to correct the utterly unmeaning *itaque abutor coroni*.
The landlord seems sometimes to have let his market-gardens
on the terms that the gardener should supply him with flowers,
which were mainly used for wreaths at entertainments, and
were far more indispensable to an ancient Roman than they are
to us.   Here Cic. writes in his usual elliptic fashion, 'and so
(*itaque* = *et ita*) let as to (give it) to whichever you can get the
flowers from,' *itaque* (loces) *ut* (ei des) *ab utro coronas* (accepturus
sis).   One cannot, of course, feel any confidence that this is what
Cic. wrote, but he certainly did not write *itaque abutor coronis*
'therefore I am plentifully using (or "wasting") garlands,
which gives no sense at all. [*Itaque abutor coronis. Itaque* seems
to lead up to some result of having 'warmed up' Motho.   *Abutor*
appears to me a corruption of *abundo* (*abūdo*).   It is just conceivable that, with this way of understanding the run of the
sentence, *abutor* may be right.]

3. Crabra, an aqueduct which extended from Tusculum to
Rome, and for the use of which Cic. paid a tax to the town of
Tusculum.

Horologium, sc. *solarium*, 'a sun-dial.'   The first sun-dial
which was used in Rome was that constructed for Catana in
Sicily in B.C. 263.   It was not till a hundred years later that
Q. Maximus Philippus constructed one for Rome (Plin. H. N.

vii. 213). They were afterwards common in private houses (Marq. Privatl. 167).

si erit sudum, 'weather permitting,' for damp might injure the manuscripts.

nullos tecum libellos. He must mean 'have you with you no works on which you are yourself engaged?' He could not ask Tiro had he any books to read, when he had access to Cicero's library at Tusculum (Fam. xvi. 20). [*Libellos*: here used as often (cf. Catullus, *lepidum novum libellum*; Prop. Ov. Mart. etc.) of the lighter poetry as opposed to the serious styles, the epic or, as here, the tragic ; for I think Cic. is alluding to a tragedy from Tiro's hand rather than a translation.]

Sophocleum, 'are you engaged on any work on Sophocles?' Perhaps Tiro contemplated a translation of some of the works of Sophocles. *Pangere* is most used of poetical composition.

Fac opus appareat, 'Let us see some fruit of your labours.' Cf. *ut huius peregrinationis aliquod tibi opus exstet*, Att. ii. 4, 3.

A. Ligurius. He is mentioned in Ep. xxi. 2. Ligurius appears in Att. xi. 9, 2 as the recipient of a letter from Quintus Cicero full of slanders against his brother Marcus.

LETTER LXIX. (ATT. XIV. 5)

1. leviter commotus, 'a little out of sorts'; cf. *commotiunculis συμπάσχω*, Ep. lv. [Cf. Fam. xv. 9 and Brut. 12, *perturbatio valetudinis*; Marcell. 23, *incertos motus valetudinis*.]

Calvena. This is the nickname by which Cic. refers to C. Matius, who was bald (*calvus*). He also calls him *Madarus* (μαδαρός) and φαλάκρωμα, or 'bald-head.' This Matius is the writer of the excellent letter about Caesar which I give below (Ep. lxxiii.) He was ever faithful to Caesar, and now was desirous that the assassins of Caesar, who was murdered on March 15 of this year, should be punished. Hence he had incurred the suspicions of Brutus.

cum signis, introduced merely for the double meaning of *signa*, 'signs' and 'ensigns.' The reference is to Caesar's troops. Cf. a previous play on *signa*, 'signs' and 'statues,' Ep. xxiii. 2.

idem postulaturas, 'will they not demand that the promises of Caesar shall be carried out?'

x

C. Asinium. C. Asinius Pollio had been in command of *Hispania Ulterior* (Dio Cass. xv. 10), and had transported thither certain troops at Caesar's command. These are here opposed to those legions who were in Spain before (*quae fuerunt in Hispania*). Cic. wrote *Annius* by an error for *Asinius*, but corrects himself immediately. *C. Asinium* is Boot's correction of *Caninium* of the mss. C. Caninius Rebilus had been Caesar's *legatus* in Gaul in 52, but he can hardly be referred to here.

Ab aleatore, 'A nice kettle of fish this, to be laid to the account of the Plunger,' that is Antonius, who is naturally enough called 'the Gambler' by Cic. (see Phil. ii. 56). However, there is no reason why we should regard *Antonius* as a gloss, because Cic. may have wished to explain to Att. whom he meant by *aleator.*

coniuratio, mentioned in Phil. i. 5; it was put down by Dolabella.

recte saperet. I have introduced into the text Dr. Reil's correction of *recta* of the mss. Cic. does not use accus. after *sapere* except *nihil, aliquid,* or an accus. expressing the taste of a thing. Cf. *sapere rectius,* Ter. Ad. v. 3, 46.

2. En! meam. I have inserted *en* as very likely to fall out before *m;* see on Ep. xliv. 1.

legari, to be appointed to a *libera legatio,* which would excuse his absence from Rome as a senator.

res prolatas, 'the vacation,' called *discessus* in Att. xii. 40, 3.

vides tamen tyranni. *Tamen* must mean 'after all'; the ellipse is '(though the tyrant is gone) *after all* we see his creatures in high place.' *Tamen* sometimes in the letters depends on a sentence easily supplied from the context as here, but not expressed. A good ex. of this use of *tamen* is in Att. x. 4, 5, where for *non tam quia maiore pietate est* Mr. Purser restores *quia non tamen maiore pietate est,* 'because he is not *after all* (in spite of my devotion to him) more filial than the other.' Cf. *qui te tamen ore referret,* 'whose face in spite of all might remind me of you,' Virg. Aen. iv. 329. So Ecl. x. 31, *tamen cantabitis,* 'yet ye will sing for me after all.' The difference between the *tamen* of the Virgilian passages and that of the Ciceronian is that the Virgilian introduce a consolatory reflection, but not the Ciceronian.

in latere, 'on our flank,' in Campania, where Caesar had given grants of land to his veterans.

εὐρίπιστα, 'easily fanned to a flame,' fr. ῥιπίζω, 'to fan' ; he detects in all these things tinder which would be easily blown into the conflagration of a revolution: νεωτερισμός, *coup d'état*.

ἅγιοι esse, 'sacrosanct.' This is the conj. of Boot for *magisse* of Z ; M¹ gives *magni sedebant*, and M² *magnis debebant*. He now rejects it for the much inferior *metu vacui esse*, which is both rash and weak. Other conjectures are *vagi esse*, which is not Latin for 'to be at large,' opp. to 'in confinement' or 'under surveillance,' and *magni esse*, which is intolerably frigid. Dr. Reid suggests *muniti esse*, comparing Tusc. v. 41, 2 Verr. v. 39, Sest. 95, Fin. i. 51.

LETTER LXX. (FAM. XVI. 23)

1. **Tu vero.** This is an answer to a question in Tiro's letter : 'Yes, finish this matter of the *professio* if you can ; tho' I know this money is not of the kind that need be declared. Yet (do so) all the same.' Antonius now required every Roman to make a specification before a magistrate of the sources of his income. Tiro consulted Cic. about some property of his which he thought would be exempt from registration. Cic. thinks it is exempt, but does not wish any question to be raised lest the completion of the transaction should be delayed.

Verum tamen. For aposiopesis following this word cf. Att. xii. 17 ; xiii. 2, 1 ; xiv. 8, *fin. ;* xvi. 3, 3.

ἐπιφορᾷ, 'defluxion.' See on Ep. iv. 1.

en ! quid egerit, 'see what he has done.' So Lehmann for *de legem quid egerit* of the mss. ; cf. *en cur magister . . . factus sit*, Phil. iii. 22. Ant. must have introduced into the Act some provision which Cic. disliked ; 'however,' says he, 'I am content if I am only allowed to stay in the country.' He had left Rome shortly after the death of Caesar.

2. **tu videris.** 'You must do what you think right,' 'you may look to emulating Servilius, you who do not despise length of days. (I do), though Att., who once knew me to be subject to alarms about myself, thinks that I am so still, and does not see in what a stronghold of philosophy I have now entrenched myself; indeed, being nervous himself, he acts the alarmist in the case of others too.' Servilius had recently died at a very advanced age, and no doubt Tiro had

suggested to Cic. that he should set before him the attainment
of a ripe old age.   Tiro seems to have done so himself with
success, for we are told he reached a hundred years of age. The
words πανικοῖς and θορυβοποιεῖ illustrate the Roman habit of
using Greek terms in reference to medical and hygienic
matters.

tamen, 'however (though not with a view of prolonging my
life, or perhaps merely "to pass to another subject"), I shall
endeavour to maintain my long-standing friendly relations with
Antony.'   Ant. and Cic. were both anxious to avoid a rupture.
But the domestic relations of Ant. were such as to tend to bring
it about.   Ant. was married to Fulvia, the widow of Cicero's
old enemy Clodius ; and his father had married the widow of
Lentulus, whom Cicero had put to death in prison for complicity
in the Catilinarian plot.

a syngrapha.   Tiro was engaged in trying to get in a debt
due to himself.   Cic. tells him to attend to that first : 'charity
begins at home.'

γόνυ κνήμης, sc. ἔγγιον.   Ar. Eth. N. ix. 8, 2.   The more
usual form of the proverb is ἀπωτέρω ἢ γόνυ κνήμη, Theocr. xvi.
18, the Lat. form being *tunica propior pallio est*, nearly answer-
ing to 'charity begins at home.'

rutam puleio.   The *puleium* or 'pennyroyal,' Gk. βλήχων,
was used by the Romans as a sweetener, and took the place of
our *sugar* even in proverbs, as here.   *Ruta*, 'rue,' was the
typical 'bitter' : 'I shall need all the sweets of your conversation to counteract the bitters in his talk.'   Lepta is mentioned
elsewhere in the letters as Cicero's *praefectus fabrum*, as owing
Cic. money, and as desirous of getting the post of manager of
some of the festivities with which Caesar entertained the people
on his return from Spain.

LETTER LXXI. (ATT. xiv. 10)

1. **Itane vero?** 'Is this the end ?   Did our hero Brutus do
his deed only to have to stay at Lanuvium, only that Trebonius
should have to slink through by-ways to his province (Asia),
only that all the acts, etc., of Caesar should have more authority
than if he were alive ?'   Cicero's first outburst of joy at the
assassination of Caesar is conveyed in a letter to C. Minucius
Basilus, which is the shortest in the whole correspondence.   It

runs : *Tibi gratulor : mihi gaudeo : te amo : tua tueor : a te amari et quid agas quidque agatur certior fieri volo.*   This tone soon gives way to one of depression, which is expressed in this and other letters, and of which the burden is *vivit tyrannis, tyrannus occidit.*

primo Cap. die. After the assassination on March 15 the conspirators occupied the Capitol, where they were joined by Cicero, Dolabella, and other *nobiles.*   They spent March 16 in appeals to the people and attempts to sound Antonius and Lepidus.   On the 17th, *Liberalia,* a meeting of the senate was held in the Temple of Tellus.   Cic. took part in the debate, and advocated a general amnesty.   The senate accepted his proposal, but added to it a ratification of Caesar's acts.   Caesar's friends, headed by L. Piso, his father-in-law, procured the consent of the senate to the publication of Caesar's will and a public funeral for his body.   Brutus subsequently addressed the people in defence of Caesar's murder, and on the following day Cic. again spoke in favour of amnesty.   Caesar's will was then read, in which Octavius was named his heir. A painful feeling was excited when the name of D. Brutus was read among the second heirs, and was intensified by the public funeral which followed, and by Antony's address on that occasion.   Watson (abridged).

oportere vocari. Edd. unanimously add *oportere,* which is not found in the mss.   It is not by any means absolutely necessary.   In animated or colloquial language the infinitive often stands where the gerundive would have been more normal ; cf. *de bonis regiis quae* reddi *ante censuerant,* Liv. xi. 5, 1 ; *censet praecidere,* Hor. Ep. i. 2, 9.   In Att. iv. 18, 4, *Cato affirmat se vivo illum non triumphare* is the reading of M^1, and the *triumphaturum esse* of M^2 is very like an obvious conjecture.   Wesenberg, however, p. 39, note, calls this use of the pres. infin. a solecism.   But why should not a vivacious use of the pres. infin. exist, like that of the pres. indic. in *imusne sessum* = 'are we going to sit down' ?   [*Vocari :* but there is no parallel in Cic. even with *censere.*   I hardly can think the inf. defensible.   I once thought that *clamare* was put for *clamando suadere.*   Possibly words like *ac suadere* have fallen out after *clamare.*]

Liberalia tu accusas, 'You condemn my conduct on the 17th of March,' in not either absenting myself from the meeting of the senate on that day in the Temple of Tellus, or speaking freely when there.   Cic. afterwards contends that *both* of these courses were impossible to him (Att. xiv. 14, 2, where I read with Boot *qui polui in senatum non venire?*)

laudatusque miserabiliter. What a theme the orator here had may be judged from the marvellous speech which Shakspeare in Julius Caesar has put into the mouth of Antony on this occasion.

tune . . . nutum? sc. *aliquid acturus es?*

cogito, 'I intend to keep moving from land to land'; to be 'a wanderer on the face of the earth.'

tua, sc. γῆ; 'yours (Epirus) is too windy.'

2. Tebassos, Scaevas, Frangones. These were veterans of Caesar's who were now in possession of properties formerly held by Pompeians.

illa, sc. *praedia.*

stantibus nobis, 'if we were not crushed'; cf. *stamus animis,* Att. v. 18, 2; *stante Pompeio vel etiam sedente,* 'if P. remained firm or even inactive,' Att. vi. 3, 4.

putarunt. For *putarunt* with a direct object Boot compares *falsum putare,* De Sen. 4.

de Curtillo scripsi. Att. xiv. 6, 1; he was one of the veterans enriched by Caesar with Pompeian property.

quod numquam accidisset, 'which never would have come about'; Cic. here records his conviction that if the Pompeians had taken a firm attitude after the murder of Caesar they would have prevailed over the Caesarians. But this interesting reflection has been taken out of the mouth of Cic. by Gronovius, who conjectured *utinam* for *numquam,* and who has been followed by most edd. I have given what Cic. wrote, not what Gron. thought he ought to have written, as I have done in the celebrated criticism of Cic. on Lucretius, where many edd. by inserting *non* have ascribed to Cic. the very opposite opinion to that which he justly expressed. See on Ep. xviii. 4.

3. Ibi . . . aditurum, 'Then Balbus met Octavius the next day, and in a conversation with me at Cumae on the same day he said that Octavius was going to take formal possession of the inheritance left him by Caesar.'

† ῥιξόθεμιν. It is hopeless to try to restore this word. Most of the attempts proceed on the hypothesis that θέμις can mean 'a contest,' which I doubt. If it could, I should conjecture *rixam an* θέμιν, 'Balbus agrees with you in thinking that before Octavius steps into the shoes of Caesar he must have it out with Antony, whether the question to be decided is to be one of might (*rixam*, 'row,' 'brawl') or one of *right* (θέμιν, 'trial,' 'suit'). [? ῥῆξιν ἀθεμιν.]

Buthrotia res. The exemption of the Buthrotians from confiscation referred to before.

adventare, the legacy of Cluvius is 'coming up to' (that is, proving nearly worth) 100,000 sesterces, about £850.

detersimus, 'I have cleared about 80,000 sesterces in the first year'; *scilicet* may mean 'that is to say,' or 'at all events.'

4. Q. pater. Quintus had divorced his wife Pomponia, of whose ill-temper we read in Ep. xxvi. She and her son Quintus had been on very bad terms, but now that she is divorced Quintus espouses her cause, and quarrels with his father about her. See Att. xiii. 38.

LETTER LXXII. (ATT. xiv. 18)

1. rem gestam Dol. Dolabella, who had acted as consul since Caesar's death, had overthrown an altar erected in honour of Caesar, and had punished very severely those who had assembled there to worship; this act Cic. praises extravagantly. See Att. xiv. 15, 1.

unis et alteris, 'more than one'; cf. Hor. Sat. i. 6, 101.

eadem causa, that is, because he would pay neither Cic. nor Att. See Att. xiv. 19, 1, *cum ex Dolabellae aritia—sic enim tu ad me scripseras—magna desperatione affectus essem,* where I believe the ms. reading as I have given it to be quite sound; Att. had intended to write *avaritia,* but by a clerical error wrote *aritia;* Cic., who understood what he meant to write, uses instead of it the *vox nihili,* which Att. actually did write. *Avaritia* is by no means synonymous with 'avarice,' it means *rapacity, closefistedness, a grasping disposition;* this was shown in Dolabella's case by his refusal to part with his money in payment of his debts, though he was abundantly supplied with ready cash, as Cic. goes on to say. His debt to Cic. was probably Tullia's dowry.

Faberii manu. Faberius had been secretary to Caesar. Antony used him to insert whatever he wished in Caesar's instructions; he thus became virtually possessed of Caesar's

fortune, and had already used some of it to buy the co-operation of Dolabella.

opem ab Ope. This is Cobet's admirable correction of
opem ab eo of the mss. Dolabella had drawn on the money
which Caesar had deposited in the temple of *Ops* for he
Parthian war. In *opem ab eo* there would be no joke. See
Att. xiv. 14, 5, *rapinas scribis ad Opis fieri*, and Phil. ii. 93.

aculeatas, 'stinging'; this word is wrongly marked
acŭleatus in L. and S.

2. Albianum. Sabinus Albius wished to purchase some
property which had been left to Cic. (Att. xiii. 14, 1).

suppetiatus es, 'you have come to my aid.' The word
suppetiari does not occur elsewhere in Cic., nor does *suppetias
ire*, but *suppetiatus* is inferred here from *suspendiatus* M [1],
suppeditatus M [2].

factum ad, 'perfectly adapted for.' *Vacillarunt* is 'they
went wrong' in the accounts.

3. De Montano. Montanus, a client of Cic., had become
security for Flaminius Flamma, who owed money to Plancus.

4. singularis vir, 'one in a thousand.'

profectum, from *proficio ;* 'I do not see that much good has
been done by (the deed of) March 15.'

Leonidae . . . De Herode. Leonides and Herodes were
writing letters to Cicero, in which they did not give a gratify-
ing account of the conduct of young Marcus, who was at Athens
pursuing his studies under them.

Saufeii, sc. *librum.* Saufeius is an Epicurean often mentioned in the letters. We have seen above (Ep. lxii. 3) that
the name of the writer is also put for the book, *e.g.* there and
Cottam, Att. xiii. 44, 3.

LETTER LXXIII. (FAM. XI. 28)

1. artibus, 'good qualities.'

propensa et perpetua, 'spontaneous and unbroken.'

ut volui scio esse. For the construction of *esse* with an
adverb cf. *Lucretii poemata ut scribis ita sunt*, Ep. xviii. 4 ; see
Corr. of Cic I.[2], p. 70.

ut par erat tua singulari bonitate. This is usually quoted as a rare instance of *par* with the abl., no other exx. being adduced except *ut constantibus hominibus par erat*, De Div. ii. 114 ; *scalas pares moenium altitudine*, Frag. Sall. Hist. iv. 55 ; *in qua par facies mobilitate sua*, Ov. Fast. vi. 804. But the ablatives here may be regarded as *ablativi modi*, 'considering your great goodness and our friendship': cf. *magnis occupationibus eius*, Fam. vi. 13, 3 ; *in Marcum benevolentia pari*, Fam. v. 8, 4 ; *summo dolore meo et desiderio*, Q. Fr. iii. 1, 9 ; *cuius dubia fortuna*, 'as his position was insecure,' Fam. xiii. 19, 2 ; *hac iuventute = cum talis sit iuventus*, Att. x. 11, 2 ; *praesertim hoc genero = cum talis sit gener meus*, Att. xi. 14, 2 ; *omni statu omnique populo*, 'whatever my state or the popular feeling may be,' Att. xi. 24, 1. [Here *te* is easily understood from *tu*, and the sense is *ut par erat te tua s. . . . resistere*. If it be thought that the *te* is necessary, it may be easily supposed to have fallen out before *tua*. *Singulari bonitate* and (*singulari* understood) *amicitia nostra* ('friendship for me'; like many things in Greek and Latin) are qualitative ablatives.]

2. **Nota mihi sunt quae . . . contulerint**, 'I am well aware what charges people have brought against me.' The verb should regularly be *contulerunt*, but the construction is a combination of *nota sunt quae contulerunt* and *notum est quae contulerint ;* cf. *audita vobis esse arbitror quae sunt acta*, Phil. vi. 1 ; *constituendi sunt qui sint in amicitia fines*, De Am. 56.

Aiunt . . . praeponendam esse. The mss. give *aiunt enim patriae amicitiam praeponendam esse*. Nearly all the edd. give *patriam amicitiae*, thus restoring what is plainly the meaning ; but Klotz reaches the same sentiment by a much more scientific method, by supposing that *patriam amicitiae non* fell out before the closely-resembling words *patriae amicitiam*.

vicerint, 'proved,' 'established their contention,' a sense which *vincere* often bears in Cic., *e.g.* De Or. i. 43 ; 2 Verr. iii. 40 ; Cluent. 124. So Plaut. Amph. i. 1, 277 ; Hor. Sat. i. 3, 115 ; ii. 3, 225.

non agam astute, 'I will not enter any subtle plea' (Jeans).

istum gradum sapientiae, 'such a height of philosophy' as to prefer the claims of the state to those of friendship (Watson).

Caesarem . . . amicum, 'I did not follow him as Caesar, but as my friend I refused to desert him.'

re offendebar, 'even though his action was distasteful to me.' He probably thought that Caesar should have given up his province.

in victoria = *cum vicisset ;* in Fam. iv. 9, 2, *in victoria* = *si vicisset ;* cf. *in damno meae laudis,* 'though I should suffer in reputation,' Fam. x. 8, 7.

minus . . . possent, 'though they had less influence with him than I.'

lege Caesaris. This is the law referred to in Ep. xlix. 7 ; see note on *aestimationem* there.

remanserunt, 'were saved from going into exile,' which they would have been obliged to do if Caesar had not come to the help of the debtors by the law just referred to.

3. iidem . . . fuerint. It was the same class of men who earned for him the unpopularity which followed his relief of the debtors at the expense (in many cases) of his own partisans, and who afterwards brought about his death.

Plecteris. *Plecti* is specially used of *vicarious* suffering, *Quicquid delirant reges plectuntur Achivi,* Hor. Ep. i. 2, 14. Hence here, 'if you will condemn our deed you must smart for it,' indicates that though he has brought his punishment on himself by his views on this question, yet he might have kept those views to himself.

gloriari . . . licere. Exclamatory infinitives are very common in the letters. There is one which has not hitherto been recognised in Att. xiii. 22, 4.

ut timerent = *timere ;* so *alterum ut te . . . diligam . . . alterum ut . . . colloquar,* Fam. i. 7, 1 ; *id quod facis ut noris,* De Pet. Cons. 42 ; *esse extremum ut irascatur,* ibid. 47 ; *vetus est lex . . . ut idem amici semper velint,* Planc. 5. See also two passages in the same work where the two constructions are found, first subj. with *ut,* and secondly accus. with infin. *caput . . . esse oratoris ut videretur,* De Or. i. 87 ; *caput esse nosse remp.* ibid. ii. 337.

4. terroribus. This is a somewhat loose use of the abl., as if he had written *nullius periculi terroribus compulsus . . . desciscam,* as he wrote *ne periculis quidem compulsus ullis,* Fam. i. 9, 11. This *ablativus causae* is very common in Cic. when the cause is an attribute or quality in the subject, as *cum alii me suspicione sui periculi non defenderent,* Sest. 20 ; *videmus alios oratores inertia nihil scripsisse,* Brut. 24. A good ex. of an ablative of the cause lying outside the subject, as in the text, is to be found in *significarunt se beneficio novo memoriam veteris doloris abiecisse*, Phil. i. 30 ; the two causes, external and internal, are combined in *eum non solum beneficio sed amore etiam et . . . iudicio meo diligebam*, Fam. i. 9, 6. A good ex. in Caesar is in the B. G. iii. 29, 2, *cum continuatione imbrium sub pellibus contineri non possent*. See Ep. lxxvii. 1.

pro civili parte, 'as heartily as a citizen can.'

velle salvam. This constr. with *velle, cupere, malle, nolle*, is rare with an adj., but frequent with a participle, as *consultum esse volt*, Div. in Caec. 6 ; *conservatas velit*, Rosc. Am. 9 ; Madv. 396, obs. 2.

vincere, used like *vicerint* above, § 2.

5. rem . . . oratione, a frequent antithesis, 'I beg you to observe that facts are more cogent than arguments, and, if you believe that law and order are for my interest, not to believe that I can have anything in common with desperadoes.'

retexam, 'undo' all my past ; cf. *novi timores retexunt superiora*, Phil. ii. 32.

quod displiceat praeterquam quod doleo, 'anything to give offence, unless the lamenting the death of a great man who was my dear friend is an offence.'

6. ludos. Caesar vowed a temple to Venus Victrix on the day of Pharsalus, and instituted games in her honour. Matius and others contributed the funds which Octavius required for the games ; cf. *vota Victoriae suae fecerit*, Fam. vi. 7, 2.

dignissimo Caesare, 'quite worthy of Caesar' ; cf. *filios dignissimos illo patre*, Fam. xiii. 79.

7. auferendi, 'carrying off' some favour ; cf. *ablaturum diploma*, Fam. vi. 12, 3 ; *auferret tribunatum*, Q. Fr. ii. 13, 3 ; *decretum abstulimus*, Att. xvi. 16 a, 5.

quae haec est adrogantia . . . conari, 'what presumption it is that they should attempt' ; cf. *O superbiam . . . gloriari*, § 3.

quod C. numquam interpellavit, lit. 'which Caesar never prevented me from doing, namely, from having what friends I pleased.' It will be convenient, the constr. being understood, to render *quod* by 'while' or 'whereas.'

8. ne aut. *Aut ne* follows as if *aut ne*, not *ne aut*, stood here ; such little irregularities are common, *e.g. ne et* for *et ne*, Att. iii. 4 ; *et ut* for *ut et*, Att. iii. 6 ; *si aut* for *aut si*, De Fin. ii. 15 ; *ut aut* for *aut ut*, Orat. 149.

recte . . . cupiam, 'always on the side of law and order.'

aperuit, because Trebatius had induced Cic. to write to Matius, who was hurt by some criticisms of Cic. on his cond ict as regards the games, etc.   Cic. attempts not very successfully to explain away his criticisms in the foregoing letter, to wh:ch this is an answer.

LETTER LXXIV. (ATT. XV. 16)

1. πεπινωμένως, 'in the true classic style.' We have had above (Ep. li. 4) εὐπινές, meaning 'archaic,' 'quaint,' 'classic,' and πίνος means the *robigo antiquitatis*, the *pretiosa vetustas* which makes a work of art valuable.   It is as if one should say new 'I have had from my son at school a letter which is quite Addi-sonian.' Cic. does not cultivate that style himself in his letters to his intimate friends, but only in his correspondence with important personages but slightly known to him.   Th s sign of 'progress' (προκοπή) on the part of his son and the praises of Herodes (though Leonides still preserves his qualifica-tory 'so far') encourage Cic. to be very hopeful.   'Indeed,' he says, 'in this matter I like to be hoodwinked, and gladl y banish suspicion.'

2. Narro tibi introduces a strong assertion ; see on Ep. vii. 1.   *Hacc loca* is probably Antium.

arbitris, 'witnesses,' 'people to overlook you.' Hor. calls a place which commands a view of the sea *maris arbiter.*

οἶκος φίλος, οἶκος ἄριστος, 'be it never so homely there's no place like home.'

me referunt pedes, 'my feet itch to return to T.' we might say ; *pes tamen ipse redit* is used in the same sense by Tibullus, ii. 6, 14.

ῥωπογραφία.   This word most probably refers to certain 'garish effects' in the neighbouring scenery—a sort of wildness on a small scale ; ῥωπικά means 'clap-trap,' 'tawdriness,' in rhetoric, as opposed to legitimate appeals to the emotions.

prognostica. Cf. the verses which Cic. quotes from his version of the Prognostica of Aratus in De Div. i. 15—

> Vos quoque signa videtis, aquai dulcis alumnae,
> Cum clamore paratis inanes fundere voces,
> Absurdoque sono fontes et stagna cietis.

ῥητορεύουσιν, 'are holding forth.' In the sequel of the passage quoted from the De Div. above he calls the frogs *ranunculos*, the diminutive form of the word, like *homunculus, virguncula, tirunculus.*

LETTER LXXV. (ATT. XV. 15)

1. L. Antonio. L. Antonius, the brother of Marcus, was *septemvir agris dividundis*, and was inclined to dispute the validity of the exemption procured for the Buthrotians by Cic. and Att. Cic. drew up a deposition setting forth what he knew about the transaction ; the matter is dealt with in detail in letters to Plancus, Att. xvi. 16 *a* and *b*.

si quidem, 'since,' as in *si quidem ut adhuc erat liberalius esse nihil potest*, Ep. xlvi. 3 ; *si quidem Homerus fuit ante Romam conditam*, Tusc. i. 3.

aedilis. L. Fadius was aedile of Arpinum ; for these aediles in country towns see Mayor, Juv. x. 101. Cic. owed some money to Arpinum, perhaps water and other rates (see on Ep. lxviii. 3). He is determined to discharge this debt in full (*vel omnes reddito*), and he countermands his orders to raise a sum of money for Statius, the steward of his brother Quintus. He wishes this sum now to be applied to the payment of Fadius, as well as another sum recently placed to his account. Boot proposes to read *a Statio*, in which case the reference would be to a sum due from Quintus and to be exacted from Statius ; but this change is not necessary.

Apud me item puto depositum. This reading cannot be right, but it is impossible to say whether a sum mentioned after the word *depositum* has fallen out, or whether that sum should be inserted before *puto* in the place of *item*, or whether we should change this last word to *idem*, and suppose Cicero to refer to a sum of money placed to his account equal to the HS. cx. which he has just mentioned.

2. Reginam odi. The reference is to Cleopatra, who was now living at Rome. Hammonius and Sara were attached to her court. It appears that the Queen had promised certain presents to Cic., desirous, no doubt, of the good offices of such a master of words. These gifts had not reached the hands of Cic., and this vexes him the more because they were gifts *qui convenoient à un homme de lettres*, as Mongault phrases it, prob-

ably valuable books or works of art, which, as he adds, were
'quite suitable to my position and character, of which I might
proclaim myself on the house-top to have been the recipient.'
The reading of the mss. is *sit* not *scit;* hence Wesenberg
would read *id me iure facere sit testis sponsor promissorum eius
II. ;* perhaps we might read *id me iure facere sit sponsor sponsor
promissorum eius II.,* 'let H. who was voucher to me for the
promises of the Queen now be vouched (guarantee) for me that I
am justified in doing what I do (in expressing my hatred for
her).' [*Testis sit* is strongly supported by Att. xv. 17, 2, *De
regina gaudeo te non laborare,* testem *etiam tibi probari.*]

Saran autem, ' As to Sara, I not only know him to be a
rascal, but I have found him impertinent to me personally.
Once and once only have I seen him at my house. On that
occasion I asked him quite politely what he wanted; he said he
wanted Atticus.' Some edd., not seeing in the conduct of
Sara anything impolite according to their code of manners,
have supposed Sara to say that he was 'looking for an Attic
orator,' thus intimating that Cic. did not deserve a place
among them, and have resorted to other elaborate devices for
importing into the sentence a breach of manners on the part of
Sara sufficiently marked to be appreciable by them. Surely it
was an act of *contumacia* in Sara to pay his first visit to a man
like Cic., and avow that he had not come to see Cic. but Att.
[*Saran.* I strongly suspect that *Serapionem* should be read.
He was one of Cleopatra's officers; cf. Dio Cass. l. 27, § 1; App.
B. C. iv. 61; *ibid.* v. 8.]

Nihil igitur cum istis, sc. *agam.*

me . . . arbitrantur, 'so far from crediting me with any
spirit, they scarcely think I have the feelings of a man';
animus is a high quality, *stomachus* is what Hamlet calls the
'gall to make oppression bitter.'

3. **Profectionem meam,** to Greece.

Erotis dispensatio, 'the mismanagement of Eros'; *dispensatio,* 'management,' is here virtually 'mismanagement'; see
note on Ep. xlix. 5.

fructuosis rebus. This refers to the rent of certain flats
which were the property of Cic., *merces insularum,* Att. xv. 17,
1. It is to be observed that he is still thinking of consecrating
a fane to the memory of his dead daughter.

impeditum impedire. Cf. *perditum perdamus,* Fam. xiv.
1, 5; *nota noscere,* Plaut. Mil. iii. 1, 42; *inventum inveni,*

Capt. ii. 3, 81 ; *actum agere*, Ter. Phorm. 419. [Cf. Plaut. Men.
ii. 1, 7, *contio quae homines occupatos occupat.*]

4. scio. This word is inserted by conjecture after *existimasse*,
which plainly depends on some verb which has been lost.
Lehmann (Quaestiones Tullianae, p. 115) would insert *perspexi*
or *perspicio* after *pertinere*, comparing with *nihil agere nisi quod
ad me pertineat facile perspicio*, Att. xii. 5, 2 ; *quatenus quidque . . . ad sese pertineat perspicere coepit*, Fin. v. 24.

ut permutetur Athenas, 'to send him a bill of exchange on
Athens to an amount which will suffice for his yearly expenses.'

LETTER LXXVI. (ATT. XVI. 3)

1. Tu vero. Here Cic. himself points to the fact that *vero*
introduces an answer to a question in the letter of one's correspondent.

igitur, resumes, as usual, after a parenthesis.

manus dedisti, 'you acted wisely in giving in, and even
thanking him.' L. Antonius had met Att. at the Tiburtine
villa of Metellus Scipio, and had assured him that should any
confiscation of the country about Tusculum be made, the property of Cic. would be safe. Cic. approves of the conduct of
Att. in not attempting to dissuade him from the design of
dividing these lands, but gratefully accepting his clemency
towards Cic. See Att. xv. 12, 2.

deseremur, 'we shall part company with our state before
we are stripped of our fortunes.' It is strange how often
deseror goes with inanimate objects in Cic.: cf. *deseror a ceteris
oblectationibus et voluptatibus*, Att. iv. 10, 1 ; *a mente*, Att.
iii. 15, 2 ; *illi quorum eminet audacia a malitia deseruntur*,
Cluent. 183.

delectare. I have unhesitatingly accepted Boot's and
Wesenberg's correction of *delectari* of the mss.; 'O Tite, si quid
ego,' the first words of the De Senectute, by which he often
refers to that treatise, may be used as the subject or as the
object of the verb, but cannot stand in any other relation to it,
cannot take the place of the ablative, for which it would have
to stand if we read *delectari*.

idem σύνταγμα, 'the same *brochure*,' the De Gloria, as we
learn from Att. xvi. 2, 6.

inculcatum. On the obscure use of the word here see a note of Dr. Reid's on Orat. 50 in Sandys. Prof. Palmer th nks the word means that faint letters in the archetype were blackened and deepened by a fresh application of the pen. [But see Att. iii. 23, 2.]

tralatum in macrocollum, 'copied on large paper,' sometimes called *protocolla*, whence our word *protocol.* The *ll* should be preserved in these words, which come from κόλλα, 'glue,' not κῶλον, 'side.'

erumpant, 'vent.' For another allusion to the parsimony of Att. see Att. vi. 1, 13, where Cic. takes him to task for serving up a cheap vegetable dinner on expensive plate, asking what would be the fare provided if the dinner-service were of earthenware. Nepos (Vit. Att. 13) says that the amount allowed by Att. for household expenses was, to his own certain knowledge, only 3000 *asses* per month, or about six guineas of our money.

2. De Xenone. We read (Att. xvi. 1, 5) that Xeno doled out the allowance of young Cic. very sparingly. To Herodes, a teacher of young Cic., and Saufeius, an Epicurean philosopher, we have often had allusions in these letters.

3. prius a tabellario. See Att. xvi. 1, 6 for an incident which certainly does not put in a pleasant light Cicero's sense of honour ; it runs thus : ' Now I must tell you why I sent my own letter-carrier with a separate packet, though I had already sent you one by young Quintus. He promises that he will be a perfect Cato, and he as well as his father begged me to make myself responsible for him, not, however, asking you to trust him till you had had plenty of time to make up your mind. Now I mean to give him a letter just such as he wants. *Don't you mind what I say in it.* I am writing now lest you should think I am really impressed by any change in the lad. Heaven grant that he may fulfil his promises ; it would be a blessing to us all ; but, for my own part—well, I will say no more.'

accedet magnus cumulus, 'there will be added the great crowning merit of your recommendation'; *com. tuae* is the gen. epexegeticus, 'in the shape of (consisting of) your recommendation,' like *merces gloriae,* 'reward in the shape of glory'; *vox voluptatis,* 'that word pleasure'; *numerus trecentorum,* 'the number 300,' Madv. 286. Cf. *vera laude probitatis,* 'real glory, which consists in uprightness,' Att. i. 17, 5 ; *aliis virtutibus continentiae gravitatis iustitiae fidei,* 'the other virtues, namely,' Mur. 23; *mercedem gloriae*, 'the reward (which consists) of glory,' Tusc. i. 15. Draeger, Hist. Syn. i. p. 466.

5. quod et Dolabellae nomen et ex attributione, 'because in my balance is included Tullia's dower, which Dol. was obliged to refund on divorcing her, and which he has not yet paid ; and because certain other debts due to me are drafts on persons of whom I know nothing ; I cannot help feeling great anxiety.' *Ex* is inserted by Boot, and either *ex* or *in* is quite requisite to make the passage intelligible at all. We have already met *attributio;* the paying of a debt to one's creditor by making over to him a debt owed to oneself would be satisfactory in proportion to the facility of collecting the debt. If one knew nothing about the person of whom one thus became the creditor, one could not feel very sure of being able to realise the money.

non concurrerent nomina, 'if it should so happen that the payments should not come up to time,' that the payments should not be made at the required time.

decemscalmis, 'ten-thowled,' that is, with ten oars.

erat etiam nunc. *Erat* is an epistolary imperfect standing for a present, and so can take with it a word like *nunc*, signifying present time. We have already had many exx. of this usage ; in the next letter to Att. (xvi. 4, 1) he writes, *ut heri tibi narravi vel fortasse hodie—Quintus enim altero die se aiebat*, 'in my letter of yesterday, or perhaps of to-day, for Q. said he would take two days,' thus describing the date of the letter, not by the day on which it was written, but by the day on which it would be received. This is a good ex. of that strange usage which makes the reader of Cicero's letters always feel as if it was the day before yesterday, or the day after to-morrow.

Ecquid . . . Hieram? 'Can you love D. without also loving H. ?' This is an ironical way of saying Hieras is as bad as Deiotarus. Hieras and Blesamius were agents of Deiotarus, who bought Armenia for their master from Antony through the intermediation of his wife Fulvia for a large sum of money. This Hieras had been ordered to do nothing without consulting Sextus Peducaeus (he is the Sextus here referred to, not Pompeius), but he never held any communication with Peducaeus or any of Cicero's friends.

LETTER LXXVII. (FAM. x. 32)

1. **Balbus,** a native of Gades, nephew of the Balbus who was so intimate a friend of Cic. and for whom the speech Pro Balbo is extant.   He is referred to as *Balbus minor* in Att. viii. 9, 4, and we read there how he was sent on a mission to L. Corn. Lentulus, who was consul in the year in which the civil war broke out.   Cic. thought that Lentulus would come over to Caesar even before Balbus could reach him (Att. viii. 11, 5).

numerata pecunia, 'ready money.'

magno pondere auri, 'a large quantity of bullion.'

exactionibus.   The *quaestor* was receiver-general of the taxes in the provinces and paymaster of the forces.   Ball us left the troops unpaid and absconded with the money, which he no doubt put at the service of Antony.

regnum Bogudis, Mauretania, including the modern Fez and Morocco.   Bogudes assisted Caesar, and subsequently Antony.

plane bene peculiatus, 'with a pretty penny in his pocket.'

His rumoribus, of the junction of Lepidus with Antony. The abl. is of the kind commented on in the note on *terroribus,* Ep. lxxiii. 4 ; or possibly 'while the present rumours prevail,' a kind of modal abl. of which exx. are given in the note on *singulari bonitate,* Ep. lxxiii. 1.

2. **eadem quae C. Caesar,** 'in imitation of Caesar.'

anulo . . . deduxit, 'he presented him with a golden ring (the badge of knighthood) and conducted him to a seat in the first 14 rows,' which in his province were reserved by Balbus for the *Equites,* as they were in Rome by the law of Roscius Otho. For the case of Laberius who acted his own mime and then took his place among the *Equites,* see Suet. Jul. 39.

quattuorviratum.   In the *municipia,* of which Gades (Cadiz) was one, the quattuorvirate corresponded to the Roman consulate, and the *decuriones* to the senate, which latter name was, however, used in the municipal towns and colonies as well as in Rome.

Sexto Varo proconsule, 57 B.C.

3. **praetextam . . . posuit,** 'he put on the stage a *fabula*

praetextata dealing with his own mission to secure the allegiance of Lentulus to Caesar.'

depressus in ludum, pressed into the calling of a gladiator, and forced to fight as such.

depugnasset, 'had fought and killed his man.'

auctorari sese nolebat, 'refused to fight as a gladiator.' *Auctorari* is not found in Cic.; it means 'to bind oneself or be bound to any service,' especially that of fighting as a gladiator; hence *auctorari* is nearly 'to be a gladiator,' 'to play the gladiator'; then the word came to mean 'to be involved in peril'; and finally 'to be bound' to anything.

manibus ad tergum reiectis, 'with his hands behind his back,' the typical gesture of ease and unconcern.

quiritanti, lit. 'to cry *pro fidem Quirites*'; hence the quantity is *quirītare*. However, Vaniçek and Fick connect the word with *queror*. From *quiritare* comes the English word to 'cry.'

C. R. natus sum. Cf. Acts of Apostles, xxii. 28.

Abi nunc. This is sometimes an expression of reproach in the comic drama, as Plaut. Mil. ii. 3, 20 (291); so *ibid.* 53 (324), *abi ludis me,* 'get out, you're playing with me'; but very often it is a word of commendation as *abi; patrissas,* 'you'll do; you're a chip of the old block,' Ter. Ad. 564. In subsequent Latin *i* or *i . . et* or *i nunc* are the phrases for invective.

circulatorem, 'a peddler,' or 'broker,' one who buys at auctions and afterwards sells at a profit; the word in later Latin means 'a cheat.' *Illicitator* is a sham bidder at an auction, one who in collusion with the auctioneer bids to raise the prices (Fam. vii. 2, 1).

portento, 'this was the kind of monster I had to deal with.'

4. Nunc, quod praestat, 'Now for the more important point.'

incitatissimam retinui, 'I kept from deserting though strongly tempted' (by the promises of Antony).

5. debetis existimare, 'you are bound to take this view that the army was kept and preserved by me for the state, and that as I have carried out the orders of the senate in that matter, so should I have done, whatever orders I had received.'

decedentes, 'attempting to desert.'

si me satis novisset. Pollio more than once complains

of the way in which he was ignored.   He had frequently
declared his desire to perish with the republic, but afterwards
joined Antony and Lepidus, and reached a good old age in h gh
favour at the court of Augustus.

praetextam, the play mentioned above.   *Poscito* takes two
accusatives, as often in Cic. and Livy as well as in Augustan
poetry.   Corn. Gallus was no doubt the poet so named.

LETTER LXXVIII. (Fam. xii. 10)

1. **Lepidus, tuus adfinis,** 'brother-in-law'; Lepidus a id
Cassius were married to sisters, daughters of D. Silanus, cois.
62, and Servilia, and therefore half-sisters of Brutus; see on Ep.
xxxv. 25.

quibus.   This probably includes only *ceteri*, not Lepidus.

ad sanitatem redeundi, 'of coming to their senses'; to
the Caesarians he ascribes *furor* and *insania ;* Lepidus is called
furiosus, Fam. xi. 18, 2 ; *furor* is attributed to him, Fam. x i.
3, 1, and to Caesar, Att. vii. 14, 1 ; cf. *insania* and *insanius*
ascribed to Caesar and his party, Att. ix. 7, 3, 5.

scelere et levitate, 'hare-brained treachery,' a hendiadys.

de Dolabella.   He was now besieged in Laodicea in Syria.
He subsequently destroyed himself when the town was carried
by the forces of Cassius.

sine capite, 'not coming from any definite source'; cf. *i*
quid sine capite manabit, Planc. 57 ; *horum criminum video*
certum nomen et caput, Cael. 31.

rumore nuntio, abl. absolute.

2. **litteris tuis,** Fam. xii. 12, 5.

ita persuasum erat civitati ut . . . arbitrarentur . . . ut.
'So established were the public in the belief that Dolabella was
crushed, and you were marching to Italy at the head of an army
that, in case the war with Antony (*haec*) should prove to be
now satisfactorily finished, we felt that we could rely on you ·
judgment and influence ; but if on the other hand it should
turn out that any check had occurred (εἴ τι πταίσαντες τύχοιμεν)
as often happens in war, then we could still rely on the strength
of the army under your command.'   *Persuasum erat civitati ut*
arbitrarentur must be taken together ; it is the second *ut (ut*

. . . *niteremur*) which is correlative to *ita*.   For *persuasum est ut* cf. *his persuaderi ut diutius morarentur* . . . *non poterat*, Caes. B. G. ii. 10.   The phrase *persuasum est ut arbitrarentur* is not unlike *in eam opinionem Caesenniam adducebat ut putaret*, Caecin. 13 ; *in eam opinionem Cassius venerat ut viderentur*, Fam. viii. 10, 2.   Mr. Jeans seems to take the first *ut* (in *ut arbitrarentur*) as correlative to *ita*, and is accordingly forced to regard the second *ut* (*ut . . . niteremur*) as if it were equivalent to *adeo ut*.   After *titubatum* we must supply *esset*, taken out of *essent* in *confecta essent*.

potuero. The fut. perf. is often used in the letters when the simple future would have been quite adequate.   Perhaps the most common instance is *videro*.

ornabo. Cassius had begged Cicero to take up the cause of his army, and make them feel that they had no reason to regret having preferred patriotism to plunder, Fam. xii. 12, 3.

gesta res . . . confido, 'some action is looked for ; and I feel sure that some action has been already set on foot, or is at hand.'   For *appropinquare* with an impersonal subject Hofm. compares *appropinquare tuum adventum*, Fam. ix. 1, 1.

3. **vos,** 'you and Brutus.'

viceramus, 'we had won,' a more vigorous expression than *vicissemus*, indicating that the victory was on the point of being achieved : the most familiar ex. of this is *sustulerat nisi*, Hor. Carm. ii. 17, 27 ; the only instance in prose given by Madvig (348 *c*) is *perierat imperium . . . si Fabius tantum ausus esset quantum ira suadebat*, Seneca, De Ira, i. 11.   Roby (1574) adds Liv. iii. 19, xxxviii. 49 ; Sen. De Ira, ii. 33 ; Cic. Nat. Deor. i. 17.

consules designatos. Plancus and D. Brutus.

magna . . . proeliorum, 'in whom we have hopes, ay, and great hopes, but at the same time anxious concern by reason of the uncertainty of the issues of war.'   When *illa quidem* is thus connected with an adj. and a noun, usually another adj. follows agreeing with the same noun, not a new noun and adj. as here.

4. **Brutum iam iamque,** 'every moment' ; but he never came.   Instead he went off to Asia.   His province, Macedonia, was much nearer than that of Cassius.

tamen. The meaning is : even though when you return you find the enemy utterly vanquished, yet the resurrection

and satisfactory establishment of the Republic will be due to
you, so many reforms are required even after the restoration of
the Republic. This is the last letter in the extant correspondence written by Cic., so far as we know. It was written at the
beginning of July. Some cannot be dated, for instance the
next two in this selection. The last *to* Cic. is Fam. **x.** 24,
from Plancus, written on July 28.

quibus erit medendum. Almost certainly an allusion to
the designs of Octavian.

LETTER LXXIX. (FAM. VII. 22)

This amusing little letter brings before us very graphically a
scene in the life of Cic. He was dining with his friend Trebatius Testa, when the question arose whether a person on
coming into a property could sue for an embezzlement committed before the property came to him. Trebatius maintained
that the heir would have an action in this case, and laughed at
Cic. for supposing that the contrary view was tenable at all.
Cic. writes that when he went home, 'though it was late and
he was quite mellow,' he looked up the authorities on the point
and found that three eminent jurists had pronounced for the
view which Trebatius thought was not tenable. 'However'
he adds, 'I agree with Trebatius and Scaevola,' the latter
authority taking the view of Trebatius that the action would
lie.

misi, 'I send herewith' the opinions copied out.

sensisse. For *sentire*, meaning 'to give an opinion,' a
juridical technical term, see Lewis and Short, s.v. iii. B
Brutus, Manilius, and Scaevola are mentioned together as jurists
in Fin. i. 12, and M. Junius Brutus is quoted as a legal
authority in De Orat. ii. 142, where see Wilkins's note. Sex.
Aelius is the jurist described by Ennius as *egregie cordatus
homo catus Aeliu' Sextus.*

LETTER LXXX. (FAM. XVI. 26)

1. Verberavi . . . convicio, 'I castigated you, but only
with the mute tongue of my mind,' 'I lashed you with abuse—
silent abuse, all to myself.' [Cf. *verberationem cessationis*, Fam.
xvi. 27, 1.]

te patrono, 'if you have only yourself for your advocate.'

. **Marcus,** the young Cicero.

vide ut, 'take care, will he be able to prove your innocence,' put as *vereor ut veniat* is lit. 'I have my fears about his coming,' hence 'I fear he will *not* come,' so *vide ut possit* means 'take care about his being able,' that is, 'take care that he does not prove *un*able.'

2. furtum cessationis, 'lest you be suspected of having attempted the thievery of indolence.' *Cessationis* is that epexegetic or definitive genitive commented on above, Ep. lxxvi. 3, note on *cumulus commendationis*. *Furtum cessationis* is 'an act of larceny (in the shape) of indolence' as a correspondent. As Cicero's mother used to seal even the empty wine-jars, lest the slaves should open full jars and, having drunk the contents, put them among the empties, alleging that they had been used by the family; so, says Cic., even when you have nothing to say, still send me a letter, that I may feel sure that you had not some news of which you have robbed me through indolence prompting you not to write, 'that you may not be suspected of having stolen a holiday' from your work as my correspondent.

Valde . . . nuntiantur, 'I always find the contents of your letters thoroughly trustworthy and charming. Good-bye. Yours very sincerely.'

INDEX TO THE NOTES (I)

The numbers refer to the pages of the notes.

)(= distinguished from.

INDEX TO THE NOTES (II)

THE END

Printed by R. & R. CLARK, Edinburgh